# Nationalism and
# Internationalism Intertwined

# European Conceptual History

The transformation of social and political concepts is central to understanding the histories of societies. This series focuses on the notable values and terminology that have developed throughout European history, exploring key concepts such as parliamentarianism, democracy, civilization and liberalism to illuminate a vocabulary that has helped to shape the modern world.

# Nationalism and Internationalism Intertwined

## A European History of Concepts beyond the Nation State

❖

Edited by
Pasi Ihalainen and Antero Holmila

berghahn
NEW YORK · OXFORD
www.berghahnbooks.com

First published in 2022 by
Berghahn Books
www.berghahnbooks.com

**Library of Congress Cataloging-in-Publication Data**
Library of Congress Cataloging-in-Publication Data
Names: Ihalainen, Pasi, editor. | Holmila, Antero, editor.
Title: Nationalism and internationalism intertwined : a European history of
  concepts beyond the nation state / edited by Pasi Ihalainen and Antero
  Holmila.
Description: New York : Berghahn Books, 2022. | Series: European conceptual
  history | Includes bibliographical references and index.
Identifiers: LCCN 2021042542 (print) | LCCN 2021042543 (ebook) | ISBN
  9781800733145 (hardback) | ISBN 9781800733152 (ebook)
Subjects: LCSH: Internationalism--History. | Nation-state--History. |
  Nationalism--Europe--History. | Europe--Relations.
Classification: LCC JZ1308 .N49 2022  (print) | LCC JZ1308  (ebook) | DDC
  327.09--dc23
LC record available at https://lccn.loc.gov/2021042542
LC ebook record available at https://lccn.loc.gov/2021042543

**British Library Cataloguing in Publication Data**
A catalogue record for this book is available from the British Library

**EU GPSR Authorized Representative**
LOGOS EUROPE, 9 rue Nicolas Poussin, 17000, LA ROCHELLE, France
Email: Contact@logoseurope.eu

ISBN 978-1-80073-314-5 hardback
ISBN 978-1-83695-063-9 paperback
ISBN 978-1-83695-201-5 epub
ISBN 978-1-80073-315-2 web pdf

https://doi.org/10.3167/9781800733145

# Contents

List of Figures and Tables

# Figures and Tables

❖

## Figures

## Tables

# Acknowledgements

Editing this book has been a pleasant journey that started as a dinner-table chat at the History of Concepts Group Conference in Aarhus in September 2016 and reached its conclusion in an almost record time for such collaborative transnational projects. After a positive review organized by the editors of *European Conceptual History* and Berghahn Books, it is time to thank several colleagues who have supported the process.

Out of tens or hundreds of ideas thrown around, only very few materialized. Unfortunately, Or Rosenboim could not continue co-editing beyond the planning stage but nevertheless helped to mould the first draft introduction. Decisive for the project was strategic funding awarded three times by Professor Minna-Riitta Luukka, the dean of the Faculty of Humanities and Social Sciences at the University of Jyväskylä. This allowed us to invite many of the authors to Jyväskylä for planning sessions in December 2017 and most of the authors to a workshop in Berlin in March 2019 as well as to hire technical editors and a native language editor. We are likewise grateful to the Finnish Institute in Berlin, led by Laura Hirvi and Mikko Fritze and coordinated by Suvi Wartiovaara, for hosting the workshop and helping us with a book launch. Numerous colleagues at the University of Jyväskylä, Pertti Ahonen, Matti Roitto, Heikki Roiko-Jokela and Petri Karonen to name but a few, and elsewhere, including Andrew Williams and Giles Scott-Smith, have provided much needed food for thought, support and encouragement.

Authors were recruited from our existing networks but also on the basis of literature searches and suggestions from colleagues. Not every expert on the history of internationalism we approached was able to contribute to a conceptual understanding of internationalism this time. Several of the recruits turned out to be Finns, even if we consciously tried to limit the number of co-patriots. Perhaps the over-representation of Finns should be taken as a reflection of the important status of conceptual history in Finnish academia and the international outlook of the latter. Chapters written by

Finnish historians are not really about national history but about the history of internationalism more generally. In the end, we did have an international and multidisciplinary team.

The authors kept to the deadlines admirably well and also contributed by commenting on other chapter drafts in a most helpful way. Collaborative chapters, written with colleagues who were either known before or became familiar during the writing process, were also a central feature of this volume. Not only did they widen the perspectives beyond particular national contexts but they also facilitated learning from co-authors, not least in combining the distant reading of digitized sources with more conventional methods of conceptual history. We were all very much motivated by Glenda Sluga's willingness to write an afterword to the volume. We really wanted to create a book that an established scholar in international history would find useful. We obviously managed to do just that as our referee concluded that this is a 'commendably coherent' volume where 'the various chapters share a common approach and add up to a consistent whole' and which 'convincingly demonstrate[s]' how national and international 'have a multi-layered history and are intricately intertwined'.

Finally, we would like to thank Dr Silja Pitkänen and doctoral student Milla Virolainen for technical editing and Dr Kate Sotejeff-Wilson for excellent language editing.

On 'Meadow Island', Toivakka, Saint John's Day or Midsummer 2021,
Pasi Ihalainen

On a sunny home terrace, Jyväskylä, celebrating internationalism by enjoying the Euro 2021 football,
Antero Holmila

# Abbreviations

| | |
|---|---|
| AfD | Alternative für Deutschland (Alternative for Germany) |
| AK | Andra Kammaren (The Second Chamber, Sweden) |
| ARA | The American Relief Administration |
| ARP | De Anti-Revolutionaire Partij (The Anti-Revolutionary Party, The Netherlands) |
| BIS | The Bank for International Settlements |
| CARE | Cooperative for American Remittances to Europe |
| CD | Chambre des députés (France) |
| CDA | Het Christen-Democratisch Appèl (The Christian-Democratic Appeal, The Netherlands) |
| CDU/CSU | Die Christlich-Demokratische Union Deutschlands (Christian Democratic Union of Germany) / Die Christlich-Soziale Union in Bayern (The Christian Social Union in Bavaria) |
| CHU | De Christelijk-Historische Unie (The Christian Historical Union, The Netherlands) |
| Con | The Conservative and Unionist Party (Britain) |
| CPN | De Communistische Partij van Nederland (The Communist Party of the Netherlands) |
| DB | Der Deutscher Bundestag |
| DTA | Deutsches Textarchiv |
| ECCI | The Executive Committee of the Communist International |
| ECCO | Eighteenth-Century Collections Online |

| | |
|---|---|
| EE | Electronic Enlightenment |
| EEC | European Economic Community |
| EFA | Greens/The European Free Alliance |
| EK | Eduskunta (The Finnish parliament) |
| EP | The European Parliament |
| EPP | The European People's Party (The European Parliament) |
| EU | The European Union |
| FDP | Die Freie Democratische Partei (The Free Democratic Party, Germany) |
| FK | Första Kammaren (The First Chamber of the Swedish parliament) |
| GATT | General Agreement of Trade and Tariffs |
| GPV | Het Gereformeerd Politiek Verbond (The Reformed Political Union, The Netherlands) |
| Greens/EFA | The Greens/European Free Alliance Group (The European Parliament) |
| HC | House of Commons |
| HE | Hallituksen esitys (Government Proposal, Finland) |
| HL | House of Lords |
| ICRC | The International Committee of the Red Cross |
| ICW | International Conference of Women |
| IFOR | International Fellowship of Reconciliation |
| IFTU | The International Federation of Trade Unions |
| IKV | Interkerkelijk Vredesberaad (Dutch Interdenominational Peace Forum) |
| ILO | International Labour Organisation |
| IMF | International Monetary Fund |
| IOC | The International Olympic Committee |
| IOE | The International Organisation of Industrial Employers |
| IWSA | International Woman Suffrage Alliance |

| | |
|---|---|
| LOESS | Local polynomial regression |
| MDM | Médecins du Monde (Doctors of the World) |
| MEP | Member of the European Parliament |
| MP | Member of Parliament |
| MSF | Médecins Sans Frontières (Doctors Without Borders) |
| NATO | The North Atlantic Treaty Organization |
| NGO | Non-governmental organization |
| NV | Nationalversammlung (National Assembly, Germany) |
| PDS | Partei des Demokratischen Sozialismus (Party of Democratic Socialism, Germany) |
| POW | Prisoner of war |
| PvdA | De Partij van de Arbeid (Labour Party, The Netherlands) |
| RD | Reichstag (Germany) / Riksdag (Sweden since 1971) |
| RO | *Revue Olympique/Olympic Review* |
| SCF | Save the Children Fund |
| S&D | Socialists and Democrats (The European Parliament) |
| SDAP | De Sociaal-Democratische Arbeiderspartij (Social Democratic Workers' Party, The Netherlands) |
| SG1 | Eerste Kamer der Staten-Generaal (The First Chamber of the Dutch parliament) |
| SG2 | Tweede Kamer der Staten-Generaal (The Second Chamber of the Dutch parliament) |
| SGP | De Staatkundig Gereformeerde Partij (The Reformed Political Party, The Netherlands) |
| SNP | The Scottish National Party (Britain) |
| SPD | Die Sozialdemokratische Partei Deutschlands (The Social Democratic Party of Germany) |
| UN | The United Nations |
| USSR | The Union of Soviet Socialist Republics |
| TLFi | Trésor de la Langue Française informatisé |

| VVD | De Volkspartij voor Vrijheid en Democratie (The People's Party for Freedom and Democracy, The Netherlands) |
| WCC | World Council of Churches |
| WHO | World Health Organization |
| WTO | World Trade Organisation |

# Introduction

# Debating Internationalisms

## Contexts, Concepts and Historiography

*Antero Holmila and Pasi Ihalainen*

❦

The experiences of the late 2010s and early 2020s – most recently the overwhelmingly nationalistic responses to the Covid-19 crisis – have made us increasingly aware of the fact that internationalism and concepts closely related to it, like cosmopolitanism, universalism or Europe, have typically lived under the shadow of nationalism. Yet, while the emergence of modern nation states with their own 'imagined communities', pace Anderson, has dominated the historian's craft since the professionalization of history in the nineteenth century, ideas that transcend the national predate nation states and nationalism. As Charlotta Wolff (Chapter 1) and several other contributors to this volume point out, ideas on borderless and universal communities within Europe emerged before the modern notions of nation state and conceptualizations of such communities as 'international'.

Many of the histories of nationalism, international relations and internationalism have focused on events, leading actors and institutions despite the fact that past discourses and conceptualizations have also shaped those histories. This volume analyses how the semantic cluster surrounding 'the international' has emerged, evolved and changed over the course of modern history, including the development of a variety of its counter-concepts. Historical events – the fodder of much international relations scholarship – are important as context for discourses on the international but to unlock their wider meanings and the underlying structures that give them their shape, the keys are concepts as used by past political agents (see also Richter 1987: 259; Koselleck 2006: 11). In this volume, we do not apply today's analytical concepts, paradigms or schools of thought from international relations research to interpret the past. From our historical, empirical perspective, conceptual history and the focus on language underscore all historical understanding; as Hans-Jürgen Goertz has noted, language dominates 'the process of cognition from beginning to end' (Goertz 2001: 13).

In terms of conceptual history, our aim is to analyse long-term discursive and conceptual constructions of the cosmopolitan, international and European, partly also global and universal, in the course of European history since the eighteenth century. Our subject is the variety of meanings of the words referring to the international and the related contested – highly political – concepts created in a variety of contexts. Concepts, unlike mere words, escape simple definitions as they 'collect, aggregate, and integrate a variety of meanings that often stem from widely differing fields, within widely differing terminologies' and not only from the contemporary world but also a wide variety of past experiences and meanings (Jordheim and Sandmo 2019: 5, 7). As Marjanen and Ros point out (Chapter 3), our present-day public discourses on the favourable and unfavourable aspects of international activities continue to recycle historical – positively and negatively charged – connotations of the international. Our chapters hence discuss both the historical trajectories of concepts reaching beyond nation states, their use in particular politicized arguments and the resulting manifold meanings. While summarizing some related history of international relations and institutions, our analyses are based on prominent texts as well as everyday political debates in which past actors defined a variety of interrelated concepts that reached beyond nation states.

As we reconstruct diverse past understandings of political, cultural and economic phenomena that reached beyond nation states, this book is not so much about the history of the agents, institutions or events of international relations, or about theoretical scholarly debates, but about the more everyday discourses on things international in a wide-ranging arena. Instead of trying to simply define what was 'cosmopolitan', 'international', 'universal' or 'European' in history, we analyse how past actors – including politicians, editors, public intellectuals and professionals – talked about the international and related terms.

As previous research on international cooperation has rarely focused on language use and has seldom been based on any systematic analysis of a vast corpora of sources, conceptual history cannot necessarily build on earlier studies focusing on international practices and their generalizations on conceptualizations and the course of political discourse. Nevertheless, previous research is the point of departure for reconstructing the past contexts in which these concepts were debated.

As part of the series *European Conceptual History*, we focus on 'the transformation of social and political concepts' and 'notable values and terminology that have developed throughout European history', though many of our chapters include elements of the international, universal and global well beyond Europe. In their *Conceptual History in the European Space* (2017), Willibald Steinmetz, Michael Freeden and Javier Fernández Sebastián emphasize the research attitude of conceptual history: it entails an awareness of the importance of language for what is sayable and doable and an emphasis on past conceptualizations by contemporaries; it does not reconstruct past 'reality' based on modern analytical concepts. Concepts constitute 'focal points of interpretation and understanding' that demonstrate 'regularities and difference in human discourse'. They are 'windows through which we can appreciate how comprehensions of the world are organized and brought to bear on action' but they are also 'constraints on the messiness of human thought and enablers of its transformation'. As Reinhart Koselleck has put it, 'concepts express what a discourse is talking about', while conceptual history 'identifies the many layered meanings contained in the actual usages of a concept'. Conceptual history does not necessarily start with words; it can also start with phenomena in search for relevant and corresponding terms (Steinmetz and Freeden 2017: 1–2, 22–23; the Koselleck quote is from Koselleck 1996, 64). This is very much the case with discourses on the international: in many empirical cases words other than internationalism itself have turned out to be the key to these debates.

Methodologically Steinmetz and Freeden have seen some common features between conceptual history and Skinnerian history of political thought. There are differences, however: conceptual history is typically not as focused on intentionality and rhetoric as a means of conceptual change as Cambridge-style intellectual history. Nor does conceptual history share the normative features and focus on linguistic structures of critical discourse analysis. In contrast to political philosophy, it is interested in meaning created in particular historical contexts rather than in the truth-value of past arguments (Steinmetz and Freeden 2017: 28–30). While many of the authors in this volume have adopted Skinnerian strategies of contextualization by focusing on linguistic conventions and considering original authorial intentions (Skinner 2002), they do not focus on the political thinking of individuals but rather on the variety of views expressed within communities – often political or intellectual elites of each national community to be precise. Debates on the international can be analysed as nexuses of multi-sited political discourses so that the previous and simultaneous activities of political agents in other historical spaces, national and transnational forums are taken into consideration. Their mobility between these forums, connected physical experiences and (transnational) discursive transfers may also be relevant for understanding any particular speech act concerning the international (Ihalainen and Saarinen 2019). Our focus is on the evolving meanings of concepts in use in political arguments: we integrate methods from discourse studies, corpus linguistics and digital humanities into the study of the history of internationalisms, to extend the repertoire of conceptual history beyond the historical semantics of *Begriffsgeschichte* or the analysis of individual speech acts by canonical thinkers in the history of political thought.

The expansion of digitized texts has led to a major turning point in conceptual history in the past few decades. Steinmetz and Freeden have seen digital humanities in conceptual history as a promise rather than a reality, due to difficulties in interpreting semantic data (Steinmetz and Freeden 2017: 32). Thanks to the rapid growth of digitized texts during the late 2010s, we take on this challenge here by tentatively integrating digital history into the study of conceptual history. In preparing this introduction and some of the chapters (Chapters 3, 7, 8, 10 and 14), we have drawn on digitized data to home in on the historical periods that saw major changes in the vocabulary of the international. Case studies that build on contextualizing and critical close reading have thus been chosen in the said chapters based on computer-assisted generation of word patterns over time. A relatively new dataset used by many of the authors consist of digitized parliamentary records from a number of European countries. However, we are aware that the historical record largely remains either undigitized or unprepared for computer-based Natural Language Processing, and as a consequence the focus of analysis cannot be determined by computer-assisted research alone.

When examining larger textual resources in conceptual history, relative word frequencies are very useful. However, we can by no means gauge the semantic value inherent in words and word patterns based on frequencies alone. We can measure the occurrence of the word *Internationalismus* at the German Reichstag in the 1930s, for instance, but without textual contexts, we cannot determine what that meant in practice. Nor can innovations in the meaning of concepts simply be measured quantitatively. Single innovative conceptualizations of the international may have been politically, economically or culturally significant, especially if they impacted the course of debate and action, while much of the everyday vocabulary of the international has been merely technical in nature, lacking ideological dimensions, such as talk about international aviation or global standards. One challenge brought about by digitized sources is the need to select representative examples of more general conceptual trends. Highlighting comparable word distributions in larger datasets, word embeddings, for instance, as opposed to mere unigram frequencies, can reveal variety in the language of the international (see Chapter 8).

## Previous Conceptual Histories of Internationalism

*Geschichtliche Grundbegriffe*, the magnum opus of German *Begriffsgeschichte*, contained a chapter on 'International, Internationale, Internationalismus' (volume 3, 1982) without discussing cosmopolitanism or universalism more extensively as we do in our volume (e.g. Chapters 1, 2 and 9). According to Peter Friedemann and Lucian Hölscher (1982: 367–69, 397), the founding of The First International by socialists in 1864 marked the beginning of the history of internationalism as a key concept in German political debate. The attribute 'international' had appeared in late eighteenth-century British and French debates on the law of nations, introduced by Jeremy Bentham in 1789 (discussed in Chapters 1, 2 and 3), but in the course of the late nineteenth century 'international' became increasingly used as a synonym for the slightly more pejorative 'cosmopolitan', reflecting the increasing international interaction of the time. In our volume, we analyse the French and British debates (Chapter 2) and explore the nineteenth-century conceptual expansion based on big data (Chapter 3) as well as in the theoretical debates of socialism (Chapter 4). For Friedemann and Hölscher, the ideological content of 'internationalism' still implied associations with expectations of a socialist world revolution in the interwar era (also Chapter 6) and, after the Second World War, socialist unity under Russian/Soviet dominance within the Eastern bloc. In the Western world, the pejorative connotations of internationalism decreased during the Cold War, even though the concept was rarely used to describe international cooperation, which reflects awareness of the continuous existence of ideological, political and cultural borders between and within the blocs (see Chapter 10). Our findings suggest that after the Second World War – especially from the 1960s to the 1980s – internationalism as a concept was highly adaptable and polyvocal. In other words, it rendered more prestige to both ideas and events across a wide spectrum of action.

Though not a representative of conceptual history, Akira Iriye's work on *Cultural Internationalism and World Order* (1997) constitutes an important starting point for analyses of the spirit of internationalism that began to emerge in the interwar period. Iriye has called this cultural internationalism, emphasizing the role of cooperation between intellectuals and artists in search of international peace and pointing at projects such as student exchange and the creation of an international language, Esperanto. '[T]he [analytical] term *internationalism* is used to refer to an idea, a movement, or an institution that seeks to reformulate the nature of relations among nations through cross-national cooperation and interchange' (Iriye 1997: 3). Following the same theme, Iriye devoted his *Global Community: The Role of*

*International Organizations in the Making of the Contemporary World* (2002) to charting out how twentieth-century internationalism evolved through the wide range of emerging international organizations. As he wrote, internationalism was a mindset, a 'global consciousness ... the idea that nations and peoples should cooperate instead of preoccupying themselves with their respective national interests' (Iriye 2002: 9–10). Our case studies show that despite the birth of new international institutions, especially the League of Nations and the United Nations (and their web of agencies and non-governmental organizations that worked in close association with the international system), the nation state remained the key unit through which internationalism was facilitated. Thus we add a fresh dimension to the current scholarly view that the international and national work in tandem as an interconnected phenomenon (e.g. Sluga 2013; Sluga and Clavin 2017; Holmila and Ihalainen 2018). As Cornelia Navari commented in her *Internationalism and the State in the Twentieth Century* (2000), internationalism was not only a matter of ideology, but also chosen as policy. Particularly useful is her observation that 'the processes which produced internationalism were informed by conceptual categories as well as by material "facts"' (Navari 2000: 3). What these conceptual categories were remained largely unexplored.

Martin H. Geyer and Johannes Paulmann's *The Mechanics of Internationalism: Culture, Society, and Politics from the 1840s to the First World War* (2001) also represents the renewed scholarly interest in internationalism at the turn of the millennium. Their work focused on the structures and practices of internationalism between the 1840s and the First World War. Their general argument illustrates approaches to the history of internationalism around 2000:

> There are good reasons for using the term 'internationalism' as a meaningful concept for analysing developments in nineteenth- and twentieth-century international relations. It is a historical term used by those advocating new international structures and organizations, economists no less than socialists, reformers as well as those rejecting the phenomenon for nationalistic reasons. (Geyer and Paulmann 2001: 3)

While recognizing the importance of the concept as such, Geyer and Paulmann focused less explicitly on concepts and language than on institutions and their transnational links. They covered matters such as standardization, passports, and governmental and monarchical internationalism, touching on themes that are discussed in this volume: the world economy (Chapter 7), socialist (Chapter 4) and feminist internationalism (Chapter

5), and the rise of internationalism in sport (Chapter 9). While Geyer and Paulmann explored the nineteenth century, we also look at the preceding revolutionary period and at twentieth-century developments in discourses when the first wave of international organizations culminated with the founding of the League of Nations.

In the 2010s, volumes on internationalism rarely had an explicit focus on conceptual history. *Internationalism Reconfigured: Transnational Ideas and Movements Between the World Wars* (2011), edited by Daniel Laqua, focuses on Europe and North America in the 1920s, addressing transnational projects connected to the League of Nations. The authors study the diversity of international thought and action beyond diplomacy, in cases combining the activities of individuals, groups and associations with intergovernmental and non-state institutions. They explore networks and transmission processes, arguing that internationalism was dependent on transnational structures and movements. While the authors were interested in national associations involved in international cooperation, 'international' organizations of the League and non-state actors, the conceptual history of 'transnational' and 'internationalism' by Patricia Clavin remains rather brief and emphasizes practices, not discourses or concepts. This leaves space for histories that show how the function of language through concepts and discourses are essential in prefiguring practices.

David Armitage's *Foundations of Modern International Thought* (2013) takes a classical intellectual history approach to how leading European political thinkers broadened their perspectives beyond nation states between the early seventeenth and mid-nineteenth centuries – ending with visions of a world of competing sovereign states. Armitage has used Google Ngrams to visualize the relative frequencies of 'global', 'international' and 'transnational' in twentieth-century English-language literature and in long-term and multiple processes of globalization and deglobalization. His discussion of how modern conceptions of international law were formed approaches conceptual history (Armitage 2013: 38, 41, 43, 45). While Armitage points at changing ways of international thinking in the British parliament, digitization has enabled us to explore those changes empirically and bring up aspects of debate that reach well beyond international law (Chapters 2, 6, 8 and 10).

This leads us to ask to what extent we should include concepts of the world and the global in our explorations of discourses of the international. While it is not in primary focus, several of our chapters touch on the concept of the world and discuss related concepts. Recently, Hagen Schulz-Forberg combined transnational and entangled history and conceptual history in his *Global Conceptual History of Asia, 1860–1940* (2014).

Schulz-Forberg challenges methodological nationalism, emphasizing the role of historical agents in conceptual entanglements as well as the inclusion of 'anti-Western' perspectives. His work is a healthy reminder of the risks of Eurocentrism in conceptual history: while writing within the series *European Conceptual History*, we need to recognize its problems and relate European conceptualizations to developments beyond Europe (see Chapter 1 on cosmopolitanism as anti-colonialism; Chapter 2 on universality and colonialism; Chapter 4 on socialist colonial politics; Chapter 6 on the importation of the controversial Leninist and Wilsonian understandings of internationalism to Europe and the world after the First World War; Chapter 9 on the rise of 'global' as an alternative to 'international' within the Olympic movement; Chapter 12 on discourses in the global South; and Chapter 13 on climate change as a global challenge). We need to ask to what extent European debates on the international have turned truly global or remained focused on relations between nation states in Europe, recycling Eurocentric views of the 'world'. At the same time, internationalist visions have been presented by numerous non-Europeans, as demonstrated by Glenda Sluga in her Afterword.

As for the concepts of the world and globalization as 'a historical process and movement that consists of everything and everyone' (Jordheim and Sandmo 2019: 2), Helge Jordheim and Erling Sandmo are comprehensive in their *Conceptualizing the World: An Exploration across Disciplines* (2019). Jordheim and Sandmo point at how language has been globalized with the rise of a number of compound words. 'The world' and 'global' have been used to refer to an infinite number of phenomena and have become temporalized to forward-looking concepts of movement and communication. A major problem related to the rise of 'globalization' and its idea of the world becoming one is that this disregards the sense of the world as a limited space, masking the risks of the process leading to a global catastrophe (Jordheim and Sandmo 2019: 2, 14–15; approached in Chapter 13). Jordheim and Sandmo focus on interaction 'between nations' or 'beyond nations' touching on the paradox of a limited globe. We consider the concepts of the world and the global whenever they have been entangled with debates on internationalism, which occurred especially in relation to the world economy as argued by Schulz-Forberg (Chapter 7), the Olympic movement (Holmila, Chapter 9), the student movement (Saksholm, Chapter 12) and environmental discourses (Kaarkoski, Chapter 13).

The work that is closest to our goal thus far is Glenda Sluga's *Internationalism in the Age of Nationalism* (2013). Sluga's book provides a general history of international ideas, associations and institutions and includes aspects of the history of the concept. Sluga explores key moments of internationalism that are highly relevant for us here, including the turn of the twentieth century, the end of the two world wars, the global seventies and what she calls the 'postinternational' 1990s. She highlights intersections of the social, political and intellectual in the history of internationalism, exploring 'imagined' and 'invented' internationalism, emphasizing entanglements with the history of nationalism and considering the interrelationship between talk on and practices of internationalism. Her comment that 'internationalism has long been regarded as a story of ideologues and radicals' (Sluga 2013: 2) is particularly noteworthy here. The chapters in this volume build on this internationalist turn, combining discourses and material circumstances to demonstrate that the discourses created by 'ideologues and radicals' have indeed framed the tone of speaking and writing about internationalism, but the story itself goes beyond their platitudes. In our opinion, Sluga is hence the best reviewer of our findings in the Afterword of this volume.

In their edited volume *Internationalisms: A Twentieth Century History* (2017) Glenda Sluga and Patricia Clavin took the study of the multiple manifestations of internationalism further – reflected in the title's plural. With their fellow authors they explored a political idea that has been central for 'war and peace, imperialism and nationalism, states and state-building'. In their view, internationalism has provided an alternative to understandings of subjectivity, identity and sovereignty that centre on the nation state, but nationalism, imperialism and internationalisms have strong ideological and intellectual connections. They welcome constructivist approaches and studies of the language of internationalism, though these perspectives are more visible in their introduction than in the actual case studies. Sluga and Clavin recognize the contextual specificity of internationalisms and refer to interaction between events and ideas, 'thought and practice', 'the entangled histories of international thinking' and 'conflicting and contested narratives' (Sluga and Clavin 2017: 5–6, 8, 12). Our volume is a response to Sluga and Clavin's call for the systematic study of the 'language' of internationalism and includes perspectives they have not covered.

A vast body of other specialist literature on internationalism is burgeoning and cannot be reviewed here in detail. Suffice it to say that the topics range from Talbot Imlay's *The Practice of Socialist Internationalism* (2017), to the fast-growing area of internationalism as seen through race and gender perspectives. One of these is Keisha N. Blain's and Tiffany M. Gill's edited volume *To Turn the Whole World Over: Black Women and Internationalism* (2019). The editors explain that this volume is less about charting concepts and more of 'an attempt to expand the contours of black internationalism theoretically, spatially and temporally' (2).

## The Structure of this Book in Relation to the Conceptual History of Internationalisms

While the European international system has evolved at least since the Treaty of Westphalia (1648), building on the principle of sovereign nation states and international law (Armitage 2013), we explore transformations in conceptualizations of the international since the eighteenth century, when the dynamic of the debate started to increase and related vocabularies to widen. Cosmopolitan Enlightenment thought (Charlotta Wolff in Chapter 1), together with traditions of French universalism, constituted the background for the radical rethinking of international relations by the French revolutionaries, which inspired reinterpretations of the implications of the law of nations in Britain (Friedemann Pestel and Pasi Ihalainen in Chapter 2). Intensified international interaction and cooperation supported considerable diversification of the language of the international in the late nineteenth century, which can be seen in the emergence of the first wave of using the term 'international' and then 'internationalism' (Jani Marjanen and Ruben Ros in Chapter 3).

The nineteenth century witnessed the rise of at least three different strands of understanding the international. Firstly, the British Empire and the rising United States constituted contexts for the growth of what has often been generalized as 'liberal' internationalism, building on the idea of the Empire as a model for global order and conceptions of national exceptionalism. Secondly, much of continental Europe carried on the traditions of diplomacy between sovereign nation states derived from Westphalia, the Congress of Vienna and the Holy Alliance. Both of these conceptions of the international contributed to the emergence of a variety of international conferences and organizations towards the end of the nineteenth century. Pressure groups emanating from the growing civil society challenged these developments, demanding the right to participate in politics both nationally and internationally, in the labour and women's rights movements. Socialist internationalism was the first to include the very word in its constructions of identity, to question the established international order based on capitalism, class societies and nation states (Pauli Kettunen in Chapter 4). It also partly inspired the first wave of feminism, while some other women's rights movements tried to change the gender order within the liberal and conservative traditions (Tiina Kinnunen in Chapter 5).

While the late nineteenth century witnessed the flowering of myriad specialized international organizations that reinforced the role of nation states, the twentieth century was an age of both internationalism and nationalism, total wars and genocide. In the wake of the First World War and the dissolution of empires, nations came together in an entirely new forum, the League of Nations, and new nations entered the international stage. A certain international optimism among revisionist socialists and some non-socialist politicians in the 1920s faded with experiences of the rise of nationalism in the 1930s (Pasi Ihalainen and Jörn Leonhard in Chapter 6). Expectations of an emerging world economy that would ensure peace evaporated with the economic crash in 1929 and the global depression that followed (Hagen Schulz-Forberg in Chapter 7). The decades after the Second World War were marked by a new type of superpower rivalry, decolonialization and the further wave of new nations appearing in the international scene. Throughout these transformations, nationalism and internationalism interacted, but internationalism was typically subordinated to the interests of nation states.

The analysis of language, both on the macro-level of serial textual data ('distant reading') and on the micro-level ('close reading'), suggests that the developments between the two world wars stimulated a further wave of internationalism. This second wave was, however, considerably delayed by the rise of National Socialist Germany and the Second World War. What we call the second wave is visible in parliamentary debates from the 1920s onwards. Figures 0.2 to 0.4 show that the term 'international' was used increasingly frequently in the British, Dutch and Swedish parliaments until the 1980s, with a steep rise since the 1960s as what can be called the third wave. Google Books Ngram Viewer on 'international*' in English, French and German similarly corroborate with an increase around 1920, a decline in the 1930s and during the Second World War, and a rapid increase during the 1960s, peaking around 1990 (see Figure 0.1).

**Figure 0.1** Juxtaposition of Google Ngrams for the word 'international' in English, German and French corpus between 1800 and 2019 (https://books.google.com/ngrams).

Figures 0.3 and 0.4, Table 0.1 and Google Ngrams in Figure 0.1 all indicate that the 'postinternational' turn, mentioned by Sluga, began towards the end of the twentieth century, when the stem 'internation*' entered into a relative decline in English, French and German literature. This seems to suggest the emergence of a 'post-internationalist age' which was less concerned with the relations between nations than with the world as a coherent whole. The word 'international' was not replaced with 'global' as expected, but there are indications in Ngram Viewer that the use of both words declined. These developments gave rise to alternative terminologies used to conceptualize the world 'beyond' the nation state as a fluid continuum rather than a constellation of nations. Of these, the scholarly terms 'cosmopolitanism' and 'transnational' rapidly gained popularity in social scientific and humanities research respectively in the first decade of the twenty-first century but have hardly found their way to public discourse.

In political theory, cosmopolitanism remains a modern normative concept which has little to do with the conceptual history of cosmopolitanism, as demonstrated by this volume (Chapters 1, 2 and 9). For us, transnational is a modern analytical concept, used (in Chapters 2, 3, 5, 6, 7, 12 and 14) when the focus is on cross-border networks functioning independently of nation states and potentially on European or global, as opposed to particular

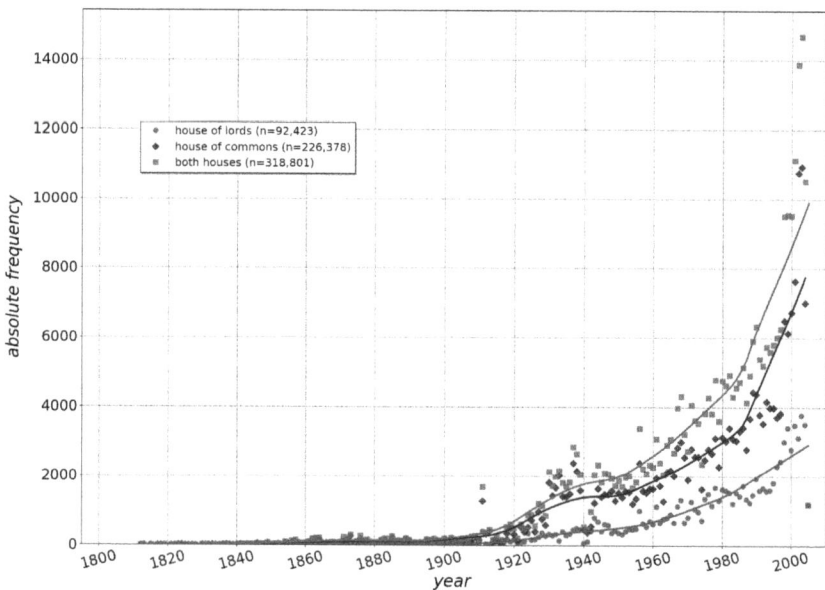

**Figure 0.2** The absolute frequency of 'international' in the British parliament (1800–2005). © Joris van Eijnatten.

national, challenges. As Tiina Kinnunen (Chapter 5) points out, in the beginning of the twentieth century 'transnational' cross-border interaction was still covered with the term international. The attribute transnational was used in public discourse before scholars began to use it in the last two decades. In historical research, the transnational perspective typically focuses on phenomena that transcend the nation state; explores processes, networks, discourses, interconnections and institutions that have had impact beyond nation states; and examines different types of cross-national transfers related to knowledge, people, currencies, information and more (Beckert 2006; Ahonen 2014; Patel 2015).

Both macro- and micro-level analyses of debates on the international suggest that this re-evaluation of internationalism began in the 1960s. For example, nation states whose official identities were constructed on membership in an established church were replaced first by more generally adopted ecumenical ways of thinking and then by purely secular ways of conceptualizing international questions (Joris van Eijnatten and Pasi Ihalainen in Chapter 8). The 1960s was also the era of decolonization and increasing cross-border mobility, both of which influenced changing values in Europe. The Red Cross, for instance, struggled to negotiate between its emphasis on

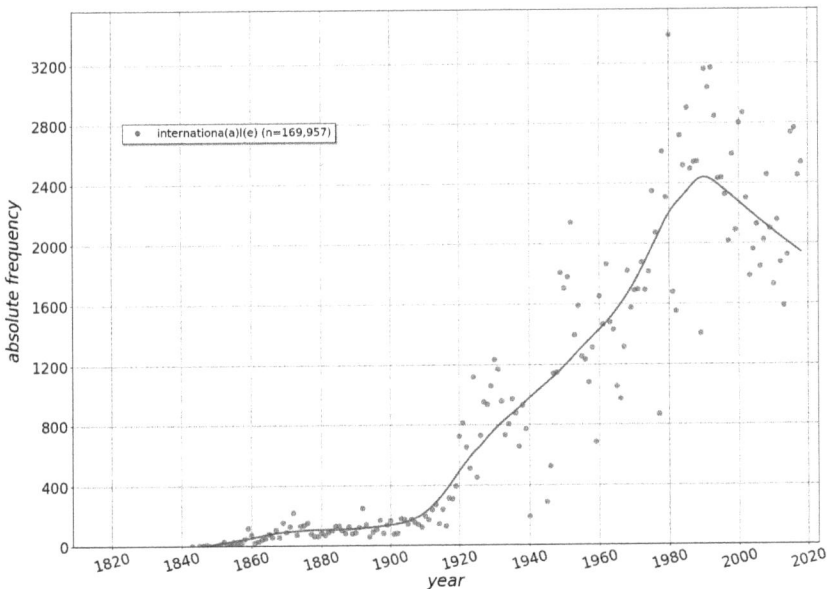

**Figure 0.3** The absolute frequency of *internationa(a)l(e)* in the Dutch parliament (1814–2018), with a clearly visible post-internationalist turn since around 1990. © Joris van Eijnatten.

humanitarian universality and the realities (and particularities) of humanitarian aid in conflicts related to decolonialization (Norbert Götz and Irène
Herrmann in Chapter 11). Similarly, the Olympic movement began to view
internationalism in sport as a universal human right rather than a reflection
of an activity centred on the nation state (Antero Holmila in Chapter 9).

Within Western European student movements, internationalism was
already a premise for all activities and, as transnational ways of thinking
gained ground, national phenomena and events were interpreted as part of
worldwide developments (Juho Saksholm in Chapter 12). The international
environmental movement was also taking new forms and affecting the ways
in which politicians saw global climate challenges, though these were not
that much discussed in the language of internationalism but often with an
emphasis on national interests (Miina Kaarkoski in Chapter 13). Finally, the
effects of European integration, first via common markets, but increasingly
also in other areas, were felt in the domestic and foreign policy debates of
EU member states. European unity continued to be frequently debated in
relation to nationhood, however (Mats Andrén and Joris van Eijnatten in
Chapter 10 and Viktória Ferenc, Petteri Laihonen and Taina Saarinen in
Chapter 14).

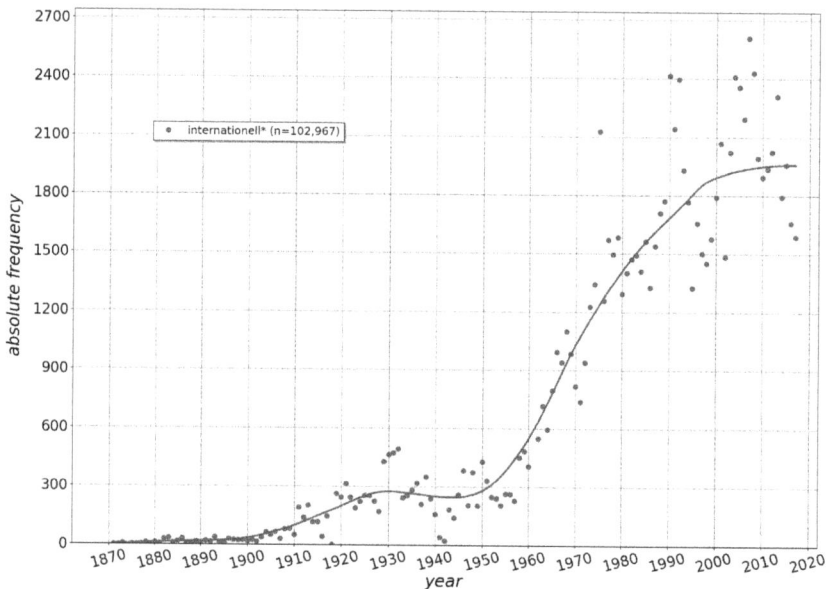

**Figure 0.4** The absolute frequency of *internationell** in the Swedish parliament
(1867–2017). © Joris van Eijnatten.

**Table 0.1** The absolute frequencies or unigram counts of 'internationali[s/z]e', 'internationali[s/z]ing' and 'internationali[s/z]ation' and related terms, with their Dutch and Swedish equivalents, as used in the British, Dutch and Swedish parliaments. © Joris van Eijnatten.

| Britain | 1861–1880 | 1881–1900 | 1901–1920 | 1921–1940 | 1941–1960 | 1961–1980 | 1981–2000 | 2001–2005 | total |
|---|---|---|---|---|---|---|---|---|---|
| globali[s/z]ation | 0 | 0 | 0 | 0 | 0 | 3 | 730 | 1,113 | 1,846 |
| globali[s/z]e | 0 | 0 | 0 | 0 | 0 | 0 | 4 | 5 | 9 |
| globali[s/z]ing | 0 | 0 | 0 | 0 | 0 | 0 | 21 | 23 | 44 |
| internationali[s/z]e | 1 | 9 | 27 | 27 | 78 | 38 | 22 | 204 | 0 |
| internationali[s/z]ing | 1 | 1 | 28 | 19 | 52 | 13 | 14 | 132 | 0 |
| internationali[sz]ation | 11 | 12 | 126 | 221 | 113 | 94 | 31 | 621 | 0 |

| Netherlands | 1861–1880 | 1881–1900 | 1901–1920 | 1921–1940 | 1941–1960 | 1961–1980 | 1981–2000 | 2001–2018 | total |
|---|---|---|---|---|---|---|---|---|---|
| globaliseren | 0 | 0 | 0 | 0 | 0 | 4 | 26 | 4 | 34 |
| globaliserend[e] | 0 | 0 | 0 | 0 | 0 | 9 | 40 | 122 | 171 |
| globalisering* | 0 | 0 | 0 | 0 | 1 | 12 | 576 | 1,096 | 1,685 |
| internationaliseren | 0 | 0 | 0 | 0 | 9 | 25 | 35 | 53 | 122 |
| internationaliserend(e) | 0 | 0 | 0 | 0 | 0 | 1 | 11 | 9 | 21 |
| internationalisering* | 0 | 0 | 0 | 1 | 22 | 122 | 866 | 777 | 1,788 |
| mondialiseren | 0 | 0 | 0 | 0 | 0 | 5 | 7 | 2 | 14 |
| mondialiserend[e] | 0 | 0 | 0 | 0 | 0 | 0 | 3 | 9 | 12 |
| mondialisering* | 0 | 0 | 0 | 0 | 0 | 25 | 97 | 95 | 217 |

| Sweden | 1867–1880 | 1881–1900 | 1901–1920 | 1921–1940 | 1941–1960 | 1961–1980 | 1981–2000 | 2001–2017 | total |
|---|---|---|---|---|---|---|---|---|---|
| internationalisera | 8 | 0 | 0 | 2 | 0 | 11 | 11 | 4 | 36 |
| internationaliserande | 0 | 0 | 0 | 0 | 0 | 0 | 2 | 0 | 2 |
| internationalisering* | 73 | 0 | 1 | 28 | 7 | 186 | 1,170 | 425 | 1,890 |
| globalisera | 0 | 0 | 0 | 0 | 0 | 0 | 0 | 2 | 2 |
| globaliserande | 0 | 0 | 0 | 0 | 0 | 0 | 0 | 1 | 1 |
| globalisering* | 0 | 0 | 0 | 0 | 0 | 0 | 537 | 1,305 | 1,842 |

## The Mission of European Conceptual History of Internationalisms

We explore conceptualizations of the international as fluctuating, contextual and contingent political, cultural and economic discourses, often, but not always, related to interests of nation states and their nationalisms. Cosmopolitan ways of thinking and transnational networks have provided alternatives to ways of thinking purely centred on the nation state, but their role in mainstream discourse has remained limited. We emphasize the discursive and contested aspects of related debates and arguments, opening up a long-term and systematic vista, from eighteenth-century cosmopolitanism to our days of transnational interaction. Translations from several languages to English are our own if not otherwise stated.

Internationalism customarily refers to cooperation between states. Within the tradition known as liberal internationalism, patriotism and nationalism have been seen not only as antonyms of internationalism but as its prerequisites and hence reconcilable. A deeper understanding of the dynamics between nationalisms and internationalisms is hence one of our goals; this helps us to comprehend challenges in international cooperation of which contemporaries were often very conscious. In the confines of one volume it is not possible to cover everything that goes beyond nations states. In line with the series *European Conceptual History*, we focus on European political cultures in a comparative and transnational perspective.

Northwest European political cultures are the primary focus of contributors: we analyse British, Dutch, Finnish, French, German, Hungarian, Swedish and Swiss debates. We consider this a legitimate choice for one substantial and three practical reasons. Firstly, many of the concepts of international cooperation first evolved in Northwest European countries and were gradually extended to cover Southern and Eastern Europe and beyond the bounds of the continent. The consideration of more peripheral countries in Northwest Europe balances conventional great-power-centred narratives. Secondly, the digitization of documents on long-term political discourse has proceeded furthest in many Northwest European countries; this makes a digital history contribution to conceptual history practical and potentially innovative methodologically. Thirdly, conceptual history – also in its comparative and transnational forms – has established itself in these countries, making it somewhat easier to recruit authors ready to contribute with diachronic analyses that proceed beyond the boundaries of their 'own' nation states. Fourthly, the group of conceptual historians we have been able to assemble mostly read Northwest European languages, which enables comparative research between countries in this cultural area.

We have done our best to break out of the nation state-centred paradigms of academic research, asking every author to justify their choice of national cases in the light of European conceptual history. Conceptualizations and discourses that extend beyond Europe – such as those of the universal and global – are considered through their relations and implications for concepts of internationalism in Europe. While empire and imperialism are not in focus here, we are aware that for centuries, Europeans have attempted to dominate global debates on international cooperation – as on almost any field of human activity. We hope that our volume contributes to the critical examination of such tendencies.

We fully recognize that not all voices can be heard through the extant sources, whether digital or analogical. The concepts whose history we analyse are abstract and not necessarily used in everyday discourses beyond political and cultural elites, even if the scope of debates was broad at times by the early and particularly the late twentieth century. We contribute to the inclusion of gender and class perspectives on the conceptual history of international cooperation. International politics has long remained a white, male and elite sphere of activity, and other perspectives are not explicitly present in many of the sources we use. Yet, the contributors have been asked to reflect on their potential significance and to include instances originating from everyday politicized debates in the media if not on the micro-level of individual citizens. Gender and class are the focus of two chapters, one on the internationalism of the first wave of feminism (Chapter 5), and the other on trade union and labour internationalism (Chapter 4).

In the beginning of the twenty-first century the future of political, economic, environmental or multilateral internationalism has been challenged by populistic, neonationalist and protectionist trends. The interconnected world manifested in the political, social, cultural and economic order of the twentieth century was depicted as being in a crisis in an age of Brexit, Trumpist policies, European populism and a number of other anti-establishment, anti-internationalist and anti-EU trends that dominated the debates of the late 2010s. The inability of international organizations to tackle effectively the climate or Covid-19 crises further calls their legitimacy into question. Is such questioning of the international exceptional or just another phase in a centuries-old negotiation between the interests of nation states and attempts to transcend or proceed beyond them? Internationalism could be seen as a phenomenon comparable to democracy and parliamentarism (Ihalainen, Ilie and Palonen 2016; Kurunmäki, Nevers and Te Velde 2018), that is, to ideals that have never been achieved in some particular phase of history but which continue to provide major goals in ongoing political debates. To understand the role of the international in the political, social, economic, cultural and ecological debates of today we need to grasp its multi-layered history as a contested concept. It may be that, like concepts of the world, our current concept of the international needs to move 'toward a broader, more comprehensive, and more complex reality' (Jordheim and Sandmo 2019: 17).

**Antero Holmila** is Associate Professor of Modern History at the Department of History and Ethnology, University of Jyväskylä, Finland. He has published widely on the histories of the era following the Second World War, including the transition from war to peace, the emergence of the Holocaust in British and Nordic collective memories, the birth of the United Nations, geopolitical thinking and the International Olympic Committee during the Cold War era. ORCID 0000-0003-2456-7223.

**Pasi Ihalainen** is Academy of Finland Professor at the Department of History and Ethnology, University of Jyväskylä, and has previously worked as a visiting professor at the universities of Freiburg, Gothenburg, Leiden and Uppsala. He has published widely on the history of political discourse and the conceptual history of nationalism, democracy and parliamentarism since the eighteenth century, applying comparative and transnational perspectives. ORCID 0000-0002-5468-4829.

# References

Ahonen, P. 2014. 'On Forced Migrations: Trans-National Realities and National Narratives in Post-1945 (West) Germany', *German History* 32(4): 599–614.

Armitage, D. 2013. *Foundations of Modern International Thought*. Cambridge: Cambridge University Press.

Beckert, S. 2006. 'AHR Conversation: On Transnational History', *American Historical Review* 111(5): 1441–64.

Blain, K.N. and T.M. Gill (eds). 2019. *To Turn the Whole World Over: Black Women and Internationalism*. Urbana: University of Illinois Press.

Friedemann, P. and L. Hölscher. 1982. 'Internationale, International, Internationalismus', in O. Brunner, W. Conze and R. Koselleck (eds), *Geschichtliche Grundbegriffe: Historisches Lexicon zur politisch-sozialen Sprache in Deutschland*, vol. 3. Stuttgart: Klett-Cota, pp. 367–97.

Geyer. M.H. and J. Paulmann (eds). 2001. *The Mechanics of Internationalism: Culture, Society, and Politics from the 1840s to the First World War*. Oxford: Oxford University Press.

Goertz, H.R. 2001. *Unsichere Geschichte: Zur Theorie historischer Referentialität*. Stuttgart: Reclam.

Holmila, A. and P. Ihalainen. 2018. 'Nationalism and Internationalism Reconciled: British Concepts for a New World Order during and after World Wars', *Contributions to the History of Concepts* 13(2): 25–53.

Ihalainen, P., C. Ilie and K. Palonen (eds). 2016. *Parliament and Parliamentarism: A Comparative History of a European Concept.* New York: Berghahn.

Ihalainen, P. and T. Saarinen. 2019. 'Integrating a Nexus: The History of Political Discourse and Language Policy Research', *Rethinking History* 23(4): 500–19.

Imlay, T.C. 2017. *The Practice of Socialist Internationalism: European Socialists and International Politics, 1914–1960.* Oxford. Oxford University Press.

Iriye, A. 1997. *Cultural Internationalism and World Order.* Baltimore: Johns Hopkins University Press.

———. 2002. *Global Community: The Role of International Organizations in the Making of the Contemporary World.* Berkeley: University of California Press.

Jordheim, H. and E. Sandmo (eds). 2019. *Conceptualizing the World: An Exploration across Disciplines.* New York: Berghahn.

Koselleck, R. 1996. 'A Response to Comments on the Geschichtliche Grundbegriffe', in H. Lehmann and M. Richter (eds), *The Meaning of Historical Terms and Concepts.* Washington DC: German Historical Institute.

Koselleck, R. 2006. 'Crisis', *Journal of the History of Ideas* 67(2): 357–400.

Kurunmäki, J., J. Nevers and H. Te Velde (eds). 2018. *Democracy in Europe: A Conceptual History.* New York: Berghahn.

Laqua, D. (ed.). 2011. *Internationalism Reconfigured: Transnational Ideas and Movements Between the World Wars.* New York: I. B. Tauris.

Navari, C. 2000. *Internationalism and the State in the Twentieth Century.* London: Routledge.

Patel, K.K. 2015. 'An Emperor Without Clothes? The Debate about Transnational History Twenty-five Years On', *Histoire@Politique* 26. https://doi.org/10.3917/hp.026.0191.

Richter, M. 1987. 'Begriffsgeschichte and the History of Ideas', *Journal of the History of Ideas* 48(2): 247–63.

Schulz-Forberg, H. (ed.). 2014. *Global Conceptual History of Asia, 1860–1940.* Abingdon and New York: Routledge.

Skinner, Q. 2002. *Visions of Politics: Volume I: Regarding Method.* Cambridge: Cambridge University Press.

Sluga, G. 2013. *Internationalism in the Age of Nationalism.* Pennsylvania Studies in Human Rights. Philadelphia: University of Pennsylvania Press.

Sluga, G. and P. Clavin (eds). 2017. *Internationalisms: A Twentieth-Century History.* Cambridge: Cambridge University Press.

Steinmetz, W. and M. Freeden. 2017. 'Introduction Conceptual History Challenges, Conundrums, Complexities', in W. Steinmetz, M. Freeden and Javier Fernández Sebastián (eds), *Conceptual History in the European Space.* New York: Berghahn, pp. 1–46.

Steinmetz, W., M. Freeden and Javier Fernández Sebastián (eds). 2017. *Conceptual History in the European Space.* New York: Berghahn.

Chapter 1

# Conceptions of Cosmopolitanism in the Intellectual Culture of the Enlightenment

*Charlotta Wolff*

The notion of a borderless community, although not conceptualized as 'international' before the nineteenth century, is obviously much older than the nation state as a concept. In medieval Europe, the self-assigned universalistic mission of Christianity had fed the idea of a cultural community, but the animosities and rivalries between European sovereigns, as well as between their developing states and the papacy, constituted a challenge to the old conception of the unity of Latin Christianity. The ideal of a universal cultural community nevertheless remained strong in medieval and early modern political theory, where it was conceptualized in terms of, on the one hand, the *res publica Christiana*, and, on the other, a universal monarchy or Christian empire, reflective of the heavenly order, which could be achieved under the rule of one sovereign (Hölzing 2011: 70–88).

The ideals of universal monarchy and Christian empire were central for legitimizing the policies of Catholic rulers such as Holy Roman Emperor Charles V. The Eurocentric ideal of a universal *res publica Christiana* as a moral superstructure lasted well into the seventeenth and eighteenth centuries and was occasionally discussed even in early nineteenth-century propaganda (see Chapter 2). As Christianity itself was split by religious dissent, the Reformations, and the long wars of the seventeenth century, universalistic ideals were articulated as necessary for the achievement of peace and stability. With the peace processes of Westphalia, diplomacy was formalized and theorized for a new mission: to maintain a balance of power essential to geopolitical stability in Europe. In this context, natural law, and the law of nations (*ius gentium*) that subsequently developed, became central for the conceptualization of relations between states. While seventeenth-century treatises on the law of nations were in Latin and therefore presented natural continuities with how a *res publica Christiana* was conceptualized, the philosophical literature of the eighteenth century and the 'Enlightenment' was increasingly in the vernacular but still recycled the classical concepts. Early eighteenth-century essays on 'international' organization and peace thus still reflected the ideals of balance and universal monarchy.

In this respect, the novelties of the eighteenth century and the Age of Enlightenment were, on the one hand, the bold proposals for perpetual peace drawn up by philosophers and thinkers such as Saint-Pierre, Rousseau, Bentham or Kant, and, on the other, the conceptualization and personal experience of a strong spirit of cosmopolitanism amidst the literary elite, known as the Republic of Letters (*république des lettres, res publica litteraria*). This development went hand in hand with the increasingly optimistic belief in progress and humanity fed by periods of relative peace in Western Europe between 1713 and 1740 and again between 1748 and 1756. After the death of Louis XIV of France in 1715, Europe in effect seemed to enter an era of cosmopolitanism, epitomized in the epistolary practices of the literary elite, with its networks of correspondence and friendship extending over the continent and the Atlantic Ocean. In terms of ideals present in dramatic literature, poetry and art, however, the second half of the century was characterized by a patriotic discourse with increasingly democratic and republican undertones. In this context, how did the intellectual elites, who described themselves in terms of a *res publica litteraria* by analogy with the *res publica Christiana*, define 'cosmopolitanism' as an ideal and as a practice?

## Cosmopolitan Visions for a Post-absolutist Europe

What we could call cosmopolitan cultural practices were commonplace in the *république des lettres* of the eighteenth century. Intellectuals, diplomats, amateurs and other educated persons of standing communicated across borders through correspondence, travelled to meet in the cosmopolitan salons of Paris, contributed to scholarly debates by publishing their writings abroad in the proceedings of the rapidly developing scientific academies or were introduced in foreign high society by common acquaintances and personal recommendations. This natural intercourse of individuals gave birth to a conscience of the existence of a community across borders, to 'cosmopolitan' as a self-description and to *cosmopoli(ti)sme* as a creed. This manifested in ambitious visions for peaceful cooperation, not only between intellectuals but also between nations and in everyday practices that impacted on language and vocabulary (Masseau 1994; Coulmas 1990).

In French, which in the late seventeenth century became the lingua franca of the Republic of Letters, *cosmopolite* (cosmopolitan), in the sense of a person travelling extensively without settling in a specific place, had been in use at least since the sixteenth century, when Guillaume Postel used the term instead of indicating his place of birth (Postel 1560; *TLFi*). The notion of a person of no fixed abode was present also in seventeenth-century usages of the word, as research in the database *Electronic Enlightenment* shows (*cosmopolite*: Daniel Coxe to Robert Boyle 1666, *EE*; Georges Pierre Des Clozets to Robert Boyle 1678, *EE*). In the sense of a 'citizen of the world', operating beyond particular states and for whom the concept of nationality is irrelevant, *cosmopolite* was increasingly used in the eighteenth century. That is also when the derived concept of *cosmopoli(ti)sme* (alternatively *cosmopolitanisme*) appeared, the marquis d'Argenson being one of the first to use it in the late 1730s to designate cosmopolitanism as an attitude and abstract ideal (*TLFi*).

René-Louis de Voyer de Paulmy, marquis d'Argenson (1694–1757) belonged to an important family of lawyers, ambassadors and ministers who served the central administration of the Bourbons from Louis XIII to Louis XV. Like his friend Voltaire, he had been educated in a Jesuit college, and like many other representatives of the French judiciary elite, he strongly opposed royal absolutism. With Montesquieu and président Hénault, he joined the Club de l'Entresol, a philosophical circle founded by the abbé Alary and the abbé de Saint-Pierre in 1724. The club gathered the aristo-cratic opposition – magistrates of the *parlements* – as well as diplomats and other intellectuals from Paris and abroad, united by French court culture and language. In this milieu, which largely corresponded to the 'first generation' of the French Enlightenment, cosmopolitanism as a practice and an ideal was strongly linked to the rejection of absolutism and the damages inflicted on society by the bellicose expansion of France under Louis XIV.

D'Argenson was slightly sceptical about human capacity for cosmopol-itanism. In a letter to Voltaire from 7 July 1739, d'Argenson stated that 'Our virtue is not advanced enough … for this perfect cosmopolitanism that would seek equally the happiness of all humankind' (7 July 1739, *EE*). Around the same time, in the late 1730s, in another of his writings, d'Ar-genson wrote that he would prefer to concentrate his love on his fatherland and be indifferent to the other inhabitants of the world: 'May a greater man embrace love for the entire globe, I admit I do not feel great enough for that' (quoted by Rathery 1859, xxxiii). Still, he was tempted by cosmopolitanism and claimed to be working on a treatise on 'to what extent cosmopolitanism can be accepted in a good citizen' (ibid.). In other words, d'Argenson gave patriotism his preference, not only because this was less demanding, but mostly because love for humankind as a whole seemed to require almost superhuman virtue.

D'Argenson's ideal was a European republic, but while his own views remained at a general and practical level, his friend Saint-Pierre drew up more ambitious plans. A Jesuit who had participated in the peace negoti-ations at Utrecht, Saint-Pierre was representative of the post-Westphalian culture of diplomacy, where international conflicts were to be resolved by civilian negotiators rather than through military action (Bély 1990: 743–51). Published in Utrecht from 1713 onwards, his *Projet pour rendre la paix per-pétuelle en Europe* was symptomatic of a certain war-weariness. To prevent conflicts in the future, it proposed forms of international organization of a kind so radical that it took 250 years before they could be concretized even partly. Saint-Pierre's *Projet*, in two volumes, breaks with tradition by reject-ing the ideals of universal monarchy (Saint-Pierre 1713: II, 49, 71, 113) and balance of powers (*équilibre des puissances*, Saint-Pierre 1713: I, vi), which he sees as leading to both an unending competition for domination and wars. Instead, he proposes a treaty of union between sovereign states, what he calls the 'European Union' (*Union Européenne*, Saint-Pierre 1713: passim), with a common deliberative assembly (*la diète générale*) invested with arbitrating powers, de facto a permanent peace congress reflective of the diplomatic experiences of the time, and a permanent council for running the affairs of the union (Saint-Pierre 1713: I, 335).

In English and French, the terminology of cosmopolitanism was scarcely used before the last third of the eighteenth century. Contrary to d'Argen-son, Saint-Pierre did not use the words *cosmopolite*, *cosmopolitisme* or even (*inter-*)*national*, which was used in French only from the beginning of the nineteenth century. *Nation* is used as a synonym for the country (including its inhabitants) ruled by a sovereign. The most interesting concepts are the ones Saint-Pierre formulates for his specific purpose, the most central being the *Union Européenne*, a concept modelled on his perception of an existing *Union Germanique* (the Holy Roman Empire, Saint-Pierre 1713: I, vii, 63, passim). His 'European Union' comprises eighteen sovereign states: France, Spain, Britain, the Dutch Republic, Portugal, the Helvetic Confederation, Florence, Genoa, the Papal states, Venice, Savoy, Lorraine, Denmark, Courland and Danzig, the Holy Roman Empire, Poland, Sweden and Russia (Saint-Pierre 1713: I, vii). The cosmopolitan community of European states is thus limited to Christian nations, but its mechanisms would be extensible to a hypothetical and pagan *Union Asiatique* (Saint-Pierre 1713: II, 204). As a weaker synonym, Saint-Pierre also uses the expressions *société européenne* and *corps européen* (Saint-Pierre 1713: I, ix, xi, passim). Interestingly, while he does not refer to cosmopolitanism as such, he not only conceptualizes the idea of a European community in terms of a political and strategic alliance, but also in terms of a common fatherland, *la commune patrie*, and a republic of peace, *république de paix*, the 'republic' here referring to the community (Saint-Pierre 1713: I, 362, 376, 378). While he rejects the idea of a universal European monarchy (*monarchie universelle, monarchie de l'Europe*) for being impractical, weak, arbitrary and subject to many inconveniencies for the rulers (Saint-Pierre 1713: II, 71), as Montesquieu did after him, Saint-Pierre's *Projet* is permeated by a universalist but Eurocentric ideal, associated with peace and with free and unhindered trade (*commerce*). This limited universalism not only reflects the liberal aristocracy's aversion towards absolutism, but also the same kind of exclusive cosmopolitanism that in practice restricted the Republic of Letters, not to speak of the cosmopolitan *beau monde*, to educated Europeans of a certain social standing. It is also a clear manifestation of an idea of a European community of interests, which had the potential to become a political superstructure.

This bold vision for peace and cooperation in a European republic was a rare but significant measure of how far the Republic of Letters could project its sense of community and of a common culture of cosmopolitanism. However, in the first third of the century, this cosmopolitanism was not yet generally conceptualized as an ideal. By contrast, cosmopolitan practices and attitudes were widely embraced by the European diplomatic and literary elites of the Age of Enlightenment, whose networks of sociability and correspondence presented a clear continuity with the Club de l'Entresol on a personal level, long after it had been dissolved by the French authorities in 1733. In the decades that followed, as we shall see, these elites would infuse the term 'cosmopolitanism' with political meaning.

## Descriptions of Cosmopolitan Practices and Attitudes

The self-celebrated practices of the Republic of Letters have been much described in previous research (Masseau 1994; Félicité 2015; Rjéoutski 2015; Wolff 2005, 2015). Interestingly, although this 'republic' de facto lived out a cosmopolitan ideal, compared to 'progress', 'Enlightenment' or 'humankind' (*humanité*), 'cosmopolitan(ism)' was rather sparsely used before the last third of the century. When the concepts were used, however, in the 1740s and 1750s, it was generally in a positive sense reflective of the spirit of the *philosophes*, who appropriated them to declare themselves cosmopolitans. Voltaire used the term *cosmopolite* in his correspondence in a pleasant and complimentary way. When writing to Frederick II on the subject of universal peace, he stated 'I am such a good cosmopolitan that I will be delighted about anything', and when addressing his friends La Condamine and Gauffrecourt, it was in the terms of 'my [very] dear cosmopolitan' (29 April 1752 and 25 January 1756, *EE*).

A work often mentioned as an example of a positive conception of cosmopolitanism representative of eighteenth-century intellectual culture is Fougeret de Montbron's *Le Cosmopolite, ou le citoyen du monde*, published in 1750 and translated into German in 1758. Despite the definite articles in the title, this is not a normative treatise but a description of the author's extensive travels. In other words, being a 'cosmopolitan' is as much a practice as a philosophical attitude. When he began his travels, the author says he 'hated his fatherland', but having grown accustomed to the 'impertinence' of so many foreigners, he has over time been reconciled with his native country. In other words, the text appears as a short lesson on the universality of human vices and virtues, regardless of place and origin (Montbron 1750: 3).

A contemporary positive and tolerant approach to cosmopolitan practices also appears in Diderot's and d'Alembert's *Encyclopédie*, a work that the editors themselves defined in the preface to the third volume as 'cosmopolitan' in the sense of tolerant and impartial: 'this dictionary is a sort of cosmopolitan work, which would do itself wrong by any marked preference or predilection' (Diderot and d'Alembert 1753: vi). In the entry 'Cosmopolitain, ou cosmopolite', the cosmopolitan is defined as 'a man who is a stranger nowhere'. The definition is illustrated by the following anecdote: 'When an ancient philosopher was asked where he came from, he answered: "I am a Cosmopolitan, which means citizen of the world. I prefer, said another one, my family to myself, my fatherland to my family, and humankind to my fatherland"'. Cosmopolitanism is thus understood as an enlarged identity that eventually embraces humankind. Significantly, the entry ends with a cross-reference to another entry, 'Philosophe' (Diderot and d'Alembert 1754: 297).

The author of the entry 'Cosmopolitain, ou cosmopolite' is unknown. However, one contributor to the *Encyclopédie* and representative of the *philosophes* who frequently used the concept was the abbé André Morellet (1727–1819). Morellet used the expression 'je suis cosmopolite' several times (five occurrences in his letters in the *EE* between 1765 and 1806). He also included his friends in this creed. He thus wrote (in French) to William Petty, First Marquess of Lansdowne (a.k.a. Lord Shelburne), 'I think you have become a little cosmopolitan by the interest you take in the happiness of all nations' (4 September 1775, *EE*); 'like me you are a cosmopolitan and a patriot at the same time' (7 May 1787, *EE*).

Morellet, like Raynal and many other French intellectuals associated with the *Encyclopédie*, was a strong supporter of American independence. Shelburne, too, as an Irish-born member of the British opposition, had demonstrated a conciliatory attitude towards the emancipation of the Thirteen Colonies, and in Morellet's letters to him, 'cosmopolitanism' was used in the context of progressive anti-colonialism. In another letter to Shelburne, Morellet wrote that 'it is precisely because of a lack of this cosmopolitanism that your government behaves in such an absurd and unjust way towards the Americans' (12 April 1776, *EE*). After the British forces led by John Burgoyne had been defeated by the Americans at the battle of Saratoga, Morellet wrote: 'As a cosmopolitan I like the good of humanity better than that of the English nation, and as a just person I cannot be unhappy to see the triumph of a cause I believe to be that of justice' (30 December 1777, *EE*). Morellet explained his enlightened vision of cosmopolitanism in a letter to Benjamin Franklin almost ten years later:

We have been told that you were very well received, and that you got all the hurrahs of the people. Those are very good and very convenient dispositions; but for the good of your country, they need to be durable, they need to expand, and all enlightened and virtuous citizens need to uphold them, so that your sage counsels and your grand visions for the happiness and liberty of America will influence the measures that are still to be taken, and will consolidate the edifice for which you have laid the foundations with some other good patriots. This is the wish I make from the bottom of my heart, not as your friend and for your glory, but as a cosmopolitan, and hoping there might be, on the face of the Earth, a country where the government might be truly busy with the happiness of humankind; where property, liberty, security, [and] tolerance could be, so to say, natural goods like the ones given by the soil and the climate; where the European governments, when they will come back from their mistakes, could go to look for models. The Greek colonies had to reignite their sacred fire in the prytaneion of their metropolis. It will [now] be the opposite, and the metropolises of Europe will go to America to look for the one that will rekindle all the principles of national happiness, which they have let die out amongst themselves. Above all, may the most complete and most illimited liberty of commerce be established amongst you: I consider it as important to the happiness of humankind gathered in society as political freedom. The latter concerns people only seldom and through a small number of things; but the liberty to cultivate, to manufacture, to sell; to buy, to eat, to drink, to dress as one likes, is a liberty of every day, of every moment; and I will never regard as free a nation that will be enslaved in all the pleasures of life, since after all it is for these same pleasures that people have come together in society. (30 October 1785, *EE*, original in French)

In the French intellectual debate, the concept of 'cosmopolitanism' – and to a slightly lesser degree 'cosmopolitan' – was thus strongly associated with the universal Enlightenment ideals of life, liberty and the pursuit of happiness put forward in the American Declaration of Independence.

In a German context, in its turn, a search on Deutsches Textarchiv indicates that the concept *Weltbürger* – world citizen – appears rather early in print. For a long time, it remained more common than *Kosmopolit* (Jordheim 2018: 304). Among the first to use it in the 1740s were Barthold Heinrich Brockes in *Irdisches Vergnügen in Gott* from 1740 (*redlicher Weltbürger*, Brockes 1740: *s.p.*, *DTA*) and Johann Jacob Bodmer in *Sammlung Chritischer, Poetischer, und anderen geistvollen Schriften* in 1743 ('He led neither an urban nor a rural life, and was in this respect truly a cosmopolitan [*Weltbürger*]', Bodmer 1743: 22, *DTA*). The concept then reappears in the 1760s, and its use increases considerably in the 1770s, when *Cosmopolit/Kosmopolit* appears as its synonym. Throughout the century, in this sample of texts, *Weltbürger* as well as *Kosmopolit* kept a mostly positive connotation often associated with humanity, philanthropy, virtue and liberty, like in Schiller's *Über die ästhetische Erziehung des Menschen* ('as a human and a cosmopolitan', 'as a liberal cosmopolitan', Schiller 1795: 11–12, *DTA*). Johan Henrich Jung-Stilling, in *Versuch einer Grundlehre sämmtlicher Kameralwissenschaften*, described the *Kosmopolit* as 'the defender of the good of humankind' (Jung-Stilling 1779: 180, *DTA*).

These cosmopolitan ideals of human fraternity and universal philanthropy were consistent with the Enlightenment philosophy of the first half of the century as well as with masonic ideals that permeated European intellectual culture to a significant but not overwhelming degree. However, from the Seven Years' War onwards, an increasingly patriotic discourse threatened this ideal.

## The Patriotic Challenge

With the rise of patriotism and democratic ideals, what role remained for cosmopolitanism as a practice and an ideal, and how did the concepts used to articulate cosmopolitanism change? Throughout the eighteenth century, 'cosmopolitanism' and 'patriotism' were used as pairs finely balancing each other. For instance, the marquis de Mirabeau, trying to understand the cause of Rousseau's unhappiness, wrote: 'it is not your quality of a cosmopolitan, since you have extended your fatherland to the whole of Europe' (3 February 1768). After the Seven Years' War, however, the term 'cosmopolitan' was gradually depreciated. In a well-known article of the *Handbuch politisch-sozialer Grundbegriffe in Frankreich*, Gerd van den

Heuvel described how this shift took place in the French context from the early 1760s. He associated this shift with the influence of Rousseau (van den Heuvel 1986). However, the rhetoric of war and the general shift to patriotic, neo-Roman discourse were probably even more important explanations.

'Cosmopolitan' had some negative potential even before, and the depreciation of the concept during the last third of the century is a matter of proportion. A research on *cosmopolit\** in the *Eighteenth-Century Collections Online* (*ECCO*) gives four results. In these examples, *cosmopolite* and cosmopolitanism are associated with indifference, as in an undated and unsigned letter in French presumably from Edward Gibbon, retrieved in the database: 'No, my dear friend, I do not want to be a cosmopolitan. Far from me [is] this sumptuous title under which our philosophers conceal an equal indifference for all humankind'. Here, cosmopolitanism appears negatively, as non-affection and non-attachment. In other words, 'cosmopolitan(ism)' could be conceptualized as a non-identity, a non-community, a rejection, indifference and negation, which might explain why it was rarely used to describe the border-crossing practices of the Republic of Letters, in an era that increasingly valued (universal) patriotism (see Chapter 2). For comparison, a search in *ECCO* on *patriot\** gives over 750 results.

Some visions of cosmopolitanism were openly negative. In a letter to Voltaire, Catherine II's favourite, General Ivan Ivanovich Shuvalov wrote that while the philosopher's lights would serve Shuvalov's fatherland, about which he declared to be 'fanatical', he was unable to become a cosmopolitan ('je ne peux me faire cosmopolite', 29 October 1762, *EE*). Similarly, in Adolph von Knigge's Über den Umgang mit Menschen from 1788, the spirit of cosmopolitanism – *Weltbürgergeist* – is something despicable, contrarily to patriotism:

> Love of fatherland is indeed a more composite feeling, but still more profound, warmer than the spirit of cosmopolitanism, for a person who is not expelled early from civil society, wandering from country to country as an adventurer, has neither property nor a sense of civil duties. (Knigge 1788: I, 132, *DTA*)

*Weltbürgergeist* is here associated with rootlessness and recklessness. Knigge also describes *Weltbürgergeist* as one of the 'big expressions' – happiness of the world, liberty, equality, human rights, culture, general Enlightenment, education, spirit of cosmopolitanism (*Glück der Welt, Freyheit, Gleichheit, Rechte der Menschheit, Cultur, allgemeine Aufklärung, Bildung, Weltbürgergeist*) – that were only bait (*Lockspeisen*) or well-intended empty words used by intellectuals for rhetorical games (ibid.: 284, *DTA*). It is remarkable that this clear rejection of the vocabulary of the Enlightenment occurs before the French Revolution and the negative reactions against it.

On the whole, the French revolutionary approach to cosmopolitanism was linked to patriotism as a universal value, and cosmopolitanism as a value was mobilized to promote patriotic, in other words revolutionary and republican, virtues, also outside France (Belissa 1998; Chapter 2). Coupled with the polarization of political concepts, this eventually gave 'cosmopolitanism' an ideological potential, although this rarely appears in the big data source databases.

With the Revolutionary Wars, the meanings of both 'cosmopolitanism' and 'patriotism' were put to the test. The positive cosmopolitanism of the mid-century had been expressed in terms of a 'universal philanthropy' or love of humankind, as a parallel to the love of fatherland, family and self (*amour-propre*). With the coalition wars, against a country with an outspoken universal-patriotic and republican mission of conquest, this essentially moral cosmopolitanism became insufficient; 'cosmopolitanism' became increasingly expressed in patriotic terms and vice versa. In 1795, German writer Jean Paul (Richter) stated in his *Hesperus, oder 45 Hundsposttage* that 'patriotism' was only a narrow form of cosmopolitanism, while philanthropy was patriotism embracing the entire world (Jean Paul 1795: 96–97).

Also in 1795, Immanuel Kant published his *Zum ewigen Frieden*. Since Saint-Pierre's *Projet*, both Rousseau and Bentham had drawn up visions for universal peace (Spector 2008; Frey 2012). Rousseau used terms such as *République européenne* and *République chrétienne*, but in his discussions of Saint-Pierre's initiatives, he expressed himself in terms of cosmopolitanism no more than Saint-Pierre himself. As demonstrated by Pestel and Ihalainen in Chapter 2, cosmopolitanism was only becoming politicized during the last decade of the century (see also Coulmas 1990: 390–97; Jordheim 2018: 311; Belissa 1998). The same absence of our key concepts is observable in Jeremy Bentham's *A Plan for an Universal and Perpetual Peace* (1786–1789) published as the fourth part of *The Principles of International Law* (1833). He uses 'nation' over a hundred times but in a traditional early modern sense as a synonym for 'country' or 'people'; his use of 'international' (which appears only in the title and in the first part) refers to the interaction between such nations, its counterpart being 'internal'. As a comparison, 'peace' appears only eleven times and 'universal' twice in the text (Bentham 1833).

The idea(l)s of peace and international organization presented by Saint-Pierre, Rousseau and Bentham enabled a clear notion of cosmopolitanism, but only Kant, writing when the concepts of 'cosmopolitan', 'nation' or 'fatherland' were becoming ideologically polarized, gave cosmopolitanism a formal role in his proposal. Kant uses both German (*Weltbürger*) and Latin terms (*cosmopoliticus*). Partly inspired by Saint-Pierre, Kant's proposal is the most utopian of the eighteenth-century peace projects, as he argues that wars could be ended if all standing armies were abolished, all countries became republics and a federation of free states was instituted to regulate the relations between them. At a legal level, Kant develops the concept of cosmopolitan law or *ius cosmopoliticum* (*Weltbürgerrecht*) as the third after *ius civitatis* (*Staatsrecht*), and *ius gentium* (*Völkerrecht*). By *Weltbürgerrecht* Kant understood the right of each peaceful individual, regardless of his or her origin, to be shown hospitality in foreign countries even after conflicts. Kant pointed out that this was not a matter of philanthropy but a lawful right (*Recht*), which is why his proposal goes further than the previous ones. Kant uses the term *Weltbürgerliche Verfassung*, a 'cosmopolitan constitution', to describe the moral and political state that results from this peaceful coexistence where *ius cosmopoliticum* is practised (Kant 1795). In this sense, Kant theorized ideas that had existed in the rich and various political and philosophical discourse of the revolutionary era without having been systemized (Hölzing 2011: 173–88; Beck 2006: 45–46).

## Conclusion

The social practices and networks of the Republic of Letters naturally affected both the self-descriptions of the multilingual elites and more theoretical reflections on cosmopolitanism and universal patriotism, such as the works by Saint-Pierre or Kant referred to above. By describing themselves in terms of a republic or as cosmopolitans, intellectuals expressed a sense of community, belonging and shared culture. The European republic (of letters) was thus, in practice, an 'imagined community' (Anderson 1983) characterized by the constant transgression of geographic, linguistic, religious and to some extent even social boundaries. Still, the social practices of the intellectual community had important exclusive mechanisms as well as inclusive ones (Lilti 2005; Edelstein 2010); eighteenth- and nineteenth-century cosmopolitanism always contained a certain amount of elitism and a nuance of carelessly 'being above' the contingencies of ordinary life.

In this context, it was only natural that 'cosmopolitanism', for long, was not an ideological concept but a practical one. Attempts to imagine what we today would call transnational communities and organizations, long before the appearance of the 'international', did not even mobilize the concept of 'cosmopolitanism'. These writers used 'cosmopolitan' much more frequently when referring to an attitude, mundane or philanthropic. The projects for peace and international organization drawn up by Saint-Pierre,

Bentham or Kant, however, were manifestations of the same enlightened creed that made European intellectuals like Morellet celebrate the spirit of cosmopolitanism as a parallel to liberty, humanity and virtue.

The French Revolution, with the appearance and more frequent use of terms such as 'national' and eventually 'international', complicated the meanings of 'cosmopolitan' and 'cosmopolitanism' and their use to describe an identity or a community. A broader study of the concept in the revolutionary era would need to take into account its relations not only to universal patriotism, but also to more exclusive concepts such as 'national interest' or 'international'. A step in that direction will be taken in the next chapter.

**Charlotta Wolff** is a professor of Finnish history at the University of Turku, Finland. Her research has focused on European culture in eighteenth-century Scandinavia, the history of elites and bourgeois experiences of modernity in nineteenth-century Finland. She currently directs two projects on intellectual culture in the Age of Enlightenment. ORCID: 0000-0001-7989-8308.

# References

## *Primary Sources*
Databases
*DTA: Deutsches Textarchiv*, available at http://www.deutschestextarchiv.de/.
*ECCO: Eighteenth-Century Collections Online*, available at https://www.gale.com/intl/primary-sources/eighteenth-century-collections-online/.
*EE: Electronic Enlightenment*, available at https://www.e-enlightenment.com/.
*TLFi: Trésor de la Langue Française informatisé*, available at the website of the Centre National des Ressources Textuelles et Lexicales, https://www.cnrtl.fr/portail/.

Printed Sources
Bentham, J. 1833. 'A Plan for an Universal and Perpetual Peace', in *The Principles of International Law*, vol. IV. Available at https://www.laits.utexas.edu/poltheory/bentham/pil/pil.e04.html.
Bodmer, J.J. 1743. *Sammlung Chritischer, Poetischer, und anderen geistvollen Schriften.* Bd 7. Zürich.
Brockes, B.H. 1740. *Irdisches Vergnügen in Gott.* Bd 6. Hamburg.
Diderot, D. and J. d'Alembert. 1753. *Encyclopédie ou Dictionnaire raisonné des sciences, des arts et des métiers.* T. III. Paris.
Diderot, D. and J. d'Alembert. 1754. *Encyclopédie ou Dictionnaire raisonné des sciences, des arts et des métiers.* T. IV. Paris.
Jean Paul. 1795. *Hesperus, oder 45 Hundsposttage.* 3rd booklet. Berlin.
Jung-Stillung, J.H. 1779. *Versuch einer Grundlehre sämmtlicher Kameralwissentschaften.* Lauten.

Kant, I. 1795. *Zum ewigen Frieden: Ein philosophischer Entwurf.* Königsberg. Available at https://korpora.zim.uni-duisburg-essen.de/Kant/aa08/341.html.

Knigge, A. von. 1788. Über den Umgang mit Menschen. Bd 1. Hannover.

Montbron, J.-L.F. de. 1750. *Le Cosmopolite ou le citoïen du monde, s.l.*

Postel, G. 1560. *De la République des Turcs.*

Rathery, E.J.B. 1859. *Introduction aux Journal et Mémoires du Marquis d'Argenson.* Paris: Renouard.

Saint-Pierre. 1713. *Projet pour rendre la paix perpétuelle en Europe.* T. II. Utrecht.

Schiller, F. 1795. 'Über die ästhetische Erziehung des Menschen in einer Reyhe von Briefen', in *Die Horen*. Bd 1. Tübingen.

## Secondary Sources

Anderson, B. 1983. *Imagined Communities: Reflections on the Origin and Spread of Nationalism.* London and New York: Verso.

Beck, U. 2006. *The Cosmopolitan Vision.* Cambridge: Polity.

Belissa, M. 1998. *Fraternité universelle et intérêt national (1713–1795): Les cosmopolitiques du droit des gens.* Paris: Kimé.

Bély, L. 1990. *Espions et ambassadeurs au temps de Louis XIV.* Paris: Fayard.

Coulmas, P. 1990. *Weltbürger: Geschichte einer Menschheitssehnsucht.* Reinbek bei Hamburg: Rowohlt Verlag.

Edelstein, D. 2010. *The Enlightenment: A Genealogy.* Chicago: University of Chicago Press.

Félicité, I. 2015. 'Relations internationales et cosmopolitisme à l'époque de Louis XIV: L'émergence d'une culture diplomatique ?', in M.-L. Pelus-Kaplan et al. (eds), *Être Citoyen du monde. Actes du Séminaire doctoral du laboratoire ICT – EA 337. Entre destruction et reconstruction du monde: Les enfants de Babel XIVe–XXIe siècles.* Vol. 2. Paris: Université Paris Diderot – Paris 7, pp. 71–81.

Frey, D. 2012. 'La guerre et la paix perpétuelle de l'abbé de Saint-Pierre à Rousseau', *Revue des Sciences Religieuses* 86(4): 455–73.

Hölzing, P. 2011. *Republikanismus und Kosmopolitismus: Eine ideengeschichtliche Studie.* Frankfurt: Campus Verlag.

Jordheim, H. 2018. 'Keeping the "Ism" in "Cosmopolitanism" – Wieland and the Origins of Cosmopolitan Discourse', *Journal of Political Ideologies* 23(3): 299–319.

Lilti, A. 2005. *Le monde des salons: Sociabilité et mondanité à Paris au XVIIIe siècle.* Paris: Fayard.

Masseau, D. 1994. *L'invention de l'intellectuel dans l'Europe du XVIIIe siècle.* Paris: Presses Universitaires de France.

Rjéoutski, V. 2015. 'La francophonie et le cosmopolitisme: Le cas de la noblesse russe (deuxième moitié du XVIIIe – début du XIXe siècle)', in M.-L. Pelus-Kaplan et al. (eds), *Être Citoyen du monde. Actes du Séminaire doctoral du laboratoire ICT – EA 337. Entre destruction et reconstruction du monde: Les enfants de Babel XIVe–XXIe siècles.* Vol. 2. Paris: Université Paris Diderot – Paris 7, pp. 93–107.

Spector, C. 2008. 'Le Projet de paix perpétuelle: De Saint-Pierre à Rousseau', in B. Bernardi and G. Silvestrini (eds), *Rousseau, Principes du droit de la guerre: Écrits sur la Paix Perpétuelle*. Paris: Vrin.

Van den Heuvel, G. 1986. 'Cosmopolite, Cosmopoli(ti)sme', in R. Reichardt and E. Schmitt (eds), *Handbuch politisch-sozialer Grundbegriffe in Frankreich 1680–1820*. Vol. 6. Munich: Oldenburg, pp. 41–55.

Wolff, C. 2005. *Vänskap och makt: Den svenska politiska eliten och upplysningstidens Frankrike*. Helsinki: Svenska Litteratursällskapet i Finland.

———. 2015. 'Le cosmopolitisme aristocratique des élites d'Europe du Nord au XVIIIe siècle: Pratiques et débats culturels', in M.-L. Pelus-Kaplan et al. (eds), *Être Citoyen du monde. Actes du Séminaire doctoral du laboratoire ICT – EA 337. Entre destruction et reconstruction du monde: Les enfants de Babel XIVe–XXIe siècles*. Vol. 2. Paris: Université Paris Diderot – Paris 7, pp. 83–92.

Chapter 2

# Revolution beyond Borders

## Conceptualizing the Universal and Cosmopolitan in the French Revolution, 1789–1815

*Friedemann Pestel and Pasi Ihalainen*

◆

At first sight, the extension of the French Revolution beyond France's borders seems to be a classic topic. Factualist accounts on revolutionary 'cosmopolitanism', 'universalism' or 'fraternity' are prominent both in historical and political theory research. The phenomena have recently gained further attention due to the transnational and global turns in post-bicentenary scholarship as well as normative uses of 'cosmopolitanism'. However, except for van den Heuvel's article on *cosmopolite* and *cosmopoli(ti)sme* in *Handbuch politisch-sozialer Grundbegriffe in Frankreich* (van den Heuvel 1986) and Helge Jordheim's work on the late eighteenth-century 'ismatization' of cosmopolitan thinking in German (Jordheim 2018: 311), there are hardly any systematic semantic analyses of these or related concepts. Many phenomenological or typological approaches to cosmopolitanism or universalism tend to carry normative implications about revolution as a transnational experience.

In this chapter, we analyse the political experiences and dynamics of the revolutionary debates of the 1790s and their aftermath in the 1800s, focusing on the relationships between nations and on cross-national contacts and transfers. Our interest lies in changing conceptualizations of what is in present-day research called the 'transnational' which the French Revolution together with the revolutionary and Napoleonic Wars gave rise to in French, British, German and Dutch political discourses. We are thereby complicating a seemingly straightforward narrative of revolutionary liberation and emancipation by looking at the ambivalences and contestations of French world discourse and by tracing subsequent discourse cycles in neighbouring countries as they responded to experiences of Revolution and increasingly uninhibited warfare.

Our approach takes its inspiration from David Armitage's and Sanjay Subramanyam's call to write 'transitive' histories, i.e. histories with defined transnational objects (Armitage and Subramanyam 2010: xiv). In our case, rather than simply speaking of 'revolutionary cosmopolitanism' or 'universalism', we intend to make clear how these concepts were used: which actors (sympathizers, foreigners, military, etc.) or institutions (such as the law) they referred to, in which way and with which limits. Aware that 'transnational' is a modern analytical category for a historical phenomenon expressed in very different terms in the Age of Revolutions, we argue that the revolutionary experiences and discourses presented a large spectrum of competing, mirroring or overlapping imaginations beyond the nation. These opened up universalist visions of an exported revolution but, at the same time, reinforced ways of thinking which were supportive of nationalism and imperialism. French revolutionaries and British parliamentarians, for instance, understood the law of nations and its implications for international relations in competing ways. When transnational interaction and exchange of ideas, goods, etc. between individuals and networks crossing borders mobilized ideas of fraternity and cosmopolitanism, the consequences were evaluated very differently in mainstream French and British political discourse.

For conceptual historians, a frequent empathic understanding of revolution linked to concepts like cosmopolitanism, universalism or humanity poses three challenges. First, while they are often positively connoted in scholarship, the risk is that these concepts reify the revolutionaries' Francocentric or expansionist imaginaries and established sympathetic readings of the Revolution, in particular with regard to hegemonic stances in revolutionary discourse on progress, emancipation or liberation. Second, in the late eighteenth century, the French term *cosmopolite* carried not only positive, but also pejorative connotations (see Chapter 1). The 1762 edition of the *Dictionnaire de l'Académie française* defined the term as 'one who does not adopt a fatherland' (Albrecht 2005: 35). On the eve of the Revolution, *cosmopolite* had established itself as the negative, or at least suspicious, 'other' to the positive 'we' category of *patriote*, the model of the new citizen, and to the idea of an upcoming regeneration of the French nation. This negative semantic pattern collides with historiographical accounts that distinguish between an early 'cosmopolitan' phase of the Revolution until 1792 and a subsequent turn towards radicalization and nationalism. Third, the growing literature on 'transnational' or 'global' aspects of the French Revolution critically assessing the French republican model and diffusionist interpretations of the Revolution places a strong emphasis on warfare, emigration and upheaval in French colonies (Armitage and Subramanyam 2010; Desan 2011; Bell 2015; Forrest and Middell 2016). Integrating these perspectives allows us to shed new light on the exclusion and violence within the Revolution that were associated with categories like 'universalism' or 'humanity'.

For these reasons, a look at France alone cannot be sufficient. We have therefore included the British debate on the 'universal', the 'law of nations' and the 'cosmopolitan' moulded by the experiences of wars against revolutionary and Napoleonic France. This panorama is complemented by transnational entanglements of revolutionary vocabularies which reflect other experiences of revolution, war and mobilization, including the Batavian Republic which emerged as a Sister Republic of France. We review uses of this political vocabulary in Franco–German relations after 1800 to highlight the impact of warfare, occupation and reform on the emergence of national consciousness.

Our analysis is based on four large source corpora. For France we relied on the debates of the revolutionary assemblies that have been edited as *Archives parlementaires* and digitized for the period between 1789 and January 1794 (both the printed and digital editions are still ongoing). Through our coverage of this short period in the French deliberations, we identified major conceptualizations of 'cosmopolitan', 'universal', 'humanity', 'fraternity', or the 'globe' (primarily designating a space beyond France) and related terms for the Constituent (1789–1791) and Legislative Assemblies (1791/92) as well as for the National Convention (1792–1795). For British and Dutch discourse, we explored the digitized records of the respective representative bodies in the Eighteenth Century Collections Online, the House of Commons Parliamentary Papers and Delpher, as well as the collocation tool of Hansard Corpus. The search terms included (selectively) the world, earth, globe, mankind/humanity, Europe/European, universal, cosmopolitan, fraternity and international, connected with the Revolution and France. As no equivalent to these legislative bodies existed for the German states, we relied on the collection of digitized newspapers and journals provided by the Bavarian State Library.

## Relating the Revolution to the World: French Debates on the Universal Nature of Revolutionary Principles, 1789–1794

French discourses on universalism derived from France's self-perceived special position within Catholic Christendom and a historical tradition that saw France as an heir to the Roman Empire. Enlightenment thinking and the Revolution's promise to 'recover' rights for all humanity fuelled ideas of placing the French nation at the centre of the universe with a particular mission. The originally religious mission was secularized by the radicalizing Revolution and targeted the European monarchies. France was to be the model for 'humanity': French revolutionaries exported the universal values of their republic in the name of humanity and by force of arms, if necessary. This exportation of Revolution was potentially unlimited, reaching from neighbouring provinces to 'Europe', the 'world' or even the 'universe'.

## Ambivalences of Cosmopolitanism

When French revolutionaries debated the relation between France and the outside, the figure of *cosmopolite* was significant. For the beginning of the Revolution until the fall of the monarchy and the radicalization of revolutionary warfare, van den Heuvel observes two usage patterns of *cosmopolite* – a more neutral one related to foreign trade and a more radical variant of *culte cosmopolite*, aiming at republican universalism (van den Heuvel 1986: 47–50). This universalism quickly took on more ambivalent meanings against the backdrop of war and terror; it began to imply exclusion as well as liberation (Desan 2013: 87). From 1793 on, *cosmopolite* became more and more assimilated into the category of 'foreigner' and thereby associated with conspiracy against and subversion of the French Republic.

In the early debates of the revolutionary assemblies, across the political spectrum, *cosmopolites* designated those uprooted individuals who had no stable links to family, society, country or region (Jean Joseph Mounier, 4 September 1789: 556; Claude Ambroise Régnier, 2 May 1790: 359; Bertrand Barrère, 9 December 1790: 358). Like 'capitalists' or professional soldiers, they either posed a threat to the regenerated society or they were expected to change their status and put down roots in it (Félix de Wimpffen, 15 December 1789: 586; Adam Philippe de Custine, 25 September 1790: 224; Pierre Louis Goudard, 30 November 1790: 135; Charles Tarbé, 15 May 1792: 405). Tellingly, the emancipation of France's Jewish community was debated as overcoming the cosmopolitan by integrating the French part of a scattered global diaspora into the revolutionary nation that would then spread its principles over the world: 'The Jews are members of this universal family which should establish fraternity among the peoples; and the revolution spreads its majestic veil over them as over you' (Emmanuel Marie Michel Philippe Fréteau de Saint-Just, 23 December 1789: 774; see also Isaac Ber-Bing, 14 October 1789: 446; Charles Louis Victor de Broglie, 24 December 1789: 779; Pétition des juifs établis en France, 13 April 1790: 723; Popkin 2015).

## Revolutionary Worldviews, Francocentrism and War

When we broaden our scope of revolutionary discourse on the world to categories such as *universel, monde, globe, humanité* and *fraternité*, we observe that French revolutionaries and their sympathizers used these terms in a Francocentric way. They correlated with invocations of *nous* and *vous*, or of the French nation and people in general, often in superlative forms such as 'the most ingenious nation in the universe' (Adresse de la ville de Coire, 2 April 1790: 517). As a general pattern, the 'world' French deputies imagined as having its eyes fixed on France was either to become more 'French', or France needed to defend itself against hostile machinations from outside. At the beginning of the Revolution, the deputies compared the situation at home to other parts of the 'world' and concluded that France had achieved more liberty than most other countries. Exceptions to this perceived superiority were Britain, before the image worsened with the declaration of war in 1793, and the United States.

When French legislators located their country in relation to the 'world' or the 'universe', they became convinced that the Revolution had a large potential impact beyond France. Based on our analysis, we can distinguish three phases of 'transnational' here. First, the deputies looked beyond borders in order to congratulate themselves on their revolutionary exceptionalism. In the debate on the Declaration of the Rights of Man in 1789, the comte de Crillon practised such self-adulation: 'The most enlightened and patriotic society that has ever been reunited among any people of the Universe will take care of a highly important work such as the constitution of a monarchy' (14 July 1789: 231). As Georges Danton's remarkable statement from June 1790 illustrates, this exceptionalist French understanding of the universal could be synonymous with patriotism: 'patriotism must have no other limits than the universe' (quoted from Vovelle 1995: 16).

In a second phase self-adulation turned into calls for this exceptionalism to be acknowledged from outside France. When talking about public finances, the Marquis de Condorcet declared in 1790: 'The National Assembly has earned itself the gratitude of humanity' (3 September 1790: 535). Finally, the revolutionaries understood their transformation of the French political order as a model of change for the world – an ambition that became closely linked to the egalitarian constitution of 1793 as 'the general code of the humanity' (Armand Gensonné, 27 October 1792: 15): 'Soon, all peoples, who are conquered by reason, will covet our constitution, which is the first example of the pact that should unite humans by the links of fraternity. Soon, liberty and equality, installed on the terrestrial globe, will alone dominate the nations and preside over the congress of humanity', declared Nicolas Guénin, mayor of Cambrai and one of the frequent radical non-members speaking to the National Convention after 1792 (30 July 1793: 5, see also *Adresse des membres du conseil général d'Annecy*, 23 June 1793: 90). With the first advances of the revolutionary armies in 1792, the belief in the universality of revolutionary principles expanded in scope: liberating the people of the 'world' from despotic repression by revolutionary propaganda, sending 'missionaries', or practising outright military 'liberation' (François Chabot, 21 August 1792: 690; Henri Grégoire, 27 November 1792: 610).

References to the broader relevance of the Revolution played a pivotal role in legitimizing French warfare against the European powers. At first, in May 1791, the Constituent Assembly had made a solemn declaration on the *droits des nations*: for all time France would profess fraternity with foreign nations, renouncing any ambition of territorial conquest (Belissa 1998: 184–97). Eleven months later, the Legislative Assembly pushed Louis XVI to declare war on Francis II of Hungary and Bohemia. On this occasion, Condorcet turned what was strictly speaking a French war of aggression into an act of defence of the 'universal liberty of humanity' (20 April 1792: 212). When the Assembly had to decree *la patrie en danger* in July 1792 as Prussia had joined Austria and France was facing foreign invasion, Marie Jean Hérault de Séchelles and others justified new measures of mobilization and delimited warfare by an early expectation of fighting a war 'to end all wars': 'The war we have undertaken in no way resembles the common wars which so often distressed and tore up the globe; it is the war of equality, liberty and the Constitution ... This war, therefore, is the last war between all foreign powers and us' (11 July 1792: 336).

Only a brief interlude sparked by the fall of the monarchy in August 1792 made the revolutionaries renounce conquests by force in the name of 'fraternity' with the peoples (Desan 2013: 96). Some months later, in their address to the National Convention, an army battalion dispatched to Mainz expected to keep on fighting until the 'universe' declared that 'humanity is free' (*Adresse du 10e bataillon de la Meurthe, à l'armée de Custine à Mayence*, 19 February 1793: 5). Indeed, the first major victories of the revolutionary army in late 1792 triggered a phase of self-fulfilling prophecies about republican universality beyond all borders:

> Legislators, declare to the Universe that all peoples who will shake off the yoke of despotism and desire the protection of the French and the reunion with their Republic will be protected and recognized as French. ... the peoples ... only wait for this desired moment to break their chains; and it is only out of fear of collapsing, by lack of your support, that they have not yet done so. (*Adresse du maire et des officiers municipaux du baillage de Berg-Zabern*, 18 November 1792: 461)

As became clear during 1793, this *fraternité universelle* was a clearly Francocentric endeavour brought about by 'the Republic regenerating the universe' that would plant tricolour flags – and French guns – over Europe, even in parts from where no calls for liberation from despotic regimes had arrived in Paris (*Adresse des administrateurs du département de la Côte-d'Or*, 5 March 1793: 608; *Lettre des amis de la liberté et de l'égalité de la ville de Gand*, 5 February 1793: 218). At first, war mobilization was directed against Austria and Prussia. For Condorcet, their support for the outlawed French émigrés marked an act of disrespect of French law and, by extension, turned the foreign monarchs into 'enemies of humanity' who were likewise betraying their own peoples (20 April 1792: 211; see also Jeismann 1992: 127). After the execution of Louis XVI, the French declaration of war on Britain and the British conquest of Toulon turned 'the new Carthage' over the Channel and its Prime Minister William Pitt into yet more 'enemies of humanity' and into violators of the 'law of nations [*droit des gens*]' (*Lettre des membres du conseil général de la commune de Nîmes*, 29 November 1793: 333; *Adresse de la Société populaire de Niort*, 12 December 1793: 350; *La Société républicaine de Montpasier*, 5 December 1793: 653). In the antagonistic logic of French republicans, defeating British 'despotism' became equivalent to 'giving liberty to the Universe' (*Adresse du conseil général du département du Nord*, 15 February 1793: 573). In September 1793, after failed attempts to 'denationalize' warfare against foreign governments (but not nations), the National Convention refrained from all *idées philosophiques* in warfare, returning to the *lois de guerre* (André Jeanbon Saint-André, 15 September 1793: 231; see also van den Heuvel 1986: 51; Belissa 1998: 356–57).

### A Cosmopolitan Nation? Inclusion and Exclusion of Foreigners and Enemies

There were significant exceptions to the general reproach that foreign states were 'despotic' or 'tyrannical'. In the revolutionary assemblies, the vocabulary of the cosmopolitan was used in numerous emphatic invocations of foreign sympathizers of the Revolution, in particular in response to addresses and declarations of solidarity with the revolutionary cause. The proceedings also reveal the important role of foreigners who spoke to the assemblies, including representatives of British and Irish Whig clubs, constitutional or reform societies and American or German Francophiles.

After the outbreak of the war with Austria and Prussia and even despite the end of the French monarchy, British and Irish revolutionary societies stuck to their solidarity with the Jacobins (Belissa 1998: 362). In their letters, addresses and speeches to the revolutionary assemblies, these Francophiles from abroad stressed the universal impact of the Revolution around categories such as 'cosmopolite', 'fraternity', 'humanity', 'citizenship' or 'citizens of the world'. Despite the ambiguity of such 'cosmopolitanism', French observers could also present a British radical like Joseph Priestley as 'a cosmopolitan and, by consequence, French man' (François Chabot, 24 August 1792: 690). Members of the British corresponding societies did not see a problem in associating themselves with the French Revolution as 'citizens of the world' (Revolution Society 1789: 9).

The most notorious of these emphatic foreigners was the Prussian noblemen Anacharsis Cloots who took residence in Paris as 'capital of the Globe' in 1789 and stylized himself as *orateur du genre humain*. As such, he became a French citizen when the Assembly presented eighteen European and American foreigners as *citoyens du monde,* elevating them to French and prospectively 'world' citizenship (Israel 2014: 266; Desan 2013; Coignard 2017: 54–63). As a French citizen, Cloots was then elected to the National Convention. Even before that, he had been admitted to speak to the deputies: in 1790, he led a delegation of twenty-one 'nations' from Europe and Asia, who had come to Paris for the *Fête de la Fédération* on Bastille Day, to demonstrate that the French Revolution had given a sign of resurrection 'in all quarters of the world' (Anacharsis Cloots, 19 June 1790: 373). A month after a Paris crowd had dethroned the king in August 1792, he made a speech in favour of the pantheonization of Johannes Gutenberg that expressed the political possibilities of that historical moment. As Cloots saw the emergence of print culture as being at the origins of the Revolution and mass mobilization, the dramatic changes in France represented for him only the first step to a *législature cosmopolite* for a *confédération universelle* leading to a *globe organisé à la française*:

> Gutenberg's art … will make you one day the representatives of one billion brothers. The Universe, put into equal departments, will forget about its old national denominations and contestations, to eternally keep fraternal peace under the aegis of a law which … will never face the slightest resistance anywhere. The Universe will form one state of united individuals, … the Universal Republic. (Cloots, 9 September 1792: 500)

Such sympathies expressed by foreign supporters to French deputies and the emotional reception of their addresses and speeches in the assemblies stood in sharp contrast with the public ostracism of fellow French citizens, performed in the interest of *l'humanité tout entière* (Charles Louis François Gabriel Morisson, 13 November 1792: 388). We find this specific world discourse applied to the 'foreigner' (Saint-Just) Louis XVI. His trial and execution served as a 'prelude to the revolutions of the entire globe' anticipating the imminent republicanization of the world (*Société populaire des Montagnards de Saint-Omer*, 30 September 1793: 333; see also *Adresse des administrateurs du directoire du département des Deux-Sèvres*, 17 February 1793: 636; Jacques Nicolas Billaud-Varenne, 9 June 1793: 221).

Moreover, the universal proscription of enemies of the Revolution targeted émigrés: 'roaming and vagabonding over the entire globe, may their torture be to find a fatherland nowhere' (Pierre Vergniaud, 18 November 1792: 493). Their condemnation resembled the early discourse on France's 'cosmopolitan' Jewry. Whereas the latter was to be integrated into the new community of citizens that formed *la patrie*, the émigrés were to be treated as the 'scum of the earth' (*Proclamation des administrateurs du département des Pyrénées-Orientales*, 29 October 1793: 6). As mentioned above, German princes hosting them in their territories were accused of violating the *droit des gens* (*Le comité diplomatique*, 22 November 1791: 291; Vergniaud, 27 November 1791: 440). As the opposite of a *citoyen de l'univers* (Mathurin Louis Étienne Sédillez, 9 February 1792: 303), the émigrés' positive contribution to the Revolution could only be indirect as the Breton deputy Joseph Lequinio declared: 'The more of them that leave France, the more fermentation will spread over the neighbouring empires; the more the attention of the other peoples will rise; and the sooner the revolution of the Universe will take place' (20 October 1792: 299). The émigrés themselves shared this revolutionary degradation of cosmopolitanism when they referred to themselves as *cosmopolites malgré eux* (Pestel 2015: 492). However, some German or Swiss magistrates did not see émigrés as possible catalysts of revolution but welcomed them as an antidote to tendencies of insurrection among the local populations (Pestel 2015: 306; Pestel and Winkler 2016: 155).

### Universality and Colonialism

A strand of cosmopolitan discourse during the French Revolution that has been underestimated to date is its colonial dimension related to slavery, the status of free people of colour and the Haitian Revolution (cf. Covo 2015). Though the revolutionaries also spoke about *l'esclavage* and 'the universal enfranchisement of nations' (Pierre François Aubry-Dubochet, 23 September 1790: 148; Antoine Adrien Lamourette, 24 August 1792: 689) in purely metaphorical terms referring to France and Europe, the impact of the Revolution in the Caribbean nonetheless resonated in the debates. This occurred early: the *cahiers de doléances* set up in 1788/89 at the local level in preparation for the Estates General put reforming slavery on the political agenda as the 'wish of humanity' (*Sénéchaussée du Boulonnais, cahier de doléances*, 426). In his opening speech at the Estates General in May 1789, Finance Minister Jacques Necker mentioned the slave trade as a 'global' evil to be remedied by the National Assembly (read by Charles Louis François de Paule de Barentin, 5 May 1789: 20). In the following months, pressure groups such as free people of colour from the colonies or the abolitionist association *Les Amis des Noirs* demanded citizen rights and denounced the oppression of a large part of *le genre humain* (*Adresse des citoyens de couleur*, 6 July 1790: 722; *Adresse de la Société des Amis des Noirs*, 21 January 1790: 273). Accordingly, the deputies conferred full citizenship to free people of colour who had two free parents in spring 1791 as an act of 'worldwide' significance (Jean Louis de Viefville des Essarts, 11 May 1791: 765).

In contrast to this emancipatory world discourse, colonial lobbyists made use of the same categories to defend the colonial system. Louis de Curt, a deputy from Guadeloupe, praised France as *première nation de l'univers* for being the first to admit representatives of the colonies to a metropolitan legislative body, in contrast to Britain and its American colonies in the 1770s. Hardly surprisingly, the Caribbean representatives were White plantation owners (26 November 1789: 265). Regarding the Assembly's projects of colonial reform, delegates from the colonies subsequently argued against lifting the *ligne de démarcation* between White people, free people of colour and Black enslaved people, citing the 'global' economic importance of the Caribbean sugar plantations. A deputy from Nantes, a centre of the French slave trade, invoked anthropological differences between the inhabitants of different *parties du monde* that justified the enslavement of Africans (*L'adresse des députés extraordinaires de la commune de Saint-Pierre de la Martinique*, 30 December 1790: 720; Joseph Michel Pellerin, 1 March 1790: 771).

With the slave insurrections in Saint-Domingue in August 1791 that marked the outbreak of the Haitian Revolution, this anti-emancipatory strand of world discourse prevailed. The subsequent interventions of Jacques Pierre Brissot in the Legislative Assembly illustrate the ambivalence between French emancipatory universality and its application to colonial slavery. Though, as a leading representative of the *Amis des Noirs*, he understood himself as an *ami de l'humanité* that included enslaved people and free people of colour, he admitted that slavery reforms should not happen at the expense of the colonists (9 November 1791: 722). Given the violence committed in the Caribbean, for him the *cri universel* for *nos frères de Saint-Domingue* implied support and solidarity exclusively for the White settlers and those free people of colour who stood on their side (30 October 1791: 522). There was no question of emancipation and little space for expressing ideas of fraternity with Black populations either (Salvador Paul Leremboure, 9 December 1791: 721; *Proclamation de l'assemblée coloniale de Saint-Domingue*, 11 February 1792: 697).

## *Into the Late 1790s: the Persistence of War*

From 1793 onwards, the political vocabulary of the cosmopolitan in France was largely discredited, marked by negative significations related to warfare, outlawed émigrés, the slave insurrections in the colonies and the suspicious figure of *l'étranger* (see Wahnich 1997). Suspected of adhering to the *République universelle* at a time when nationalism was mobilized to support external and internal warfare, the emphatic Anacharsis Cloots ended his career under the guillotine calling upon the 'fraternity of nations' (Polasky 2015: 269; see also Polasky 2019: 114). Linked to a nationalist turn in the French understanding of 'patriotism', the political discourse revolving around the 'world' or 'humanity' became strongly tinctured with Francocentric universality. This implied the spread of French republicanism abroad but evolved from scenarios of solidarity and liberation to controversies about hierarchy, sovereignty or conquest, and finally annexation and occupation. For the later 1790s, existing research suggests that the ambivalent power relations between revolutionary France, Europe and the world prevailed throughout the Revolutionary Wars (van den Heuvel 1986: 52–53). Persistently reproached for lacking patriotism in a nation under political and military strain, cosmopolitanism in France remained largely discredited.

In contrast to these shifts in French political discourse, throughout the 1790s and early 1800s 'cosmopolitanism' in Germany remained a largely positive concept, complementary to the nation and patriotism (*Allgemeine Literatur-Zeitung*, 24 June 1795; 4 December 1802; 8 February 1805; see also Weichlein 2006). This stability created a tension with European warfare from 1792 as German cosmopolitanism was understood as being in opposition to French Jacobinism, regicide and expansionism or even to revolution as such, but also to British hegemony (*Allgemeine Zeitung*, 20 June 1798; *Allgemeine Literatur-Zeitung*, 19 April 1799). Michael Jeismann has poignantly observed the diverging Franco-German conceptions of 'humanity' in that respect: whereas German propagandists interpreted this in terms of 'Germankind', French authors equalled the Revolution with humanity (Jeismann 1992: 132). By politicizing cosmopolitanism at different degrees, German observers reframed the concept as the disinterested, peaceful, observing other of revolutionary universality without being reduced to national terms (Albrecht 2005: 301; Klinger 2008: 213).

## British Reactions to French Revolutionary Universality and Fraternity

Next, we turn to analysing how French revolutionary claims to universality and fraternity on behalf of all humanity and the world were received by

British parliamentarians – as representatives of the leading military opponent of the French Republic from 1793. According to David Armitage, as
the British Empire expanded in the late eighteenth century, parliamentary
debates became increasingly international. Knowledge of international law
was increasing, particularly after the publication of Robert Ward's *Enquiry
to the Foundation and History of the Law of Nations in Europe* (1795), critical
of French republican attempts to redefine the law of nations, and James
Mackintosh's *Discourse on the Study of the Law of Nature and Nations* (1799)
(Armitage 2013: 135–36, 150, 152–53).

Early revolutionary discourse on universality vindicating the 'inalienable
rights of mankind' – or norms of international law – had been based in both
Britain and France on shared ideals of rights and liberty inspired by anti-slav-
ery debates. As the Revolution radicalized and the implications of popular
sovereignty were extended, British corresponding societies joined this radicalization. The abolition of the French monarchy and the outbreak of war
between Britain and France in February 1793, however, made any interaction
with French revolutionaries appear treasonous (Alpaugh 2014: 594–96, 607;
cf. Dupuy 2016: 245, 255). Initial enthusiasm about the Revolution by Richard
Price and others turned into rising anti-revolutionary loyalism in favour of
the status quo. While Charles James Fox and especially Thomas Paine were
ready to interpret the sovereignty of the people and democracy in radically
new ways, William Pitt turned into a defender of the established mixed constitution and redefined traditional concepts for that purpose. Edmund Burke
became the leading critic of revolutionary principles. Governmental voices
increasingly represented French revolutionary liberty as a threat to the
British laws, liberties and constitution and questioned the motives of British
radical societies, accusing them of republicanism supportive of 'the assumed
sovereignty of the universe' claimed by the French (Mori 2003: 35, 37;
Ihalainen 2010: 488–93).

### Opposition to French Universality

In Parliament, the French threat to the balance of power was the real issue,
while more explicit opposition to French claims of expansive universality
emerged towards the end of the 1790s. Discourse on the British parliament
as the defender of 'the universal liberties of mankind' rose as a reaction to
revolutionary ideas on universal suffrage (Thomas Erskine, HC, 26 May
1797: 584). As Peter Burrell put it, the rulers of France aimed at 'universal
domination' on the European continent: while talking about justice, good
faith and humanity to persuade neighbouring peoples, they committed
atrocities to attain universal dominance (HL, 2 November 1797: 82). For
William Fitzwilliam, little had changed in France since the *ancien régime*,

with the government still aiming at a 'universal empire', this time through 'Jacobinical' deeds (HL, 2 November 1797: 86). Britain was typically seen as the major opponent of such 'universal domination', particularly after the French government declared that the British constitution was incompatible with that of the French Republic (John Proby, HC, 10 November 1797: 184; Henry Dundas, Secretary at War, HC, 4 December 1797: 341). According to Prime Minister Pitt, the French held 'principles which professed to be universal' and were 'intended to be established and perpetuated among all nations of the earth' but, in practice, entailed perpetual changes in native constitutions and rulers (HC, 3 February 1800: 324–25). They still seemed to aim at 'universal empire' in Europe and globally (William Elliot, HC, 24 November 1802: 124, 129). In 1805, Pitt completed a memorandum on the deliverance and security of Europe after discussions with Russians, implying the existence of a concept of Europe, balance of power, 'public law' and constitutional order opposed to French warfare and hegemony (Jarrett 2013: 39–41).

The revolutionary principle of popular sovereignty was another major challenge. As George Canning, a rising Tory politician, put it, the French republicans destroyed all freedom by claiming that power originated from the people. According to him, no class had been involved in creating or was ready to preserve such power. Popular sovereignty implied despotism free from laws at home and military despotism 'proposing to maintain itself by universal peace' abroad (HC, 3 February 1800: 489). The rise of popular sovereignty implied major transformations in the law of nations as it questioned treaties traditionally based on dynastic and feudal rights. This interpretation resulted from the revolutionary process: the revolutionary assemblies gradually concluded that popular will should be the basis of the law of nations – only to find themselves opposed by the rest of Europe, and international tensions rising surrounding interpretations of such law. It remained difficult to deduce what the will of the people was, who they were, and to what extent foreign peoples' attitudes towards the Revolution mattered at all (Kolla 2017: Introduction). In the British parliament, few sympathizers of the Revolution would have negotiated with France in the name of 'universal order and civilization' (Charles James Fox, HC, 18 October 1796: 114); most viewed Britain as the leader of the anti-French alliance (Richard Brinsley Sheridan, HC, 20 April 1798: 21).

The war between Britain and France continued almost without intermission until 1814/15. Napoleon, too, was viewed in Britain as aiming at 'universal domination' in the style of an early modern universal monarchy (Dwyer 2010: 306). British universalist conceptualizations were evolving in a direction not so different from the French; the British, too, considered it their duty to defend the entire 'civilized world'. 'Civilization' was becoming a counter-concept of its supposed opposite, the French Revolution (den Boer 2005: 55). Prime Minister Henry Addington called France 'the common enemy of the civilized world' due to its tendency to 'subjugate' other nations (HC, 22 November 1803: 26). The role of the British parliament was to defend liberty on behalf of Europe and 'the whole civilized world', Britain and France being 'tried at the tribunal of the nations of the world' as alternative centres of universality (John Doyle, HC, 23 January 1807: 540, 544; also George Hibbert, HC, 12 March 1807: 100; and Beilby Porteus, Bishop of London, HL, 9 February 1807: 693).

### British Emphasis on the Law of Nations

The philosopher Jeremy Bentham coined the term 'international' in 1789 to more clearly express the law of nations that extended beyond one nation state and mainly concerned relations between them (also Chapters 1 and 3). Bentham considered his neologism 'sufficiently analogous and intelligible' (*An Introduction to the Principles of Morals and Legislation*, London, 1789: cccxxiv) but 'international' did not yet find its way into public discourse. In Parliament, it remained reserved for references to 'international law' or to 'international forces/troops' fighting against Napoleon (Dillon, HC, 5 April 1807: 515). Foreign Secretary Lord Castlereagh recognized 'a code of international law' in line with regulations created in connection with the Treaty of Westphalia (1648) as the basis of 'rights acknowledged and maintained by every nation' and as regulation for 'intercourse with her neighbours' (HC, 18 February 1813: 596).

The law of nations – as a counter-revolutionary if not even counter-Enlightenment concept – remained the expression for international law going beyond a single nation (Armitage 2013: 39–41). It was typically invoked to justify foreign policy action in any part of the Empire or Europe as Britain was believed to have a duty 'to instruct other states in the law of nations' (Edvard East, HC, 17 March 1794: 620). French revolutionary discourse provoked debates on international law particularly as the French 'violated the law of nations by a decree, declaring war against all Governments, and forcing those countries, into which their armies should enter, to form a constitution of their own', imposing the sovereignty of the people (Edmund Burke, HC, 28 December 1792: 218). By contrast, French positive references to *le(s) droit(s) des nations* only extended to republics that had broken with the rights of kings and 'tyrants'. As an enemy, the British monarchy was accused of violating these laws when occupying the French port city of Toulon or supporting royalist insurrectionists in the Vendée (Billaud-Varenne, 17 September 1793: 307; *La Société républicaine de Niort*,

12 December 1793: 350). As we shall see, the Revolutionary Wars consolidated a gap between two different concepts of 'laws of nations' – the French republican and expansionist, the British aiming at balance of power, full national sovereignty, and imperial public order (Belissa 2006).

British parliamentarians contributed to the construction of the alternative British concept of the law of nations. While some sympathizers of the Revolution rejected intrusions to the internal affairs of France as a violation of the law of the nations (Charles Stanhope, HL, 4 April 1794: 201; Charles James Fox, HC, 17 April 1794: 174), the majority presented British military campaigns as justified by the same token. Once a war was threatening in 1793, Prime Minister Pitt said that the French were applying their 'new code of law of nations ... to establish their Government wherever they should carry their arms' while only causing universal anarchy (HC, 4 January 1793: 296). When the war broke out, he presented the French as 'taking themselves the office of the arbiters of Europe ... in entire contradiction to whatever had been sanctioned by established practice' (HC, 1 February 1793: 390–91). He insisted that the French regicide should be put on trial on the basis of 'the laws of humanity' (HC, 23 April 1793: 304). Later on, peace with France was opposed with references to the political instability of its regime (George Canning, HC, 30 December 1794: 25–26). The war was not 'a dispute between nations in general at war, but was of a particular nature', concerning the very type of government in France (Charles Grey, HC, 26 January 1795: 305). The Prime Minister consistently insisted that 'every principle of the law of Nations' justified Britain resisting 'a system hostile to the interests of this country and safety of Europe' (William Pitt, HC, 16 January 1795: 324). According to him, the French were applying a 'private law of their own making, a mere internal regulation' as opposed to 'the universally received maxims and laws of nations' (HC, 30 December 1796: 564).

The British political elite increasingly saw themselves as the primary defender of the 'European' law of nations – the concept itself remaining highly Eurocentric. According to George Spencer, 'the principles advanced by France would go to subvert all the acknowledged laws of nations' so that 'the laws and Constitution of France' would be 'paramount to the laws of Europe' (HL, 30 October 1796: 40). William Grenville expressed the same view this way: the Directory was totally mistaken to suggest that 'the French Republic possessed the only supreme power in Europe, and that all other countries might be parcelled out by them at pleasure into what they were pleased to call Republics' (HL, 30 December 1796: 32). The Prime Minister condemned France for inventing a 'sacred law of nature' that extended beyond the French borders and tried to bypass 'by a new code of their own, all recognized principles of the law of nations'. For Pitt, 'the Laws of Nature and Nations' were the authority on which the British parliamentarians should build as opposed to 'the inherent principles of the French Revolution' (William Pitt, HC, 3 February 1800: 306, 318–19, 321).

All this was contestable. In the inaugural session of the representative institution of the Batavian Republic, the Speaker presented the British as isolated, 'cursed by all the peoples of the world', when fighting a war to establish 'a tyranny over humanity' (Pieter Paulus, *Dagverhaal*, 1 March 1796: 7). They were violating the 'most sacred laws of nations' (*heiligste rechten der Volken*) through their measures against Dutch shipping, carrying on commercial rivalry between the two nations (*Extract uit de Decrete*, vol. 1, 1796: 392; Vitzinga, *Dagverhaal*, 1 December 1797: 28).

During the Napoleonic Wars, British parliamentary discourses on the law of nations typically concerned justifying British military measures with French violations of the law of nations. Sometimes the British government also faced allegations that it had broken international law. Senior opposition parliamentarians might argue that Britain held a particular responsibility as the only imperial power to consistently defend the legal basis of international relations. Thomas Erskine, the former Lord Chancellor who had defended Thomas Paine and the London Corresponding Society against charges of treason raised by the government, protested in 1808 against the bombardment of Copenhagen and the seizure of the neutral Danish fleet. He described the long process through which 'civilized nations have emerged from a state of continual insecurity and violence, by the establishment of an universal public law' and insisted that this 'ought to be held sacred and inviolate by all governments, as binding the whole civilized world under one politic and moral dominion'. It remained 'the duty and the interest of G[reat] Britain, and her pledge to the world, to maintain inviolate the acknowledged principles of public law' (HL, 21 January 1808: 32–34). Britain was to be 'the shield, the disinterested protector, and the saviour of Europe; and the nations of the earth might expect to have their chains broken' (HL, 8 February 1808: 356), reflecting allegories of British global exceptionalism as evoked in 'Rule Britannia'. If Britain failed to do its providential duty, the impact of the French Revolution would become permanent and universal, destroying 'all the sanctions of morals and policy, which the wisdom of ages has ripened into universal law, for universal security and peace' (HL, 8 March 1808: 929).

The tendency to identify Britain as the primary champion of international law was also expressed by Charles Abbot, the Speaker of the House of Commons, in his speech at the opening of Parliament in 1813. For Abbot, the British 'national character' was based on the responsibility to work for the benefit of all 'Europe', indeed 'mankind' and 'humanity', that counted on British leadership and example, learning 'what was the spirit of those ancient institutions, what the genius of that international law'. Britain possessed 'inexhaustible resources of power consolidated by justice, and operating only for the benefit of mankind' (HC, 4 November 1813: 37–38). This conceptualization of the 'international' community was not that different from the French: it was based on a universalist (imperialist) notion of setting an example which the other nations should follow. The rise of such a notion of Britain as *the* champion of international law that regulated relations between nations in Europe would support the emergence of Anglophone and Anglocentric worldviews.

### French Fraternity as Revolutionary Influence
British experiences of the radicalized Revolution also left a legacy of pejorative discourse on French fraternity as transnational ideological interaction. As 'liberty' in its British form remained an overwhelmingly positive concept and the French concept of 'equality' was too challenging a notion to be discussed, 'fraternity' was the third term of the revolutionary slogan that was constantly attacked.

In late 1792, the approaching military conflict was audible in the words of the Home Secretary. Henry Dundas interpreted French talk about fraternity as a mere disguise to 'the aggrandisement of their dominions, and the establishment of their own Government' (HC, 13 December 1792: 59). Edmund Burke presented the French Declaration of the Rights of Man as comparable to the Koran in that it ordered the French to propagate the revolutionary doctrine and violently conquer countries that did not submit to their 'system of fraternizing' (HC, 13 December 1792: 85–86; 28 December 1792: 219). In the debate on war, Prime Minister Pitt cited the declaration of the French National Convention on 19 November 1792 addressed to foreign peoples and granting 'fraternity to all those people who should be desirous to gain their freedom, and offer them assistance for that purpose'. Pitt's interpretation of this as a revolutionary threat was clear: the French were hostile 'to the human race' when offering the peoples 'fraternity' with the purpose of subverting governments and abolishing the constitution. The British should not worry, as their fellow subjects would welcome the hostile subtext of this message (HC, 1 February 1793: 389; 12 February 1793: 445, 457). The British government saw the French revolutionary system as having changed so that its declarations of 'universal liberty and fraternity' stood for 'universal conquest' (Grenville, HL, 1 February 1793: 73).

The Terror in France only reinforced such views. While some hoped by 1795 that 'the spirit of Jacobinism and fraternization' was declining (William Wilberforce, HC, 27 May 1795: 396), the discourse rejecting fraternity continued unabated. A bishop might concede that war was not the preferable way of communicating to the French that their 'fraternizing system must be given up', yet assured his fellow peers that the British stood united to 'protect the people themselves from the insidious machinations of their demagogues, from the bloody tyranny of French fraternities' (Richard Watson, HL, 27 January 1795: 74, 82).

The Prime Minister presented British liberty as the major counterforce to 'French fraternization' (William Pitt, HC, 13 March 1797: 33), citing the Netherlands and Switzerland as warning examples of countries destroyed by French or Jacobin 'fraternity' (William Drummond, HC, 2 November 1797: 12; Richard Temple, HC, 14 February 1797). The only way to gain 'French fraternity' seemed to be murdering legitimate monarchs, destroying parliaments and overturning constitutions (Richard Temple, HC, 10 November 1797: 162). During the Irish rising of the late 1790s, parliamentarians were shocked by attempts to import 'French fraternity and French liberty' and to destroy British 'liberty' and Empire (William Grenville, HL, 18 December 1798: 301; George Grey, HC, 7 February 1799: 731). The Irish were advised to prioritize 'the English connection to French fraternity' (Richard Temple, HC, 14 February 1797: 88, 94, 97; Gilbert Elliot, HL, 11 April 1797: 394).

Those on the other side of the Revolutionary Wars saw French fraternity very differently. The Dutch States General spoke favourably about 'the closest fraternity between two nations yet mentioned in the history of the human race' (HL, 2 June 1795: 515) when referring to the bonds between revolutionary France and the Batavian Republic. In their National Assembly, F.M.W. Ruisch thanked these strong ties to 'our sister, the most powerful republic of the world' for domestic peace in the Netherlands (*Dagverhaal*, 8 March 1796: 42). The Dutch parliamentarians typically saw revolutionary France as the model of liberty and equality when formulating their own republican constitution (J.A. de Mist, 22 April 1797: 716). They did not hesitate to associate themselves with 'the largest, the most famous, the bravest of all republics in the world, our ally' (Speaker H. Midderigh, 23 January 1798: 428), which demonstrates the centrality of the concept of republic for a revolutionary understanding of international relations. The Batavian Constitution, once completed in 1798, was described as 'the seal on the friendship and alliance between this Republic and her sister the French' (*Dagverhaal*, 18 May 1798: 86). The Sister Republics not only accommodated supranational ideals borrowed from France into their native political traditions but could at times be innovative (Desan 2011: 148; Serna 2016: 39–42; Oddens and Rutjes 2015: 17–19, 27, 29; Jourdan 2015: 187, 198–99). Yet direct French domination over Dutch politics had become evident and increased under Napoleon, leading to annexation by France in 1810.

In Britain, rejections of French fraternity did not cease with the fall of the Republic in France. Napoleon's plans to invade Britain seemed to carry on the anarchy and despotism threatening European constitutions. Parliamentarians believed, however, that the Irish had become sufficiently aware of 'the horrors of French fraternity' (John Berkeley Burland, HC, 22 November 1803: 18–20), their rebellion having been no more than 'conspiracy, fomented by the intrigues of France' (John Browne, HL, 22 November 1803: 5). In 1805, Prime Minister Pitt claimed that, after 'bondage which has been introduced by republican fraternity' and 'by the audacity of jacobinism [sic]', the French government was offering 'avowed despotism', revolutionary ideas being still disseminated across borders (HC, 8 February 1805: 320–21). This statement made James Martin emphasize that there was no longer 'an organised republic existing in Ireland, and ready to fraternize with the then democratical [government] of France' (HC, 8 February 1805: 335). Foreign Secretary George Canning recommended that other nations model themselves on the British, rather than the French: 'It was to be hoped that any nation whose intercourse and union with Great Britain were intimate, would gradually imbibe the feelings of Great Britain' (HC, 31 May 1809: 827).

### The Few Cosmopolitans in Britain, the Netherlands and Germany

Expressions of cosmopolitan attitudes in countries surrounding France after the experiences of the Revolutionary and Napoleonic Wars were few. A parliamentary instance of the competing meanings of 'cosmopolitan' can be found from 1807, again with reference to revolutionary influence in Ireland. As Henry Grattan suggested that the British constitution should be suspended in Ireland due to the continuous presence of 'cosmopolitan principles' there (HC, 13 August 1807: 1205), two colleagues responded by defending both parliamentary government and the positive connotations of the cosmopolitan. John Ingram Lockhart defined the British parliament itself as one of 'cosmopolitan beneficence' (HC, 13 August 1807: 1211), only to be echoed by Richard Brinsley Sheridan that 'our cosmopolitan and philanthropic parliament' was pursuing the right policies in Ireland (HC, 13 August 1807: 1216). 'Cosmopolitan' could thus stand both for rejected (transnational) revolutionary ideas and for British imperial policies defined as beneficial and even philanthropic for all peoples. This illustrates the presence of two competing imperialist concepts of universality.

In Germany, a peculiar kind of ambiguity was attached to the term 'cosmopolitan', recalling its anti-revolutionary connotations in the British parliament. After debates on *Weltbürgertum* led by Schiller, Kant and Fichte in the 1790s (see Chapter 1) and occasional associations of cosmopolitanism

with Freemasonry conspiracy theories (Jordheim 2018: 313), as a consequence of the Napoleonic conquests German evocations of cosmopolitanism
after 1800 became increasingly associated with patriotism and political and
cultural independence from French dominance. The concept of a 'citizen
of the world' had clearly become politicized and an object of competing
definitions. In 1811, the *Jenaische Allgemeine Literatur-Zeitung* concluded
for a patriotic definition: 'The inauthentic cosmopolitans [*Kosmopoliten*]
want a constitution to be common to all peoples... The true citizen of the
world [*Weltbürger*] is the faithful son of his people' (28 February 1811).
Through the conceptual couple *Kosmopolit/Weltbürger* we can see two
competing variants of conceptualizing cosmopolitanism, one embracing
French hegemony (and thus the 'foreign' form of the word), the other
prioritizing German patriotism and meeting the French revolutionary
challenge with the idea of a federal German nation. As Georg Schmidt has
argued, universalizing a plural understanding of Germanness was a strategy
to counter national marginalization (Schmidt 2016).

   This nationalization of cosmopolitanism marked some similarities with
the British discourse; German patriotism around 1810 was conceived as
cosmopolitan insofar as it targeted French 'universal despotism'. In that
sense, it was a political principle beyond borders (*Jenaische Allgemeine
Literatur-Zeitung*, 1 January 1814; *Erlanger Real-Zeitung*, 14 June 1814).
Only Napoleon-friendly papers from the Confederation of the Rhine or
the Kingdom of Westphalia praised the Emperor's continental system as
the historical completion of European unification (*National-Zeitung der
Deutschen*, 22 September 1808; *Le moniteur westphalien* supplement, 25
December 1811; Coignard 2017: 119). With Napoleon's defeat, cosmopolitanism was once again clearly negative. Patriotic calls for national unity
replaced the category of the 'world' with the 'nation', and, in contrast to its
earlier German usages, cosmopolitanism became associated with hegemony
and Bonapartism (*Deutsche Blätter*, 21 March 1814; 31 May 1815; 1 January
1815; *Allgemeiner Anzeiger der Deutschen*, 3 October 1814; *Berlinische
Nachrichten von Staats- und gelehrten Sachen*, 24 August 1815).

## Conclusion

Using Reinhart Koselleck's conceptual historical 'veto of the sources',
which 'forbids us to dare or admit interpretations that evidence from the
sources simply unmasks as ... inadmissible' (Koselleck 1977: 45–46), we
have demonstrated that revolutionary world discourse was far more contested than many accounts of the revolutionaries' early 'cosmopolitanism'
suggest. The revolutionary assemblies debated cosmopolitanism by and

large as a negative concept. Since 1789 categories such as 'cosmopolitan', 'fraternity', 'humanity', 'universe' or 'the world' marked lines of inclusion and exclusion from a revolutionary community that centred on France and Frenchmen (and excluded groups such as women, émigrés, aristocrats, priests, Jews, people of colour or enslaved people). Towards the outer world, this community was open only as long as 'outsiders' acknowledged the principles of the Revolution or cooperated with revolutionary France for their own emancipatory interests, as in the Batavian Republic. Revolutionary world discourse left little room for pluralism; thus, it made an easy transition from liberation, emancipation and regeneration to war, enmity and extermination. These findings give rise to questions on the evolution of revolutionary world discourse between the French Revolution of 1789 and the emergence of Marxist discourse on world revolution and universal revolutionary emancipation beyond borders, which culminated in 1917 (see Chapter 4).

Contrasting French revolutionary discourses with British and German counter-discourses has revealed how relative the concepts were. Condemning French universality and fraternity as no more than new names for universal domination, the British gradually re-conceptualized their role as the defenders of the right kind of law of nations. The law of nations still overshadowed the emerging concept of 'international' as an institutional framework was still lacking, and only emerged as an outcome of the conflicts considered here. Therefore, the consolidation of the concept of international, the political threshold of the Congress of Vienna, the institutionalization of the congress system as international security cooperation and the operational modes of the Concert of Europe all merit further investigation on a conceptual level (see de Graaf, de Haan and Vick 2019: 2; see Chapter 3).

The British also mobilized the category of Europe and by implication the entire 'civilized' world against the French concept of universal popular sovereignty and liberation and against French warfare and expansion. British cosmopolitan and universalist discourse was presented as an alternative but, similar to French attempts to hegemony, it assumed that Britain was the leader and model for a better world. British parliamentarians believed that Britain had a particular responsibility to ensure that the law of nations was observed consistently; this constitutes a starting point for later Anglophone contributions to rethink the international order. By contrast, in German discourse we observe the opposite tendency to turn national: at the end of the Napoleonic Wars, the 'true' cosmopolitan was portrayed as a patriot.

**Friedemann Pestel** is lecturer in Modern European History at Albert-Ludwigs-Universität Freiburg, Germany. He was a visiting fellow at the German Historical Institutes in Paris and London, the Universities of Vienna and Bordeaux and the Freiburg Institute for Advanced Studies. His research interests and publications cover the French and Haitian Revolutions, political migration in the Age of Revolutions, the history of classical musical life and memory studies. He is currently working on a global history of orchestral touring in the twentieth century. ORCID 0000-0001-9481-4010.

**Pasi Ihalainen** is Academy of Finland Professor at the Department of History and Ethnology, University of Jyväskylä, and has previously worked as a visiting professor at the universities of Freiburg, Gothenburg, Leiden and Uppsala. He has published widely on the history of political discourse and the conceptual history of nationalism, democracy and parliamentarism since the eighteenth century, applying comparative and transnational perspectives. ORCID 0000-0002-5468-4829.

## References

### Primary Sources

*Archives parlementaires*, digital edition, available at https://sul-philologic.stanford.edu/philologic/archparl/.

Digital Newspaper Collection of the Bavarian State Library, available at https://digipress.digitale-sammlungen.de/.

Hansard Corpus (British Parliament), available at https://www.english-corpora.org/hansard/, including House of Commons (HC) and House of Lords (HL) debates since 1803.

Revolution Society 1789. *At the Anniversary Meeting of this Society*.

UK Parliamentary Papers (ProQuest): Debates 1774–1805 (from *The Parliamentary Register*).

### Secondary Sources

Albrecht, A. 2005. *Kosmopolitismus: Weltbürgerdiskurse in Literatur, Philosophie und Publizistik um 1800*. Berlin: De Gruyter.

Alpaugh, M. 2014. 'The British Origins of the French Jacobins: Radical Sociability and the Development of Political Club Networks, 1787–1793', *European History Quarterly* 44(4): 593–619.

Armitage, D. 2013. *Foundations of Modern International Thought*. Cambridge: Cambridge University Press.

Armitage, D. and S. Subrahmanyam. 2010. 'Introduction: The Age of Revolutions, c. 1760–1840 – Global Causation, Connection, and Comparison', in D. Armitage and S. Subrahmanyam (eds), *The Age of Revolutions in Global Context, c. 1760–1840*. Basingstoke: Palgrave Macmillan, pp. XII–XXXII.

Belissa, M. 1998. *Fraternité universelle et intérêt national (1713–1795): Les cosmopolitiques du droit des gens*. Paris: Éditions Kimé.

———. 2006. *Repenser l'ordre européen (1795–1802): De la société des rois aux droits des nations*. Paris: Éditions Kimé.

Bell, D.A. 2015. 'Global Conceptual Legacies', in D. Andress (ed.), *The Oxford Handbook of the French Revolution*. Oxford: Oxford University Press, pp. 642–58.

Coignard, T. 2017. *Une histoire d'avenir: L'Allemagne et la France face au défi cosmopolitique (1789–1925)*. Heidelberg: Universitätsverlag Winter.

Covo, M. 2015. 'Race, Slavery, and Colonies in the French Revolution', in D. Andress (ed.), *The Oxford Handbook of the French Revolution*. Oxford: Oxford University Press, pp. 290–307.

den Boer, P. 2005. 'Civilization: Comparing Concepts and Identities', *Contributions to the History of Concepts* 1(1): 51–62.

Desan, S. 2011. 'Internationalizing the French Revolution', *French Politics, Culture & Society* 29(2): 137–60.

———. 2013. 'Foreigners, Cosmopolitanism, and French Revolutionary Universalism', in S. Desan, L. Hunt and W.M. Nelson (eds), *The French Revolution in Global Perspective*. Ithaca: Cornell University Press, pp. 86–100.

Dupuy, P. 2016. 'British Radicals and Revolutionary France: Historiography, History and Images', in A. Forrest and M. Middell (eds), *The Routledge Companion to the French Revolution in World History*. London: Routledge, pp. 241–59.

Dwyer, P. 2010. 'Napoleon and the Universal Monarchy', *History* 95(319): 293–307.

Forrest, A. and M. Middell (eds). 2016. *The Routledge Companion to the French Revolution in World History*. London: Routledge.

Graaf, B. de, I. de Haan and B. Vick. 2019. 'Vienna 1815: Introducing a European Security Culture', in B. de Graaf, I. de Haan and B. Vick (eds), *Securing Europe after Napoleon – 1815 and the New European Security Culture*. Cambridge: Cambridge University Press, pp. 1–18.

Heuvel, G. van den. 1986. 'Cosmopolite, Cosmopoli(ti)sme', in R. Reichardt and E. Schmitt (eds), *Handbuch politisch-sozialer Grundbegriffe in Frankreich 1680–1820*, vol. 6. Munich: Oldenbourg, pp. 41–55.

Ihalainen, P. 2010. *Agents of the People: Democracy and Popular Sovereignty in British and Swedish Parliamentary and Public Debates, 1734–1800*. Leiden: Brill.

Israel, J.I. 2014. *Revolutionary Ideas: An Intellectual History of the French Revolution from the Rights of Man to Robespierre*. Princeton: Princeton University Press.

Jarrett, M. 2013. *The Congress of Vienna and Its Legacy: War and Great Power Diplomacy after Napoleon*. London: I. B. Tauris.

Jeismann, M. 1992. *Das Vaterland der Feinde: Studien zum nationalen Feindbegriff und Selbstverständnis in Deutschland und Frankreich 1792–1918*. Stuttgart: Klett-Cotta.

Jennings, J. 2011. *Revolution and the Republic: A History of Political Thought in France since the Eighteenth Century*. Oxford: Oxford University Press.

Jordheim, H. 2018. 'Keeping the "Ism" in "Cosmopolitanism" – Wieland and the Origins of Cosmopolitan Discourse', *Journal of Political Ideologies* 23(3): 299–319.

Jourdan, A. 2015. 'The National Dimension in the Batavian Revolution: Political Discussions, Institutions, and Constitutions', in J. Oddens, F. Jacobs and M. Rutjes (eds), *The Political Culture of the Sister Republics, 1794–1806: France, the Netherlands, Switzerland, and Italy*. Amsterdam: Amsterdam University Press, pp. 187–200.

Klinger, A. 2008. 'Deutsches Weltbürgertum und französische Universalmonarchie', in A. Klinger, H.-W. Hahn and G. Schmidt (eds), *Das Jahr 1806 im europäischen Kontext: Balance, Hegemonie und politische Kulturen*. Cologne, Weimar and Vienna: Böhlau, pp. 205–32.

Kolla, E.J. 2017. *Sovereignty, International Law, and the French Revolution*. Cambridge: Cambridge University Press.

Koselleck, R. 1977. 'Standortbindung und Zeitlichkeit: Ein Beitrag zur historiographischen Erschließung der geschichtlichen Welt', in R. Koselleck, W.J. Mommsen and J. Rüsen (eds), *Objektivität und Parteilichkeit in der Geschichtswissenschaft*. Munich: Deutscher Taschenbuch-Verlag, pp. 17–46.

Mori, J. 2003. 'Languages of Loyalism: Patriotism, Nationhood and the State in the 1790s', *The English Historical Review* 118(475): 33–58.

Oddens, J. and M. Rutjes. 2015. 'The Political Culture of the Sister Republics', in J. Oddens, F. Jacobs and M. Rutjes (eds), *The Political Culture of the Sister Republics, 1794–1806: France, the Netherlands, Switzerland, and Italy*. Amsterdam: Amsterdam University Press, pp. 17–32.

Pestel, F. 2015. *Kosmopoliten wider Willen: Die monarchiens als Revolutionsemigranten*. Berlin: De Gruyter.

Pestel, F. and M. Winkler. 2016. 'Provisorische Integration und Kulturtransfer: Französische Revolutionsemigranten im Heiligen Römischen Reich deutscher Nation', *Francia* 43: pp. 137–60.

Polasky, J.L. 2015. *Revolutions without Borders: The Call to Liberty in the Atlantic World*. New Haven: Yale University Press.

———. 2019. 'Liberté sans frontières: La circulation des idées nouvelles', *Annales historiques de la Révolution française* 397: 99–125.

Popkin, J.D. 2015. 'Revolution and Changing Identities in France, 1787–99', in D. Andress (ed.), *The Oxford Handbook of the French Revolution*. Oxford: Oxford University Press, pp. 236–53.

Schmidt, G. 2016. 'Deutsche Europautopien: Nation, Kosmopolitismus und Universalismus um 1800', in K. Ries (ed.), *Europa im Vormärz: Eine transnationale Spurensuche*. Ostfildern: Thorbecke, pp. 47–59.

Schor, N. 2015. 'The Crisis of French Universalism', *Yale French Studies* 100: 43–64.

Serna, P. 2016. 'The Sister Republics, or the Ephemeral Invention of a French Republican Commonwealth', in A. Forrest and M. Middell (eds), *The Routledge*

*Companion to the French Revolution in World History*. London: Routledge, pp. 39–59.

Vovelle, M. 1995. 'Entre cosmopolitisme et xénophobie: Patrie, nation, république universelle dans les idéologies de la Révolution française', in M. O'Dea and K. Whelan (eds), *Nations and Nationalisms: France, Britain, Ireland and the Eighteenth-Century Context*. Oxford: Voltaire Foundation, pp. 11–26.

Wahnich, S. 1997. *L'impossible citoyen: L'étranger dans le discours de la Révolution française*. Paris: Michel.

Weichlein, S. 2006. 'Cosmopolitanism, Patriotism, Nationalism', in T. Blanning and H. Schulze (eds), *Unity and Diversity in European Culture c. 1800*. Oxford: Oxford University Press, pp. 77–99.

Chapter 3

# International

## From Legal to Civic Discourse and beyond in the Nineteenth Century

*Jani Marjanen and Ruben Ros*

If the nineteenth century was the age of nation building, it was also crucial for constructing an international imaginary. This imaginary expanded hand in hand with the gradual breakthrough of the nation as a essential unit in ordering the world. While the national perspective was overwhelmingly positive (although not completely), the international imaginary was more ambiguous. Comparing different things, ranging from habits to goods and laws, as nationally delineated enforced the idea of the nation state as a unit and had mostly positive connotations. A more sinister element, relating to international threats to the local way of life, also formed an important part of the late nineteenth-century international imaginary. Both the positively and negatively laden connotations form layers of meaning (Koselleck 2000) that are still with us in public discourse around what is truly international and whether it is good for us.

In this chapter, we trace the conceptual history of the international from the coinage of the word in the late eighteenth century to its considerable expansion in meaning and increased variation in how it was valued in the second half of the nineteenth century. It pays special attention to international civic organizations as bodies that epitomize the transformation in how the international sensibilities were established. These came about as a result of the international imaginary and also helped to change notions of what was international. As such, international organizations do not form a coherent category for collective action. Everything from international NGOs to governmental bodies or criminal organizations can be included under this umbrella (Götz 2008). Nor is it self-evident how international an organization needs to be in order to achieve international status. While scholars of international NGOs have paid much attention to what aspects of these organizations are international and what is non-governmental today (Reinalda 2009; Davies 2014), we pay more attention to the historical language use. The aim is to write a history of transnational concepts that deals with how they circulate and are adapted in crossing borders (Marjanen 2017). Organizations that labelled themselves international did it for a purpose, and in the course of the nineteenth century the word itself started to lend organizations and activities called international a certain prestige. In this chapter, we seek to understand how this came about, but also point out that the prestige of the international was contested. In doing so, we draw on earlier work published in the lexicon *Geschichtliche Grundbegriffe* (Friedemann and Hölscher 1972; see also Chapters 1 and 2), but expand the focus by using digitally available newspapers from several different countries and aiming for more robust quantification.

As organizations started to label themselves as international, the term became generally more appealing. The International Committee of the Red Cross (1863), the International Workingmen's Association (First International, 1864), the Institute of International Law (1873), the International Council of Women (1888), and the International Olympic Committee (1894) are prominent cases of organizations with high levels of influence in their respective fields. All of them consciously used the word 'international' rhetorically. For the early organizations this might have been a bold move, as other terms such as universal or general were available and might have worked better, but as more organizations, exhibitions and meetings were labelled international, the word gained higher status. The early international organizations and events were, in the spirit of Reinhart Koselleck's famous phrasing, indicators and factors in how the vocabulary of the international evolved in the latter half of the nineteenth century (Koselleck 1972).

Before this important juncture in the transformation of worldviews, eighteenth-century organizations also crossed borders and had contacts that in today's vocabulary are often termed transnational (see Chapters 1 and 2). To address the novelty in nineteenth-century conceptualizations of international civic life, in this chapter we also discuss how eighteenth-century Freemasons and economic societies conceptualized their cross-border activities and reconceptualized them after the language of international became common in the context of associations. Studies on internationalism rightly focus on the twentieth century (Sluga 2013; Sluga and Clavin 2017) but do not go back as far as the eighteenth century as is customary in literature on Enlightenment cosmopolitanism. In this chapter, we shift the focus back into the nineteenth century, in order to highlight the connections in how both international and national imaginaries developed.

As the term 'international' grew in popularity during the course of the nineteenth century and entered new domains of language, it helped to shape a worldview that saw nations as equal in the sense that they could reasonably be represented in international organizations. Nations were obviously not seen as being equal in terms of development, progress or power, but in the sense that most had a more or less equal right to exist and were part of a shared historical trajectory. The language of the international was crucial in facilitating the synchronizing of different nations (Jordheim 2014; 2017). Before it, the language of crossing borders in civic organizations was different. The synchronizing aspect means that today's distinction between the transnational and international is sometimes confusing in a nineteenth-century setting. Today, the term 'transnational' is used to describe cross-border migratory patterns and civic engagement as distinct from more rigid international activities based on individuals or organizations representing their nation states (e.g. Dahinden 2017). This distinction was not relevant for the nineteenth century because of the strength of the national framework; then, the word 'international' did not yet yield such rhetorical power that the coinage of related terms could be transformed into cultural capital.

## The Introduction of International Law

The word 'international' was famously coined by Jeremy Bentham in his *An Introduction to the Principles of Morals and Legislation*, first printed in 1780 (Friedemann and Hölscher 1972: 369; also Chapters 1 and 2). Bentham's intention was not to propose a word for general use, but to find a specific term for understanding legal issues between nations. He was unsatisfied with the terminology and explanations offered by his teacher, William Blackstone, as to what the law of nations was really about. Bentham thought that Blackstone's definition of the law of nations was not specific about how it related to natural law, or even clear whether or not it was about law at all (Janis 1984). Bentham hence introduced a distinction between internal and international jurisprudence. He wrote that persons who are the object of the law 'may, on any given occasion, be considered either as members of the same state, or as members of different states: in the first case, the law may be referred to the head of *internal*, in the second case to that of *international* jurisprudence' (Bentham 1780: cccxxiv). At first glance, this division appears mechanical and not even very important for Bentham: He was simply seeking terminological clarity by introducing a neologism that was not meant to carry a lot of weight in his overall analysis. He reserved the word for relations between sovereigns only, and excluded legal matters relating to individual persons from different states, which indicates not an ad hoc coinage, but a term he had thought through (Suganami 1978; Sylvest 2004; Mazover 2013: 19–22). In a footnote, Bentham even remarked that the 'word *international*, it must be acknowledged is a new one; though, it is hoped, sufficiently intelligible. It is calculated to express, in a more significant way, the branch of law which goes commonly under the name of the law of nations' and that the chancellor Henri François d'Aguesseau (1668–1751) had made a similar remark by proposing the term *droit entre les gens* (law between peoples) (Bentham 1780: cccxxiv; see also Vollerthun 2017: 1–8; Roshchin 2013).

Both Bentham and d'Aguesseau proposed new expressions, but did not regard international law or law between peoples as something new. They simply attempted to propose more accurate descriptions of an old phenomenon. While d'Aguesseau's term did not catch on, Bentham's terminology gradually became more commonly used than the discourse on the law of nations, also in French translation as *droit international*. The term spread from Spanish and Portuguese in the South and to Danish and Swedish in the North. In German and other Germanic languages, however, the term *Völkerrecht* (or translations of it) remained predominant. Regardless of the terminology, the practice of emphasizing a continuity from the early modern discourse of the law of nations to the modern discourse of international law was and still is commonplace (Sylvest 2004).

Perhaps unsurprisingly the term 'international law' spread internationally, to use the word in a modern way, but for Bentham and many early nineteenth-century authors, this remark would not have made sense. For them, the international was strictly reserved for the legal sphere and it was about a collision between national systems or, perhaps more accurately, about conflicting legal matters between states. In this period, phenomena (like the spread of a word) were not conceived as international. Books with 'international' in the title, like Frederick Eden's (1823) *An Historical Sketch of the International Policy of Modern Europe* or Henry Wheaton's (1836) *Elements of International Law*, also reserved the word for the legal sphere.

Newspapers in different European countries show similarly early employment of the concept in legal discourse. In the Netherlands, the adjective 'inter-nationale' appeared for the first time in 1818, when the *Leydse Courant* (12 April 1818) included a report translated from English on the Congress of Aix-la-Chapelle, where the Sixth Coalition against Napoleon had discussed the 'permanence and utility of [this] inter-national agreement'.[1] The concept was adopted more widely in the late 1820s and early 1830s. The Francophone newspapers were important in this process, as were newspapers printed in the Caribbean and Indonesian colonies (e.g. *Le Journal de la Haye*, the *De Curaçaosche Courant* and the *Surinaamsche courant*). Although the adjective was employed predominantly in a legal sense, it was by no means void of political connotations. As early as 1835, *Le Journal de la Haye* (19 August 1835) spoke of 'principes de justice internationale et le patriotisme élevé' and the increasingly vocal liberal press frequently employed the concept in their pleas for 'free international exchange' (*Algemeen Handelsblad*, 24 February 1838).

One by-product of the coinage of 'international law' was the gradual appropriation of 'international' as a modifier for other nouns, for a broader application than its first users intended. Use of the word changed in parallel with changes in the use of 'nation' as a super concept of the era. While the language of nationhood certainly involved much disagreement and contestation, in general the nation was gradually attached to almost everything in society from economy to political institutions and culture (Kemiläinen 1964; de Bertier de Sauvigny 1970; Gschnitzer et al. 1978; Hengchen et al. 2021). It became especially closely associated with state matters, which may have made the term 'international' more flexible. As more things could be conceived as national, more things could potentially be international.

Contemporaries noted the growing popularity of the term (Mazover 2013: 21–22), which can also be evidenced through quantitative assessments of its use in historical data. At the moment, the largest dataset available is Google Ngrams, which, despite errors in optical character recognition and some uncertainty in the contents of the different language corpora, indicates a gradual growing relative frequency for the word 'international' in Spanish, French, English and German (Figure 3.1). Our use avoids most of the pitfalls of Google Ngrams which have been thoroughly discussed in the literature (see Pechenick, Danforth and Dodds 2015) and shows that in all four languages occurrences are rather few in the first part of the nineteenth century, whereas the latter part shows growth. Relative frequencies provide some comparability over time and across languages, but based on the graph alone it is hard to observe more than a general growing trend.

The relative frequency plots show that while 'international' entered the lexicon in the late eighteenth and the first half of the nineteenth century at least in English, German, French and Spanish (and clearly many other languages), it did not become frequent until towards the middle of the century (see also Friedemann and Hölscher 1972).[2] The first uses of terms are often instructive, but looking at frequencies helps us to get beyond the 'religion of the first occurrence' (Dufoix 2017: 15) that often ascribes more influence to early linguistic innovators than they deserve. To trace the development in the mid-nineteenth century, we looked at which words (mostly nouns)

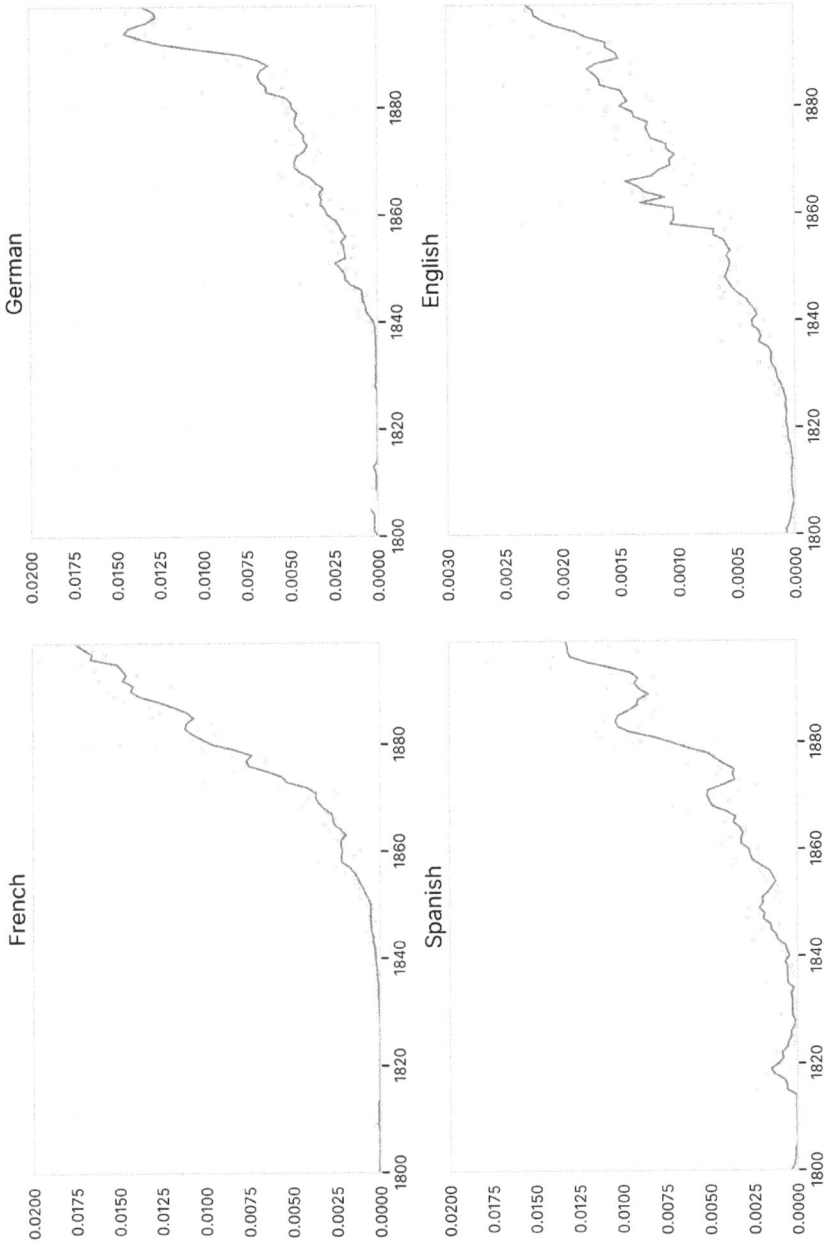

**Figure 3.1** Relative frequency of the word 'international' in French, Spanish, English and German on Google Ngrams (https://books.google.com/ngrams).

the word international modified. We did this for the Gale Cengage dataset of nineteenth-century British newspapers (Hengchen et al. 2021). A plot showing the yearly number of unique bigrams (sets of two words) with international as the first word indicates that not only did 'international' become used more frequently, but also that it was used to modify a growing number of different nouns, meaning that its use expanded in this period.

Because bigrams contain two words, they provide minimal context in which the word international was used. Based on word embeddings and *k*-means clustering, we can group the accompanying words thematically (for more elaborate examples, see Hengchen et al. 2021). In short, the embeddings can be used to compare the context in which a particular word usually appears in the data (its distribution), and group words that have similar distributions (Gavin 2018; Wevers and Koolen 2020). This models the context of language use, but not the material context of newspapers or different sections within them.

Figure 3.3 portrays fourteen groups of words that are analysed for the whole nineteenth century. Similarity in distribution often entails some sort of semantic or thematic similarity, but the division into a particular number of groups leads to groups that are regarded as similar in distribution, but do not necessarily appear to naturally belong together. Some groups seem more coherent than others. We explored the same data with different numbers

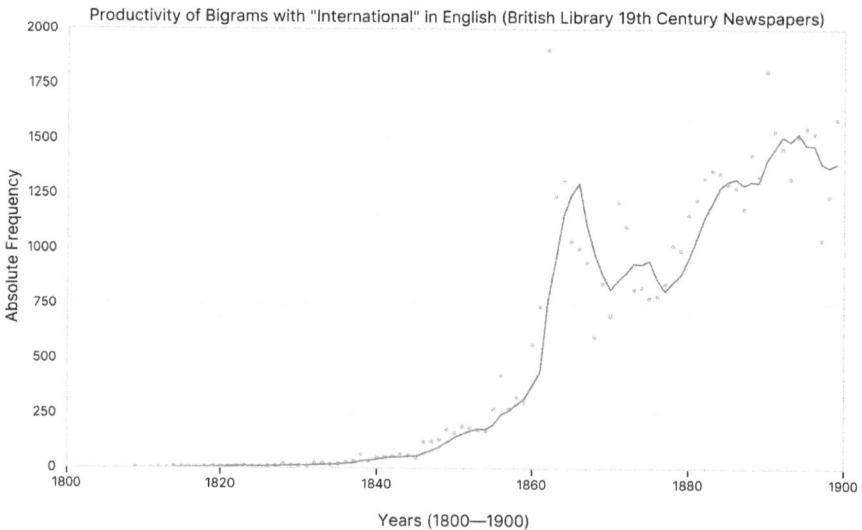

**Figure 3.2** Annual number of unique bigrams with 'international' as the first word in nineteenth-century newspapers in the British Library. Gale Nineteenth Century British Newspaper Collection.

of groups, and while the groups themselves are different in those cases, the main ruptures and trends are the same with fewer or more groups.

Using word embeddings and $k$-means clustering, the complete vocabulary was placed in fourteen clusters. The frequency of the words in similar clusters is summed and normalized for every year. After experimentation with different cluster sizes (4–20), a $k$ of fourteen proved to yield the best insight into long-term changes.

**Figure 3.3** Normalized cluster distribution of the bigrams with 'international', 1820–1900 in nineteenth-century British newspapers. Gale Nineteenth Century British Newspaper Collection.

Like the bigram frequencies (Figure 3.2), the diachronic cluster distribution (Figure 3.3) shows a rather sudden rupture in the mid-nineteenth century. Until the 1840s the discourse of international law (visible in the 'relations, disputes, peace' and 'law, arbitration, congress' clusters) remained dominant. However, the figure also shows that the legal discourse itself changed. Driven by the conflicts that erupted in the late 1840s and 1850s, the legal language of the term 'international' became geared towards the political questions surrounding the European balance of power. The cluster of words such as 'relations', 'disputes' and 'peace' demonstrates this focal shift toward diplomacy. Instead of philosophical considerations on 'morality' and 'principles', legal discourse gravitated towards 'dissensions', 'grievance', 'crisis' and 'antagonism', words that first appeared in the international vocabulary in 1854, 1855, 1858 and 1859, respectively. While the immediate post-Napoleonic era has been interpreted as a new period in European security culture (de Graaf, de Haan and Vick 2019), the discourse on international disputes and peace became common only mid-century. The word 'international security' did so even later, in the twentieth century.

The lexical shift toward international diplomacy as manifested in the cluster distribution also offers clues for the sudden rise of clusters related to 'exhibitions', 'awards' and 'engagements'. When, in the 1850s, 'international' was used to denote a sphere of diplomatic action, other gatherings and activities at the international level were also increasingly named international. The early 1850s appear as a turning point in the extension of the concept beyond diplomacy. It is here that we find examples of contestation and terminological competition. The 1851 London Exhibition, for example, was initially referred to as the 'Universal Exhibition'. Four years later, the event in Paris was called the 'Paris International Exhibition'. Similarly, the Belgian mathematician Adolphe Quetelet, who was inspired by the London Exhibition, drafted a plan 'to invite scientists from over the world who are engaged in statistical work to gather in a universal congress of statistics'. In 1853, by the time Quetelet had organized the congress in Brussels, it was branded the 'International Congress for Statistics' (Prevost and Beaud 2015: 5). Although 'universal' remained in use in the context of exhibitions and conferences, it was 'international' that became the prime denominator for these events. It seems that 'universal' captured cross-border activities, but 'international' was perhaps more apt for incorporating the national perspective that had become so dominant by the mid-nineteenth century. International was not only a way of crossing borders; it was a way of enforcing the nation.

Exhibitions and conferences were not the only contexts to embrace the vocabulary of the international. A decade before the sudden rise in the 'exhibition' cluster, the 'telegraph, college, board' cluster displays an increase in frequency, caused primarily by the establishment of the International Postage Association (1851) and the spread of 'international postage' as a concept (Murphy and Yates 2015).

Besides the labelling of civil and political actors, 'international' was gradually used more in terms related to the world economy. Many products originating abroad were referred to as international, as were a multitude of companies that aimed to increase their stature by using the adjective. Moreover, the rise of terms such as 'markets' (1871) and 'capital' (1873) indicates an understanding of international trade not just as exchange between nationally rooted parties, but as a distinctively international or global system of commerce. The conceptual emergence of the 'world economy' (a bigram used extensively after 1880; see Chapter 7) was accompanied by new discussions (e.g. on bimetallism and standards of measurements) and the reframing of old ones (on tariffs) as related to international trade.

From a purely quantitative perspective, the nineteenth century saw a gradual increase in international public discourse. Judging from the British newspaper data, it seems that much of this has to do with the breakthrough of civic organizations, fairs and exhibitions as international. The legal discourse dominant in the early century did not disappear, but rather the language of international expanded into new domains. This development can be traced in book titles containing the word international. The word first appeared in the catalogue of German-language books in the Berlin State Library[3] in Friedrich List's *Das nationale System* (1841); the first volume dealt with 'international trade' (*international Handel*). We must bear in mind that international law was discussed in German as *Völkerrecht*, so that excludes much of the legal discourse that we would expect to be labelled international in other European languages at this time. Still, the legal discourse is strong. In 1848, we find a book that deals with 'international relations' (*international Verhältnisse*) from a legal point of view (Stedmann 1848). In 1855, books were published on international patent legislation (Kleinschrod 1855) and international publishing contracts (Enslin 1855). Words included in the titles of books signal key matters for the author or publisher, and are as such signs of the discourse on the international becoming more established. The number of titles that included the word 'international' increased from the mentioned two in the 1850s to fifteen titles in the 1860s. We find ninety-one titles in the 1870s, 110 titles for the 1880s, and 109 for the 1890s, meaning that the last three decades of the nineteenth century saw a steady stream of books about something international. As in the British newspaper data, we encounter a broadening of the scope of the term, with print material about the international exhibition in

Paris in 1867 (Internationale Ausstellung 1867) and an organization called the International Association for the Advancement of Social Sciences (Neumann 1863).

## Were the Freemasons, Economic Societies and Bible Societies International?

Bentham and d'Aguesseau, who introduced the word international, thought that international law had existed before, but was poorly described. Similarly, present-day scholars of transnational and international civil society, like Thomas Davies, argue that the roots of what he calls transnational civil society can and should be sought between the 1760s and 1860s, when new international NGOs emerged alongside existing international religious organizations (Davies 2014: 3–4, 19–44). Another scholar of international organizations, Bob Reinalda, sees the Congress of Vienna as a turning point for international non-governmental and governmental organizations alike (Reinalda 2009: 37–42). Both Davies and Reinalda point to organizations that did not describe themselves as international; here, however, we are more interested in what terminology such organizations did use and what changed once they introduced the language of the international to describe themselves.

The Freemasons are an early civic organization that crossed borders, with lodges all over Europe and beyond. Their forms of organization as a brotherhood, with a hierarchical structure between lodges, entailed cross-border activity. Their membership also transcended national boundaries as representatives were frequent visitors to lodges in other countries and were instrumental in creating networks among elites in different parts of the world (Jacob 1991; Harland-Jacobs 2007; Prescott 2013). Most outsider assessments of the Freemasons have had a critical tone ever since the eighteenth century. Part of this criticism was the recurring accusation of cosmopolitanism directed toward the Freemasons from the 1780s onwards in the German-speaking lands (Hardtwig 1990: 799; Jordheim 2018). Within the Masonic movement the word 'international' was introduced into the names of organizations such as the Bureau international de relations maçonniques and the Association maçonnique internationale, both established in the 1870s (Berger 2020: 8), which corresponds with the overall internationalization of the language relating to civil society.

Outsider critiques of Freemasons as cosmopolitans also picked up the language of the international. For example, conservative Vienna newspapers wrote in 1893 about the 'internationally allied Freemasonry' that had brought misfortunes upon the ruling families of Tuscany and Naples (*Das*

*Vaterland*, 20 January 1893: 1)[4] and in the following year about 'the influence of the foreign international-Jewish Freemasonry' (*Ostdeutsche Rundschau*, 8 May 1894: 1). In 1895, *Das Vaterland* (26 September 1896: 1) reported on the 'first international congress against Freemasonry', but lamented how internationality did not really materialize as the event was dominated by Italians speaking their language. The sentiment in the report and later commentary was that while the 'Masons were international, also the anti-Masonic movement must be international' (*Das Vaterland*, 3 October 1896: 2). A further trope in the same genre used the label *Freimaurerei international* (*Grazer Volksblatt*, 4 March 1906), as a reference to the Communist international. In this case, the label 'international' was used to discredit both Freemasons and communists, but associating the two served to rhetorically evoke a sense of dangerous and radical politics.

It is clear that Freemasons were described as international only after other organizations had been labelled as such. But doing so introduced new themes to the discourse; the description of the Freemasons as international follows the earlier traditions of discrediting Freemasons as cosmopolitan. In these critical texts, it is not only the organization that is seen as 'international' and therefore dangerous, but also every individual Freemason.

Other eighteenth-century organizations with arguably border-crossing imaginaries were labelled international only after the term made a breakthrough in the mid-nineteenth century. While Freemasons were often portrayed as suspiciously cosmopolitan and indifferent to the domestic good, another form of eighteenth-century civic life, the economic societies, were seen as devoted to local improvement, many with a geographically defined area of interest such as a country or town. The origins of societies aimed at improving local economic conditions through the production and dissemination of new knowledge relating to agriculture, manufacturing, commerce and the arts can be located in the establishment of the *Honourable Society of Improvers in the Knowledge of Agriculture in Scotland* (1723) and *The Dublin Society for Improving Husbandry, Manufactures and Other Useful Arts* (1731). Further societies were established around Europe, especially around the Seven Years' War and after the French Revolution, by which time most bigger towns in Europe hosted such a society (Stapelbroek and Marjanen 2012).

By the mid-eighteenth century, we find statements in which economic societies from elsewhere are regarded as models (or at least predecessors). The economic societies did not constitute any kind of international organization, with national or local chapters, but rather held notions of comparability across borders and cultivated contacts. The London-based Society for the Encouragement of Arts, Manufactures and Commerce (founded 1754) noted in its early publications that 'there are Societies for the Encouragement of Arts, Manufactures and Commerce in the Part of *Great Britain* called *Scotland*, and also in *Ireland*' (*Premiums by the Society, Established at London, for the Encouragement of Arts, Manufactures and Commerce*, 1758: 31). In a similar statement the Economic Society of Berne (founded 1759) pointed to other peoples as a source for emulation: 'It is our noblest intention to teach our countrymen to make use of the examples of other peoples who have taken useful sciences to a higher level' (*Ökonomische Gesellschaft zu Bern* 1761: IV).

The transnational imaginary of similar societies is manifested in lists of predecessors and models from other countries. In Sweden, the Patriotic Society (founded 1766) wrote how 'Patriotic and Oeconomic Societies in Berne, in London, in Dublin, in Brittany, in Saren and in Silesia [have in their] encouragement of Agriculture, the Arts and Commerce become so well known ... that they need no further introduction at this particular moment' (*Hushållnings Journal*, 1776: 3–4). Such lists became a general feature of the foundation of any new society, and functioned as a way of creating prestige for the foundation (and its founders) by laying claim to a tradition of similar societies. This tradition would not be called international, but it involves expressions like 'other countries' and, in the early nineteenth century, 'foreign'. At the same time, comparative remarks presented other countries as predecessors or models that could and should be emulated, thus turning improvement and development into issues of lagging behind and catching up (Marjanen 2013).

The societies were also similar in that they had networks of corresponding and honorary members abroad; scientific societies and academies used cross-border networks as sources of information and prestige, but economic societies focused more on the local state and applying knowledge (Stapelbroek and Marjanen 2012). Activities that would undoubtedly be called international or transnational today were discussed in terms of the honorary, corresponding and foreign. Talking about something as international did not lend prestige to the activities.

Besides economic societies, other bodies shared structural similarities. Early nineteenth-century bible societies, relief programmes or campaigns for the abolishment of slavery all had local structures, but also engaged in exchanges across borders and dealt with issues that could not be addressed solely in a domestic context (Davis 2013; Reinalda 2009). However, the language of the international was not used to describe their activities then as it would today. Instead, this collective action in organizations that required input from different nations was described as civic. As legal systems met in Benthamian international law, associations met in international civic life.

## Explicitly International Civic Organizations

It is difficult to identify a clear turning point when it started to make sense to perceive civic organizations as and consequently call them international. This renaming required three gradual changes in civic life. First, associations were increasingly seen as fulfilling a societal task. While associations designed to focus on a particular problem had existed for quite some time, by the early nineteenth century most European countries had associations that dealt with a large array of topics ranging from music, economy, education and literature to very specific tasks like drainage. These associations were at least meant to take care of issues relating to the common good (Im Hof 1982; Dülmen 1992). Second, they were perceived as nationally delineated. Associations that were specifically Finnish, Swedish, Norwegian, Dutch, Spanish or Swiss, to mention a few interesting cases of economic societies, decided to define their area of influence as coinciding with the nation (Marjanen 2013). As the nation became increasingly considered a unit to identify with politically, associations became one forum among others in which the nation could be represented. Different countries, regions and imperial substructures had their particular circumstances, but nonetheless associations provided a channel for citizens to be part of the nation by advancing the common good on a national level. Third, the membership of the associations in general was growing. While scientific societies, lodges and secret societies were aimed at a select elite, associations started to recruit more broadly and accepted paying members if they subscribed to the society's aims without necessarily (or even probably) being active in meetings or on a personal level (Stenius 1987). Some associations, like the London Corresponding Society, even aimed to maximize their membership to ultimately include everyone (Thompson 1968: 24; see Chapter 2).

With associations that sought to benefit the common good, and included a larger crowd that participated in representing the nation, the door was open for coming together internationally. At this time, the international was primarily reserved for representing the nation and happened when representatives met – an idea best crystallized in the 'principle of the Olympic games' (Stenius and Haggrén 2005: 81; see Chapter 9). For most of the nineteenth century, phenomena were not generally described as being international in themselves, as in the 1890s' examples for Freemasons mentioned above or phrases like 'international fame'.

The first associations to describe themselves as international seem to have been rather ephemeral. The International Association founded in Scotland in the 1830s aimed at evoking solidarity and peace with the motto 'all mankind are brothers', but was short-lived (Davies 2014: 30; Saunders

1847: 29). What was remarkable about this association was the brevity of its name and the assumption that one organization could cover issues related to the international. This may be a sign that the International Association saw itself as the only one of its kind and did not expect that other such organizations would be needed in future.

According to Davies, the first international organization by name and structure was the Société générale des naufrages dans l'intérêt de toutes les nations, founded in 1835. The society was the product of its founder Auguste Godde and his extensive networks in France and abroad. Through active branding and networking, the secretariat of the society in Paris managed to organize chapters on several continents and raise large amounts of funds for the cause of lifesaving and preventing shipwrecks. By the early 1840s Godde faced criticism for the way in which he led the society, which ultimately split into two. A competing faction started publishing the journal *L'Internationale* in 1842 (Davies 2018). At some point the society started using the name Société internationale des naufrages, but this seems to have been a gradual process as both names were used in parallel. In the publications of the society, we cannot find a reason for the change in name. It seems that 'international' was simply introduced as a variation on the word 'general' (e.g. Godde de Giancourt 1841). In British newspapers from 1840 onward reports that refer to the International Shipwreck Society indicate that the new name was established by then (*Southampton Herald*, 11 January 1840).[5]

While the International Association and the International Shipwreck Society remain isolated examples, international cooperation gained more formal organizational structures in the following years. The best-known cases are perhaps the International Committee of the Red Cross (founded 1863) and the International Workingmen's Association in Britain (from 1864), both of which combined physical meetings of participants from different countries and causes that involved different nationalities. Like in the word clusters in Figure 3.3, what was mostly described as international were the exhibitions, conferences, committees and meetings. While of course the organizations themselves can be seen as international, contemporaries mostly used the word to talk about their activities. For instance, the Dutch *Rotterdamsche Courant* mentions how 'the Count Lallemand and Doctor Fauvel will represent France on the international sanitary conference that will gather in Constantinople' (14 December 1863). Similarly, a typical report in the Swedish newspaper *Nya Dagligt Allehanda* (8 April 1892) narrates how Edvard Edholm travelled as the representative of the Swedish Red Cross to the 'international Red Cross conference in Rome'. While other texts write about the Red Cross itself as international, its internationality stems from the conferences and meetings. Henry Dunant's book, *Une souvenir de Solférino* (1862) helped to spark enthusiasm for the foundation of the International Committee of the Red Cross; it was a call for an international relief society (Société internationale de secours), but here too, the gatherings were central. Dunant argued that if jurists, industrialists, statisticians, agronomists, economists and others organized international congresses, so should people dealing with relief (Dunant 1862: 107, 113).

The International Workingmen's Association revolved around congresses organized in London and Continental Europe, but it was soon called 'The International' giving both the noun and the adjective new layers of meaning as well as increased political valence. Its most important resolution was an 'international combination of efforts, by the agency of the Association, in the struggle between labour and capital' (International Workingmen's Association 1868: 3; Chapter 4). As in the case of the Red Cross, international cooperation was seen as paving the way for dealing with problems in the future, but in the First International the term itself gained a layer of meaning with a set of connotations of socialist and anarchist activity, making it politicized in a new way (see especially Friedemann and Hölscher 1972 and Chapter 4).

At this time, the international had become something that went beyond congresses and meetings and was also an arena of action that could feed into other levels in society. This is most visible in the field of jurisprudence and the establishment of the Institute of International Law in 1873, which marked in very concrete terms the rise of international law as a field. The men who engaged with the Institute used the international arena to formulate political objectives that could then be argued for in the national arena of politics. Some ideas were realized nationally, whereas others morphed into something quite different in their transition from international to national (Koskenniemi 2001: 2–6, 11–97). Nevertheless, the international had become a space of its own that was tied to the nation but that could also be used as an additional platform for states and individuals to perform politics.

## International Contested: Truly International and Internationalism

The powerful rhetoric of international cooperation and especially its role in the workers' movement led to reactions. Predominantly positive perceptions of the international became coupled with fear of foreign or international influence. The Dutch newspaper *Algemeen Volksblad voor Nederland* (19 December 1872) included a letter to the editor warning against the wrong kind of international activism:

I do know men amongst the so-called 'Internationals' that I value highly because of their honesty, but the horrors of their commune and the programme of the International in France and Spain makes me doubt their honesty and makes uniting with them impossible for the true Dutchman. Moreover, they are not *truly* [original italics] international; when pointing them to the needs of Spain, France and Italy, to what they did there or want to do there, the answer is 'yes, but you cannot blame the Dutch chapter, in every country the International complies to national laws'. Why? Do they not believe in eradicating the differences between the nations? Otherwise they would not be bothered by the laws of individual nations ...

At this point the internationals, the International as an organization and what it meant to be truly international was contested both within the working men's movement and from the outside. The claim that some things could be truly international is revealing: it supposes that some things pretend or fail to be international for various reasons. In the above case, 'true international' means following international ideals everywhere and not compromising with local conditions. In other cases, it could be about attracting authors from '*all* countries' (*The Aldine Press* 1870), or about elevating something (e.g. a collection of historical documents) to be truly international by adding foreign material to it ('Gleanings' 1872), but calling something truly international could give it negative connotations.

A further sign of contestation and a marker of negative valuation toward the discourse of the international is the emergence of the term 'internationalism'. As with most isms, the relationship between the root and the suffix is complicated. Typically, the introduction of the ism is late and inverts the valuation of the word. Similarly, while there is a relationship between national and nationalism, the nineteenth-century discourse on things national was largely positively laden, whereas the ism, nationalism, became popular at the turn of the twentieth century and was predominantly used in a negative sense. Some isms have been coined as positive descriptions of self-identified doctrines or practices, but in most cases the coinage of an ism is a sign of contestation and criticism (Kurunmäki and Marjanen 2018a; 2018b; Kettunen 2018; Chapter 4).

The word 'internationalism' was first used in the 1840s and occurred in the 1870s as a clear reaction to the First International, but became common at roughly the same time as nationalism, that is the turn of the twentieth century (as is evident from Google Ngrams and the newspaper datasets consulted). It is not surprising that the two words go hand in hand as speaking of things international was clearly tied to the change in discourses about the nation, as also indicated by the shift from universal to international exhibitions.

Internationalism lent itself to other juxtapositions than nationalism. Our survey of newspapers published in France, Austria, the Netherlands and Sweden provides ample examples of this in the use of 'internationalism', which can be roughly grouped in five categories. First, it was used to describe practices of crossing borders in the form of conferences (*Neue Freie Presse*, 24 November 1875: 8). Second, it could refer to the present state of things, as in a Dutch statement about international crises: 'In this time of cosmopolitanism and internationalism all our plagues and afflictions become cosmopolitan and international plagues and afflictions' (*Arnhemsche courant*, 28 August 1877). Third, it was often a synonym of socialism or a particular strand of it: 'An agreement was reached to squash internationalism, communism, socialism and all kinds of "ism" that could lead to a revolution' (*Bohusläns Tidning*, 15 October 1872). Fourth, it could be used as a very negatively laden label for conspiratory internationalism with antisemitic and anti-Masonic overtones: 'Carbonism in Italy, Freemasonry in France, in England and in Austria, internationalism in Switzerland and Belgium, socialism in Germany – that all is the same thing under different names. It is a single society that at this moment holds the fate of Europe' (*De Grondwet*, 21 April 1878). Fifth, it could be used as a policy pursued by states, but then it was often connected either to socialism or to internationalism as a description of our times. In the latter three cases the tone was most often negative, but some positively laden examples also occur. Regardless of the valuation, at this time 'internationalism' did not refer to any kind of established ideological position of its own, although the suffix might lead one to think so (cf. Mazover 2013: 2).

While the discourse of internationalism differs somewhat from that of the international, the emergence of the former is nonetheless a sign of the semantic and political tensions that arose once the whole notion of the international became more laden with semantic baggage toward the end of the nineteenth century. At this point the international was partly detached from the conferences and exhibitions; several things were described as being international in themselves. As a result, the word became useful as a rhetorical device in individual speech acts. In criticisms of Masonic activity, the Freemasons were presented as an international threat regardless of whether or not they met in congresses. The policy of internationalism pursued by particular states was not necessarily tied to representing one's nation abroad, but was oriented towards shaping a different future world through political activities. The future was international regardless of whether particular authors liked it or not.

The new political nature and temporal directionality of internationalism ran parallel with several tonal shifts in the discourse on the international in the last decades of the century. As tensions rose between the European powers, terms such as 'international agitation', 'international jealousy' and 'international frictions' (re)surfaced frequently in the 1880s and 1890s. Compared to earlier periods of interstate tensions, the discourse on the international in these decades appears to be slightly different. From the 1890s onwards, newspapers all over Europe came to speak of international space on a higher level of generality. It was 'international politics' (another bigram that rose rapidly in frequency after 1880) that was in a permanent state of crisis. Terms such as 'international catastrophe' (first appearing in 1880), 'international fear' (1880), 'international panic' (1890) and 'international turmoil' (1898) reveal how the optimistic internationalism showcased in the exhibitions, conferences and associations was mirrored by an understanding of the international order as being in a permanent state of dissension and deadlock (Atkinson and Dodds 2002: 27–30). This crisis imaginary also speaks to a heightened actuality, as becomes clear from the rising frequency of 'current international problems, questions and trends' (Jordheim and Wigen 2018).

In this context of an increasingly abstract notion of 'the international' with its connotations of crisis and conflict, we encounter the emergence of other concepts. Most important in this respect is the concept of the 'world'. Both the noun 'world' and the adjective 'global' have a long history, but only in the 1890s were they used to refer to a unified space consisting of competing nations, cultures or civilizations (Jordheim and Sandmo 2018; Braun 1992). This relatively new conception of the world contained aspects that also marked the concept of international(ism). 'World politics' was used to refer to international diplomacy as a whole, but also to describe specific state policies aimed at both friendly cooperation and imperialist expansion. The latter aspect became dominant in line with fin-de-siècle fears for the near future. In *World Politics*, one of the first works to explicitly discuss the term as such, Ernest Hargrove wrote about the 'gloomy prospects' of 'the condition of the world at the present time', arguing that 'all classes, no matter their trade or occupation, are affected by events occurring on the other side of the globe', and for this reason 'correct diagnosis [of world politics] is necessary if malady is to be cured' (Hargrove 1898: 1–18). The German concept of *Weltpolitik* added an extra dimension to the concept: the German Kaiser used the term to refer to an aggressive expansionist foreign policy (Bach and Peters 2002). Similarly to the conception of internationalism as a specific policy outlook, *Weltpolitik* was used to denote policies of intervention. This, in turn, opened the door for discussions on the desirability of such policies.

## Conclusion

The rise of an international imaginary was heavily intertwined with the emergence of the national perspective as a dominant way of structuring the world. When coined in the late eighteenth century, the term 'international' was designed to grasp the encounter of national legal traditions. After the term extended from the legal sphere to cover financial and civic activities, it still was bound to the nation. Apparently an alternative to describing exhibitions as universal, talking about them as international allowed for national variations and comparison rather than universalization (see also Steinmetz 2020). At the same time, the comparability of national peculiarities in an international setting provided a kind of synchronization that made nations part of the same trajectory of progress and decline (Jordheim 2014; 2017). As more and more organizations established international meetings, led by the International Committee of the Red Cross and the International Workingmen's Association, the word 'international' started to acquire more layers of meaning, making it contested and more frequent in public discourse. In this process a more abstract notion of the international arose; it gained a future orientation as it represented a promise or a threat. In this sense, it became detached from representatives of different nations coming together, but rather became something in itself. It was now possible to have an international reputation or stand for internationalism as a loosely defined doctrine. Whatever was described as international was no longer only the sum of its national parts, but something more.

**Jani Marjanen** is a researcher at the University of Helsinki, where he gained his PhD in 2014. He specializes in the language of economic patriotism in Scandinavia, the theory and method of conceptual history, public debate in Finland in the nineteenth century and the history of ideology. He is one of the editors of *Contributions to the History of Concepts*. ORCID: 0000-0002-3085-4862

**Ruben Ros** is a PhD candidate at the Luxembourg Centre for Contemporary and Digital History. He is especially interested in conceptual history and computational methods. His previous research focused on the conceptual history of nationalism and the rise of 'the foreign' as a spatial category in nineteenth-century Europe. His doctoral project is to model technocratic reasoning in twentieth-century Dutch and British parliamentary debates. ORCID: 0000-0002-5303-2861

## Notes

We thank Gale Cengage for access to nineteenth-century British newspapers and Mikko Tolonen, Eetu Mäkelä and Simon Hengchen at the Helsinki Computational History Group for infrastructural support. Jussi Kurunmäki and Johan Strang kindly commented on an earlier draft of the text. This work has been supported by the European Union Horizon 2020 research and innovation programme under grant 770299 (NewsEye).

1. Dutch newspapers have been accessed at https://www.delpher.nl/.
2. Apart from Google Ngrams the claim is also based on the *Oxford English Dictionary* (https://www.oed.com), *Svenska Akademiens Ordbok* (https://www.saob.se), *Dictionnaire de l'Académie Française* (https://www.dictionnaire-academie.fr/) and *Deutsches Textarchiv* (http://www.deutschestextarchiv.de/).
3. http://stabikat.de.
4. Austrian newspapers have been accessed through Austrian Newspapers Online at https://anno.onb.ac.at/.
5. British newspapers have been accessed through British Library Newspapers at https://www.gale.com/intl/c/british-library-newspapers-part-i.

## References

### Primary Sources

*Algemeen Handelsblad.*

*Algemeen Volksblad voor Nederland.*

Bentham, J. 1780. *An Introduction to the Principles of Morals and Legislation.* London: T. Payne & son.

*Bohusläns Tidning.*

Dunant, H. 1862. *Un souvenir de Solférino.* Geneva: Jules-Guillaume Fick. Available at https://gallica.bnf.fr/ark:/12148/bpt6k1060754/f110.item.r=international.

Eden, F. 1823. *An Historical Sketch of the International Policy of Modern Europe, as Connected with the Principles of the Law of Nature and of Nations, Concluding with Some Remarks on the Holy Alliance.* London: John Murray.

Enslin, A. 1855. *Über internationale Verlagsverträge mit besonderer Beziehung auf Deutschland.* Berlin: Enslin.

'Gleanings'. 1872. *The College Courant* 10(24): 288.

Godde de Giancourt, A. 1841. *Société générale internationale des Naufrages: Traité pratique de moyens de sauvetage, contenant des détails complets sur l'emploi de la Balistique des projectiles porte-amarres.*

*Grazer Volksblatt.*

*De grondwet.*

Hargrove, E.T. 1898. *World Politics.* New York: R.F. Fenno & Co. Available at http://archive.org/details/cu31924031323235.

*Hushållnings Journal.*

International Workingmen's Association. 1868. *Resolutions of the Congress of Geneva, 1866, and the Congress of Brussels, 1868*. London. Available at http://archive.org/details/resolutionsofcon00inte.

Internationale Ausstellung. 1867. *Internationale Ausstellung zu Paris 1867: Katalog der Österreichischen Abtheilung*. 2. Aufl. Vienna: K. K. Central-Comité.

*Le Journal de la Haye.*

Kleinschrod, C.T. von. 1855. *Die internationale Patentgesetzgebung nach ihren Prinzipien nebst Vorschlägen für ein künftiges gemeines deutsches Patentrecht*. Erlangen: Enke.

*Leydse Courant.*

List, F. 1841. *Das nationale System der politischen Oekonomie: Der internationale Handel, die Handelspolitik und der deutsche Zollverein*. Stuttgart: Cotta.

'Literature'. 1870. *The Aldine Press*.

*Neue Freie Presse.*

Neumann, S. 1863. *Die internationale Assoziation für den Fortschritt der sozialen Wissenschaften: ein Rückblick auf den ersten Kongress derselben in Brüssel 1862.*

*Nya Dagligt Allehanda.*

Ökonomische Gesellschaft zu Bern. 1761. *Abhandlungen Und Beobachtungen Durch Die Ökonomische Gesellschaft Zu Bern*. Vol. 3. Bern.

Saunders, J. (ed.). 1847. *The People's Journal, Aims to Combine, in the Direct Service of the People (Using That Word to Express a Nation, Rather Than a Class), a Greater Amount of Literary and Artistical Talent Than Has Ever Before Been Known in This Country in Connexion with Any Similar Publication*. People's Journal Office.

Society for the Encouragement of Arts, Manufactures, and Commerce. 1758. *Premiums by the Society, Established at London, for the Encouragement of Arts, Manufactures and Commerce*. London.

*Southampton Herald.*

Stedmann, K. 1848. *Bericht der relativen Minorität der vereinigten Ausschüsse für internationale Verhältnisse und Centralgewalt über den Waffenstillstand vom 26. August in dem Herzogthume Schleswig*. S.l.

*Das Vaterland.*

Wheaton, Henry. 1836. *Elements of International Law: With a Sketch of the History of the Science*. Philadelphia: Carey, Lea & Blanchard.

*Secondary Sources*

Atkinson, D. and K. Dodds. 2002. *Geopolitical Traditions: Critical Histories of a Century of Geopolitical Thought*. London: Routledge.

Bach, J. and S. Peters. 2002. 'The New Spirit of German Geopolitics', *Geopolitics* 7(3): 1–18. https://doi.org/10.1080/714000978.

Berger, J. 2020. *Mit Gott, für Vaterland und Menschheit? Eine europäische Geschichte des freimaurerischen Internationalismus (1845–1935)*. Göttingen: Vandenhoeck & Ruprecht. https://doi.org/10.13109/9783666564857.

Bertier de Sauvigny, G. de. 1970. 'Liberalism, Nationalism and Socialism: The Birth of Three Words', *The Review of Politics* 32(2): 147–66. https://doi.org/10.1017/S0034670500013607.

Braun, H. 1992. 'Welt', in *Geschichtliche Grundbegriffe: Historisches Lexikon zur politisch-sozialen Sprache in Deutschland*. Stuttgart: Klett-Cotta, vol. 7, p. 433–510.

Dahinden, J. 2017. 'Transnationalism Reloaded: The Historical Trajectory of a Concept', *Ethnic and Racial Studies* 40(9): 1474–85. https://doi.org/10.1080/01419870.2017.1300298.

Davies, T. 2014. *NGOs: A New History of Transnational Civil Society*. New York: Oxford University Press.

————. 2018. 'Rethinking the Origins of Transnational Humanitarian Organizations: The Curious Case of the International Shipwreck Society', *Global Networks* 18(3): 461–78. https://doi.org/10.1111/glob.12189.

Davis, M. 2013. 'Reappraising British Socialist Humanism', *Journal of Political Ideologies* 18(1): 57–81. https://doi.org/10.1080/13569317.2013.750175.

Dufoix, S. 2017. *The Dispersion: A History of the Word Diaspora*. Leiden: Brill. https://doi.org/10.1163/9789004326910.

Dülmen, R. van. 1992. *The Society of the Enlightenment: The Rise of the Middle Class and Enlightenment Culture in Germany*. New Jersey: Wiley.

Friedemann, P. and L. Hölscher. 1972. 'Internationale', in R. Koselleck, O. Brunner and W. Conze (eds), *Geschichtliche Grundbegriffe: Historisches Lexikon zur politisch-sozialen Sprache in Deutschland*. Stuttgart: Klett-Cotta Verlag, vol. 3, pp. 367–97.

Gavin, M. 2018. 'Vector Semantics, William Empson, and the Study of Ambiguity', in *Critical Inquiry* 44(4): 641–73. https://doi.org/10.1086/698174.

Götz, N. 2008. 'Reframing NGOs: The Identity of an International Relations Non-Starter', in *European Journal of International Relations* 14(2): 231–58. https://doi.org/10.1177/1354066108089242.

Graaf, B., I. de Haan and B. Vick (eds). 2019. *Securing Europe after Napoleon: 1815 and the New European Security Culture*. Cambridge: Cambridge University Press. https://doi.org/10.1017/9781108597050.

Gschnitzer, F. et al. 1978. 'Volk, Nation, Nationalismus, Masse', in O. Brunner, W. Conze and R. Koselleck (eds), *Geschichtliche Grundbegriffe: Historisches Lexikon zur politisch-sozialen Sprache in Deutschland*. Stuttgart: Klett-Cotta Verlag, vol. 4, pp. 141–431.

Hardtwig, W. 1990. 'Verein: Gesellsschaft, Geheimgesellschaft, Assoziation, Genossenschaft, Gewerskschaft', in O. Brunner, W. Conze and R. Koselleck (eds), *Geschichtliche Grundbegriffe: Historisches Lexikon zur politisch-sozialen Sprache in Deutschland*. Stuttgart: Klett-Cotta Verlag, vol. 6, pp. 789–829.

Harland-Jacobs, J. 2007. *Builders of Empire: Freemasons and British Imperialism, 1717–1927*. Chapel Hill: The University of North Carolina Press. Available at http://search.ebscohost.com/login.aspx?direct=true&db=nlebk&AN=461013&site=ehost-live&scope=site.

Hengchen, S. et al. 2021 'A Data-Driven Approach to Studying Changing Vocabularies in Historical Newspaper Collections', *Digital Scholarship in the Humanities* 36 (Supplement 2): ii109–ii126. https://doi.org/10.1093/llc/fqab032.

Im Hof, U. 1982. *Das gesellige Jahrhundert: Gesellschaft und Gesellschaften im Zeitalter der Aufklärung.* Munich: Beck.

Jacob, M.C. 1991. *Living the Enlightenment: Freemasonry and Politics in Eighteenth-Century Europe.* New York: Oxford University Press.

Janis, M. 1984. 'Jeremy Bentham and the Fashioning of "International Law"', *The American Journal of International Law* 78(2): 405–18.

Jordheim, H. 2014. 'Introduction: Multiple Times and the Work of Synchronization', *History and Theory* 53(4): 498–518.

————. 2017. 'Europe at Different Speeds: Asynchronicities and Multiple Times in European Conceptual History', in W. Steinmetz, M. Freeden and J.F. Sebastián (eds). *Conceptual History in the European Space.* European Conceptual History 1. New York: Berghahn, pp. 47–62.

————. 2018. 'Keeping the "Ism" in "Cosmopolitanism" – Wieland and the Origins of Cosmopolitan Discourse', *Journal of Political Ideologies* 23(3): 299–319. https://doi.org/10.1080/13569317.2018.1503770.

Jordheim, H. and E. Sandmo. 2018. *Conceptualizing the World: An Exploration across Disciplines.* New York: Berghahn.

Jordheim, H. and E. Wigen. 2018. 'Conceptual Synchronisation: From Progress to Crisis', *Millennium* 46(3): 421–39. https://doi.org/10.1177/0305829818774781.

Kemiläinen, A. 1964. *Nationalism: Problems Concerning the Word, the Concept, and Classification.* Jyväskylä: Jyväskylän kasvatusopillinen korkeakoulu.

Kettunen, P. 2018. 'The Concept of Nationalism in Discussions on a European Society', *Journal of Political Ideologies* 23(3): 342–69. https://doi.org/10.1080/13569317.2018.1502943.

Koselleck, R. 1972. 'Einleitung', in O. Brunner, W. Conze and R. Koselleck (eds), *Geschichtliche Grundbegriffe: Historisches Lexikon zur politisch-sozialen Sprache in Deutschland.* Stuttgart: Klett-Cotta Verlag, vol. 1, pp. XIII–XXV.

————. 2000. *Zeitschichten: Studien zur Historik.* Frankfurt am Main: Suhrkamp.

Koskenniemi, M. 2001. *The Gentle Civilizer of Nations: The Rise and Fall of International Law 1870–1960.* Cambridge: Cambridge University Press.

Kurunmäki, J. and J. Marjanen. 2018a. 'A Rhetorical View of Isms: An Introduction', *Journal of Political Ideologies* 23(3): 241–55. https://doi.org/10.1080/1356931 7.2018.1502939.

————. 2018b. 'Isms, Ideologies and Setting the Agenda for Public Debate', *Journal of Political Ideologies* 23(3): 256–82. https://doi.org/10.1080/1356931 7.2018.1502941.

Marjanen, J. 2013. *Den ekonomiska patriotismens uppgång och fall: Finska hushålln-ingssällskapet i europeisk, svensk och finsk kontext 1720–1840.* Helsinki: Helsingin yliopisto.

_____. 2017. 'Transnational Conceptual History, Methodological Nationalism and Europe', in W. Steinmetz, M. Freeden and J.F. Sebastián (eds), *Conceptual History in the European Space*. New York: Berghahn, pp. 139–74.

Mazower, M. 2013. *Governing the World: The History of an Idea*. London: Allen Lane.

Murphy, C.N. and J. Yates. 2015. 'Afterword: The Globalizing Governance of International Communications: Market Creation and Voluntary Consensus Standard Setting', *Journal of Policy History* 27(3): 550–58. https://doi.org/10.1017/S0898030615000226.

Pechenick, E.A., C.M. Danforth and P. Sheridan Dodds. 2015. 'Characterizing the Google Books Corpus: Strong Limits to Inferences of Socio-Cultural and Linguistic Evolution', *PLOS ONE* 10(10): e0137041. https://doi.org/10.1371/journal.pone.0137041.

Prescott, A. 2013. 'Relations Between the Grand Lodges of England and Sweden During the Long Eighteenth Century', *Journal for Research into Freemasonry and Fraternalism* 3(2): 185–222. https://doi.org/10.1558/jrff.v3i2.185.

Prevost, J.-G. and J.-P. Beaud. 2015. *Statistics, Public Debate and the State, 1800–1945: A Social, Political and Intellectual History of Numbers*. London: Routledge.

Reinalda, B. 2009. *Routledge History of International Organizations: From 1815 to the Present Day*. London: Routledge. https://doi.org/10.4324/9780203876572.

Roshchin, E. 2013. '(Un)Natural and Contractual International Society: A Conceptual Inquiry', *European Journal of International Relations* 19(2): 257–79. https://doi.org/10.1177/1354066111422118.

Sluga, G. 2013. *Internationalism in the Age of Nationalism*. Pennsylvania Studies in Human Rights. Philadelphia: University of Pennsylvania Press.

Sluga, G. and P. Clavin (eds). 2017. *Internationalisms: A Twentieth-Century History*. Cambridge: Cambridge University Press. https://doi.org/10.1017/9781107477568.

Stapelbroek, K. and J. Marjanen. 2012. 'Political Economy, Patriotism and the Rise of Societies', in K. Stapelbroek and J. Marjanen (eds), *The Rise of Economic Societies in the Eighteenth Century: Patriotic Reform in Europe and North America*. Basingstoke: Palgrave Macmillan, pp. 1–25.

Steinmetz, W. 2020. 'Introduction: Concepts and Practices of Comparison in Modern History', in W. Steinmetz (ed.), *The Force of Comparison: A New Perspective on Modern European History and the Contemporary World*. New York: Berghahn, pp. 1–32.

Stenius, H. 1987. *Frivilligt, jämlikt, samfällt: Föreningsväsendets utveckling i Finland fram till 1900-talets början med speciell hänsyn till massorganisationsprincipens genombrott*. Helsinki: Svenska litteratursällskapet i Finland.

Stenius, H. and H. Haggrén. 2005. 'Det nordiska samarbetets vardagspraktiker: Vad vet vi om dessa förutom att de har varit/är viktiga?', in L. Häggman (ed.), *Finland i Norden: Finland 50 år i Nordiska rådet*. Helsinki: Pohjola-Norden, pp. 79–90.

Suganami, H. 1978. 'A Note on the Origin of the Word "International"', *British Journal of International Studies* 4(3): 226–32.

Sylvest, C. 2004. 'International Law in Nineteenth-Century Britain', *British Yearbook of International Law* 75(1): 9–70. https://doi.org/10.1093/bybil/75.1.9.

Thompson, E.P. 1968. *The Making of the English Working Class.* London: Penguin Books.

Vollerthun, U. 2017. *The Idea of International Society: Erasmus, Vitoria, Gentili and Grotius.* J. L. Richardson (ed.). Cambridge: Cambridge University Press.

Wevers, M. and M. Koolen. 2020. 'Digital Begriffsgeschichte: Tracing Semantic Change Using Word Embeddings', *Historical Methods: A Journal of Quantitative and Interdisciplinary History*, May, 1–18. https://doi.org/10.1080/01615440.2020.1760157.

Chapter 4

# Internationalism in Socialist Conceptualizations of Politics in the Late Nineteenth and Early Twentieth Centuries

*Pauli Kettunen*

In the book that came to serve as the foundation of 'proletarian internationalism', the *Manifesto of the Communist Party* (1848), we do not find the word 'internationalism', nor even 'international'. Socialists, including the two young authors of the pamphlet, Karl Marx and Friedrich Engels, only later conceptualized and advocated its message as 'internationalism'. Writing a conceptual history of socialist internationalisms provides an opportunity to get beyond the conventional images portraying a linear progress from narrow national perspectives to wider international ones. Being sensitive to the historicity of concepts means avoiding use of the terms 'international' and 'internationalism' for anything beyond a national perspective; a tendency to do this is notable in studies on Marx's internationalism (e.g. Bottomore 1983; Bellamy Foster 2000).

There is a good case for arguing that 'international' and 'internationalism' pushed aside earlier imperial or cosmopolitan images of the world that were not bound to the nation (Armitage 2012; Sluga 2013; Jordheim 2018; Chapter 1). By means of the concepts of international and internationalism, socialists in the late nineteenth century adopted a notion of a world order consisting of interdependent nations and a world history proceeding through the interplay of class-divided nations and the conflicts between nationally organized social classes. Rival political manifestations of this notion emerged, even among those socialists and socialist movements that represented, interpreted and revised the legacy of Marx and Engels in the late nineteenth and early twentieth centuries. I focus on those socialists.

In the first part of the chapter, I examine the adoption and usage of 'international' and 'internationalism' as concepts in socialist vocabularies until the First World War. The data mainly consists of texts that include reflection on these concepts, that is, writings of leading socialists in debates on programmes, policies and modes of organization. In the late nineteenth century discussions on the so-called labour question, the relationship between the notions of international economy and national society appeared as a major issue. In the second part, I examine how socialists defined their politics in relation to this nexus of the social and economic, the national and international. I focus on a confrontation between two future visions that emerged after the First World War and created a context for rival socialist internationalisms, namely the confrontation between international social policies institutionalized in the International Labour Organization (ILO) and proletarian world revolution inspired by the Bolshevik Revolution in Russia. I discuss socialist views on this confrontation between the world wars, especially those appearing in texts produced by the ILO, the International Federation of Trade Unions, the Labour and Socialist International and the Communist International.[1]

## Internationalism in Class Struggle

### *National Form and Cosmopolitan Substance*
From the mid-nineteenth century until the 1980s, the period when social-ist futures played an important role in political imagination whether as promises or threats, the most frequently cited part of the *Manifesto* was its last sentence: 'Workers of the World, unite!'.[2] Since the 1980s, struggles between socialist and capitalist visions have rarely provided any effective framework for imagining futures. The *Manifesto* resurfaced in discussions on postmodernity and globalization, but a different part had gained greater popularity. It is the chapter depicting the revolutionary role of bourgeoisie:

> Constant revolutionising of production, uninterrupted disturbance of all social conditions, everlasting uncertainty and agitation distinguish the bourgeois epoch from all earlier ones. ... The bourgeoisie has through its exploitation of the world market given a cosmopolitan character to produc-tion and consumption in every country. ... The bourgeoisie, by the rapid improvement of all instruments of production, by the immensely facilitated means of communication, draws all, even the most barbarian, nations into civilisation. (Marx and Engels 1848: ch. 1)

Thus, the bourgeoisie was breaking down old social structures and transforming the world into a whole of global connections and transfers. This world did not appear as an international order. Instead, it had 'a cosmopolitan character'. However, the chapter on bourgeois revolution was not just a praise of the innovative cross-border capacities of capitalism, but it motivated the historical mission of the working class.

For the authors of the *Manifesto*, the national centralization of political power was a phase of bourgeois revolution and nations still played a role as the main framework of political struggle. However, they were made of pre-bourgeois elements and were eroding in the post-national bourgeois world. The working class, while rising to fulfil its historical mission as the force of universal emancipation, would further boost the cosmopolitan transformation.

A crucial precondition for this was the national organization of the working class. According to the *Manifesto*, 'Though not in substance [*Inhalt*], yet in form, the struggle of the proletariat with the bourgeoisie is at first a national struggle. The proletariat of each country must, of course, first of all settle matters with its own bourgeoisie' (Marx and Engels 1848: ch. 1).

The authors specified their view on the relationship between form and substance when defining the role of Communists: 'In the national struggles of the proletarians of the different countries, they [Communists] point out and bring to the front the common interests of the entire proletariat, inde-pendently of all nationality' (Marx and Engels 1848: ch. 2). In a few later texts they explicitly applied the word 'cosmopolitan' to this common inter-est of the entire working class, that is, to the 'substance' of class struggle.[3] It is worth noting that in the vocabulary of Marxism-Leninism established in the Stalin era, 'cosmopolitan' and 'cosmopolitanism' were tools of condem-nation and strongly opposed to 'proletarian internationalism' (see below).

Marx and Engels did adopt the adjective 'international' into the vocab-ulary they used to conceptualize and direct working-class movements. However, even in the 'provisional rules' of the International Working Men's Association, founded in London in 1864, Marx avoided using this adjective to define the mission of the working class. In his formulation, 'the emancipation of labour is neither a local nor a national, but a social problem, embracing all countries in which modern society exists'.[4] In these rules, as well as in his 'inaugural address' for this association that soon became known as the (later the First) International, Marx used the word 'international' to describe not the mission itself, but two factors that would make the working class capable of fulfilling it.

First, in Marx's vision of world history, nations were at different phases of development. It was crucial for the working class to learn from experiences in other countries, especially those at the forefront of progress, to be able to develop the right national forms of class struggle. This was an 'international' learning process. Second, the power of the ruling classes was institutionalized not only in the national structures of domination and the cosmopolitan formations of world market noted in the *Manifesto*, but also in 'international' politics, which included rivalry, conflicts, wars, alliances and diplomacy. In the inaugural address of the International in 1864,[5] Marx emphasized that recent experiences had 'taught the working classes the duty to master themselves the mysteries of international politics'. They should 'vindicate the simple laws of morals and justice, which ought to govern the relations of private individuals, as the rules paramount of the intercourse of nations'. He concluded that: 'The fight for such a foreign policy forms part of the general struggle for the emancipation of the working classes'.

Thus, foreign policy was one topic of the working-class struggle, in which the national form and the cosmopolitan substance should be correctly conceived. Controversies related to this emerged within the International, creating preconditions for the concept of the international to become an 'ism'.

In their account of the ramifications of the Franco-Prussian war and the failure of the Paris Commune, Marx and Engels in 1872 assessed that the war had caused 'disorganization' in the International, but also created new preconditions for anti-bourgeois working-class solidarity. They noticed that among German migrant workers in America, a sharp divide between 'internationalist' and 'chauvinist' groups had emerged.[6] In a letter in 1874, Engels admitted that the International could no longer exist as it had. It had been founded at a time when 'the common, cosmopolitan interests of the proletariat could be put in the foreground', yet it had dissolved and a new, theoretically more advanced and coherent International was needed.[7]

Marx and Engels adopted 'internationalism' as a concept for the right way of combining the national form and the cosmopolitan substance of working-class struggle, realized in international proletarian collaboration. However, a tendency to subordinate the cosmopolitan substance to the national form emerged in working-class movements, and counter-concepts to internationalism were needed. Concerning views associated with international politics, 'chauvinism' became the most popular tool of critique. The adoption of 'nationalism' as a counter-concept to internationalism in socialist discourse deserves special attention here.

## Nationalism as a Counter-Concept to Internationalism

The old word 'nation' was a core term of the French Revolution, referring to the universal principle of citizenship that overcame the particularism of the privilege-based old regime. However, even before it became a popular conceptual tool in political debates at the end of the nineteenth century, 'nationalism' referred to ideas and practices that violated universal principles such as Catholicism (Kettunen 2018: 344–45).

'Nationalism' did not gain any central role in the vocabularies of Marx and Engels or that of their late nineteenth-century disciples. During one of his periods in prison, Wilhelm Liebknecht, a founder of the Marxian social democratic party in Germany (1869), began to collect a lexicon of foreign-origin words, meant to help ordinary people understand newspaper texts. His *Volks-Fremdwörterbuch* was published in 1874 and later in many editions, the ninth one in 1907. The lexicon included *Internationalismus* and *Kosmopolitismus*, but not *Nationalismus*.[8]

The failure to understand the international duties of the German working class was one of the main criticisms Marx and Engels levelled against Ferdinand Lassalle and the Lassallean wing of the German labour movement. This argument was included in Marx's critique of the Gotha Programme of Die Sozialistische Arbeiterpartei Deutschlands that was formed in 1875 by uniting the Lassallean and Marxian parties. While sharply criticizing the lack of concrete working-class internationalism in the programme, he nevertheless did not use the concept of nationalism.[9]

In the First International, the conceptual pair of internationalism and nationalism occasionally appeared, notably in disputes on how Irish workers should organize. In 1872, the British trade unionist and General Council member of the International, John Hales rejected any nationality-based Irish working-class organization, because, as he argued, the 'fundamental principle' of the International 'was to destroy all semblance of the nationalist doctrine, and remove all barriers that separated man from man'. Engels strongly opposed this, pointing to the national subordination of the Irish people: 'In a case like that of the Irish, true Internationalism must necessarily be based upon a distinctly national organization'.[10]

In 1882, after the end of the First International, the young Marxian theoretician Karl Kautsky asked Engels to give his authoritative statement in a dispute concerning Polish socialists and the requirements of internationalism. In Engels' view, 'there are *two* nations in Europe which do not only have the right but the duty to be nationalistic before they become internationalists: the Irish and the Poles. They are internationalists of the best kind if they are very nationalistic'.[11] By using the word 'nationalistic' in a provocative way, Engels apparently wished to warn his fellow socialists against condemning all kinds of national aspirations as violations of internationalism.

The relationship between the so-called national awakening and socialist labour movement became an acute question in multinational European empires, especially in the Habsburg Monarchy (Konrad 1976). With his book *Die Nationalitätenfrage und die Sozialdemokratie* (1907), Otto Bauer achieved a position as a leading Marxist – 'Austro-Marxist' – theoretician of this question. One of his conceptual contributions was an explicit distinction between internationalism and cosmopolitanism.

In Bauer's view, socialists should recognize the importance of nations, entities based on cultural experience and community rather than territory, and he argued for national autonomy within a multinational (Austrian) political framework. He distinguished between two tendencies of workers' 'revolutionary instinct', both of which had their roots in specific historical preconditions of working-class struggle. Workers in subordinated nations developed 'naïve nationalism', identifying their class struggle with the national one, whereas in fully developed (*gesättigte*) nations, they tended to direct their struggle not only against the dominant classes but also against the nation, thus adopting 'naïve cosmopolitanism'. By advocating 'conscious internationalism' (*bewusster Internationalismus*), social democracy would overcome both forms of instinctive thought. While Bauer argued for the progress from cosmopolitanism to internationalism, he nevertheless found 'cultural cosmopolitanism' a necessary element within 'proletarian internationalism', in connection with international working-class solidarity, and struggle against imperialism and for the liberty and self-government of all nations. Such internationalism had developed in the large nation states (*Nationalstaaten*) yet continued to face big challenges in multinational states (*Nationalitätenstaaten*).[12]

In addition to the naïve nationalism among the workers of subordinated nations, Bauer identified a type of nationalism in dominant nations nourished by 'revisionist' politics. Participating in the dispute Eduard Bernstein had raised in the German Social Democratic Party and in the Second International, Bauer argued that revisionist politics, based on national cooperation with fractions of the bourgeoisie, failed to create international counterforces to economic competition between workers of different nationalities. In the Austrian empire, German workers had adopted an 'unreflected hate' against foreign, especially Czech workers, who competed with lower wages and could be recruited as strike breakers. The hate, stemming from real experiences, was doomed to grow if trade unions failed to organize workers on an international basis (ibid.: §33 and §34).

### Internationalism and Patriotism

Opposing the recruitment of foreign workers as strike breakers was one of the first concrete incentives and practices of international working-class collaboration (Prothero 2018). International solidarity and national protectionism were two sides of the same coin. In proletarian rhetoric, it was easy to turn accusations of a lack of patriotism against the capitalists who willingly promoted their class interests by employing foreign workers. This was the case, for example, in Finland, an autonomous Grand Duchy in the Russian empire, where Russian strike breakers played an effective role in many industrial conflicts (Stenius 1978).

International collaboration was a means of strengthening the national capacities of the organized working class, by opposing strike breaking, providing financial support and especially transferring political ideas. The internationals played a role in these communicative activities. The network later called the Second International was launched in 1889 as a practice of international socialist conferences, dominated by the ideological leaders of German and French socialist parties, and it had a permanent bureau from 1900 (Haupt 1964; Dogliani 2017). Defining the socialist views to be applied in national politics was the main ambition of its conferences.

Marxian condemnation of anarchism framed the Second International debates. Yet it did not solve the problem of reform and revolution that arose in debates on the role of parliamentary action and universal suffrage, including women's political rights (Eley 2002: 86–108). Kautsky and other 'orthodox' Marxists solved the dilemma by distinguishing between short-term reforms and the final goal. Reforms, together with the rise of the working class, its experiences of exploitation and the educational efforts of social democratic parties, would increase proletarian class power. The final goal would be achieved when the proletariat grew capable of conquering the state power – actually, of receiving the majority in a democratized parliament – and the crisis-prone capitalist system has proved unsustainable. Bernstein and other revisionists began to interpret the gradual reforms of political institutions and societal conditions, as such, as changes leading towards a socialist society – an idea Bernstein had learned from the Fabian Society in Britain, with Beatrice and Sidney Webb as its most prominent representatives (Hyrkkänen 1986: 167–95).

Those advocating socialist participation in existing state institutions expected that this would change, and was already changing, foreign policies and international relations.[13] Bernstein in Germany and Jean Jaurès in France were among the most prominent socialists to argue that patriotism, unlike nationalism, was compatible with internationalism.

'In all countries where the working class has become influential it develops a new patriotism of its own', Bernstein wrote in 1907. It is based on 'the equal democratic right of the nationalities'. Instead of 'altering the boundaries on the map of Europe, which under present circumstances could only be accomplished by means of bloody wars', the correct way of promoting this development was 'altering the constitutions of those States which have become historical'. In the Marxian discourse, 'historical' was an attribute of peoples that had developed a national self-consciousness, and Bernstein obviously saw this as the basis for more national autonomy rather than for new sovereign nation states. In any case, Bernstein believed that ongoing change 'enables the working class to combine with its patriotism the most effectual peace policy that the world has ever known'.[14]

For Jean Jaurès, patriotism, reshaped by the increased political influence of the working class, combined the willingness to defend national independence and to protect international peace. This was the main message of his large book *L'armée nouvelle* (1910). He rejected 'l'internationalisme abstrait et anarchisant', which failed to understand that internationalism and patriotism, rightly conceived, required and enabled each other. Internationalist socialist proletarians should actively participate in national defence, thus reforming and democratizing the army and making it capable of protecting both international peace and national independence (cf. French parliamentary debates in Chapter 6).[15]

### Internationalism and Imperialism

Socialists associated imperialism and its core, colonial politics, with the centralization and concentration of capital, the formation of trusts, cartels and groupings of financial capital, anti-free-trade protective tariffs, colonial expansion, and violence and militarism. Accounts of the role of these phenomena in the transition from capitalism to socialism diverged, however, and greatly contributed to the split of Second International Marxism.

As a step in his turn to revisionism, in the 1890s Bernstein was inspired by Jaurès and the Fabians to elaborate an idea of 'socialist colonial politics'. He accepted colonial politics as the extension of civilization from nations at a higher level of culture to those at a lower level, but criticized the exploitative and conflict-laden capitalist forms in which undemocratic states conducted it. Free trade was the opposite of imperialism and a key element of socialist colonial politics (Hyrkkänen 1986). Kautsky did not approve any vision of a socialist transformation through incremental reforms. Just after the First World War began, however, he envisioned a possibility of 'ultra-imperialism', a tendency within imperialism that might decrease its war-generating powers even before the socialist revolution (Gronow 2015).

The left wing of the Second International were convinced that capitalism and imperialism, and imperialism and militarism, were inseparable. The First World War was a decisive evidence of those connections, and only two alternatives existed, *Sozialismus oder Barbarei*, as Rosa Luxemburg put it after 'a world historical catastrophe; the surrender of the international social democracy'.[16] In what became the best-known socialist account of imperialism – *Imperialism, the Highest Stage of Capitalism* (1917)[17] – Vladimir Ilyich Lenin sharply rejected any assumptions that a phase of post-imperialist capitalism would precede the transition to socialism. The tendencies towards ultra-imperialism or the 'general cartel'[18] could never overcome the contradictions and conflicts of imperialism. They could be only solved by proletarian revolution, turning the imperialist war into a class war against the bourgeoisie and their allies, including those socialists – 'social chauvinists' – that had betrayed internationalism and committed themselves to national warfare when the First World War broke out.

The so-called Zimmerwald International, founded in 1915, was an incoherent grouping of those who did not approve the integration of socialist parties and trade unions in national war efforts (Eley 2002: 127–31). In Germany, Bernstein, Kautsky and Luxemburg found themselves in an equally incoherent new party, the Independent Social Democratic Party, founded by the critics of war policies in 1917 and divided over the German Revolution.

Controversial conclusions from a wide range of dramatic experiences coloured the socialist horizons of expectation after the First World War. Recent and current experiences included wartime policies of national integration and associated ideological conflicts, a new regulating role of the state in national economies and the postwar international economic crisis, the revolutionary collapses of multinational empires and the conflict-laden projects of new nation states, radical working-class mobilization and the extension of parliamentary political democracy. Responses to these led to irreconcilable divisions among the heirs of the Second International Marxism.

However, it would be far too simple to depict the outcome as a divide between social democracy focusing on national parliamentary action for social reforms and communism attempting to extend the Bolshevik Revolution into a proletarian world revolution, and defining Bolshevism as the universal proletarian mode of action. In postwar struggles on the future world order, there were advocates of divergent socialist internationalisms and divergent critiques of capitalism. In what follows, I relate the socialist internationalisms to intergovernmental efforts at harmonizing the relationship between the international economy and national society, notably those institutionalized in the ILO.

## Socialist Internationalisms and International Social Policy

### Social and Economic, National and International

The project to protect labour on an international level, or an international social policy, has a longer history than that of socialist working-class internationals. The ILO begins its historical self-descriptions with a social policy plan that Robert Owen, a Welsh manufacturer and one of the visionaries later called Utopian socialists, submitted to the congress of European great powers in Aachen in 1818. In the late nineteenth-century international discussions on the 'social question' or 'labour question', we can distinguish between six arguments that were contrasted or intertwined (Kettunen 2006).

According to the first argument, social political reforms were necessary to diminish the social and political threats of class conflicts caused by the international economy. The second argument was that international economic competition presented obstacles to national social policies that weaken a nation's competitiveness. Alternatively, international economic competition could be seen – so the third argument went – as the point of departure for international social norms that would be binding for all competing countries and firms. According to a fourth argument that appeared at an early stage in the discussions, national social policies would support the success of national economies by improving workforce quality and productivity and by increasing purchasing power.

Another influential argument took two forms: that the logic of the capitalist economy would itself either produce the solutions to the problems it had caused or generate the powers that would overthrow it. The former variant was manifested in efforts to show that demands for economic efficiency and social harmony could be realized through scientific management techniques or by employers providing social welfare for their workers. The latter variant was the main message of the revolutionary socialist critique of capitalism.

Besides fundamental critique of capitalism, the motives of national and international social policies (the third and fourth argument above) were included in the political visions of Second International Marxism. On one hand, the internationalism of class struggle was associated with not only the final goal of socialism, but also its short-term objectives, including social policy reforms and improvements to working conditions. Bauer had pointed out in 1907 that international solidarity was a precondition for a successful national struggle: it was necessary to restrict the scope of capitalists and nations to compete by lowering labour costs. On the other hand, socialist political argumentation was that immediate working-class demands for better wages, shorter working hours and social insurance actually corresponded to the best national economic interest; capitalists who opposed these demands were blinded by their narrow class interests and short-sighted greed (Kettunen 1994: 97–101, 124–25).[19] The working class was not only the agent of the transition from capitalism to socialism and, hence, of the emancipation of humanity; it was also the true bearer of the national interest when struggling for its own short-term objectives.

After the First World War, all six arguments described above played a role in the struggles between different visions of societal change. These visions were internationalized in a new way through the experiences of war, political upheavals and radical mass mobilization.

### International Social Policy versus Proletarian World Revolution

The ILO was founded after the First World War as an autonomous part of the League of Nations. It arose from the long project for establishing international social norms yet, with good reason, it has been characterized as 'the answer of Versailles to Bolshevism' (Tikriti 1982: 125). With the foundation of the ILO, the vision of world revolution was confronted by the vision of an international social policy.

The ideology behind the League of Nations presupposed that the world after the breakdown of multinational empires would be an international order of sovereign national states, completed by a civilizational legitimation of continued colonial policies. The foundation of the ILO expressed a further element of this ideology, a view that this order required international regulation of certain internal affairs within national societies. Political stability within countries was a precondition for international political stability. Internal political stability depended on placing social limitations on the free play of the capitalist economy. These social limitations had to be enshrined at the international level because international economic competition prevailed in the world. This argumentation can be found behind the lofty formulations in that section of the Treaty of Versailles that contained the charter of the ILO.[20]

Furthermore, the ILO came to express a view that the international order of sovereign nation states required self-imposed restriction of state autonomy even in relation to society. The organization of the ILO was based on tripartite representation. In both the national delegations of international labour conferences and the governing body of the whole organization, workers and employers had (and have) their representatives besides those of the governments. Among official international organizations, this structure was unique. Governments were supposed to nominate worker and employer delegates from the candidates proposed by the most representative organizations of these two groups, a rule that would cause numerous disputes on mandates. In its very structure, the ILO came to universalize an image of an industrial society in which organized capital and organized labour together with the government generate social regulations, resolving the tensions between the international economy and national society.

Tripartite representation was a far from unproblematic principle. According to the left-wing socialist critique, the organizational structure of the ILO was aimed at integrating the working class into the bourgeois state. Reformist socialists could see the recognition of workers' unions as an extension of political democracy, whereas for many employers, it was a threat. However, corporatist representation of economic interests in national political processes could also be understood as a means to limit the threats seen as inherent in universal suffrage, which made its breakthrough after the First World War. It was possible to interpret tripartism as a representation of the different functions of society rather than of conflicting interests – an argument that was later used to facilitate the ILO membership of the Soviet Union and Eastern bloc countries (Kettunen 2013: 223–25).

Both employer and worker delegates were organized as groups and guided to define their views with support of their own international organizations. The International Organization of Industrial Employers was founded in 1919 to meet the requirements of ILO activities (Haas 1964: 203–206). The foundation of the ILO gave impetus to trade union internationalism as well. Within the ideological framework of the Second International, an international trade union secretariat had been organized in 1901, and in 1913 the International Federation of Trade Unions (IFTU) was founded. After the war, in 1919, it was reconstituted with the same name, also called the Amsterdam International; in the 1920s and 1930s one of its main activities was to lead the workers' group in the ILO (Van Goethem 2006: 133–56).

### Amsterdam versus Moscow

From the very beginning, the ILO and the Amsterdam International were harshly condemned by Bolsheviks and the Third International, or the Communist International (Comintern), also founded in 1919. There was no middle course between 'imperialism and socialism, the dictatorship of the bourgeoisie and the dictatorship of the proletariat, the League of Nations and the Third International', a Bolshevik trade union leader in 1919 asserted to 'all the workers of Europe and America' (Tossdorff and Fowkes 2016: 61).

However, the dichotomy was far from clear-cut in the labour movement, especially in trade unions that channelled postwar radical working-class mobilization. A transition to socialism appeared both necessary and possible – necessary, as capitalism seemed unable to solve the economic crisis,[21] and possible due to either the assumed revolutionary capacities of the working class or the opportunities offered by the extension of parliamentary political democracy.

Several socialist parties tried to oppose the division between the revitalized reformist Second International and the Third International, although the so-called Two-and-a-Half International, led by Austrian socialists, only lasted a couple of years (1921–1923) before its affiliation with the Second International in the Labour and Socialist International. In trade unions, rival political orientations ranged from anarcho-syndicalism to social Catholicism, both of which had their own organizational traditions and forms. In the ideology of the Amsterdam International, a socialist political dimension connecting trade unions and labour parties remained strong, and during the initial postwar years, the assumption that the international socialist transition was real was widely shared. One of the two Dutch secretaries of the Amsterdam International, Edo Fimmen, who was also the general secretary of the International Transport Workers Federation, defined the goal as 'the liberation of the working classes, the abolition of all wars and the attainment of World Peace'. His fellow secretary Jan Oudegeest – a much less radical trade unionist – wrote in 1920: 'World revolution is to lead the people to Socialism' (Van Goethem 2006: 29).

Radical statements did not prevent the Comintern from categorizing the Amsterdam International as a 'yellow' union, that is, an organization founded to support employers. The attraction of the Third International was a real threat for the IFTU. In 1920, a trade union international was founded in connection with the Comintern (Tossdorff and Fowkes 2016). While the founding of the Red International of Labour Unions (Profintern) indicated a defeat of 'ultra-leftist' views, rejecting traditional forms of working-class action and focusing on the immediate completion of world revolution, for non-communist trade union leaders it indicated the challenge stemming from the Bolshevik Revolution and Soviet Russia. One of the first research projects the ILO carried out was on Soviet Russian labour conditions. This was needed because 'the mind of the working classes' was affected by the stories of great achievements in Soviet Russia, as the French trade unionist Léon Jouhaux, the leading figure of the ILO workers' group, argued in January 1920.[22]

The result of the postwar period of political upheavals was a widely unexpected situation: the Bolshevik power was stabilized in Russia, while 'recasting bourgeois Europe' (Maier 1975) occurred in different national modes. The colonial powers, however, faced possible world revolution in their colonies. Connecting the efforts for proletarian world revolution and the support for the national liberation of suppressed and colonized peoples was a crucial part of the Comintern programmes. In his report to the 1927

International Labour Conference, ILO Director Albert Thomas, a French socialist who had served as Minister of Armament in a wartime government, paid attention to political unrest in the Dutch East Indies. In his view, it indicated a combination of nationalism and communism that 'may be in the future a very serious complicating factor in the administration not only of the Netherlands East Indies, but of other colonial areas'.[23]

In the struggle between 'Amsterdam and Moscow' the IFTU managed to reinforce its position. The Soviet efforts at a 'united front' – between the Soviet and British trade unions in the mid-1920s and between the Soviet, Norwegian and Finnish trade unions at the end of 1920s – gained sympathy among the invited partners, but eventually failed (Calhoun 1976; Lorenz 1982).

The First Five-Year Plan (1928–1932) in the Soviet Union attracted international attention, but while the Comintern's diagnoses of the emerging crisis of capitalism were incisive, the political conclusions it drew were catastrophic. Social democracy would be an integral part of the fascist responses to the crisis of monopoly capitalism. In the process of 'rapid fascization of the reformist trade union apparatus and of its fusion with the bourgeois State, a particularly harmful role is played by the so-called "left" wing of the Amsterdam International'. Those leaders, for example Fimmen, were forming 'an active and constituent part (and by far not the least important) in the system of social fascism'.[24] Communist optimism relied on the fact that 'the treacherous social-fascist role of the leaders of the Social Democratic and Amsterdam Internationals is being more and more clearly recognized by broad sections of the working class'.[25]

Nevertheless, by the mid-1930s a distinction between bourgeois democracy and fascism was drawn in the motivations and justifications of communist politics at both international and national levels. This appeared in a changing attitude to the League of Nations and, subsequently, the ILO, both of which the Soviet Union joined in 1934;[26] in the same year, the United States joined the ILO, yet not the League (Lorenz 2001). Popular front tactics were first applied in France and Spain and confirmed in the seventh congress of the Comintern in 1935. Friendly communication on options for anti-war cooperation was achieved between the Comintern and the two social democratic internationals (the Labour and Socialist International and the Amsterdam International).[27] Profintern was wound up in 1937, although negotiations about the membership of Soviet trade unions in the Amsterdam International failed. However, the victory of the IFTU in the battle between trade union internationals did not cover the fact that not only the vision of proletarian world revolution but also the visions of trade union internationalism and international social policy had waned.

## International Social Policy and a Model of National Society

In the ILO discussions, the concept of internationalism mostly appeared in critical accounts of practical achievements. Thomas, the first Director of the ILO, used the concept in this way in his reports to the annual international labour conferences. 'A living internationalism' – 'la vie international réelle' in the native language version of his 1925 report – could not be built 'on the perpetual repetition of a few principles, or on continual sentimental proclamations of human fellowship and love of justice'. Nor were the criteria of internationalism fulfilled by scientific and educational work to spread knowledge about the similar problems each state sought to solve 'by their own independent efforts': true internationalism would require 'wholehearted and effective' collaboration.[28]

In his critique of the lack of internationalism, Thomas made active use of the statistics of ILO conventions ratified by member states. In his 1931 report, he admitted that the social policies of different countries had much in common, yet 'in these early stages of internationalism' the only concrete criterion of internationalism were the ratifications, and he was not satisfied with this.[29] In 1919–1939, the international labour conferences, including the special conferences on maritime issues, accepted sixty-seven conventions.[30] These ranged from the restriction of working hours, the protection of women and children, and social insurance, to the prohibition of forced labour and the conditions of indigenous workers. A convention became a part of national law after a member state had ratified it. However, exactly as Thomas had complained in 1925, any international harmonization of social norms was achieved through national solutions rather than through subordination to international regulation.

Working hours are a good example. In accordance with the old demand of the international socialist movement that had played a central role in the wartime and postwar radical mobilization (Cross 1989), the first ILO convention in 1919 restricted the workday to eight hours. However, relatively few countries ever ratified this convention; none of the Nordic countries did. Supporters of the convention waited in vain for its ratification by the leading industrial state, Britain. However, the eight-hour day was quite widely adopted in practice during the early 1920s for industrial labour. During the Great Depression, the Labour and Socialist International and the Amsterdam International together demanded the introduction of a forty-hour week, Otto Bauer being one of the most prominent advocates of this international norm.[31] The IFTU ascribed huge significance to this objective as a solution to all current problems: 'The forty-hour week means the end of unemployment, the end of the crisis, industrial recovery, the defeat of Fascism, the downfall of economic nationalism, etc.'[32] A convention to this effect was accepted at the ILO conference of 1935, but by the outbreak of the Second World War, only one country, New Zealand, had ratified this convention.

The ILO exercised greater influence on changes in labour law and wider social policy by producing and transmitting knowledge than it did through international law. It produced arguments and comparative knowledge, not least statistical classifications and categorizations (Wobbe and Renard 2017), which could be used in national contexts and political struggles. The ILO was a forum and facilitator of what can be characterized as the comparative reflexivity of national politics.

During the 1930s, the ILO leadership contributed to the propaganda of 'economic planning' and Keynesian ideas concerning the desirability of contracyclical economic policy. The director's reports to international labour conferences praised the Scandinavian social democratic novelties of anti-crisis policies and Franklin D. Roosevelt's New Deal. Nevertheless, the systems of economic planning in National Socialist Germany and Fascist Italy were also presented in the ILO's journal, *International Labour Review*, and the five-year-plan in the Soviet Union evoked considerable interest (Kettunen 1994: 132–35).

However, all these examples of economic planning were associated with what the ILO leadership criticized as 'economic nationalism'. The Great Depression had 'caused a sort of instinctive, unreasoning reaction which has led States and nations to withdraw into themselves' and 'made them temporarily sceptical or uncertain as to the utility of internationalism', as Thomas cautiously noted in his report in 1932.[33] Two years later, the new director, the British liberal Harold Butler, was deeply concerned about the dangerous implications of economic nationalism: 'The application of economic nationalism is beginning to generate tensions and antagonisms between nations, which in the long run are bound to affect their political relations'.[34]

In the IFTU's analysis, the crisis of capitalism resulted from the structural imbalance of overproduction and under-consumption, worsened by the business economic limits of rationalization. In collaboration with the Labour and Socialist International, the IFTU elaborated programmes that extended rationalization into economic planning, not only at national but also at international level. It demanded the foundation of a 'World Economic Council' and the integration of Europe into an 'economic unity',[35] but these demands had very little practical impact and came to indicate the weakness of trade union internationalism. Economic recovery had taken a 'dangerous direction' towards national protectionism, autarchy, isolation and armament, the secretariat of the IFTU concluded in 1937. This direction was set by fascism 'in which the democratic countries have also been involved'.[36]

In collaboration but not without tension, the ILO and the Economic and Financial Organization of the League of Nations opposed economic nationalism. After the Great Depression, international expert collaboration and networking to prevent economic crises was organized, and it came to play a role in shaping the post–Second World War economic order, not least regarding relationships between the economic and the social (Clavin 2013a and 2013b; see also Chapter 7). Nevertheless, in 1939 the IFTU's conclusions about the ILO were pessimistic. The great hope born with the creation of the ILO 'has grown very dim' (Van Goethem 2006: 151).

At the end of the 1930s, it was clear that the ILO had played a more effective role as an advocator of a model of national society than as an agency of binding international regulation. It was far from evident that the model of national society that the ILO had advocated, combining workers' rights, social policies and economic success, would be the winner. Developments in the Nordic countries seemed to correspond to this national model, and an internationalist dimension appeared in the reinforced social democratic collaboration for 'Nordic democracy' (Kurunmäki and Strang 2010; Kettunen 2013), but this went against the mainstream expansion of fascism in Europe. The other pole of the post–First World War confrontation between international social policy and world revolution, in turn, had developed into an international system of Bolshevized national parties, defending the Stalinist socialism in one country against what were defined as its external and internal enemies (McDermott 1998). It was in this context that 'proletarian internationalism' gained an established central position in the vocabulary of 'Marxism-Leninism'.

### *Proletarian Internationalism and Socialism in One Country*

'What is internationalism?' Lenin posed and answered this question in 1918 when condemning 'the renegade Kautsky', a critic of the Bolshevik understanding of the dictatorship of the proletariat. According to Lenin, Kautsky was 'absolutely convinced that he is an internationalist and calls himself one', but had, in fact, adopted a political view that 'means substituting petty-bourgeois nationalism for internationalism'.[37] Lenin did not need to qualify internationalism with any specifying attribute. Only those who held the correct view on proletarian revolution and proletarian dictatorship were internationalists.

The expression 'proletarian internationalism' was not used systematically in Lenin's vocabulary. Any true internationalism was proletarian. At the Comintern's second congress in 1920 Lenin declared 'the struggle against opportunist and petty-bourgeois pacifist distortions of the concept and policy of internationalism'. When contrasting the petty-bourgeois view on internationalism with true internationalism, he did provide the latter with the attribute 'proletarian'. Petty-bourgeois nationalism proclaimed as internationalism 'the mere recognition of the equality of nations' and preserved 'national self-interest intact', whereas

> proletarian internationalism demands, first, that the interests of the proletarian struggle in any one country should be subordinated to the interests of that struggle on a world-wide scale, and, second, that a nation which is achieving victory over the bourgeoisie should be able and willing to make the greatest national sacrifices for the overthrow of international capital.[38]

The second demand implied the leading role of the Soviet Russian party in the international communist movement. However, 'proletarian internationalism' was not yet established as *the* concept referring to this principle. The two main rivals after Lenin, Leon Trotsky and Joseph Stalin, had divergent views on true internationalism, yet by the end of the 1920s 'proletarian internationalism' was not a central concept in their political theories. In his critique of the idea of socialism in one country in 1928, Trotsky demanded that in order to meet the requirements of 'the epoch of imperialism, i.e. of *world* economy and *world* politics under the hegemony of finance capital', the Comintern had to be 'a world communist party'. In his view, 'the national orientation of the proletariat must and can flow only from a world orientation and not vice versa. Herein lies the basic and primary difference between communist internationalism and all varieties of national socialism'.[39]

A decisive step in the rise of 'proletarian internationalism' to become a central concept of communism seems to have been an article by Stalin in 1931, condemning 'Trotskyist' interpretations of the history of Bolshevism and defining guidelines for the 'right' history writing. Stalin connected the concept with the leading role of Soviet communism: 'the consistent and thoroughly revolutionary internationalism of the Bolsheviks is a model of proletarian internationalism for the workers of all countries'.[40]

By the seventh congress of the Comintern in 1935, proletarian internationalism had become a necessary element of 'Marxist-Leninist' rhetoric. 'The task of educating the workers and all working people in the spirit of proletarian internationalism is one of the fundamental tasks of every Communist Party', Georgi Dimitrov, the secretary general of the Comintern, proclaimed in the report he delivered at the conference. The aim of his report was to motivate popular front politics against fascism and, consequently, to point out that national sentiments were not only compatible with but were a part of proletarian internationalism. The revolutionary proletariat would rescue human culture and raise it 'to its highest flowering as a truly national culture – *national in form and socialist in content* – which is being realized in the Union of Soviet Socialist Republics before our very eyes'.[41]

The Spanish Civil War became a failed test of popular front politics, and the Hitler-Stalin Pact closed the window of opportunity for the popular front. After Britain and France had declared war on Germany, the Comintern accounts of 'the second imperialist war' to some degree revitalized a vision of world revolution (Rentola, forthcoming). After the beginning of 'the Great Patriotic War' and the alliance with the Western great powers, world revolution was again pushed aside, and the Comintern was wound up in 1943.

## Conclusion

The historical mission of the working class, as Marx and Engels defined it in the mid-nineteenth century, was neither national nor international. By putting an end to the era of class-based societies and emancipating humanity, the working class would complete the cosmopolitan transformation the bourgeoisie had started and advanced. Since the 1860s, 'international' was established as an attribute to the activities that made the working class capable of fulfilling its mission, and 'internationalism' referred to the right way of connecting the national form and the universal or cosmopolitan content of working-class struggle.

The adoption of 'international' and 'internationalism' in socialist vocabulary reflected a breakthrough for the notion of a world order based on nations and relationships between them. Socialists continuing or revising the legacy of Marx and Engels recognized that the national and the international were two necessary and mutually compatible aspects of working-class action, but nationalism was contrasted with internationalism. Opposing nationalism was no socialist privilege: nationalism was, and is, seldom a concept of self-identification. In socialist rhetoric it emerged as a specific counter-concept to internationalism. Prefixing 'national' with 'inter-' and then suffixing it to become 'internationalism' seems to have preceded the practice of adding '-ism' to 'national'. Thus, nationalism was a counter-concept to internationalism rather than the other way around.

At the beginning of the twentieth century, the concept of internationalism was at the centre of controversies within the socialist movement. Divergent opinions were adopted by distinguishing between nationalism and patriotism, by combining patriotism and internationalism, and by contrasting internationalism with imperialism and militarism. Following the collapse of the Second International in 1914, then wartime and postwar experiences, these controversies deepened into the final split of the Marxian heritage.

One fissure between future visions after the First World War opened up between international social policy and proletarian world revolution. Rival socialist internationalisms were shaped in relation to this confrontation.

On one pole of this opposition, the International Labour Organization, with its tripartite corporatist organization, became a forum for the trade union internationalism dominated by reformist socialism, with a wide range of ideological and national variations. During the Great Depression, the ILO intermediated and advocated ideas of economic planning, yet it had to recognize the dominance of economic nationalism in its practical applications. The social democratic internationals (the International Federation of Trade Unions and the Labour and Socialist International) were badly weakened by the expansion of fascism in Europe, and they achieved little support for their demands for a world economic council and European economic integration.

On the other pole, the vision of proletarian world revolution developed into an international system of Bolshevized national parties that defended Stalinist socialism in one country against all those defined as its external and internal enemies. In this context, 'proletarian internationalism' gained an established central position in the vocabulary of 'Marxism-Leninism'. The conceptual ingredients of Marxism-Leninism established in the 1930s under Stalin's leadership were revitalized after the Second World War and sustained after the Stalin era. The years during and immediately after the war seem to have clarified some conceptual distinctions. While the wartime rhetoric raised 'patriotism' into the top category of positive concepts, after the war the anti-Western and antisemitic cultural campaign confirmed 'cosmopolitanism' as a concept referring to enemies. Until the collapse of the Soviet Union, as established in its authoritative texts, the conceptual system of Marxism-Leninism deployed four concepts. These were used in contrasting or complementary pairs: 'In contrast to the nationalist and cosmopolitan, the internationalist is a patriot. Internationalism and patriotism are as inseparable as the nationalism and cosmopolitanism which oppose it'.[42] Adding 'proletarian' in front of 'internationalism' told a communist that internationalism, including confidence in the leading role of the Soviet Union, was her or his binding duty. The *Manifesto of the Communist Party* was authorized as the foundation of proletarian internationalism, yet a close reading of this text was not the way of creating the Marxist-Leninist vocabulary.

**Pauli Kettunen** is Professor Emeritus of Political History at the University of Helsinki. His research topics include social movements, welfare state and labour relations, nationalism and globalization and the conceptual history of politics. He has led several large research projects, including a Nordic centre of excellence in welfare state research. ORCID 0000-0002-0323-7914.

## Notes

1. In the first part of the chapter, I refer to collections of digitized socialist texts, especially Marxists Internet Archive (https://www.marxists.org/). In the second part, I make use of the archive of the IFTU at the International Institute for Social History in Amsterdam; the online collection of the archives of Labour and Socialist International at the same institute (https://search.iisg.amsterdam/Record/ARCH01368); ILO documents, including reports of the director and records of conferences and the governing body, available in the Labordoc ILO Digital Repository (https://labordoc.ilo.org/discovery/search?vid=41ILO_INST:41ILO_V2); and documents of Communist International in the three-volume compendium, selected and edited by Jane Degras (1956, 1959, 1965), which are accessible in the digitized version from the Marxists Internet Archive (https://www.marxists.org/).

2. *Proletarier* from the original sentence 'Proletarier aller Länder, vereinigt euch!' had a gendered translation 'Working Men' in the English edition of 1888 that was authorized by Engels. The phrase has entered the popular imagination in English as 'Workers of the World, unite!' The following quotations are from the 1888 edition, available at https://www.marxists.org/archive/marx/works/1848/communist-manifesto/.htm.

3. Engels to Friedrich Adolph Sorge, 12 September 1874, available at https://www.marxists.org/archive/marx/works/1874/letters/74_09_12.htm. See also speeches by Marx and Engels on Poland, available at https://www.marxists.org/archive/marx/works/1875/03/24.htm.

4. The International Workingmen's Association 1864. General Rules, October 1864, available at https://www.marxists.org/history/international/iwma/documents/1864/rules.htm.

5. Inaugural Address of the International Working Men's Association 1964, available at https://www.marxists.org/archive/marx/works/1864/10/27.htm.

6. Marx and Engels 1872.

7. Engels to Friedrich Adolph Sorge, 12 September 1874 (see endnote 3).

8. The meaning of the word *Nationalitäts-Prinzip* was close to how later researchers have used 'nationalism': 'a theory according to which people with the same origin and language should be united also in political terms' (Liebknecht 1907).

9. Marx 1875.

10. Minutes of the General Council of the First International, Council Meeting, 14 May 1872, available at https://www.marxists.org/archive/marx/iwma/documents/1872/minutes-may-14.htm.

11. Engels: Nationalism, Internationalism and the Polish Question, letter to Karl Kautsky, 7 February 1882; available at https://www.marxists.org/archive/marx/works/1882/letters/82_02_07.htm.

12. Bauer 1907: §31.

13. See e.g. the debate on militarism and international conflicts in Internationaler Sozialisten-Kongress zu Stuttgart, 18. bis 24. August 1907, available at https://archive.org/details/internationale00inte/mode/2up.
14. Bernstein 1907.
15. Jaurès 1910, quoted on p. 559.
16. Luxemburg 1913 and Luxemburg 1916. The quotation is from the latter book, ch. 1.
17. Lenin 1917.
18. A forecast proposed by Rudolf Hilferding in Hilferding 1910.
19. For example, the Finnish Kautskyan social democrat Otto Wille Kuusinen, who later became a prominent actor in the Comintern and the Soviet Communist Party, argued in this way in the Finnish parliament in 1909.
20. Preamble of the Constitution of the International Labour Organization, available at http://www.ilo. org/public/english/about/iloconst.htm.
21. This argument for the necessity of socialism featured strongly in the founding congress of the IFTU in 1919, which took place in Amsterdam (20 July to 2 August). Socialisation, IFTU 7. IISG, Amsterdam.
22. Minutes of the Second Session of the Governing Body of the International Labour Office held in Paris, 26–28 January 1920: 20–22. Not surprisingly, the Soviet government did not cooperate, and the ILO had to make use of the study data available in existing publications. Report of the Director, International Labour Conference, Third Session, Geneva, 1921: 217–19.
23. Report of the Director, International Labour Conference, Tenth Session, Geneva, 1927: 210; on colonial politics in the ILO, see Maul 2007.
24. Extracts from the theses of the tenth plenum of the Executive Committee of the Communist International [ECCI] on the economic struggle and the tasks of Communist Parties, July 1929, The Communist International 1919–1943 documents, volume III, 1929–1943: 55.
25. Extracts from a circular letter on factory cells of the organization department of the ECCI endorsed by the political secretariat, December 1930, The Communist International 1919–1943 documents, volume III, 1929–1943: 148.
26. The Soviet Union sent a delegation to the international labour conferences in 1935–1937. In December 1939, it was expelled from the League of Nations and the ILO because of its aggression against Finland. It rejoined the ILO only after Stalin's death, in 1954.
27. Dokumente betr. die Beziehungen zur Komintern: Telegramme der Komintern, ein Bericht von F. Adler über den 7. Kongreß und Zuschriften und Anträge zu dieser Frage. 5 Bl. Labour and Socialist International Archives, IISG, available at https://search.iisg.amsterdam/Record/ARCH01368/ArchiveContentList#1441.
28. Report of the Director, International Labour Conference, Seventh Session, Geneva, 1925: 365–66.
29. Report of the Director, International Labour Conference, Fifteenth Session, Geneva, 1931: 2.

30. See ILO website for details.
31. Antrag Bauer 22 February 1931. Dossier betr. die Sitzung in Zürich, 21.–22. Februar 1931. 382. Anträge von O. Bauer betr. die Fünftagewoche und Indien. 9 Bl. Labour and Socialist International Archives, IISG, Amsterdam, available at https://search.iisg.amsterdam/Record/ARCH01368/ArchiveContentList#2320.
32. General Council, Copenhagen, 21–23 May 1935, Item 7 of the Agenda, the 1936 International Labour Conference, IFTU 98, IISG, Amsterdam.
33. Report of the Director, International Labour Conference, Sixteenth Session, Geneva, 1932: 13; see Chapter 6 on reactions.
34. Report of the Director, International Labour Conference, Eighteenth Session, Geneva, 1934: 79.
35. Fifth Ordinary International Trade Union Congress, Stockholm, 1930, IFTU 31; VI. Ordentlichen Internationalen Gewerkschaftskongress, Brüssel, 1933, IFTU 42, 43, IISG, Amsterdam.
36. Report of the Secretariat on the Activities of the International Federation of Trade Unions during the period 1 January 1936–30 April 1937; To the IFTU General Council meeting, 1937, IFTU 102, IISG, Amsterdam.
37. Lenin 1918, ch. 'What Is Internationalism?'.
38. Lenin 1920.
39. Trotsky 1928.
40. Stalin 1931.
41. Quotations from the chapter on 'The Ideological Struggle against Fascism' in Dimitrov 1935.
42. Konstantinov et al. 1982: 290.

# References

## *Primary Sources*
### Archives
International Institute for Social History (IISG), Amsterdam.
  International Federation of Trade Unions Archives
  Labour and Socialist International Archives, online collection, https://search.iisg.amsterdam/Record/ARCH01368.
Labordoc – ILO Digital Repository, available at https://labordoc.ilo.org/discovery/search?vid=41ILO_INST:41ILO_V2.
Marxist Internet Archive, https://www.marxists.org/.

### Books and Other Writings
Bauer. O. 1907. *Die Nationalitätenfrage und die Sozialdemokratie,* available at https://www.marxists.org/deutsch/archiv/bauer/1907/nationalitaet/.
Bernstein, E. 1907. 'Patriotismus, Militarismus und Sozialdemokratie', *Sozialistische Monatshefte* 13(6): 434–440, the English edition published in the *Social Democrat*, available at https://www.marxists.org/reference/archive/bernstein/works/1907/07/patriotism.htm.
*The Communist International 1919–1943: Documents.* Selected and edited by Jane Degras. Volumes I–III. 1956, 1959, 1965. New York: Oxford University Press.

Dimitrov, G. 1935. *The Fascist Offensive and the Tasks of the Communist International in the Struggle of the Working Class against Fascism. Main Report delivered at the Seventh World Congress of the Communist International*, the English edition included in Dimitrov's *Selected works*, Vol 2 (1972), available at https://www.marxists.org/reference/archive/dimitrov/works/1935/08_02.htm.

Hilferding. R. 1910. *Das Finanzkapital. Eine Studie über die jüngste Entwicklung des Kapitalismus*, available at https://www.marxists.org/deutsch/archiv/hilferding/1910/finkap/index.html.

Jaurès. J. 1910. *L'armée nouvelle*, available at https://gallica.bnf.fr/ark:/12148/bpt6k932623s/f1.item.r=559.

Konstantinov, F.V. et al. 1982. *Fundamentals of Marxist-Leninist Philosophy*. English translation from a revised Russian edition. Moscow: Progress.

Lenin, V.I. 1917. *Imperialism, the Highest Stage of Capitalism*, the English edition included in Lenin's *Selected works*, Vol. 1 (1963) available at https://www.marxists.org/archive/lenin/works/1916/imp-hsc/.

———. 1918. *The Proletarian Revolution and the Renegade Kautsky*, the English edition included in Lenin's *Collected Works*, Vol. 28 (1974) available at https://www.marxists.org/archive/lenin/works/1918/prrk/index.htm.

———. 1920. *Draft Theses on National and Colonial Questions For The Second Congress Of The Communist International*, the English edition included in Lenin's *Collected Works*, Vol. 31 (1965) available at https://www.marxists.org/archive/lenin/works/1920/jun/05.htm

Liebknecht, W. 1907. *Volks-Fremdwörterbuch*, 9th edn. Stuttgart: Dietz.

Luxemburg, R. 1913. *Die Akkumulation des Kapitals. Ein Beitrag zur ökonomischen Erklärung des Imperialismus*, available at https://www.marxists.org/deutsch/archiv/luxemburg/1913/akkkap/index.htm.

———. 1916. *Die Krise der Sozialdemokratie [Die "Junius"-Broschüre]*, available at https://www.marxists.org/deutsch/archiv/luxemburg/1916/junius/.

Marx, K. 1875. *Kritik des Gothaer Programms*. Marx-Engels Werke, Band 19, available at http://www.mlwerke.de/me/me19/me19_013.htm.

Marx, K. and F. Engels. 1848. *Manifest der Kommunistischen Partei*, available at https://www.marxists.org/deutsch/archiv/marx-engels/1848/manifest/index.htm; the English edition of 1888 (*Manifesto of the Communist Party*) available at https://www.marxists.org/archive/marx/works/1848/communist-manifesto

———. 1872. *Die angeblichen Spaltungen in der Internationale. Vertrauliches Zirkular des Generalrats der Internationalen Arbeiterassoziation*. Geschrieben Mitte Januar bis Anfang März 1872. Marx-Engels Werke, Band 18, available at http://www.mlwerke.de/me/me18/me18_007.htm.

Stalin, J. V. 1931. *Some Questions Concerning the History of Bolshevism. Letter to the Editorial Board of the Magazine "Proletarskaya Revolutsia"*, the English edition included in Stalin's *Works*, Vol. 13 (1954) available at https://www.marxists.org/reference/archive/stalin/works/1931/x01/x01.htm.

Trotsky, L. 1928. *The Third International After Lenin. The Draft Program of the Communist International: A Criticism of Fundamentals*, published in English in 1929, available at https://www.marxists.org/archive/trotsky/1928/3rd/ index.htm

## Secondary Sources

Armitage, D. 2012. *Foundations of Modern International Thought*. Cambridge: Cambridge University Press.

Bellamy Foster, J. 2000. 'Marx and Internationalism', *Monthly Review* 52(3): 11–22.

Bottomore, T. (ed.). 1983. *A Dictionary of Marxist Thought*. Oxford: Blackwell.

Calhoun, D.F. 1976. *The United Front: The TUC and the Russians, 1923–1928*. Cambridge: Cambridge University Press.

Clavin, P. 2013a. *Securing the World Economy: The Reinvention of the League of Nations, 1920–1946*. Oxford: Oxford University Press.

————. 2013b. 'What's in a Living Standard? Bringing Society and Economy Together in the ILO and the League of Nations Depression Delegation, 1938–1945', in S. Kott and J. Droux (eds), *Globalizing Social Rights: The International Labour Organization and Beyond*. Basingstoke: Palgrave Macmillan, pp. 233–48.

Cross, G. 1989. *A Quest for Time: The Reduction of Work in Britain and France, 1840–1940*. Berkeley: University of California Press.

Dogliani, P. 2017. 'The Fate of Socialist Internationalism', in G. Sluga and P. Clavin (eds), *Internationalisms: A Twentieth-Century History*. Cambridge: Cambridge University Press, pp. 38–60.

Eley, G. 2002. *Forging Democracy: The History of the Left in Europe, 1850–2000*. Oxford: Oxford University Press.

Van Goethem, G. 2006. *The Amsterdam International: The World of the International Federation of Trade Unions (IFTU), 1913–1945*. Aldershot: Ashgate.

Gronow, J. 2015. *On the Formation of Marxism: Karl Kautsky's Theory of Capitalism, the Marxism of the Second International and Karl Marx's Critique of Political Economy*. Leiden: Brill.

Haas, E.B. 1964. *Beyond the Nation-State: Functionalism and International Organization*. Stanford: Stanford University Press.

Haupt, G. 1964. *La deuxième internationale 1889–1914: Étude critique des sources, essai bibliographique*. Paris: Mouton.

Hyrkkänen, M. 1986. *Sozialistische Kolonialpolitik: Eduard Bernsteins Stellung zur Kolonialpolitik und zum Imperialismus 1882–1914*. Helsinki: Finnish Historical Society.

Imlay, T. 2017. 'Socialist Internationalism after 1914', in G. Sluga and P. Clavin (eds), *Internationalisms: A Twentieth-Century History*. Cambridge: Cambridge University, pp. 213–41.

Jordheim, H. 2018. 'Keeping the "Ism" in "Cosmopolitanism" – Wieland and the Origins of Cosmopolitan Discourse', *Journal of Political Ideologies* 23(3): 299–319.

Kettunen, P. 1994. *Suojelu, suoritus, subjekti: Työsuojelu teollistuvan Suomen yhteis- kunnallisissa ajattelu- ja toimintatavoissa*. Helsinki: Suomen Historiallinen Seura.

————. 2006. 'Power of International Comparison – A Perspective on the Making and Challenging of the Nordic Welfare State', in N.F. Christiansen et al. (eds),

*The Nordic Model of Welfare – a Historical Reappraisal.* Copenhagen: Museum Tusculanum Press, pp. 31–65.

———. 2013. 'The ILO as a Forum for Developing and Demonstrating a Nordic Model', in S. Kott and J. Droux (eds), *Globalizing Social Rights: The International Labour Organization and Beyond.* Basingstoke: Palgrave Macmillan, pp. 210–30.

———. 2018. 'The Concept of Nationalism in Discussions on a European Society', *Journal of Political Ideologies* 23(3): 342–69.

Konrad, H. 1976. *Nationalismus und Internationalismus: Die österreichische Arbeiterbewegung vor dem Ersten Weltkrieg,* Ludwig Boltzmann Institut für Geschichte der Arbeiterbewegung, Materialien zur Arbeiterbewegung 4. Vienna: Europaverlag.

Kurunmäki, J. and J. Strang (eds). 2010. *Rhetorics of Nordic Democracy.* Helsinki: Finnish Literature Society.

Lorenz, E. 1982. 'Norwegens Gewerkschaften zwischen Amsterdam und Moskau: Versuche eines Brückenbaus', in *Internationale Tagung der Historiker der Arbeiterbewegung. 16. Linzer Konferenz 1980.* Vienna: Europaverlag, pp. 182–200.

Lorenz, E.C. 2001. *Defining Global Justice: The History of U.S. International Labor Standards Policy.* Notre Dame: University of Notre Dame Press.

Maier, C.S. 1975. *Recasting Bourgeois Europe: Stabilization in France, Germany, and Italy in the Decade after World War I.* Princeton: Princeton University Press.

Maul, D. 2007. *Menschenrechte, Sozialpolitik und Dekolonisation: Die Internationale Arbeitsorganisation (IAO) 1940–1970.* Essen: Klartext.

McDermott, K. 1998. 'Bolshevisation from above or below? The Comintern and European Communism in the 1920s', in T. Saarela and K. Rentola (eds), *Communism: National & International.* Helsinki: SHS, pp. 105–17.

Prothero, I. 2018. 'The IWMA and Industrial Conflict in England and France', in F. Bensimon, Q. Deluermoz and J. Moisand (eds), *'Arise Ye Wretched of the Earth': The First International in a Global Perspective.* Leiden: Brill, pp. 54–65.

Rentola, K. (forthcoming). 'The Strange Resurrection of the World Revolution: A New Reading'.

Sluga, G. 2013. *Internationalism in the Age of Nationalism.* Philadelphia: University of Pennsylvania Press.

Stenius, H. 1978. *Utländska arbetare i inhemska arbetstvister före första världskrigets utbrott.* Licentiate thesis in history. University of Helsinki.

Tikriti, A.-K. 1982. *Tripartism and the International Labour Organization: A Study of the Legal Concept – Its Origins, Function and Evolution in the Law of Nations.* Stockholm: Almqvist & Wiksell.

Tossdorff, R. and B. Fowkes. 2016. *The Red International of Labour Unions (RILU) 1920–1937.* Leiden: Brill.

Wobbe, T. and L. Renard. 2017. 'The Category of "Family Workers" in International Labour Organization Statistics (1930s–1980s): A Contribution to the Study of Globalized Gendered Boundaries between Household and Market', *Journal of Global History*, 12(3): 340–60.

Chapter 5

# Progress, Nation and Great Women in Constructing the Idea of Feminist Internationalism

*Tiina Kinnunen*

⬦

> We have been baptised in that spirit of the 20th century which the world calls Internationalism; it is a sentiment like love, or religion, or patriotism, which is to be experienced rather than defined in words. And yet, those of us who have come under its exalting influence recognize in it a motive more impelling than any we have experienced before.
>
> —C.C. Catt, 'Address by Mrs. Chapman Catt', 1909

This is how Carrie Chapman Catt, the President of the International Woman Suffrage Alliance (IWSA), tried to encapsulate the idea of feminist internationalism in her address to its conference in London in 1909. Internationalism was linked with emotions and experiences. At the heart of this experience was the feeling of belonging to a community of feminists that crossed borders and created bonds of organizational and personal sisterhood between feminist activists from different countries. A century later, Swedish historian Lovisa af Petersens introduced the idea of 'emotional energy' that characterized international conferences around which women's internationalism became visible, for themselves and for larger audiences (af Petersens 2006: 33).

Emotional expressions of belonging expressed by international activists are found in both public and private sources. In her memoirs, published in

1924, Dutch women's rights activist Aletta Jacobs reminiscences about the beginning of her international career:

> In July 1899, the great International Conference of Women … was to take place in London. … For months I had been looking forward to meeting many of the women from distant lands with whom I had been corresponding for years. Each time I received a letter asking, 'Will I be seeing you in London?' my heart skipped a beat and I was delighted to reply that yes, indeed, I would be attending. (Jacobs 1924: 125)

Jacobs was one of the most actively engaged feminist internationalists in the period from the late nineteenth century until the post-First World War years. Alexandra Gripenberg from the Grand Duchy of Finland was another renowned activist. She was in London in 1899 too and wrote from London to her associates in Finland that delegates at the International Conference of Women (ICW) meeting 'declared love to each other' (Gripenberg to Ennola, 23 June 1899).

Not only did the encounters with like-minded activists in international surroundings arouse emotions, they were also highly instrumental in creating channels for producing and circulating feminist knowledge. At the conference dinner in London, Charlotte Perkins Stetson asked Jacob about her interest in translating a work of hers (Jacobs 1924: 126). The work was *Women and Economics*, one of the so-called travelling books, read in the original and in translations around the globe. Translations exemplify how feminist internationalism was committed not exclusively to feeling, but also to doing. In addition to translating, the 'doing' included corresponding across borders, reading and writing in journals and books about other nations and international events, participating in conferences and travelling to promote feminist goals. Reflecting this activism, we have an increasing body of knowledge about what activists did for international feminism in organizations and as individual activists. As a result, Francisca de Haan, Margaret Allen, June Purvis and Krassimira Daskalova have emphasized that transnational connections were inherent to the modern women's movement since its beginnings around 1800 (de Haan et al. 2013: 2; also Midgley et al. 2016; on the twentieth century, see e.g. Sluga 2017).

Feeling and doing were crucial aspects of cementing an international feminist community. Little attention, however, has been paid to how internationalism was perceived and what notions were attributed to it. The introductory quotation by Catt suggests that her contemporaries also gave little thought to the conceptual meaning of internationalism. In this chapter, I contribute to the body of research into feminist internationalism during the first wave of feminism since the 1890s by examining attributes and concepts that were associated with the terms 'international' and 'internationalism'. The aim is to answer this question: how were the ideas of the international and internationalism conceptualized and verbalized?

## Analysing Feminist Conceptualizations of the International

This period covered here spans from the late 1890s to the 1910s, when international encounters and organizing reached a peak prior to the First World War. The major international organizations were established in 1888 (the ICW) and 1904 (the IWSA). The source material includes a selection of documents associated with international activism: firstly, coverage in four feminist journals (the Finnish *Koti ja Yhteiskunta*, the Swedish *Dagny* and the Austrian *Dokumente der Frauen* and *Neues Frauenleben*) and secondly, printed reports of conferences of and connected to the ICW and the IWSA. These reports include general addresses and national accounts of developments within various fields of feminist work. Some memoirs and unpublished letters of prominent activists were used, the latter however as a descriptive material, without going into the methodology of autobiographical studies. In addition to the four journals that were examined systematically, a small sample of published writings by some leading figures were included to enlarge the spectrum of feminist views. Among these individual writers of letters, memoirs and other texts were the British-Australian radical suffrage activist Dora Montefiore, the German moderate leader Helene Lange, the Finnish suffrage activist Annie Furuhjelm and the above-mentioned Aletta Jacobs and Alexandra Gripenberg.

By paying attention to Northern and Central European feminist journalism and to a handful of individual feminists outside Britain and the United States, in this chapter I give voice to activists often overshadowed by their Anglo-American colleagues in contemporary contexts and later research. Jacobs and Furuhjelm were actively engaged in the IWSA, whereas Gripenberg and Lange contributed to the ICW. International activism was a truly broad phenomenon, but as Leila J. Rupp has demonstrated, the ideal of sisterhood across borders had its limits. Anglo-American feminism often presented itself as the most advanced and thus the model for other nations (Rupp 2010).

In topical research, the concept of transnationalism often replaces internationalism. From the 1890s to the 1910s the contacts, connections and cross-border interaction between individuals and within organizations that the term 'transnational' conveys today were included in the contemporary term 'international'. At the same time, the term remained contested as it had strong connotations with socialism (see Chapter 4). Among socialist women, cross-border contacts and connections were intense. Accordingly, the prominent Russian revolutionary Alexandra Kollontay challenged non-socialist internationalism and declared, exuding self-assurance: 'A new danger is threatening the domination of the bourgeoisie – women workers are resolutely adopting the path of international class organisation' (Kollontay 1918). Non-socialist women did not content themselves with a socialist framing of internationalism. Alexandra Gripenberg's comment in her letter to the President of the ICW, Lady Aberdeen, exemplifies that they made a claim of their own: 'And the socialists dominate everywhere, and they hate all other international ideas with the exception of socialism' (Gripenberg to Aberdeen, 26 January 1908). Without contesting the significance of socialist internationalism within the history of feminism, I focus here on non-socialist feminism.

The research proceeded as follows. Journals were selected based on two principles: they are accessible online and range from moderate to more radical positions. In so doing, the journals reveal the variety of feminist agendas and journalism in Europe. The Finnish *Koti ja Yhteiskunta* (Home and Society) represented a moderate line. Alexandra Gripenberg edited it from 1889 until its closure in 1913. Apart from being an activist with the ICW, Gripenberg was a leading figure of the Finnish Women's Association (Suomen Naisyhdistys, established in 1884), which was part of the Finnish-nationalist Fennoman movement. The Swedish *Dagny* was a mouthpiece of the Fredrika Bremer Association (Fredrika-Bremer-Förbundet, established in 1884); its programme was quite close to that of its Finnish sister organization (apart from the Fennoman aspect). *Dagny*, which was published from 1886 until 1913, had several editors-in-chief over the years. In Finland, the more radical women had their own journals but in Sweden, *Dagny* had the ambition of representing the non-socialist field as a whole (Samuelsson 2014: 19–67). The Austrian *Dokumente der Frauen* (Documents of the Women) and *Neues Frauenleben* (New Woman's Life) represented a radical agenda, formulated as liberal (*freiheitlich*), with connections to the radical wing of the women's movement in Germany. Auguste Fickert, leader of the General Austrian Women's Association (Allgemeiner Österreichischer Frauenverein, established in 1893), co-edited *Dokumente der Frauen* in 1899–1902; from 1902 until her death in 1910, she edited *Neues Frauenleben* (Hacker 2006: 131–34).

In the digital search, the word 'international' in Finnish (*kansainvälinen*) and Swedish (*internationell*) emerged predominantly in relation to the international organizations (ICW and IWSA) and in particular, related conferences. Based on this finding, key conferences were examined in terms of their media coverage and the printed reports they produced. The following were selected: 1899 London (the ICW conference and the related International Women's Conference), 1904 Berlin (the ICW conference and the related International Women's Conference), 1906 Copenhagen (the IWSA conference), 1909 London (the IWSA conference), and 1911 Stockholm (the IWSA conference). The IWSA was established in 1904 in conjunction with the Berlin conference to strengthen women's struggle for the vote in their respective countries.

The next step was to collect the media coverage of the conferences in the respective four journals and related descriptions in other materials. The data was read closely, with a focus on attributes that were associated with 'international' and 'internationalism'. In what follows we focus on 'progress', 'nation' and 'greatness / Great Women', since these terms proved substantial for the idea of 'international' in these contexts. 'Progress' conveyed the goal of emancipation, democracy and humanity that would enable women's participation in public work on an equal footing with men and equality within the private sphere of family. 'Progress' included the process of achieving this goal, such as raising feminist consciousness. The emphasis on 'nation' shows the significance of the national as the basis for the international; the international was typically seen as a compilation of national entities. 'Great Women' emphasized women's agency, and how some women were experienced as capable of leading others.

## Progress

> When the history of the Women's Movement is written in the future, I believe it will reflect that the year 1904 was an important one in the annals of their cause. There is little doubt that the recent Berlin Congress brought together forces and influences whose centrifugal power it is difficult to estimate; has encouraged the weak, has strengthened the brave; and has given to women working all over the world in the cause of their sister women a feeling of solidarity and of sisterhood such as they never possessed before! (Montefiore, 1904b: 475)

This quotation addresses the consciousness of progress that characterized the feminist imaginary of the first wave. Progress referred to the definite goal of women's equal citizenship but also the single achievements within education, in professional and political life, and in terms of legal rights. Feminist activists always related progress in women's rights to both national and international development more generally. The women's cause concerned the whole civilization, as for instance *Dokumente der Frauen* put it, inspired by the spirit in London in 1899 (*Dokumente der Frauen* 9 / 1899: 237). Reflecting this widely shared understanding, the Finn Annie Furuhjelm wrote in her memoirs how women's rights were human rights and their establishment, in one country after another, served all of humanity (Furuhjelm 1939: 78–79). The exchange of ideas, models for campaigns in single countries and various other forms of interaction was a tool to promote progress country by country, and at the same time to strengthen consciousness of progress everywhere and envision a shared victory. The national reports and speeches given at conferences formed a discourse characterized by the very idea of the triumphal march of women towards freedom in every nation.

As President of the IWSA Carrie Chapman Catt gave the following expression to the way in which achievement in one country (in this case the introduction of voting rights in Australia and Norway) inspired and empowered women in other nations and provided them with arguments to push their own governments to follow suit: 'They stand like mile-posts pointing the way to every other nation, and in those mile-posts there is something of compulsion, for they tell every other nation that it will be forced by the destiny of things to march along that self-same path' (Catt 1909: 66).

Within the international community, pioneering countries were celebrated as examples of 'progress' and thus models for others (e.g. *Neues Frauenleben* 7/1911: 182). At the same time, feminist media did not shy away from publishing critical comments on the status of women in particular countries. For instance, in 1899, in a reflection on the London conference, *Dokumente der Frauen* wrote how 'shameful' the status of women was on the labour market in countries under the influence of the Napoleonic Code, whereas England and Scandinavia were beacons of hope and demonstrated a European capacity to go forward (*Dokumente der Frauen* 9/1899: 238). This type of commentary undoubtedly ranked nations in a perceived hierarchy and strengthened prevailing prejudices about national characteristics (Kinnunen 2016). I suggest, however, that hierarchization may have been instrumental in strengthening solidarity between women, because women in particular countries could not be blamed for underdevelopment as they had no influence within the political sphere. Women from countries with 'delayed' emancipation sparked sympathy for their agency in difficult circumstances (e.g. Montefiore, 1904a: 363–64).

## Nation

'Sisterhood' was how the idea of an international feminist community has typically been expressed and circulated (Rupp and Taylor 1999: 363–86). In the media coverage of the conferences, the idea of a community based on solidarity and togetherness across borders (*Dagny* 25/1911: 294) manifested itself in narratives of face-to-face encounters. At conferences, women came together from long distances, exchanged experiences, shared knowledge, socialized with each other at official events and participated in a rather opulent social programme. For critical voices, the descriptions of this socializing manifested the upper- and middle-class characteristics of feminism (e.g. *Neues Frauenleben* 6/1904: 6). An alternative reading of these descriptions reveals the significance of meeting each other in person. The expression 'hand in hand' (e.g. *Koti ja Yhteiskunta*, 15 September 1899: 67) in the media coverage illustrates this aspect. As a metaphor, this expression refers to feminism as a shared, international campaign to promote gender equality and women's rights as human rights (e.g. Stritt 1899: 641).

The media coverage depicted the encounters as meetings of individuals, but national thinking and categorizations played into the narration (e.g. Stritt 1899: 647). The international activists of the first wave of feminism did not typically identify with cosmopolitanism. In this respect, the internationalisms of the feminist and labour movements showed similarities (see Chapter 4): internationalism was conceptualized as 'nations coming together' rather than polemicizing feelings of national belonging, rejecting nationalist identity, or envisioning nationless or stateless cosmopolitanism (e.g. Lange 1900: 1–4). A compilation of national symbols, flags and folklore at international conferences manifested the significance of the internationalists' national identifications (e.g. Bosch 2009; Rendall 2014: 153). The organizations themselves, with their national affiliations, were based on the very logic of 'multiplication of the national', as Susan Zimmermann defines it (Zimmermann 2010: 154).

The idea of 'nations coming together' was occasionally exemplified by describing women as embodiments of their respective countries and the related national characteristics. For instance, at a garden party, 'Sweden and Norway' were walking 'hand in hand' (*Koti ja Yhteiskunta*, 15 September 1899: 67). This way of investing women with national attributes, instead of seeing them as individuals, is undoubtedly problematic. Nevertheless, this depiction can be read as radical: it presented women as public persons (equal to men), representing their nations, instead of regarding them as persons belonging to the private sphere due to their gender.

For feminists in this period, at least those engaged in international bonding, the national aspect was not synonymous with exclusive, aggressive nationalism. Yet, internationalism did not erase feelings of national pride and the custom of comparing nations: organized conferences tended to produce a mentality of comparison and competition. As an example, Aletta Jacobs and her Dutch compatriots organized the IWSA conference in Amsterdam in 1908. In her memoirs, her statement about its alleged success exemplifies this very mentality: '[I]n my opinion the Amsterdam conference was never surpassed by any other meeting of the IWSA and was perhaps only equalled by the 1911 Stockholm conference' (Jacobs 1924: 145).

Some leading figures reflected critically on internationalism as opposed to the nation state. The German Helene Lange wrote in her memoirs about how internationalism provided her with an opportunity to exchange experiences across borders and to establish friendships. Despite this appreciation, she underlined that every serious effort towards feminist aims had a national basis. She addressed some 'shortcomings' of other nationalities, too (Lange 1900: 4; Lange 1928: 233–37).

This national basis became audible through the variety of languages spoken at conferences. The policy of the international organizations to include three working languages (English, French and German) to some extent acknowledged the diversity within the field. At the ICW in Berlin in 1904, Marie Stritt concluded her opening words with a saying in Latin, 'the international language': 'Fortiter in re, suaviter in modo' ('Forcibly in action, gently in manner'; Stritt 1904: 6). The formulation is interestingly ambiguous. On the one hand, it can be interpreted as a statement of the unity of the 'civilized' countries, in terms of a shared history since Antiquity. On the other, it might have been a gentle expression of criticism towards the Anglo-American dominance of the international organizations.

The Anglo-American dominance within the ICW and IWSA impacted conceptualizations of the nation in terms of self-governing nations or federal states. Multinational empires with women negotiating their various identifications could be difficult for British, US American and other Western leaders to handle (e.g. Zimmermann 2010: 153–69; Zimmermann 2006). Recalling her work as an international campaigner for women's suffrage, Aletta Jacobs pointed to difficulties with these multinational and multilingual circumstances. In Prague, she tried to balance conflicting Austro-German and Czech claims: 'It was not easy task to get across the message that we intended to remain completely neutral, that we refused to take sides' (Jacobs 1924: 609).

Despite the policy of non-intervention in domestic affairs of the respective nations and empires, on some points the international community openly criticized the suppression of small (European) nations by major imperial powers. At conferences, this criticism was translated into expressions of sympathy towards representatives of these nations. This was the case with Finland during the Russification period. In her memoirs, Annie Furuhjelm recalls how Mrs Fawcett's public expression of sympathy at the 1906 Copenhagen IWSA conference touched her deeply and she could not help kissing her hand (Furuhjelm 1939: 126). Women's involvement in the Finnish national struggle constituted an important step towards emancipation. They were given active and passive voting rights in the 1906 reform. In her speech in Copenhagen, Annie Furuhjelm proudly underscored this national aspect of the victory (e.g. *Dagny* 15/1906: 323; see also Ihalainen and Kinnunen 2022).

## Great Women

> There were many grounds for gratitude and admiration. When one hears speakers like Mrs Fawcett, Mrs Catt and Miss Shaw, one's heart throbs with excitement, hope and admiration. (*Koti ja Yhteiskunta*, 15 July 1904: 83)

The idea of greatness was largely present in the nineteenth-century mentality and cultural production of the Western world, historical writing included: narratives of Great Men and masculine heroes were produced and circulated in great numbers. Reflecting the zeitgeist, the idea of greatness and genius also permeated collective feminist cultures. The related construction of feminist 'herstory' was truly political as it selected useful lives and shed light on those aspects that best served various feminist – political and related didactic – purposes (Hüchtker 2019). Reflecting the entanglements of the national with the international within feminist movements, narratives of female genius and heroic women in the past circulated across borders and were consumed in various national contexts (Kinnunen 2019: 319).

Greatness was not only attributed to women of the past. On the contrary, contemporary women's lives and deeds became the subject of narration within the framework of greatness and exemplarity. Female pioneers and their achievements in different professions were news in feminist media. In the media coverage of international conferences, featuring Great Women was a recurrent topic and image. For instance, when describing the opening ceremony of the IWSA conference in Stockholm in 1911, *Neues Frauenleben* spared no superlative in describing the greatness of author Selma Lagerlöf, who had won the Nobel Prize in literature in 1909. Particularly praiseworthy was the fact that despite her genius, she supported her sisters' yearning for freedom (*Neues Frauenleben* 7/1911: 182).

For feminists across borders, Selma Lagerlöf embodied women's capacity in the artistic and intellectual realm. However, feminist internationalism was narrated primarily with a focus on female activists with the capacity – and resources – to move across borders, communicate with people from different national backgrounds and act as an inspiration beyond the bounds of their

own nation (Rupp 2010; Bosch 1999). The followers invested this group
of Great Women with a belief that they had a special talent and power of
leadership that spanned across borders. They personalized female internationalism at its best.

At the conferences, homage was paid to Great Women in several ways.
In Berlin in 1904, the confections at the tables of the conference dinner
were wrapped in paper with photographs of 'the outstanding persons of
the women's cause' (*Koti ja Yhteiskunta*, 15 July 1904: 80). In the media
coverage, the greatness of the selected women was shown to derive from
their intellectual capacities combined with their high-minded mental and
moral characteristics. For instance, Anna Pappritz, a German leader of the
transnational movement against prostitution, was embraced for 'having a
razor-sharp brain', combined with high idealism (*Dagny* 12/1904: 280).
Remarks on the appearance of the respective women were also included, and
very often entangled with their alleged elevated moral characteristics and
capacities. Helene Lange, for instance, appeared as a well-balanced person,
characterized by motherliness and humour (*Dagny* 12/1904: 279; see also
e.g. *Neues Frauenleben* 9/1906: 13).

A pleasant voice and an impressive art of rhetoric were often included
as components of greatness (e.g. *Dagny* 13/1899: 272–73; *Dagny* 14/1906:
300; *Neues Frauenleben* 9/1906: 10; Stritt 1899: 45). The skills of public
performance were emphasized because they manifested women as respectable figures, equal to male leaders. A related skill, necessary in creating an
international community, was translating. The German Käthe Schirmacher
earned much appreciation and admiration for her knowledge of foreign
languages and her talent of interpreting swiftly from German to French to
English (*Dagny* 15/1906: 321–22).

The writers of the media reports did not shy away from commenting (in
positive terms) on the activists' appearance. To point out women's greatness
in terms of their intellect, rhetorical skills and other qualities that were not
traditionally seen as feminine challenged the gendered assumptions and
concepts of genius and heroes. I suggest that this challenge was cushioned
to some degree by pointing out women's appearance and looks as feminine.
The Italian Teresa Labriola, for instance, was 'lovely to see', due to her
female grace (*Dagny* 15/1906: 324; also *Dagny* 12/1904: 279). Positive references were made to the appearance of eminent women that contrasted with
traditional images of feminine grace, for example, the 'monumental head' of
the German suffragist Anita Augsburg (*Dagny* 24/1911: 294).

My findings are in line with the conclusions of previous research on
Anglo-American hegemony in international activist circles. In the examined media coverage of the international conferences, several of the Great

Women were from the United States or Britain. While women from other European countries were credited for their greatness and leadership qualities, one American figure was superior in terms of the acclaim bestowed on her person. This was Susan B. Anthony. Around 1900, Anthony held a unique status in the international canon of Great Feminists. In her lifetime, Anthony was described across borders as a Great Woman who sacrificed her whole life to work for women's rights globally (e.g. Gripenberg 1890: 17–21). After she died, her memory was revered at international encounters (e.g. *Neues Frauenleben* 9/1906: 12). One phrase stands out and is recurrent in descriptions of her lifetime and posterity: she was the 'uncrowned queen' (e.g. *Koti ja Yhteiskunta*, 15 July 1904: 78; *Dagny* 12/1904: 280). This tribute tells us about the active agency of feminist media in creating an imagined community that included women across borders.

The shared emotional community around Susan B. Anthony was quite exceptional, as admiration and gratitude emerged irrespective of the individual writer's position on the moderate-to-radical continuum. Not only did the division between moderate and radical groupings affect feminist movements in national contexts; it also affected identifications with the international organizations. For instance, the international ICW activist Alexandra Gripenberg was convinced that only one international feminist organization was needed, namely the ICW. In her own journal *Koti ja Yhteiskunta*, she embraced Isabel Aberdeen, the leader of the ICW, for her intellectual quality, her capacity to see the women's cause as an issue that served all humanity, and 'the nobility of her heart' (*Koti ja Yhteiskunta*, 15 July 1904: 77). Gripenberg regarded the IWSA critically as she thought that it unnecessarily split the feminist front and was too subject to the radical influence of socialist women and sexual radicals (Kinnunen 2016: 660). For the women in the *Neues Frauenleben* circle, the ICW was too moderate or even conservative in its politics. The role of the German Empress in the social programme of the 1904 Berlin conference made the author of the journal's report sharply question the relevance of royal connections for feminism (*Neues Frauenleben* 6/1904: 6).

Despite Alexandra Gripenberg's criticism of the IWSA, she praised Susan B. Anthony, who was actively involved in its establishment. Without contesting Anthony's feminist standpoint, radically focused on suffrage and in conjunction with their identification with the IWSA, the feminists in the *Neues Frauenleben* circle cultivated an attitude of deep admiration towards Anthony (*Neues Frauenleben* 9/1906). Helene Lange shared the moderate feminists' appreciation for Anthony, in contrast to her otherwise critical attitude towards feminists in the USA. She wrote retrospectively that for her, Anthony was the only truly respectable representative of American feminism, due to Anthony's pure, religious motives to promote suffrage (Lange 1928: 235).

Previous research shows that contacts, connections and interaction based on shared goals and visions created loving relations, friendships and acquaintances between feminists at national and international levels (e.g. Göttert 2000; Borgström and Markusson Winkvist 2018). Reading the media coverage of the journals indicates the emergence of another type of bonding. The figures revered as Great Women, who were the leaders of a campaign for women's rights and ultimately universal emancipation, became the objects of intense emotion. Admiration and gratitude constituted the pillars of this emotional community that spanned across borders. The journals not only took the role of a neutral medium, they actively co-created the international canon of Great Women and the related emotionality.

The admiration of women who were perceived as the embodiment of intellectual and moral greatness and thus invested with the quality of leadership created a strong emotional community among women across borders. The media coverage about these Great Women was a means of verbalizing the need for leadership of one's own gender that characterized feminist communities at both national and international levels. These women embodied the capacity to lead their 'sisters' on the path of progress and provided them with new patterns of femininity. This cultivation of admiration and gratitude seems to contrast with the discourse of equal sisterhood. This view does not recognize the nineteenth-century women's need for leaders of their own gender (see e.g. Kinnunen 2019).

## Conclusion

In her analysis of twentieth-century feminist internationalisms, Glenda Sluga shows that after the First World War, the growing number of international organizations and associations within and through which feminist agendas were advanced entwined with issues of permanent peace, humanitarianism and social justice (Sluga 2017: 84). In this chapter, I focused on the pre-war period and on the two major organizations, the ICW and IWSA. Women's citizenship in various countries gathered apace in the aftermath of the First World War, making it possible for women to widen the scope of their agency to include the newly established International Labour Organization, the League of Nations and, later, the United Nations. Before the war, women were empowered by the right to vote in only a handful of countries.

In this chapter, I have focused on feminist conferences. Not all activists were able to travel abroad to meet fellow activists, so defining internationalism exclusively in terms of conferences would be elitist and misleading.

However, they did play a significant role in creating feminist discourses and influencing feminist identifications. They indisputably formed a nexus of feminist relations.

> Under the influence of this new spirit we realise that we are not enlisted for the work of our own countries alone, but that before us stretches the task of emancipating the women of the civilized world. Nay, more, since in the progress of things the uncivilized are destined to become civilized, our task will not be fulfilled until the women of the whole world have been rescued from those discriminations and injustices which in every land are visited upon them by law and custom. (Catt 1909: 63)

This collective 'we' had the potential to empower and encourage women in their journey towards an emancipated identity and agency. The vision of a future world with women's rights as human rights was shared across borders, even if citizenship rights were bound to individual nation states or to some extent to sovereign parts of empires. International solidarity was thought to be a tool in this process. Activists from Britain and the United States impacted the internationalism of the nineteenth century in general, and the work of the ICW and IWSA, in particular. Paying attention to voices from Central and Northern European feminist communities helps to balance the Anglo-American dominance. Yet the fact remains that non-Western voices were marginal in the media coverage, as the focus was on 'civilized' countries. In an evolutionary spirit, however, Carrie Chapman Catt envisioned a process that would emancipate women in the whole world.

It was through images of Great Women, representing their nations and walking hand in hand in harmony with their counterparts from other countries towards democracy and modernity, that the media coverage conveyed the concept of internationalism. They not only walked the way of progress and promoted it, but embodied progress through their intellectual and moral capacities. By so doing, these exemplary women paved the way for all women. Women as active embodiments of both their respective national backgrounds and human progress constituted a strong claim on a new future of women's agency and international solidarity. The discourse about nation, progress and great individuals characterized nineteenth-century Western thinking. In this respect, too, the feminists were typical representatives of their time. In her analysis of twentieth-century feminisms, Sluga reminds us that this history was as much about internationalism as imperialism and nationalism. This is also true of the relation between nationalism and internationalism in the long nineteenth century. It is important to emphasize that nationalism and internationalism were not mutually exclusive. On the contrary, the international was 'a multiplication of the national' (Zimmermann 2010: 154). Despite occasional competition and the habit of creating hierarchies, the overall mentality was not based on aggressive confrontation.

Feminist internationalism was an emotional force, creating 'emotional energy' within and between women to work for the common cause. It was about both doing and conceptualizing. All these aspects are inherent in 'The Women's Battle Song' adopted at the London 1909 IWSA conference as 'an international hymn' (*The International Woman Suffrage Alliance* 1909: 55). We end with the first verse:

> Forward, sister women!
> Onward ever more,
> Bondage is behind you,
> Freedom is before.
> Raise the standard boldly,
> In the morning sun;
> 'Gainst a great injustice,
> *See the fight begun!*

**Tiina Kinnunen** is Professor in Finnish and Northern European History at the University of Oulu. Her publications on the history of feminisms include 'A Model Country or a Peripheral Anomaly? The Finnish Women's Suffrage and Female MPs in Transnational Debates, 1906–19', in T. Kaiser et al. (eds), *Entering the Parliamentary Stage – Women in Parliament and Politics in International Comparison*, Droste (forthcoming in 2022), co-written with Pasi Ihalainen. ORCID 0000-0003-1450-0228.

# References

## Primary Sources
### Archival Sources
Finnish Literature Society. Literature Archives, Alexandra Gripenberg's Collection. Letters from Alexandra Gripenberg to Hildi Ennola.
Helsinki City Archives. The Archives of the Finnish Women's Association, Alexandra Gripenberg's Collection. Letters from Alexandra Gripenberg to Lady Isabel Aberdeen.

### Printed Sources
Borelius, H. 1906. 'Rösträttskvinnor vid kongressen i Köpenhamn, 7–11 August 1906', *Dagny* 15.

Catt, C.C. 1909. 'Address by Mrs. Chapman Catt', in *The International Woman Suffrage Alliance, Report of the Fifth Conference and First Quinquennial*. London: Samuel Sidders & Co.

*Dagny – månadsblad för litterära och sociala intressen.*

Deutsch, R. 1911. 'Der IV Internationale Frauenstimmrechts-Kongress in Stockholm. 12–19. juni 1911', *Neues Frauenleben* 7.

*Dokumente der Frauen.*

Furuhjelm, A. 1939. *Gryningen*. Helsinki: Söderströms.

G.A. 1899. 'Från International Council och kvinnokongressen i London', *Dagny* 13.

Gerber, A. 1904. 'The Intern. Council of Women', *Neues Frauenleben* 6.

Gripenberg, A. 1890. 'Elizabeth Cady Stanton och Susan B. Anthony', in *Biografiskt Album: Med 13 porträtter i ljustyck*. Utgifvet af Finsk Qvinnoförening. Helsinki: G. W. Edlunds Förlag.

———. 1899. 'Kansainvälinen Naisten kongressi Lontoossa', *Koti ja Yhteiskunta*, 15 September.

———. 1904. 'Kansainvälinen naisten kongressi Berliinissä', *Koti ja Yhteiskunta*, 15 July.

*The International Woman Suffrage Alliance, Report of the Fifth Conference and First Quinquennial*. 1909. London: Samuel Sidders & Co.

Jacobs, A. 1996 [1924]. *Memories: My Life as an International Leader in Health, Suffrage, and Peace*. New York: The Feminist Press at the University of New York.

Kleman, E. 1911. 'Den internationella rösträttskongressen', *Dagny* 25.

Kollontay, A. 1984 [1918]. 'International Socialist Conferences of Women Workers', in A. Kollontay, *Selected Articles and Speeches*. Moscow: Progress Publishers, available at https://www.marxists.org/archive/kollonta/1907/is-conferences.htm.

*Koti ja Yhteiskunta.*

Lange, H. 1900. 'National oder international', *Die Frau: Monatsschrift für das gesamte Frauenleben unserer Zeit* 8(1).

———. 1928. *Lebenserinnerungen*. Berlin: F. U. Herbig.

Montefiore, D. 1904a. 'The Women's Congress in Berlin', *New Age*, 9 June, available at https://www.marxists.org/archive/montefiore/1904/06/berlin-congress.htm.

———. 1904b. 'Women's Progress', *New Age*, 28 July, available at https://www.marxists.org/archive/montefiore/1904/07/womens-progress.htm.

*Neues Frauenleben.*

Schwimmer, R. 1906. 'Die internationale Stimmrechtsversammlung in Kopenhagen', *Neues Frauenleben* 9.

Stritt, M. 1899. 'Der internationale Frauenkongress in London', *Die Frau: Monatsschrift für das gesamte Frauenleben unserer Zeit* 6(11).

———. 1904. 'Eröffnungsrede', in *Der Internationale Frauenkongress in Berlin 1904: Bericht mit ausgewählten Referaten herausgegeben im Auftrage des Vorstandes des Bundes Deutscher Frauenvereine von Marie Stritt*. Berlin: Verlag von Carl Habel.

Theimer, C. 1899. 'Nature sometimes indulges in curious freaks', *Dokumente der Frauen* 9.

Wahlström, L. 1904. 'Internationella kvinnokongressen i Berlin II', *Dagny* 12.

Wallerstedt, J. 1906. 'Internationella kvinnorösträttskongressen i Köpenhamn 1906', *Dagny* 14.

*Secondary Sources*

Borgström, E. and H. Markusson Winkvist (eds). 2018. *Den kvinnliga tvåsamhetens frirum. Kvinnopar i kvinnorörelsen 1890–1960*. Stockholm: Appell förlag.

Bosch, M. 1999. 'Colonial Dimensions of Dutch Women's Suffrage: Aletta Jacob's Travel Letters from Africa and Asia, 1911–1912', *Journal of Women's History* 11(2): 8–34.

———. 2009. 'Between Entertainment and Nationalist Politics: The Uses of Folklore in the Spectacle of the International Woman Suffrage Alliance', *Women's Studies International Forum* 32: 4–12.

Göttert, M. 2000. *Macht und Eros: Frauenbeziehungen und weibliche Kultur um 1900 – eine neue Perspektive auf Helene Lange und Gertrud Bäumer*. Sulzbach: Ulrike Helmer Verlag.

de Haan, F. et al. 2013. 'Introduction', in F. de Haan et al. (eds), *Women's Activism: Global Perspectives from the 1890s to the Present*. London: Routledge, pp. 1–12.

Hacker, H. 2006. 'Fickert, Auguste (1855–1910)', in F. de Haan et al. (eds), *A Biographical Dictionary of Women's Movements and Feminisms: Central, Eastern, and South Eastern Europe, 19th and 20th Centuries*. Budapest: CEU Press, pp. 131–34.

Hüchtker, D. 2019. 'Vergangenheit, Gefühl und Wahrheit: Strategien der Geschichtsschreibung über Frauenpolitik und Frauenbewegungen in Galizien an der Wende vom 19. zum 20. Jahrhundert', in A. Schaser, S. Schraut and P. Steymans-Kurz (eds), *Erinnern, vergessen, umdeuten? Europäische Frauenbewegungen im 19. und 20. Jahrhundert*. Frankfurt: Campus Verlag, pp. 284–311.

Ihalainen, P. and T. Kinnunen. 2022. 'A Model Country or a Peripheral Anomaly? The Finnish Women's Suffrage and Female MPs in Transnational Debates, 1906–19', in T. Kaiser et al. (eds), *Entering the Parliamentary Stage – Women in Parliament and Politics in International Comparison*. Düsseldorf: Droste.

Kinnunen, T. 2016. 'The National and International in Making a Feminist: the Case of Alexandra Gripenberg', *Women's History Review* 26(4): 652–70.

———. 2019. 'Feminist Biography in Finland and Sweden around 1900: Creation of Bonds of Admiration and Gratitude', in A. Schaser, S. Schraut and P. Steymans-Kurz (eds), *Erinnern, vergessen, umdeuten? Europäische Frauenbewegungen im 19. und 20. Jahrhundert*. Frankfurt: Campus Verlag, pp. 312–37.

Midgley, C., A. Twells and J. Carlier (eds). 2016. *Women in Transnational History: Connecting the Local and the Global*. London: Routledge.

af Petersens, L. 2006. *Formering för offentlighet: Kvinnokonferenser och Svenska Kvinnornas Nationalförbund kring sekelskiftet 1900*. Stockholm: Stockholm University.

Rendall, J. 2014. 'A Transnational Career? The Republican and Utopian Politics of Frances Wright (1795–1852)', in O. Janz and D. Schönpflug (eds), *Gender History in a Transnational Perspective: Networks, Biographies, Gender Orders*. New York: Berghahn, pp. 144–61.

Rupp, L.J. 2010. 'Constructing Internationalism: The Case of Transnational Women's Organizations, 1888–1945', in K. Offen (ed.), *Globalizing Feminisms 1789–1945*. London: Routledge, pp. 139–52.

Rupp, L.J. and V. Taylor. 1999. 'Forging Feminist Identity in an International Movement: A Collective Identity Approach to Twentieth-Century Feminism', *Signs* 24(2): 363–86.

Samuelsson, L. 2014. 'Dagny: En tidskrift för den nya dagens kvinna', in A. Nordenstam (ed.), *Nya röster: Svenska kvinnotidskrifter under 150 år*. Möklinta: Gidlunds förlag, pp. 19–47.

Sluga, G. 2017. 'Women, Feminisms and Twentieth-Century Internationalisms', in G. Sluga and P. Clavin (eds), *Internationalisms: A Twentieth-Century History*. Cambridge: Cambridge University Press, pp. 61–84.

Zimmermann, S. 2006. 'Nation und Internationalismus: Kooperationen und Konflikte der Frauenbewegungen der Habsburger Monarchie im Spannungsfeld internationaler Organisation und Politik', in W. Heindl, E. Király and A. Millner (eds), *Frauenbilder, feministische Praxis und nationales Bewusstsein in Österreich-Ungarn 1867–1918*. Tübingen: A. Francke Verlag, pp. 119–67.

———. 2010. 'The Challenge of Multinational Empire for the International Women's Movement: The Habsburg Monarchy and the Development of Feminist Inter/national Politics', in K. Offen (ed.), *Globalizing Feminisms 1789–1945*. London: Routledge, pp. 153–69.

# Chapter 6

# Non–Socialist Internationalisms before and after the First World War

*Pasi Ihalainen and Jörn Leonhard*

While socialist internationalism has been explored in a sophisticated body of literature (Eley 2002; Chapter 4), there has been a tendency to lump non-socialist conceptualizations together under the generalizing category 'liberal internationalism', especially as regards the interwar era. A major challenge to non-socialists or 'bourgeois' politicians sympathetic to international cooperation in the aftermath of the First World War was that the very term 'international' had become associated with the Socialist International and transnational class struggle against nationalism and capitalism (Sluga 2013: 4). 'Internationalism', in particular, appeared in the aftermath of the Bolshevik Revolution as the counter-concept to nation states and bourgeois political and social order, implying in its most radical form the creation of a dictatorship by the international proletariat (Koselleck 1992: 403). In practice, however, nation states and internationalism did not necessarily exclude each other in socialist thought, and labour internationalism had been overshadowed by revisionist social democrats supporting national defence during the First World War. As a consequence of the division of the left, internationalism had also become associated with failed pacifist projects.

Wartime propagandistic ideas of a league of nations, circulated in order to win over world opinion and advocated by the US President Woodrow Wilson above all, pushed the victorious states to plan new practical solutions for international cooperation, while the losing side – especially Germany – would soon view such projects as merely new forms of Western hegemony. The anti-German atmosphere among the Western powers led to the exclusion of Germany and its allies from the League of Nations. Soviet Russia denounced the League as capitalist and anti-revolutionary, forming a counter-force with the Communist International at the same time when the League was formed, in spring 1919 (Mazover 2013: 173–75), and encouraging communist parties that continued to challenge the capitalist order in the spirit of Marxist internationalism. In these circumstances, liberals and conservatives needed to either redefine 'internationalism' as peaceful cooperation between capitalist nation states, replace it in discourses on international cooperation with alternative expressions, or continuously denounce 'internationalism' as antinationalist and anticapitalist. Their practical solution was often to prioritize nation states in cooperation and to look for common ground in opposing Bolshevism (Sluga 2013: 5). Revisionist social democrats found themselves between ideals of labour internationalism and the search for democratic and parliamentary reformism within nation states, which made them look for a third-way compromise while continuously being subjected to liberal and conservative accusations of Marxist internationalism.

In this chapter, we first discuss the prewar and wartime transformations of the concept of internationalism and then proceed to analyse the multi-sited, polyvocal and conflicting non-socialist conceptualizations of internationalism in national parliaments and the party press in the interwar years, demonstrating similar tendencies in different national contexts and seeking explanations for divergent long-term developments. Even if they rarely proclaimed any gospel of internationalism, liberal and conservative politicians played key roles in national governments trying to construct a new international order between pressures from communist internationalism and far-right anti-internationalism – or as the ones who questioned the realism of internationalism. These non-socialist views became decisive especially once the pressures increased in the 1930s, and hence attention needs to be paid to liberal and conservative expressions of ideologically acceptable international cooperation and their opposition to it.

The available digitized data on discourses of internationalism are extensive; to enable cross-national comparability, we limit our focus to explicit talk about 'internationalism' in parliaments. Some related debates – such as those on 'the world'– are excluded by this limitation. In order to understand the dynamics of the ideological debate on internationalism we need to pay attention to competing socialist conceptualizations (on socialist theorists, see Chapter 4) and far-right arguments to which the liberals and conservatives were responding.

In much of the previous research, 'internationalism' has been used as an analytical category, with only limited references made to its actual usage by past politicians. The conventional interpretation of British 'liberal internationalism', for instance, is that it tried to reconcile nationalism and internationalism with global free trade. The 'liberal internationalists' carried on prewar debates on the nature and causes of war, ethics, law and the ways to secure peace. Rationality, morality, political progress, order, justice and prosperity in international relations were their themes. The Bolshevik Revolution and far-right reactions after the First World War added to the goal of preventing revolutions to this agenda. While the institutional solutions of the League of Nations were increasingly emphasized after the war and economic and social interdependence seen as a way to build an international society, beliefs in moral evolution, democracy and peace attained through education remained characteristic of 'liberal internationalism' (Holbraad 2003: 38, 42−43; Sylvest 2009: 2−4, 10−11, 197−99; Trentmann 2009; Pugh 2012: 2, 8). Such ways of thinking are discernible in interwar parliamentary debates, too, but we demonstrate that the representatives of liberal parties were often hesitant to articulate them so distinctly. Instead of emphasizing internationalism as an ideal, they rather pointed at the practical benefits of international cooperation for nation states.

'Conservative internationalism' is even more difficult to discern as an empirical phenomenon in interwar political discourse. Using such an analytical category, Holbraad calls 'conservative internationalism' the oldest version of international thought based on realist traditions that built on the primacy of sovereign states. The Russian Revolution connected liberals and conservatives in a common fight not only against Bolshevism but also against more moderate forms of socialist internationalism. Unlike many liberals, conservatives remained doubtful about the League due to its tendency to bypass conference diplomacy between sovereign states. Later in the interwar era, conservatism tended to be overshadowed by far-right nationalist movements (Holbraad 2003: 11−13, 15, 22). Conservative ways of thinking were again reflected in parliamentary discourse, especially with regard to the great powers, but we demonstrate that interwar economic and geopolitical circumstances could have enabled expressions of conservative internationalism. Most distinctly in the Nordic countries, caught between the Soviet threat and the prospects of rising rightist extremism in Germany and at home, experiences of the benefits of international cooperation made some conservatives reconceptualize internationalism.

In order to reveal the common and peculiar features of liberal and conservative interwar discourses on internationalism within the great powers, we discuss examples from the British, French, German, Swedish and Finnish parliaments. Britain was a leading actor in the construction of the League whose conservative and liberal politicians conceptualized international cooperation primarily from the perspective of its empire (McCarthy 2011), while fears of Bolshevism and National Socialism kept criticisms of internationalism alive. The French right prioritized national interests (Mouton 1995: 3–4), while French socialists emphasized international solidarity among the workers. This made national debates highly confrontational. In Germany, optimistic non-socialist conceptualizations of internationalism were overshadowed by the Treaty of Versailles that reinforced doubts about internationalism linked to the concepts of democracy and parliamentarism as 'un-German' (Jörke and Llanque 2016; Leonhard 2018a). In our analysis, Sweden represents a former great power which redirected its international cooperation in the postwar situation though building on a tradition of neutrality, while Finland was a newly independent nation state aiming at strengthening national sovereignty with engagement in the new legalistic international order (Jonas 2019).

We begin by analysing longer-term changes in conceptualizations of internationalism from the late nineteenth century, through the First World War and to the postwar peace conferences, taking transatlantic and global perspectives into consideration. We then contrast these with conceptualizations of the League in national parliaments in the immediate postwar situation and proceed to discuss rising liberal optimism and continuous conservative scepticism in different national contexts during the 1920s. This leads us to analyse how weakening internationalism tended to be overtaken by nationalism during the 1930s but also to point at some noteworthy countercurrents.

## 'Internationalism' During and Immediately After the First World War

Prior to the First World War, two major trends existed in the semantics of 'internationalism', reflecting major developments since the last decades of the nineteenth century. First, the concept represented a new idea of stability between states in international relations, often coupled with connotations of pacifism. Lord Hobbart used the word 'internationalism' in 1867 with reference to Richard Cobden, champion of the free trade movement in Britain. He described Cobden's political mission which had aimed at an international federation of states based on a universal state of law in the international sphere:

> What is certain is, that for the complete realisation of internationalism in its ultimate result, political association, it is requisite that nations in general should possess a very large measure of real political liberty ... Complete

political liberty once established in the world, some form of international federation would be the natural result. (Hobbart 1867: 38–39)

Second, 'internationalism' was used to describe various processes of internationalization (Hervé 1910; Chapters 3 and 5). Even when Marx and other leading socialists used the concept in the last third of the nineteenth century, it did not have a particularly ideological meaning, thereby provoking semantic dichotomies or counter-concepts. Nor did it necessarily signify transnational solidarity among workers of all countries, as was the case for contemporary concepts of 'cosmopolitism' or 'fraternization' (see Chapter 4). In 1883, August Bebel summed up what characterized the international in his own epoch: 'international trade and shipping agreements, international post treaties, international exhibitions ... our trade and traffic, all this and many other examples prove the international character, which the relations between different civilized nations has developed'. Although explanations of social origins still referred to nation and nation state, Bebel had no doubt that 'we find ourselves in an age of internationalism' (Bebel [1879] 1883: 195; see also Friedemann and Hölscher 1995: 394).

The semantic horizon of the concept – the description of internationalization in many political, economic, scientific and cultural areas – began to change at the beginning of the new century. Critics of contemporary colonial practice like John Hobson formulated a clear dichotomy between imperialism and internationalism, the latter denoting an international system that would allow peace and stability by overcoming the former. This definition would be taken up by socialist authors and became radicalized during the First World War. In his influential book on imperialism, published in 1905, Hobson wrote: 'Not only does aggressive Imperialism defeat the movement towards internationalism by fostering animosities among competing empires: its attack upon the liberties and the existence of weaker and lower races stimulates in them a corresponding excess of national self-consciousness' (Hobson 1905: 3–4; Groh and Walther 1995: 216).

During the same year the liberal German politician Friedrich Naumann summed up different layers of meaning, resulting from experiences of the nineteenth century, to underline a growing antagonism between the national viewpoint and internationalism. The concept came under growing pressure when identified with anti-patriotic behaviour and doubtful loyalty. Naumann referred to the 'viewpoint of proletarian internationality' (*Standpunkt proletarischer Internationalität*) on the one hand, and to an anti-patriotic mentality of Catholics in their own 'internationalism' on the other, reflecting the long shadow of both antisocialist legislation and anti-Catholic *Kulturkampf* in the German Empire since its foundation in 1871. According to his interpretation,

internationalism referred to an imagined future instead of a concrete political agenda among Social Democrats, whereas Catholics' internationalism
in his view reflected the ideal of a community of life not defined by nations
(Naumann 1906: 125; Friedemann and Höscher 1995: 395). Naumann's
diagnosis was important because it anticipated a development that would
dominate the first years of the First World War: a negative view of internationalism as a potential instrument to weaken nation states and their societies
engaged in war. When proofs of loyalty became ever more important on the
military and home fronts after August 1914, internationalism could easily be
identified as another variant of defeatism and nourished various stab-in-the-
back narratives even before it became prominent in Germany in late 1918.

Since late 1916, a number of developments combined and paved the way
for 'internationalism' to become a key concept during and immediately after
the First World War. The combination of war weariness, war and revolution
in Russia and various peace initiatives in 1917 marked a major watershed
in the development of the concept. Thus before the war's global end, the
Paris Peace Conference peace treaties and the foundation of the League of
Nations, an ideological polarization was under way. From 1917 onwards, the
concept was coupled with competing scenarios for how to end the war and
create a new international order that had to be different from the status quo
ante 1914.

The first scenario, which integrated 'internationalism', unfolded in the
course of 1917 when the Russian Revolution demonstrated that a long-
awaited fundamental change could be actively implemented. In this context
'internationalism' began to overshadow 'internationality', which had been an
established key concept before 1914, and became the polemical counter-concept to both 'nationalism' and 'imperialism' (Leonhard 2018b: 581–90). As
early as 1916, the socialist Alexander Trojanowski pointed to this fundamental ideological dichotomy, brought about by the war and condensed in
the two counter-concepts of internationalism and imperialism:

> It is now a question of life or death of the International. Either it will become,
> after a period of hesitation, errors and lack of organisation, the real weapon
> of the international workers' movement and stand on stable ground, or else it
> will become a sort of church asylum which has no real function. Either inter-
> nationalism or imperialism. (Trojanowski 1916: 32; Lenin [1917] 1974: 59)

Whereas Lenin insisted on the 'internationalism of deeds' in contrast to
the false 'internationalism of words' which he used polemically in his critique of moderate socialists, Karl Liebknecht claimed that if 'legitimacy and
nationality' could be identified as the two natural enemies of Napoleon, the

contrast was now between socialism and 'proletarian internationalism' on one side and 'German imperialism' on the other (Liebknecht [1918] 1968: 502, cited in Lenin [1917] 1974; Friedemann and Hölscher 1995: 395–96). Behind these definitions lay the expectation of a chain of socialist revolutions that would result in world revolution. Very soon, however, the limits of this prospect became obvious, not only in the contained revolutionary upheavals in Germany, Austria and Hungary, but also in the Russian Civil War.

The second scenario was identified with Woodrow Wilson when the American president developed his own variant of an end to the war and a future world order. Against the background of the Bolshevik takeover and their first decrees advocating self-determination in Europe and colonial societies, an ideological competition between different understandings of 'internationalism' developed. In the European perception of Wilsonian 'internationalism' became a synonym of 'New Diplomacy' while American war propaganda fostered the export of the new vocabularies to many societies, not only to crumbling European continental empires, but also to colonial societies in Asia or Africa. For all their ideological differences, Lenin and Wilson shared this focus on the international dimension, beyond the European states and their imperial protrusions: for the former, an international civil war would revolutionize all class societies; for the latter, a 'people's war' would achieve the democratic principles of self-determination. In September 1918, Wilson developed his vision of 'internationalism' as a supranational order: the world war should end not in the resumption of traditional foreign policies but in a global internal policy: 'national purposes have fallen more and more into the background and the common purpose of enlightened mankind has taken their place' (Wilson, 'An Address at the Metropolitan Opera House', 27 September 1918, cited in Steigerwald 1994: 37).

In American discourse, 'internationalism' reflected a very national perspective that affected debates globally. Unlike the German discussion of war aims, the concept of the nation held by liberal intellectuals in the United States did not start from annexationist ambitions but focused on a new social and national democracy and a new vision of loyalty for the heterogeneous immigrant society of the United States. Progressivists advocated an international system of collective security that would include the United States and became identified with 'internationalism'. But the global perception of Wilson's agenda neglected the fact that its main focus remained national politics. Thus, Herbert Croly emphasized that a 'national purpose' would redefine the common good beyond materialist culture and class interests. This vision of the nation was supposed to overcome both the stateless individualism of the pioneering age and the one-sided material and economic egotism of the second half of the nineteenth century in the United States. *The New Republic*, mouthpiece of the Progressivists, gave expression to these hopes of American liberals. In April 1917, following America's entry into the war, it wrote: 'Never was a war fought so far from the battlefield for purposes so distinct from the battlefield' (*The New Republic*, 19 February 1916: 62–67 and 21 April 1917: 338; see also Leonhard 2018b: 630–31).

As a result of war weariness and the ever more difficult mobilization of home fronts, ideological polarization grew sharper in all societies after late 1916. On top of defensive operations against the left and right at home, many liberals had to face ideological competition from democratic egalitarianism and the Bolshevik Revolution, bound together by 'internationalism'. The persuasiveness of liberal ideas had to be measured against the new political, social and international models represented by Lenin and Wilson. Petrograd provided laboratory-like conditions for demonstrating how war and revolution were interlinked, and how traditional institutions such as dynasty, monarchy and empire could be swept aside in short order. These dramatic experiences explain why the vocabulary around 'internationalism' enabled contemporaries to formulate their expectations vis-à-vis the construction of peace when the war came to an end. At the same time, 'internationalism' had already acquired layers of meaning that went beyond the liberal–communist dichotomy. It was used to underline the internationalization of new problems generated by the war. Issues like the integration and repatriation of refugees and prisoners of war stretched across national boundaries, and the League of Nations and other organizations such as the Red Cross expanded their activities in this context.

Furthermore, 'internationalism' had a utopian dimension: its promise to overcome the very principle of war. The abstract line from individual through family and nation to a single humanity was already a leitmotiv during the war. In 1916 Ernst Joël referred 'to the paradoxical fact today ... that the community of the truly patriotic is an international, supranational' community (Joël 1916: 162). Henri Barbusse, the author of the savagely critical war novel *Le Feu*, emphasized in 1918: 'Humanity instead of nation. The revolutionaries of 1789 said: "All Frenchmen are equal." We should say: "All men." Equality demands common laws for everyone who lives on earth' (Barbusse 1920: 92; see also Leonhard 2018b: 904). This hope, that the war and its enormous sacrifices should not have been in vain and that they should lead to the creation of a new global order, is probably the most influential claim that became associated with 'internationalism' at the end of the war.

The complexity of 'internationalism' became particularly obvious in the context of a crumbling multi-ethnic empire towards the end of the war. The German-Austrian Social Democratic Party understood itself 'as a democratic and international party' and supported the principle of national self-determination. But it also called upon fellow parties to fight 'any attempt by their nations' bourgeoisies' to 'enslave other nations in the name of the freedom of their own nation'. This was an attempt to halt the spread of irredenta nationalism in all parts of the monarchy. Advocating 'internationalism', the right to national self-determination was to be based only on 'the full victory of democracy' and 'the international class struggle' (quoted in Neck 1968: 42–43).

The victory of democracy would bring statehood to all people of the crumbling multi-ethnic empires. But by the same token, 'German Austria [would be separated] from the Austrian mixture of peoples as a distinctive polity' (quoted in Neck 1968: 44). The problem in defining 'internationalism' here was to prevent national self-determination from fuelling limitless competition among different nationalisms, and to reject aggressive nationalism directed against ethnic minorities as a distinguishing characteristic of the bourgeoisie. How could the Habsburg Monarchy continue to exist in a new age of 'internationalism'? In 1918, Karl Renner for one still spoke in favour of a Habsburg 'state of nationalities', which could 'offer an example for the future national organization of humanity' (quoted in Mazower 1998: 45; see also Leonhard 2018b: 799–800).

In the immediate postwar period, when the Bolsheviks were paralysed by civil war and the Allies intervened in the former Russian Empire, the semantics of 'internationalism' were influenced by the American political agenda. Wilson based his vision on a very suggestive analysis of the factors he believed had caused the world war: a misguided European system of militarization and the uncontrolled development of state power, secret diplomacy and autocratic empires which had suppressed the rights and interests of national minorities. He promised a counter model to the exhausted variants of European liberalism. This shifted the traditional focus on the balance of power and the sovereignty of states to international law, the idea of collective security, the League of Nations as an international forum and the premise of national self-determination as the basis for drawing new maps. Here 'internationalism' represented a quasi-universal democratization of both societies and the international order that bridged the gap between domestic politics and the international system.

Wilson's and Lenin's ideas were applicable not just to national minorities within continental European empires but, from 1917 onwards, they had a global meaning, in China and Korea as well as in India or in South America. The result was not a simplistic 'Wilsonian Moment', as if one could translate Wilson's ideas and American war propaganda into liberation movements seeking emancipation from colonial or quasi-colonial oppression (Manela 2007). Instead, a new postwar variant of the tension between universalism and particularism arose, between internationalist rhetoric and local conditions – this allowed particular constellations, conflicts and interests to be integrated into global entanglements. However, Wilson's vision was controversial from the first, particularly in the United States. Former US President Theodore Roosevelt criticized Wilson's internationalism and vision of the League of Nations – they would negate US sovereignty and force the United States to support military interventions: 'We are no internationalists, but we are American nationalists' (*Chicago Tribune*, 27 August 1918; see also Knock 1992: 169; Berg 2017: 153; Leonhard 2019: 410–11).

Outside the United States, many political actors used 'internationalism' to formulate their expectations and interests vis-à-vis the Paris Peace Conference. The German reference to a 'Wilson peace' stood in this context (Leonhard 2019: 137, 229, 261, 440, 459, 822–23 and 950). The new government in Berlin formed after the Revolution of November 1918 and the new chief diplomat, Count Brockdorff-Rantzau, relied on what they regarded as American guarantees for a moderate peace without victors, reparations or annexations, based on Wilson's fourteen-point programme. A takeover by moderate social democrats and liberals and the transition from military monarchy to democratic republic were seen as prerequisites for a new postwar Germany to be admitted to the League of Nations. When the German peace conference delegation assembled in Paris in May 1919, Carl Legien as chairman of the German trade unions pointed out that by their revolution, the German people could count on the solidarity of European workers' movements. After the collapse of the monarchical nation, this 'internationalism' was Germany's only possible future (Stampfer 1957: 237; Leonhard 2019: 958).

In the course of the Paris Peace Conference, 'international' became identified with a whole spectrum of new institutions. The internationalization of political deliberation in the League of Nations proved partly successful as there now existed a public forum, albeit without executive power, to implement collective security. 'Internationalization' could be seen in action in the League of Nations' administration of the free city of Danzig, the Saarland and the mandatory territories. In contrast to the prewar period a range of institutions promoted the meaning of 'internationalism' in their names, such as the International Labour Organization (Leonhard 2019: 703–705; see Chapter 4).

As a result of the Peace Conference, however, 'internationalism' became an extremely contested concept. The hitherto unknown number of war victims which had to be legitimized through the results of the peace, ever radicalizing war aims, the ideal of a new international order which would make future wars impossible, new mass markets for public deliberations and the new relation between 'international' and 'domestic' politics in an age of mass media and democratic franchise: all these factors contributed to a massive disillusion and disappointment with the peace settlement. Referring to the widening gap between expectations and outcomes and the contradictions of the peace treaties, John Maynard Keynes saw 'internationalism' as being under enormous pressure: 'Our power of feeling or caring beyond the immediate questions of our own material well-being is temporarily eclipsed ... We have been moved already beyond endurance, and need rest. Never in the lifetime of men now living has the universal element in the soul of man burnt so dimly' (Keynes 1919 [1971]: 188–89; Leonhard 2019: 629).

When the conditions of the Versailles Treaty became obvious, the 'Wilson peace' as a synonym of a fair internationalism was met with bitter resentment in Germany. To the nation state not admitted to the League of Nations, 'internationalism' now seemed to denote either broken promises and the unfair order implemented by the victorious powers or else the danger of civil war, stimulated by Bolshevik dreams of internationalist class struggle. Turning away from and countering 'internationalism' paved the way for multiple national revisionisms. These could easily be used in domestic conflicts – thus, foreign political revisionism fuelled political conflicts and ideological polarization within postwar societies.

That was the case not only in Germany – or Hungary – but also in Italy. Here the *vittoria mutilata* corresponded well to the various stab-in-the-back myths and narratives of conspiracy or treachery which would further weaken the reputation of postwar liberal political regimes and contribute considerably to the rise of Fascism (Gibelli 2010: 472–75). For the defeated Germans, the economic and monetary legacy of the peace settlement together with the question of war guilt linked any domestic political conflict easily to the trauma of Versailles. This poisoned German political culture and prevented the evolution of a positive republican narrative after 1918. When Adolf Hitler developed his *Weltanschauung* in the early 1920s to give his new party a basis and to position it above the spectrum of other parties, he referred to Marxism. Despite the obvious ideological polarization, he stated that the *völkische Weltanschauung* needed a kind of weapon, 'similar to the way in which the Marxist party organization creates ample space for internationalism' (Hitler 1939 [1925]: 375; Braun 1992: 502). In the course of the 1920s and early 1930 he developed an enemy image in which capitalism, the idea of a Jewish conspiracy, Bolshevism and internationalism became amalgamated. By insisting that 'internationalism' and 'democracy' were inseparable he found a key concept in his fight against the democratic republic which he portrayed as un-German (Hitler, speech given on 1 May 1923, quoted in Siebarth 1935: 86; Hitler, speech given on 27 January 1932, quoted in Siebarth 1935: 78; Friedemann and Hölscher 1995: 396).

## The Immediate Reception of the League of Nations in National Parliaments

As the contexts of discourses on internationalism were radically different in victorious Britain and France, disappointed Germany, neutral Sweden and newly independent Finland – despite shared transnational trends – we discuss the national parliamentary debates separately while considering their remaining transnational connections. In the postwar situation, a wartime focus on the security of the nation state continued everywhere. The non-socialist parties wished to carry on policies based on the truce, L'Union sacrée *Burgfrieden* or *borgfreden*, which implied that political forces considered disloyal to the nation should be excluded. A further unifying theme in discourse on internationalism was anti-Bolshevism – except for the extreme left.

Not even the British press and parliament were overwhelmingly enthusiastic about the Convention of the League of Nations (Holmila and Ihalainen 2018). *The Times*, a moderate conservative voice, associated internationalism with Bolshevism and the destruction of nation states (14 January 1919: 3; 30 January 1919: 3), while the left-liberal *Manchester Guardian* called for 'a stronger internationalism' (20 March 1919: 12). The conservative *Daily Telegraph* wrote that the League gave rise to 'the highest hopes for a better regulation of the world's affairs' but doubted whether human nature could be changed or the public opinion trusted (23 July 1919: 8). In Parliament, Robert Cecil, a rare conservative spokesman for the League, assured members that patriotism and the notion that 'all nations are part of a larger whole' were mutually supportive and that the League supported the interests of the British Empire (HC, 21 July 1919: 987). MPs typically prioritized international law, financial questions and the conditions of workers, whereas the peers focused on morality and law while recognizing the existence of an 'international spirit' (Ihalainen and Sahala 2020). 'Liberal internationalism' was most explicitly summarized in the Lords by James Bryce, a member of the International Court, who viewed the League as based on 'the feeling that the world has now become one[,] one in a new sense never dreamed of before; that the fortunes of each people affect those of all other peoples, and that the well-being of each makes for the well-being of all'. The League rested on 'the belief that the community of the world requires that a new spirit should prevail in international relations – a spirit which seeks to substitute friendship for enmity' (HL, 24 July 1919: 1019). Even if the Empire remained the starting point for conceptualizing international cooperation, George Curzon, the acting foreign secretary and a well-known imperialist, emphasized his belief in

> the international spirit, the kind of idea that the future unit is not to be the race, the community, the small group, but is to be the great world of mankind, and that in that area you try and induce a common feeling, you try and produce co-operation which will be a better solvent of international difficulties. (HL, 24 July 1919: 1029)

Both men represented official optimism regarding a new start in international relations after the victory over Germany, while some backbenchers criticized the Treaty of Versailles for its hard peace terms on Germany and French nationalist interpretations of the League (Holmila and Ihalainen 2018).

In France, the government and public opinion indeed prioritized national security, seeing the League as a means to control German militarism (Henig 1995: 30–32, 36, 43) even if doubtful about its military power. In parliament, internationalism was associated with either opportunities opened up or threats posed by socialist ideology and the labour movement. Party-political polarization over internationalism followed partly from the very name of the socialist party, *Section Française de l'Internationale Ouvrière*, which defined socialism through internationalism and turned *internationaliste* into a party denomination. Such a practice differs from the German, Swedish and Finnish social democratic parties whose names made more explicit reference to the respective nation states. French debates typically led the right to prioritize patriotism over internationalism and the left to allege that 'the internationalism of capital' ran the world. Deeply ideological trajectories made the debates focus on political divisions within France rather than on international cooperation.

In Germany, the League was generally seen as a new form of British and French imperialism imposed on weaker nations and violating German interests (Carr 2001: 78–80). As we have seen, some had initially held positive views on the League, expecting mild terms of peace from Wilson, but by May 1919 the Treaty of Versailles and the League with it were interpreted as further means to repress Germany. Even if several neutral states supported German membership of the League as a counterweight to France (Wintzer 2006: 78), internationalism remained a highly pejorative term for most German non-socialists. In the National Assembly, it was a contested party-political concept associated with Marxist internationalism. Even left-liberals were disappointed when they realized that the Austrians had been denied self-determination. Gertrud Bäumer argued in anti-internationalist terms, denouncing 'shallow internationalism' in favour of 'the holiness of the nation' (NV, 15 July 1919: 328:1907). While moderate Social Democrats insisted that their internationalism served the interests of the 'fatherland', the extreme left carried on Marxist discourse on proletarian internationalism (Wilhelm Keil, NV, 14 February 1919: 326:79; Oscar Cohn, NV, 30 July 1919: 328:2100), which only provoked the right. The right emphasized the suffering that such 'international – or, as it was earlier called, cosmopolitan – thinking' had caused the German people (Franz Heinrich Költzsch, NV, 15 April 1919: 327:1058) or suggested that 'the illusion of internationalism' and 'the international solidarity of the proletariat' had been destroyed by the war once the workers had supported their governments against Germany (Gottfried Traub, German Nationalists, NV, 9 July 1919: 328:1411), which, by implication, the German socialists had not done.

Sweden joined the League in 1920 simultaneously with Denmark, the Netherlands, Norway and Switzerland. The Swedish membership entailed both the rejection of previous pro-German policies and the reinforcement of Western parliamentary democracy as established with a recent suffrage reform (Ihalainen 2017, 2019a). The Liberal–Social Democratic coalition represented the membership as a way to contribute to a new judicial community of states while denying the 'supranational' (*överstatlig*) aspects of the League (the liberal *Dagens Nyheter*, 18 February 1920). Liberal Prime Minister Nils Edén combined discourses on the universal and national good when emphasizing Swedish connections to 'the uniting world culture' as 'a limb of the entire humanity' and the need to think about 'the great universal problem of justice and peace in the world' as part of national security (AK, 18 February 1920: 18:25–26). He did not deny the tendency of the League to serve the interests of the Western powers (Nils Edén, AK, 18 February 1920: 18:23). His coalition partner Hjalmar Branting, the revisionist Social Democrat leader, turned to the older vocabulary of 'universality' instead of ideologically charged 'internationalism' (AK, 18 February 1920: 18:27–28, 54), while Gustav Möller of the same party did not hesitate to welcome the rise of 'the international state' out of labour initiatives (FK, 3 March 1920: 19:48; see Chapter 4). The Right Party responded by emphasizing the looming dangers of socialist internationalist democracy (Ernst Trygger, FK, 3 March 1920: 19:23, 113), defending national sovereignty, cultural ties to Germany and inherited great power identity but rejecting any idea of Swedish politicians turning 'internationalists', as their duty was to view international relations from the perspective of Sweden, not of all 'humanity' (Arvid Lindman, AK, 18 February 1920: 18:13, 16–18; 3 March 1920:

23:33–4). Whereas the Swedish Liberals joined the Social Democrats in the rhetoric of an internationalist breakthrough, the Swedish Conservatives retained their nationalist stand.

Finland, which had recently experienced a civil war with German, Russian and Swedish interventions, was invited to join the League on British initiative in 1920, partly in order to solve a border dispute with Sweden and to gain an anti-Bolshevist ally against Soviet Russia. The non-socialist coalition presented the membership as supportive of independence and implicitly also as a way to stabilize Finland as a Western parliamentary democracy. In a country with historical experience of defending the constitution against Russian authoritarianism, the international legalism of the League was welcomed (Ihalainen 2019a). According to Conservative Prime Minister Rafael Erich, the League allowed small states to retain independence while offering them the chance to be heard by the great powers. In the face of the Bolshevik threat, Finland was seeking 'legal protection and also factual political guarantees' as well as 'broader possibilities for such peaceful international interaction' (EK, 4 May 1920: 474–75). The liberal organ *Helsingin Sanomat* welcomed membership (13 May 1920: 2) while the conservative *Uusi Suomi* remained sceptical (8 May 1920: 4). Some Finland-Swedish activists rather welcomed 'new nationalism' that would stop 'vulgar internationalism' and 'internal Bolshevism' (P.L. Bolinder to Swedish-speaking students in Helsinki, *Aftonbladet*, 21 May 1919: 5). As in other countries, Finnish liberals who were supportive of the League referred to national interests existing side by side with the creation of a legal international order. Conservative scepticism remained strong everywhere and took over in France, Germany and Sweden, whereas the leaders of the Finnish conservatives (National Coalition Party) welcomed Western internationalism as a survival strategy of a small nation. In Britain, the League was accepted as an extension of the Empire.

## Rising Liberal Optimism and Continuous Conservative Scepticism in the 1920s

In the 1920s, conservative internationalism remained exceptional in Britain and hardly existed in France, Germany or Sweden but found some support among Finnish conservatives, as practical internationalization progressed. Liberal defenders of internationalism, too, were fewer than might be expected from the generalizing category of 'liberal internationalism'; the liberals continued to qualify internationalism by defining it as cooperation between nation states and prioritizing bilateral over multilateral collaboration.

Robert Cecil, a founding father of the League, was a lonely figure as a conservative defender of internationalism. As the League was criticized in

an Oxford debate as being based on 'the spirit of internationalism' supportive of a revolution that endangered English nationalism and all civilization,
Cecil defended 'the growing spirit of internationalism', insisting that public
opinion and the League constituted 'the conscience of mankind' fortified
by 'co-operation among the nations' (*The Manchester Guardian*, 24 October
1919: 8). The other Conservatives were critical of emerging democratic
Germany and feared both the growth of the Labour Party and the progress of
revolutionary Bolshevism (Parson 2007: 4, 310–11, 313–14, 324–27). Their
fears made Labour leaders cautious: while Arthur Henderson defined his
party as the supporter of 'true internationalism' (*The Manchester Guardian*,
1 January 1920: 4), Prime Minister Ramsay MacDonald emphasized the
patriotism of the same (*The Daily Telegraph*, 7 October 1924: 11). As the
Conservatives were so strong, even the moderate left presented internationalism as a way to advance national interests in order to demonstrate their
legitimacy.

The Conservatives remained highly critical of internationalism throughout the 1920s. In the beginning of the decade, Britain was involved in a
war in Ireland and crises in Egypt and India, which made the value of
internationalism appear doubtful. Arthur Balfour, a former prime minister, denounced cosmopolitan and socialist internationalism, insisting that
nationalism remained the strongest political force and welcoming an alternative internationalism based on cooperation between nation states. According
to him, 'true internationalism' could not be achieved with destructive 'cosmopolitanism' that attacked 'not the excesses of nationalism, but nationalism
itself' and pretended that 'patriotism is played out'. While 'international
comprehension' in the sense of understanding the aims and points of view
of other countries was needed, it was to be 'carefully cultivated by the best
statesmen and writers of the day, who are themselves secure against the
odious charge of being the friends of every country but their own' (*The
Daily Telegraph*, 7 July 1920: 10). J.D. Rees, a former colonial administrator,
defined internationalism as 'the negation of patriotism and the abnegation
of everything of which we should be proud', concluding that 'instead of
extending internationalism I long myself to see it abolished completely off
the face of the earth' (HC, 1 November 1920: 106). Field Marshal Henry
Wilson remained 'an intense nationalist' and did not believe 'in this period of
the world's history in internationalism' (*The Manchester Guardian*, 26 April
1922: 8). Beliefs that all British socialists cooperated with Moscow against
the British Empire made Richard Glover attack the alleged Labour '"Anti-
Britishism", camouflaged as internationalism, aimed at our national life by
destroying our national confidence'. For Glover, '[t]he continued preaching
of internationalism … had damaged the moral strength of the nation, which

brought in its train weakness and unemployment' (*The Daily Telegraph*, 18 August 1926: 10). By 1926 even Cecil had to concede that growth in international spirit had been precarious and that patriotism was 'a splendid thing' (*The Manchester Guardian*, 15 October 1926: 6). After his resignation from the British delegation to the League, he was criticized for having 'in his ardent advocacy of a new internationalism ... ignored the fact that this country is an island, able and entitled to avoid foreign commitments' (*The Daily Telegraph*, 31 August 1927: 9). Austen Chamberlain, Cecil's successor, was instead thanked for having spoken in the League both for the British Empire and internationalism (*The Daily Telegraph*, 12 September 1927: 10).

Meanwhile, the Liberals welcomed 'a sane internationalism' standing for 'a European as opposed to a merely insular outlook' (*The Manchester Guardian*, 16 March 1920: 8). H.H. Asquith and Edward Grey, together with Robert Cecil and J.R. Clynes of the Conservatives and Labour, signed a declaration supportive of the League 'leading men from nationalism to internationalism' as citizens would control foreign policy and censor 'national egoism' (*The Manchester Guardian*, 7 April 1920: 6). Yet the Liberals continued to emphasize that internationalism based on patriotism served best the interests of nation states. Grey criticized socialist and communist internationalists for having taken over the word 'international' and denouncing patriotism (*The Daily Telegraph*, 7 July 1920: 10). According to Victor Finney,

> the vital spirit of nationalism would [not] be lost in following the international ideal [as] an international conception should mean a call to each nation to act according to the highest standard and to develop to the best possible condition, so that its contribution to the life of the whole world should be the best it could make. (*The Manchester Guardian*, 16 October 1925: 11)

Fred Maddison, secretary of the International Arbitration League, called for the rise of 'a world patriotism and for a fuller realisation of the fact that humanity was never contained alone in any one particular nation' (*The Manchester Guardian*, 23 November 1928: 13). Economic internationalism was viewed positively: every Englishman was 'in his daily life an internationalist' thanks to international trade (Callisthenes, *The Manchester Guardian*, 16 November 1934: 10). Liberal internationalism existed but was mainly concerned with economic cooperation benefiting nation states.

Such non-socialist discourse on internationalism is hardly traceable in France: the parliamentarians continued to view internationalism as an aspect of socialist ideology, particularly as the wartime *union-sacrée* style of politics no longer worked. A leading conservative newspaper close to the foreign ministry attacked 'the error of internationalism itself' (*Le Temps*, 12

January 1922: 2), warning about 'revolutionary internationalism and Soviet propaganda' (*Le Temps*, 19 February 1923: 2). For Vincent Auriol, a leading socialist, the destiny of France and the cause of world peace were inseparable yet the socialist understanding of patriotism and internationalism could be reconciled (CD, 15 March 1921: 1244; see Chapter 4 on Jean Jaurès). Such revisionist formulations were needed as even the radical (liberal) leader Édouard Herriot insisted that 'sincere internationalism' superimposed itself on 'true patriotism' (*Le Petit Parisien*, 19 November 1922: 2). Raoul Péret, the President of the Chambre des députés, expressed the views of the centre-left even more directly: 'We are ... for the homeland against internationalism' (*Le Petit Parisien*, 5 May 1924: 3). After 1923, there was an attempt to overcome antagonism with Germany but this was called into question by the political and economic crisis of the Weimar Republic.

Quite similar patterns can be found in the German Reichstag though with an earlier and more distinct rise of far-right discourse motivated by the rejection of the Treaty of Versailles as fraudulent internationalism. An old polarization between the German organic national *Kultur* and the supposedly individualistic and materialistic *Zivilisation* (allegedly supported by a worldwide Jewish conspiracy) grew stronger. Some intellectuals were supportive of a stronger international law and receptive to liberal democratic thought (Harrington 2016: 3–4, 8); attempts to build cross-cultural understanding between the French and Germans emerged as well (Passman 2009: 1–2), but such activities were not much reflected in parliamentary discourse. Antisocialist liberals continuously found it difficult to argue for any 'Western' form of democracy or internationalism, given their traditional concern that social democratic internationalism challenged the German nation state (Leonhard 2019: 86, 88–89). The nationalistic, antisocialist and anti-Bolshevist conservatives were opposed to internationalist projects, approaching the far right in their argumentation (Parson 2007: 4, 6, 8, 323–24). Politicians actively engaged in international cooperation, such as the right-liberal Gustav Stresemann, had to find alternative ways to legitimate their actions. One way to interpret the international in a German way had been provided by the rise of *Völkerrecht* and expectations of international solidarity between all moderate social democratic governments. Another was to cooperate with other defeated nations excluded from the League as in the case of Russia in the Treaty of Rapallo. A further method was the socioeconomic discourse on the world economy (*Weltwirtschaftspolitik*) that aimed at overcoming German diplomatic isolation while avoiding the political connotations of communist internationalism (see Chapter 7).

The Conservatives dominated parliamentary discourse on 'internationalism', blurring far-right authoritarian discourses with medical vocabulary to construct persuasive images of a pandemic to be healed with nationalism. Such rhetoric built on the narrative that the war had been lost due to domestic treason and on the interpretation of all compliance policies as expressions of anti-German Western internationalism. Count Kuno von Westarp of the pan-German Nationalist People's Party condemned all internationalism as Marxism, insisting that 'the delusions of internationalism, the interests of class struggle and inciting agitation' should be replaced with 'the unanimous unity of the German people' (DR, 12 March 1921: 348:2865). Such *völkisch* thinking was presented as 'a necessary reaction to the aberrations of internationalism', the German people having 'become ill from the poison of internationalism' and likely to recover once the youth turned to nationalism (Wilhelm Bazille, Nationalist, DR, 18 July 1922: 356:8691).

This anti-internationalist discourse turned expressly antisemitic (*Vorwärts*, 20 February 1920: 2), carrying on traditions that surfaced in other countries as well. Albrecht von Graefe presented 'Jewish Marxism and Jewish capitalist internationalism' as antitheses of every 'strong, national, civic heart' (DR, 25 November 1922: 357:9166). Count Ernst zu Reventlow (German Völkisch Freedom Party) equated and questioned 'the idea of internationalism and the forces of judaized vision of the world' (DR, 28 August 1924: 381:1038), claiming that internationalism originated from 'the Jewish blood' of German leftist politicians (DR, 11 February 1930: 426:3962). For him, the League constituted 'the leading supporter of disintegrating internationalism, Jewishness' (zu Reventlow, DR, 24 November 1926: 391:8173). He accused Social Democrats of advancing 'internationalism at any cost, also at the cost of the loss of German sovereignty' (zu Reventlow, DR, 6 July 1927: 393:11342) and the Weimar coalition of subordinating the German economy to 'internationalist foreign policy and capitalist internationalism' (DR, 5 March 1928: 395:13188). Stresemann's ideas about a United States of Europe and his alleged 'Europeanization of Germany' appeared in the rhetoric of the far right as identical with the decomposition of the German state (DR, 11 February 1930, 426:3962). Authoritarian far-right rhetoric climaxed in Joseph Goebbels' definition of internationalism as 'plain treason' that undermined the German nation:

> Being an internationalist can mean nothing other than belonging to the morally and spiritually poor and lacking. ... As what is called internationalism in Germany today is no longer a connection between the German nation and the world, but outright treason, ... nothing other than undermining the national sense of honour, nothing other than the systematic destruction of the national existence of the German people. (DR, 8 June 1929: 425:2220)[1]

The liberals did not really respond to these condemnations. Their representatives spoke cautiously for international cooperation, refrained from defending it or simply denounced internationalism. The German Democrats prioritized national feeling over both chauvinism and communist internationalism (*Vorwärts*, 12 December 1920: 17). Adolf Korell, who had been expelled from the Rhineland by the French authorities, emphasized 'national sense and national allegiance ... in an age of delirious unspiritual internationalism' by which he meant Bolshevism and Entente nationalism taking revenge on Germany (DR, 28 June 1924: 381:436). Within the Catholic Centre Party, 'Christian internationalism' that considered the nation and humankind as a whole might still have found advocates (Heinrich Brauns, *Vorwärts*, 15 June 1921: 2), but Deputy Speaker Johannes Bell was doubtful of 'theoretical pacifism or any internationalism' while still speaking for German involvement 'in the organism of the European whole' (*der europäische Gesamtorganismus*; DR, 20 May 1925: 385:1963) through the League. The Social Democrats remained the only party to speak for internationalism in revisionist terms, prioritizing national work for 'the international liberation of the peoples' over any 'boundless internationalism' (*Vorwärts*, 17 June 1922: 2) of communism. Rudolf Breitscheid hence responded to nationalist attacks by insisting that 'our internationalism is nothing else but the embodiment of national interests on a broader basis' (*Vorwärts*, 28 January 1925: 2) and arguing, as a German delegate to the League: 'We know that through this internationalism the way has gone onwards and upwards and will continue to go onwards and upwards despite the burdens that are placed upon us' (DR, 11 February 1930: 426:3915).

What may surprise in the case of Sweden is the lack of outspoken liberal discourse on internationalism, despite their initially positive stand on the League, and the unwillingness of their conservatives to compromise. The Right Party hence dominated non-socialist discourse, insisting that labour internationalism hardly had a place in an international order based on nationality (*Aftonbladet*, 20 October 1920: 11) and rejecting the 'fad internationalism of social democracy' (*Aftonbladet*, 3 August 1929: 4). The Social Democrats consequently distinguished themselves from communist internationalism, including Nobel Peace Prize winner Hjalmar Branting who was not ready to give up nations in favour of 'cosmopolitan collaboration' (*Dagens Nyheter*, 20 June 1922: 8). Those who developed the ideology of a people's homeland (*folkhemmet*) maintained that working-class internationalism constituted the strongest foundation for 'healthy nationalism' (Arthur Engberg, *Dagens Nyheter*, 13 July 1931: 13). Yet they denounced the way of distinguishing between national and international interests formulated by the Right Party's Foreign Minister Ernst Trygger as 'national egoism' (Olof

Olsson, FK, 15 February 1930: 9:21—22). In Swedish discourse, the Social Democrats profiled themselves as able to reconcile internationalism with nationalism.

In Finland, the Social Democrats were no longer the only advocates of internationalism as ideological confrontations following the civil war led to the construction of competing internationality, if not internationalism. According to two women MPs, the Social Democrats opposed alliances between nationalism and 'international capitalism' (Olga Leinonen, EK, 3 February 1922: 1876) and supported education that strengthened 'the feeling of democracy' and 'the spirit of internationality' (Hilda Seppälä, EK, 6 December 1924: 1503). Socialist theory was seen to imply that the ongoing internationalization and rise of the world economy made class distinctions international, strengthening solidarity across borders and weakening nationalism (*Suomen Sosialidemokraatti*, 7 January 1928: 5; see Chapter 4). Some liberals recognized the Social Democratic transformation from 'international perspectives' to ones 'suitable for a political party in an independent state' (Kaarlo Vuokoski, EK, 17 December 1926: 2078), while others continued to criticize Finnish socialists for being exceptionally ambivalent about nationality (*Helsingin Sanomat*, 24 January 1926: 4). The liberal organ *Helsingin Sanomat* advised the bourgeois parties to support 'international interaction' provided that the advancement of the cause of the nation was ensured, as that only entailed progress (5 August 1923: 2).

The Finnish conservatives not only prioritized the nation state but also allowed right-wing criticisms of internationalism. The National Coalition Party questioned the motives of the Social Democrats, emphasizing 'the national' in the Finnish Constitution as opposed to 'the internationalist, international way of thinking in a social democratic sense' (Kaarlo Kares, EK, 17 December 1926: 2063). 'A patriotic way of thinking and the national principle' were presented as the right foundations of international politics and the Social Democrats were advised to denounce Jewish 'international Marxism' (Johannes, *Uusi Suomi*, 1 August 1931: 2) which was willing to 'destroy national borders and national defence in order to realise an international order through a general violent war' (Juho Vennola, EK, 27 September 1927: 334). The Finnish conservatives were clearly in danger of turning to antisemitism in their antisocialism.

One suggested way to strengthen 'national undercurrents' as opposed to socialist internationalism was that 'the bourgeois world would create an international' of their own (Antisosialisti, *Uusi Suomi*, 28 September 1924: 9; also 19 June 1928: 7). The conservative organ welcomed the growing 'internationalization' of economy, technology and manners as natural development (*Uusi Suomi*, 14 July 1925: 4). It wrote that even if 'internationality [*kansainvälisyys*] does not have in most circles among us any beautiful tone', 'international life' was becoming increasingly interconnected and efficient in terms of economy and technology (*Uusi Suomi*, 21 September 1927: 9). The vernacular *kansainvälisyys*, or 'internationality' in a more technical sense, was easier for the conservatives to approve than the ideologically loaded and foreign *internationalismi*. This may be partly explained by the generally positive sense of the word *kansa* (people/nation), which referred to both national sovereignty and to people's power, and the word combination identifying Finland with civilized (Germanic) nations, thus realizing an old emancipatory Fennoman goal. Rightist leaders believed in 'the principles of modern internationality and international solidarity' within the League as favourable to small nations (Rafael Erich, *Uusi Suomi*, 7 December 1923: 9). In a striking counterpoint to the Lutheran foundation of Finnish national identity, *Uusi Suomi* encouraged the Church of Finland, too, to become more international (29 July 1928: 5). The Fennoman conservatives were overcoming their prejudices towards internationality, welcoming scientific, economic, cultural, political and potentially even confessional internationalization.

## Weak Internationalism Overtaken by Nationalism in the 1930s

In this section we demonstrate the weakness of internationalist discourse in the British and French parliaments after Hitler's accession to power in 1933. National histories were entangled so that transnational perceptions of what was happening in Germany were translated to other contexts; foreign and domestic politics became permeable. There was a general feeling of a crisis, not just of internationalism but also of democracy. Nordic conservatives, by contrast, found themselves between National Socialist Germany and the Soviet Union, and chose to believe in international cooperation as their strategy of national survival.

In Britain, a Labour minority government was replaced by a Conservative one in the early 1930s, which amplified Conservative voices critical of internationalism, particularly as the economy was declining and fascism making progress on the Continent. For a typical Conservative there was no way of forgetting 'a reasonable nationalism in our new internationalism' (John Buchan, HC, 9 May 1932: 1625). After Hitler's rise to power a supporter of Anglo-American cooperation assured the House of Commons that the British government had done more than any other 'to establish the spirit of internationalism' (James Henderson Stewart, National Liberals, HC, 27 April 1933: 366). The generally acknowledged problem was that Germany had 'removed pacifism and internationalism from her vocabulary' and was instead preaching 'the gospel of militarism and war' (Seymour Cocks,

Labour, HC, 13 November 1933: 665). An increasing number of rightists concluded that '[i]n this changing world internationalism is madness' (J. Gibson Jarvie, *The Daily Telegraph*, 17 November 1933: 12). By 1937, Ralph Rayner saw it as 'extremely dangerous to teach pacifism, internationalism, and the brotherhood of man' in schools (HC, 14 June 1937: 112–13). In the days of appeasement, which still counted on legalistic practices in international politics, the Conservatives revived nationalistic, imperialistic, antisocialist and downright anti-internationalist rhetoric. Prime Minister Neville Chamberlain attacked socialism – with an implicit reference to the ongoing Spanish Civil War – as 'always at the mercy of its own extremists and attempting to handle foreign affairs on no other principle than that of a cloudy internationalism', which opened the way to communism and fascism (*The Daily Telegraph*, 29 June 1937: 14). Colonial Secretary Malcolm MacDonald (National Labour) directed British internationalism towards the Empire, speaking for 'a practical internationalism' among 'the free and equal nations of the earth' as a model to others (*The Daily Telegraph*, 24 May 1938: 13). The Empire, or idealistic dreams about it, continued to constitute an alternative to internationalist projects for all British parties, despite obvious challenges to the imperial order.

The French right did not hesitate to declare that 'the international-ists … in France, support German policy' (*Le Temps*, 7 January 1931: 1) and to complain about 'the dangerous follies of internationalism and the indolences of Europeanism' (*Le Temps*, 11 April 1931: 2). For them, given that the Paris Commune (1871) challenged the government during the Franco-German War, 'socialist internationalism is indeed anti-patriotism' (*Le Temps*, 15 April 1931: 1). The radical liberal Herriot wished for under-standing between France and Germany, looking for a compromise in a typically liberal manner: 'No illusory internationalism, but no surly nation-alism either' (*Le Petit Parisien*, 8 November 1931: 2). The socialist Frédéric Brunet drew conclusions that provoked non-socialists: 'We have reached the point where we must choose: we must continue to be closely nationalist or become truly European or more completely internationalist' (CD, 19 November 1931: 3948). During confrontational debates, centrists were likewise critical of 'doctrinaire internationalism' and policies of one-sided disarmament by the socialists 'in the face of nationalist German socialism', condemning associated Marxism as a non-French, German ideology (Jean Autrand, CD, 21 January 1932: 84). On the centre-right, Prime Minister André Tardieu rejected both 'negative nationalism', for denouncing all negotiations, and 'reckless internationalism', for promoting 'firmness' and 'conciliation' (*Le Petit Parisien*, 7 April 1932: 1). After 1933, leftist discourse on internationalism declined. In the words of Jean Montigny, the pacifist general secretary of the Radical Socialists and delegate to the League of Nations, the antagonistic ideologies of 'racism and international-ism, Hitlerism and communism, and, finally, fascism and democracy' were confronting each other in Europe in ways that made the situation worse than in 1913 (CD, 31 July 1936: 2325).

Internationalism had indeed become one of the major scapegoats of the National Socialists. They depicted social democracy which had carried on internationalist discourse in the Reichstag as 'un-German', 'anational', 'anti-national' and 'inter-national' (*Vorwärts*, 14 February 1933: 3). On 30 January 1934, Reichskanzler Adolf Hitler denounced 'the more or less nationally embellished bourgeois democracy', 'the unconcealed Marxist internationalism' and 'parliamentary government' as destructive of the interests of the German nation (DR, 458:8). Internationalism stood in his regime for a Bolshevist and Jewish conspiracy against the nation, the two representing ideological and racial internationalism.

Among Swedish and Finnish conservatives, the rise of dictatorship in Germany and pro-fascist right-wing movements in their own countries led to the emergence of more positive stances towards parliamentary democ-racy as Nordic legacy; dictatorship was defined as antinational (Kurunmäki 2010: 45, 47, 76). Such rethinking also concerned international cooperation: mainstream conservatism recognized the League as a forum for negotiation, counting on its potential to develop into 'a good instrument for international understanding' (Emanuel Björck, AK, 19 February 1936: 10:40). Professor Gösta Bagge, the conservative leader, maintained that Sweden should strive for better international relations through the League despite its obvious weaknesses (AK, 22 May 1937: 34:53); the chairman of his parliamentary group, Fritiof Domö, was more doubtful (FK, 1 June 1938: 40:35−36). In domestic battles, 'the misunderstood internationalism' of socialism was still attacked, particularly once Thorvald Stauning, the Social Democratic Prime Minister of Denmark, had said that 'the national' should be prioritized as 'internationalism does not belong to the values of the day' (*Aftonbladet*, 28 June 1935: 4). *Dagens Nyheter* reported on such debates on international-ism without taking a stand, maintaining liberal ambiguity. In the Riksdag, defences of the League as the only solid organization of the international community were heard (Carl Axel Reuterskiöld, FK, 19 February 1936: 10:2). By 1939, even Social Democrats had tended to lose faith (Östen Undén, FK, 9 June 1939: 39:46−47). All major parties had nevertheless turned international in the sense of sympathizing with the League, despite their disappointment with its achievements.

In Finland, too, the far-right challenge reinforced pragmatic attitudes towards democracy and internationalism among mainstream conservatives:

they distanced themselves from German developments, were unwilling to revive the divisions of the Civil War and counted on the backing of the League under Soviet pressures. When some rightists demanded that the Social Democrats 'leave the paragraphs on the international out of their pro- grammes' or otherwise the party should be banned (Pekka Pennanen, EK, 26 April 1933: 2870), R.A. Wrede of the conservative Swedish People's Party (who had been critical of universal suffrage and parliamentarism in 1918) concluded that internationalism was no crime and that the Finns benefited from international organizations (Hesekiel, *Suomen Sosialidemokraatti*, 16 June 1933: 4); for him, the League giving Åland to Finland rather than Sweden was a case in point. The far right did borrow anti-internationalist discourse from Germany, condemning 'Marxism of Jewish origins' and 'lib- eralism favouring internationalism' (*Helsingin Sanomat*, 9 December 1933: 7). As they insisted that Marxism and internationalism should be stopped like in Germany, a centrist MP shouted: 'No Nazi speeches are needed here!' (K.R. Kares, EK, 8 December 1933: 1520). Far-right conspiracy the- ories, critique of 'the sickly nature of parliamentarism' (Eino Tuomivaara, EK, 13 March 1934: 665; Hilja Riipinen, EK, 22 March 1938: 272; 5 April 1938: 420) and a suggestion that all the other parties were compromisingly 'international' gave rise to hilarity (Reino Ala-Kulju, EK, 13 March 1934: 705). Due to their experiences of pre-independence Russification and fears of Bolshevist internationalism, the Finnish centre-right had become stout supporters of Western international cooperation based on legal norms. This was also increasingly the stand of the Social Democrats who appeared supportive of the nation state, denouncing the 'perverted internationalism' of communism (*Suomen Sosialidemokraatti*, 14 July 1931: 6). Before the Winter War in 1939, they emphasized the connected patriotism and inter- nationalism of their party even more strongly (K.-A. Fagerholm, *Suomen Sosialidemokraatti*, 31 October 1939: 3). The Winter War itself, which the League was unable to prevent, united the two sides of the Civil War in defence of Western civilization.

## Conclusion

We have shown that many British and Scandinavian liberals viewed inter- nationalism optimistically in the aftermath of the First World War but on the condition that international cooperation supported what they considered positive nationalism or patriotism within nation states. Given the strength- ened Bolshevist tone of internationalism the liberals remained cautious about openly advocating it, with the exception of a few British and French demands for 'sane' and 'sincere' internationalism. In Britain, the usual argument for the League was that it enabled the reconciliation of nationalism and internationalism while safeguarding the interests of the Empire.

Typically, non-socialist discourse in all countries studied drew negative associations between internationalism and socialism and by implication with communism, suggesting that internationalism stood for anti-patriotism. Anti-Bolshevism was a common theme in most references to internationalism but its connotations varied depending on the motives of the speakers. Internationalism had established itself as a disputed political concept after the First World War but the interwar period saw its connotations multiply, either returning to the nineteenth-century descriptive language of international cooperation or approaching ideas about a world economy and legally bound international order. Such developments were brought to an end by the rise of Hitler.

In the Nordic countries, a pragmatic non-socialist concept of internationality emerged between the two world wars. Whereas the Swedish Liberals and Social Democrats were stout supporters of League internationalism and the Finnish non-socialists increasingly counted on its legalism, the Swedish right was initially sceptical and the Finnish conservatives typically blamed all socialists of internationalism undermining the nation state. Several factors nevertheless made the Swedish and Finnish conservatives opt for international cooperation as opposed to far-right nationalism: the economic benefits of practical international cooperation, the Soviet threat, the warning example of National Socialist Germany, the legalism of the League that reminded them of national constitutional traditions and the redefinition of democracy as a national legacy all made them distance themselves from anti-internationalism and see potential in 'bourgeois' internationalism instead.

Internationalism was at no stage approved by the French or German right, which did not prevent them from cooperating transnationally to counter Bolshevism without using the concept (Gerwarth and Horne 2012). 'Internationalism' retained its socialist or Marxist tone, much like 'democracy', despite revisionist assurances of social democratic dedication to both internationalism and the *patrie/Vaterland*. Liberals did not defend internationalism in explicit terms: in France they continued to talk derisively about socialist internationalism; in Germany parliamentary discourse on internationalism was dominated by the anti-internationalism of the far right, while the liberals found it increasingly difficult to defend international cooperation or Western democracy after their disappointment with Wilson's promises and the Treaty of Versailles. The rise of National Socialism reinforced conservative doubts about internationalism in Britain and France, while Swedish and Finnish conservatives mainly moved towards majority democracy and League internationalism. Insinuations of subversive socialist internationalism were not entirely rejected despite the revisionist parties consistently emphasizing their denouncement of communism and their dedication to the nation states. National Socialist discourses were imitated by the far right, but for the mainstream conservatives economic, political and even cultural internationalism turned into a survival strategy for Nordic democracy between communism and National Socialism.

**Pasi Ihalainen** is Academy of Finland Professor at the Department of History and Ethnology, University of Jyväskylä, and has previously worked as a visiting professor at the universities of Freiburg, Gothenburg, Leiden and Uppsala. He has published widely on the history of political discourse and the conceptual history of nationalism, democracy and parliamentarism since the eighteenth century, applying comparative and transnational perspectives. ORCID 0000-0002-5468-4829.

**Jörn Leonhard** is Full Professor in Modern European History at the History Department of Freiburg University. From 2007 to 2012, he was one of the Founding Directors of the School of History of the Freiburg Institute for Advanced Studies. In 2015, he was elected as a member of the Heidelberg Academy of Sciences. ORCID 0000-0002-7213-1611.

## Note

1. 'Wir meinen, daß dann Internationalist sein nichts anderes heißen kann, als zu den moralisch und geistig Minderbemittelten und Enterbten zu gehören. (Sehr wahr! bei den Nationalsozialisten.) Denn was heute in Deutschland unter der Marke Internationalismus umgeht, ist nicht mehr eine Inbeziehungsetzung der Deutschen Nation zur Welt, sondern glatter Landesverrat, (sehr wahr! bei den Nationalsozialisten) ist nichts anderes als Unterhöhlung des nationalen Ehrbewußtseins, nichts anderes als systematische Vernichtung der nationalen Existenzen des deutschen Volkes.'

## References

### *Primary Sources*

Databases

Hansard Corpus: House of Commons (HC) and House of Lords (HL), available at https://hansard-corpus.org.

Journal officiel de la République française. Débats parlementaires, Chambre des députés (CD), available at https://gallica.bnf.fr.

Riksdagstryck, Riksdagsprotokoll, Andra Kammaren/Första Kammaren (AK/FK), available at https://riksdagstryck.kb.se/tvakammarriksdagen.html.

Valtiopäiväasiakirjat, Eduskunnan pöytäkirjat (EK), available at https://avoindata. eduskunta.fi/#/fi/digitoidut/.

Verhandlungen des Deutschen Reichstags (Nationalversammlung 1919/DR), available at https://www.reichstagsprotokolle.de/.

Newspapers
Aftonbladet
Chicago Tribune
Dagens Nyheter
The Daily Telegraph
Helsingin Sanomat
The Manchester Guardian
The New Republic
Le Petit Parisien
Suomen Sosialidemokraatti
Le Temps
The Times
Uusi Suomi
Vorwärts

Writings and Speeches
Barbusse, H. 1920. *La lueur dans l'abîme*. Paris: Clarté.

Bebel, A. [1879] 1883. *Die Frau in der Vergangenheit, Gegenwart und Zukunft*. Hottingen-Zürich: Schweizerische Volksbuchhandlung.

Hervé, G. 1910. *L'internationalisme*. Paris: V. Giard & E. Briére.

Hitler, A. 1939 [1925]. *Mein Kampf: Jubiläumsausgabe*. Munich: Zentralverlag der NSDAP.

Hobart, R. 1867. 'The "Mission" of Richard Cobden', *Macmillan's Magazine*, January 1867: 38–39.

Hobson, J.A. 1905. *Imperialism: A Study*. London: George Allen & Unwin.

Joël, E. 1916. 'Kameradschaft', in K. Hiller (ed.), *Das Ziel: Aufrufe zu tätigem Geist*. Munich: Müller.

Keynes, J.M. [1919] 1971. 'The Economic Consequences of the Peace', in *The Collected Writings of John Maynard Keynes*, vol. 2. London: Macmillan.

Lenin, W.I. [1917] 1974. 'Die Aufgaben des Proletariats in unserer Revolution', in *Werke*, vol. 24. East Berlin: Dietz.

Liebknecht, K. [1918] 1968. 'Nach altem Klischee', in H. Schumacher et al. (eds), *Gesammelte Reden und Schriften*, vol. 9. East Berlin: Dietz.

Naumann, F. 1906. *Demokratie und Kaisertum*. Berlin: Hilfe.

Siebarth, W. 1935. *Hitlers Wollen: Nach Kernsätzen aus seinen Schriften und Reden*. Munich: Zentralverlag der NSDAP.

Stampfer, F. 1957. *Erfahrungen und Erkenntnisse: Aufzeichnungen aus meinem Leben*. Cologne: Verlag für Politik und Wirtschaft.

Trojanowski, A. 1916. *Brauchen wir eine Internationale?* Zurich: Grütliverein.

## Secondary Sources

Berg, M. 2017. *Woodrow Wilson: Amerika und die Neuordnung der Welt*. Munich: C. H. Beck.

Braun, H. 1992. 'Welt', in O. Brunner, W. Conze and R. Koselleck (eds), *Geschichtliche Grundbegriffe: Historisches Lexikon zur politisch-sozialen Sprache in Deutschland*, vol. 7. Stuttgart: Klett-Cotta, pp. 433–510.

Carr, E.H. 2001. *The Twenty Years' Crisis, 1919–1939: An Introduction to the Study of International Relations*. Basingstoke: Palgrave Macmillan.

Conway, M. 1997. *Catholic Politics in Europe 1918–1945*. London: Routledge.

Eley, G. 2002. *Forging Democracy: The History of the Left in Europe*. Oxford: Oxford University Press.

Friedemann, P. and L. Hölscher. 1995. 'Internationale, International, Internationalismus', in O. Brunner, W. Conze and R. Koselleck (eds), *Geschichtliche Grundbegriffe: Historisches Lexikon zur politisch-sozialen Sprache in Deutschland*, vol. 3. Stuttgart: Klett-Cotta, pp. 367–97.

Gerwarth, R. and J. Horne. 2012. *War in Peace: Paramilitary Violence in Europe after the Great War*. Oxford: Oxford University Press.

Gibelli, A. 2010. 'Italy', in J. Horne (ed.), *A Companion to World War I*. Malden: Wiley-Blackwell, pp. 464–78.

Groh, D. and R. Walther. 1995. 'Imperialismus', in O. Brunner, W. Conze and R. Koselleck (eds), *Geschichtliche Grundbegriffe: Historisches Lexikon zur politisch-sozialen Sprache in Deutschland*, vol. 3. Stuttgart: Klett-Cotta, pp. 171–236.

Harrington, A. 2016. *German Cosmopolitan Social Thought and the Idea of the West: Voices from Weimar*. Cambridge: Cambridge University Press.

Henig, R. 1995. *Versailles and After 1919–1933*, 2nd edn. London: Routledge.

Holbraad, C. 2003. *Internationalism and Nationalism in European Political Thought*. New York: Palgrave Macmillan.

Holmila, A. and P. Ihalainen. 2018. 'Nationalism and Internationalism Reconciled: Visions for a New World Order after the First World War Versus History Politics during and after the Second World War', *Contributions to the History of Concepts* 13(2): 25–53.

Ihalainen, P. 2017. *The Springs of Democracy: National and Transnational Debates on Constitutional Reform in the British, German, Swedish and Finnish Parliaments, 1917–1919*. Helsinki: Finnish Literature Society.

———. 2019a. 'Internationalization and Democratization Interconnected: The Swedish and Finnish Parliaments Debating Membership in the League of Nations', *Parliaments, Estates and Representation* 39(1): 11–31.

———. 2019b. 'The Fragility of Finnish Parliamentary Democracy at the Moment when Prussianism Fell', *Journal of Modern European History* 17(4): 448–68.

Ihalainen, P. and A. Sahala. 2020. 'Evolving Conceptualisations of Internationalism in the UK Parliament: Collocation Analyses from the League to Brexit', in P. Paju,

M. Oiva and M. Fridlund (eds), *Digital Histories: Emergent Approaches within the New Digital History*. Helsinki: Helsinki University Press, pp. 199–219.

Jonas, M. 2019. *Scandinavia and the Great Powers in the First World War*. London: Bloomsbury Academic.

Jörke, D. and M. Llanque. 2016. 'Parliamentarism and Democracy in German Political Theory since 1848', in P. Ihalainen, C. Ilie and K. Palonen (eds), *Parliament and Parliamentarism: A Comparative History of a European Concept*. New York: Berghahn, pp. 262–76.

Kaiser, W. 2007. *Christian Democracy and the Origins of European Union*. Cambridge: Cambridge University Press.

Knock, T.J. 1992. *To End All Wars: Woodrow Wilson and the Quest for a New World Order*. Oxford: Oxford University Press.

Koselleck, R. 1992. 'Volk, Nation, Nationalismus, Masse', in O. Brunner, W. Conze and R. Koselleck (eds), *Geschichtliche Grundbegriffe: Historisches Lexikon zur politisch-sozialen Sprache in Deutschland*, vol. 7. Stuttgart: Klett-Cotta, pp. 141–431.

Kurunmäki, J. 2010. '"Nordic Democracy" in 1935: On the Finnish and Swedish Rhetoric of Democracy', in J. Kurunmäki and J. Strang (eds), *Rhetorics of Nordic Democracy*. Helsinki: Finnish Literature Society, pp. 37–82.

Leonhard, J. 2018a. 'Another "Sonderweg"? The Historical Semantics of "Democracy" in Germany', in J. Kurunmäki, J. Nevers and H. te Velde (eds), *Democracy in Modern Europe: A Conceptual History*. New York: Berghahn, pp. 65–87.

———. 2018b. *Pandora's Box: A History of the First World War*. Cambridge: Belknap Press.

———. 2019. *Der überforderte Frieden: Versailles und die Welt*. Munich: C. H. Beck.

Manela, E. 2007. *The Wilsonian Moment: Self Determination and the International Origins of Anti-Colonial Nationalism*. Oxford: Oxford University Press.

McCarthy, H. 2011. *The British People and the League of Nations: Democracy, Citizenship and Internationalism, c. 1918–45*. Manchester: Manchester University Press.

Mazower, M. 1998. *Dark Continent: Europe's Twentieth Century*. New York: Vintage.

———. 2013. *Governing the World: The History of an Idea, 1815 to the Present*. New York: Penguin.

Mouton, M.-R. 1995. *La Société des Nations et les intérêts de la France (1920–1924)*. Bern: Peter Lang.

Neck, R. (ed.). 1968. *Österreich im Jahre 1918: Berichte und Dokumente*. Vienna: Verlag für Geschichte und Politik.

Parson, G. 2007. *Conservative Visions and Political Change in Germany and Great Britain after the First World War, 1918–1924*. PhD dissertation. Rochester: University of Rochester.

Passman, E. 2009. *The Cultivation of Friendship: French and German Cultural Cooperation, 1925–1954*. PhD dissertation. Chapel Hill: University of North Carolina.

Pugh, M.C. 2012. *Liberal Internationalism: The Interwar Movement for Peace in Britain*. New York: Palgrave Macmillan.

Sluga, G. 2013. *Internationalism in the Age of Nationalism*. Philadelphia: University of Pennsylvania Press.

Sluga, G. and P. Clavin. 2017. 'Rethinking the History of Internationalism', in P. Clavin and G. Sluga (eds), *Internationalisms: A Twentieth Century History*. Cambridge: Cambridge University Press, pp. 3–14.

Steigerwald, D. 1994. *Wilsonian Idealism in America*. Ithaca: Cornell University Press.

Steinmetz, W. and M. Freeden. 2017. 'Introduction: Conceptual History: Challenges, Conundrums, Complexities', in W. Steinmetz, M. Freeden and J. Fernández-Sebastián (eds), *Conceptual History in the European Space*. New York: Berghahn, pp. 1–46.

Sylvest, C. 2009. *British Liberal Internationalism, 1880–1930: Making Progress?* Manchester: Manchester University Press.

Trentmann, F. 2009. *Free Trade Nation: Commerce, Consumption, and Civil Society in Modern Britain*. Oxford: Oxford University Press.

Wintzer, J. 2006. *Deutschland und der Völkerbund 1918–1926*. Paderborn: Schöningh.

Yearwood, P.J. 2009. *Guarantee of Peace: The League of Nations in British Policy 1914–1925*. Oxford: Oxford University Press.

# Chapter 7

# Securing Peace by Trade?

## The 'World Economy' and International Organization

*Hagen Schulz-Forberg*

⬥

> The case of the world economy demonstrates very impressively that good
> order on the national level is required to assure working order also on the
> international level.
>
> —Wilhelm Röpke, *International Order and Economic Integration*

From a semasiological perspective, the concept of the 'world economy' is
astonishingly young. It is not mentioned literally until the nineteenth century
although there clearly is an older onomasiology of the world economy. When
it began to appear more frequently after the Napoleonic Wars, particularly in German as *Weltwirtschaft*, it was used by liberal economists. While
Karl Marx obsessively collected information about all things economic in
all parts of the world in the mid-nineteenth century, he did not comment
on it. On the opposite pole to Marx's work, in Adam Smith's *The Wealth
of Nations* (1776), the world economy is just as absent. Smith's and David
Ricardo's work did have an important influence on the semantics of the
world economy, however. In particular, Smith's boundless conception of
market relations both inspired liberal economists across Europe and aroused
fears about possible obstacles to the state's control over its territory via
national legal frameworks, causing Johann Gottlieb Fichte to write about *Der
geschlossene Handelsstaat* (the closed trading state) as early as 1800. Fichte
rigorously argued in relation to his conception of the state as a 'community
of free and reasonable beings' and believed freedom and autonomy could
be undermined by economic dynamics. While his intervention caused some
reaction in German (pushing Ludwig Hestermann to publish *Der offene*

*Handelsstaat* [the open trading state] in 1802), it remained very much a local German affair until Fichte's work received closer attention between the 1900s and 1930s and then again during the 1970s (Hoffmann 2018).

The liberal currency of the 'world economy' is revealed by a look at its semantic field, which includes first and foremost free trade as a guarantor of peace and thus security. The world economy was conceptualized as a progressive force creating ever-greater riches and ever-tighter relations, which would take war off the agenda for nation states. And while Marx might not have contested the concept directly, liberal authors throughout depicted Marxism, collectivism and socialism as a threat to the world economy based on free trade and private property that were identified as a necessary condition for a peaceful arrangement of the world.

Sparsely mentioned in the early decades of the nineteenth century, the concept of the world economy became more widely used before the First World War, again particularly in German. The frequency of usage increased significantly in the 1920s and 1930s in English and French, too. In the interwar period, the world economy was perceived to be in crisis and in need of reanimation. After the Second World War, usage of the term decreased and then rose again in the 1960s. By the 1980s, 'global economy' soars in usage and 'world economy' plummets.

The 'world economy' saw two periods of steep increase in usage, from the 1920s to the 1940s and from the 1960s to the 1980s. It is certainly not a coincidence that Fichte's reflections on the closed trading state were discussed more intensely in these decades, too. Semantically, the 'world economy' took shape in the nineteenth century. It became more nuanced during the interwar period, before a further semantic shift went hand in hand with a terminological shift and 'global economy' became the hegemonic term in English. Perhaps most importantly, the world economy was politicized in the twentieth century within both national and transnational forums of

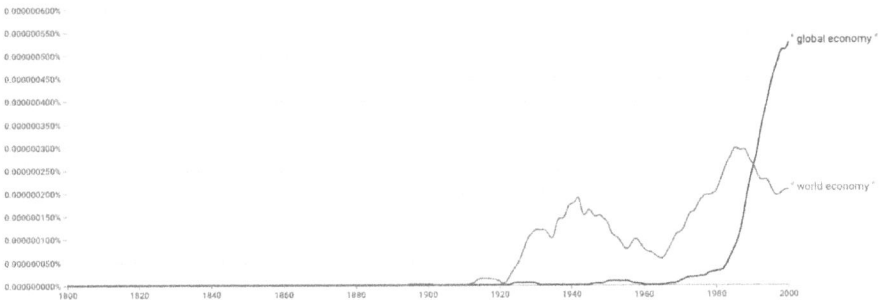

**Figure 7.1** Ngram viewer search for 'world economy' and 'global economy', 1700–2000 (https://books.google.com/ngrams).

communication. Identified as crucial for social and political peace, the form and function of the economy – nationally and globally – became a matter of central political importance.

In this chapter, I illustrate the history of the concept through its English, French and German usage by following transnational and national formations of the world economy. The first part describes its emergence as a concept and its early meaning until the First World War, highlighting the development of *Weltwirtschaft* in German publications in the *Weltwirtschaftliches Archiv* since 1913. The second part looks at the 1920s and 1930s, more specifically publications by the League of Nations and the Bank for International Settlements (BIS, the world's first transnational financial institution founded in 1930); the *Economist*; and key economic journals published in English and French, *Economica* and *Révue d'économie politique*. Leading economists and League experts published there, translated and reviewed each other. Together, they formed an important network for the exchange of ideas, shaping the meaning of the world economy both on the transnational and the national level. Building on these two parts, a concluding reflection discusses the rise of the concept and change in its semantics after the Second World War.

Independent of national languages and traditions in economic thought, economists across Europe mostly agreed on how to define the world economy. It was a modular construction, made up of nation states. The economy within nation states was conceptualized as based on private contractors with the state playing a limited (if any) role as an economic actor. The national level was configured as the recognized political economic space within which markets were conceptualized as freely as possible while developing national idiosyncrasies rooted in each specific national legal framework. Single political economies then became individual contractors on the level of the world economy, and, ideally, conducive to its proper functioning. This interdependent construction of the world economy was seen as necessary for peaceful and prosperous relations within and between countries. Threats to this seemingly fragile international order could easily be depicted, mostly in forms of socialism and economic nationalism. In the absence of a world state, national and international security and peace needed a world economy, as liberals had argued since the nineteenth century.

## The 'World Economy' until 1914

Figure 7.1 (above) displays the concept's use in English. When the search is broadened to German and French, Google's Ngram Viewer reveals similar results between the 1920s and 1980s. In French, économie *mondiale* took off to a very limited degree in the early twentieth century and then grew just as fast and steeply as in English from the 1920s to the mid-1940s. It then fell in usage frequency like its English sibling. Unlike 'world economy' (in English), however, *économie mondiale* kept rising in French usage from the mid-1970s until 2000. It was not superseded by *économie globale* – a phrase that has been used in French since the 1940s, yet not to the same degree as *mondiale*. Here, the fact that what is called globalization in a number of European languages (e.g. German *Globalisierung*, Italian *globalizzazione*, Spanish *globalizaciòn*, Danish *globalisering* and Polish *globalizacija*) is predominantly called *mondialisation* in French may explain the persistent use of 'world' instead of 'global' in French.

In German, *Weltwirtschaft* was used more widely as a concept slightly earlier than in English and French. After the Cold War, *Weltwirtschaft* did not fall in usage as steeply as its English sibling. Again, the reason may be found in the specific linguistic context. *Weltwirtschaft* was established in German and while the usage of *Globalwirtschaft* (global economy) has increased since the 1980s, *Weltwirtschaft* remained the dominant term. In addition to the deeper semantic roots of *Weltwirtschaft* in German, the policy of *Globalsteuerung* (global steering) had already given a certain meaning to the prefix 'global' since the late 1960s, focusing on the demand side of the economy.

In German, the concept was established earlier than in French or English, as evidenced by the foundation of the Kiel-based Institute for the World Economy (*Institut für Weltwirtschaft*) in 1914 (preceded by three years as a department of the city's Christian Albrecht University). The first theories of *Weltwirtschaft* appeared in the 1820s. Karl Heinrich Rau used *Weltwirtschaft* in his 1826 handbook on political economy, *Grundsätze der Volkswirthschaftslehre* (as well as in reprints in 1833, 1837, 1841 and 1847).

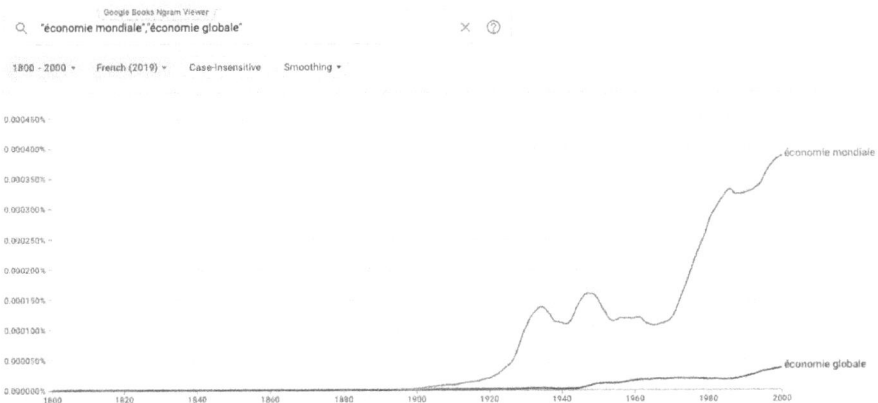

**Figure 7.2** Ngram viewer search for *économie mondiale* and *économie globale* in French, 1800–2000 (https://books.google.com/ngrams).

He introduced a fundamental definition of agents in the world economy: only 'educated peoples', the 'civilized' could be such. For him, the world economy was the geographically aggrandized version of the national political economy (*Volkswirtschaft*, see Rau 1825). Claiming that the economy transcended national boundaries, Rau argued that the notion of a world economy was 'not inadmissible', but one might be able to deduce its laws from the national political economy (Rau 1847: 18). Eduard Baumstark pointed out the interdependence of *Volks-* and *Weltwirtschaft*. The 'term *Volkswirthschaft* was', he reasoned, 'thoroughly defended by Rau, which simultaneously clarified its relation to the idea of a world economy' (Baumstark 1835: 86).

*Volkswirtschaft* emerged particularly in the writings of Rau and in the translation of Ricardo. When the latter's *On the Principles of Political Economy and Taxation* (1817) was published in German as *Grundgesetze der Volkswirthschaft und der Besteuerung* (1837), Eduard Baumstark provided the translation, based heavily on the French translation of Ricardo's work by Jean-Baptiste Say (Tribe 2017).

As a scientific discipline, political economy grew out of cameralism with its particular mix of economics, policy-making and state administration (Nokkala and Miller 2019). The term 'political economy' was being used by the late eighteenth century: in 1791 Alexander Hamilton used it in his function as finance minister of the newly independent United States of America, and in 1805, Thomas Malthus was endowed with the very first chair in political economy, at the East India Company headquarters in Hertfordshire. In France, Say popularized the concept of political economy, not only through his famous letters to Malthus, but also through his very accessible *Catéchisme d'économie politique* (1815), which became the first European business school textbook in economics and was widely translated. Born during the Enlightenment, political economy was essentially about statecraft and incorporated other economic forms, such as private or local economies.

'World economy' developed in interdependence with 'political economy' (with its variations and translations). The early version of the concept – proclaiming that single political economic entities were its constituents just like individual economic actors were the constituents of political economies – is found throughout Europe in the nineteenth and early twentieth centuries. Importantly, political economies were not only related, but interdependent. This dependency was enshrined in treaties and thus rooted in international law. The world economy was a construction based on the contracts binding political economies to each other. As the co-founder of the *Verein für Socialpolitik*, Gustav Schmoller, wrote: 'The sum of those contemporary political economies that touch and have grown mutually dependent is what we call the world economy' (Schmoller 1900: 21). A self-declared liberal, Schmoller still faced a lot of criticism by his contemporaries, particularly those who thought he betrayed Manchester liberalism and the work and ideas of Adam Smith. He and his colleagues in the historical school of economics were stigmatized as 'socialists of the chair' (*Kathedersozialist*, Oppenheim 1872; Ashley 2018). Despite his pioneering of state interventions and social welfare measures – which were an ethical necessity for him – he remained a liberal at heart, and did not question the free market as a core concept of political economies co-constructing the world economy (Taussig 1905; Backhaus 1993; Balabkins 1993; Peukert 2001; Magnusson 2004). Schmoller saw the world economy ushering in historical change: 'Ever since, a new epoch has begun: the world economy interferes ever more forcefully with the single political economies; the long-existing tendencies toward world economic dominance and colonial acquisition create a number of world empires much larger than the hitherto prevalent nation states' (Schmoller 1900: 315).

This world economy was not only encroaching on the economic leverage of individual countries, it was also based on a division of labour within nation states, wrote Schmoller (1900: 353). But national economies were here to stay. It would be wrong to assume, Karl Bücher reasoned in 1893, that the world economy would simply absorb them and that political economies would be superseded and overcome to morph into one single economy. This view prevailed across Europe. As early as 1893 Schmoller reasoned about the dependence of national political economies on the world economy. Yet, it was the interplay between political economies that made the world economy (Bücher 1893: 89); their design was of utmost importance. The advent of a new constitution of economic relations – the age of the world economy – was shared in French as well when the *Journal des économistes* claimed that one would not need to be a prophet to believe 'in the imminent advent of a world economy' (1896: 202).

In 1906, Ernst von Halle began the annual publication of the three-volume series, *Die Weltwirtschaft*, through to 1908. In it, he divided the world economy into an international overview, the various parts of German industry, and *Das Ausland* (foreign countries). Germany's involvement in the world economy was closely connected to its economic rise and place among colonial powers associated with such economic prowess. Beginning in 1910, Bernhard Harms, the first director of the Kiel institute, began publishing the series *Probleme der Weltwirtschaft* (Issues of the World Economy). In 1913, the academic journal *Weltwirtschaftliches Archiv* initiated its remarkable output under the editorship of Harms. Furthermore, books like Richard Calwer's *Jahrbuch der Weltwirtschaft* (1903–1912) and Sigmund Schilder's

*Entwicklungstendenzen der Weltwirtschaft* (1912) show the increase in usage of the concept. By then, for liberals at least, the world economy was well developed; proposals that were not based on free trade were seen as outliers. While the social democrat, Eduard Bernstein, believed that there was no alternative to adapting national economies to the world market, he also proposed to overcome the tension between free trade and tariff walls simply by abandoning both (Bernstein 1911: 430).

Schilder pointed out that utopian 'fantasies' of the world economy were most unlikely in their Marxist-socialist form, as proposed by Bernstein. Further 'fantasies', according to Schilder, were what he labelled 'world empire fantasies' built on ever-expanding customs unions, 'social liberal fantasies' about co-operatives of global scope that foregrounded the labour market, and fantasies of a future in which 'steerable airplanes' would rule the world (Schilder 1912: 223–39). Countering these few contemporary alternative perspectives on the 'world economy' and the much older discussion of the tensions between the national and the international in Fichte's *Der geschlossene Handelsstaat* (1800), Schilder maintained that free trade was not a fantasy but had become accepted as the basis of the world economy. Gustav Schmoller most poignantly wrote in 1900: 'Out of national economy, the world economy developed most recently, which finds its ideal in world peace and in the victory of free trade' (Schmoller 1900: 371).

In the 1910s, Harms not only defined the term in all its breadth but also explored how to teach about the world economy. Following his book on *Volkswirtschaft und Weltwirtschaft* (1912), from 1913 the journal *Weltwirtschaftliches Archiv* became a focal point of discussion, publishing an impressive quantity of articles annually, its authors including leading European economists from John Maynard Keynes to Friedrich von Hayek, Luigi Einaudi and Wilhelm Röpke.

Harms's opening article for *Weltwirtschaftliches Archiv* was a critique of existing liberal approaches, which he judged to be either too assumption-heavy, as in older liberalism, or without theoretical foundation, as for Schmoller and others in the historical school. Older liberalism, Harms insisted, assumed that political economies dissolved increasingly and simultaneously engaged in the construction of one single economy and a world state to run it. If this could not be achieved, at least free world trade without any tariffs would be established. Harms argued that such a simplistic conceptualization of the world economy – the achievement of peace through free trade – was the fundamental error of nineteenth-century liberals.

For Harms, the world economy was not an abstract idea of future becoming. It was very tangible. Based on intensifying economic relations, interdependence and diversification would increase, he reasoned. At the same time, the world economy did not just unfold on its own, but was shaped by contract-based relations. It was an intergovernmental creation heavily dependent on transport routes and costs. Up until the First World War, global commodity exchanges had grown in an unprecedented manner and political economies had become complex, related entities. Harms maintained that single economic units defined the political economy of a given country through their relations with each other and the state. The latter defined the room for manoeuvre for economic actors through laws, currency exchange rates and taxation policies. The agency of the state made the economy 'political', creating specific complexities within its confines that Harms saw as national economic systems. These systems were mutually dependent (Harms 1913: 10).

One key observation Harms made was based on his discussion of the semantics of *Volkswirtschaft*. *Volk* sounded close to *völkisch*, he conceded, a term related to the ethnicity-based concept of *Kulturnation* that defined the nation by common language and culture. To Harms, however, *Volk* simply described the citizens living in a state. It was neither a cultural disclaimer nor an ethnic one. Criticizing Schmoller for his racist undertones and his exclusive, culture-based description of *Volkswirtschaft* ('Men of the same race and the same language, bound together by uniform feelings and ideas, mores and legal rules', Schmoller 1901: 21), he maintained that a shared language or ethnicity was not what made *Volk* for economics; at least it should not: 'The world economy is the inclusive notion of all relations and their reciprocities that exist between the earth's single economies and are regulated and promoted by a highly developed transport system and international contracts' (Harms 1913: 14).

Economics, Harms claimed, needed to be law-bound, based on rules and policies originating at state level. Where the national political economy was based on the laws of a particular state, the world economy was based on the treaties between states. On balance, all states in some way had a treaty with all states, he pointed out. Political economy in any state was at the same time world economy (Harms 1913: 13).

For Harms, the theoretical source for such a world economy was the *homo oeconomicus*. He called his theory *reine Ökonomik* (pure economics). The pure essence from which all theory derived was captured by two simple traits of what he did not hesitate to call human nature: 1) to reach the fulfilment of desires, human beings choose the path of least resistance; and 2) private property constitutes an eternal human social institution (Harms 1913: 18–19).

While Harms set his theoretical marks, the concept of the world economy was already present in international circles of experts and policy makers, as was the shared notion that it required close attention. The practice of gathering international expertise to tackle a common, more global problem had its origins before the First World War; the Carnegie Endowment for International Peace began its work in 1910 with the economic section holding its first conference in Berne from 2 to 15 August 1911. Gathering leading economists from a string of countries (including Eugen von Böhm-Bawerk, Lujo Brentano, Charles Gide, Leonard Trelawny Hobhouse, Alfred Marshall and Gustav Schmoller) as well as the editor of the *Economist* at the time, Francis Hirst, the conference inaugurated a vast agenda for research into the economy's relation to war and peace.

At the time of the conference, the old liberal assumption that trade inherently had peaceful effects needed careful scrutiny. Does protectionism really lead to war? What is the effect of territorial annexations on the economic development of both the annexed and the annexing parties? In particular, what is the effect of annexation on what was then called 'semi-civilized' or 'entirely savage' countries? What is the effect of the workers' movement? And of the women's movement? These questions were fleshed out by the invited economists and sparked research for decades to come. The whole complexity of world affairs was on the table and the world economy appeared as a possible source of both peace and war, calling for the right political arrangements. The tensions emerging from power hierarchies within the world economy were also on the agenda and the mere theoretical assumption of equal relations based on law superseded. As one of the participants summed it up: 'World economic development was accomplished mostly because of capital investment of rich countries into less developed countries. ... The commission estimates that it would be useful to conduct precise research into the emerging mutual dependencies that this state of affairs created among different countries' (Gide 1911: 559).

## The 'World Economy' in the Interwar Period

Even before the First World War, the perspective on the economy had partially changed: it needed political handling and not only legal framing and it had possibly unsettling, even violent consequences. Designing a world economy that sustained a peaceful world order was increasingly on the agenda after 1918. By the time the Great Depression hit European economies, the concept of the world economy had come even more into focus and the economic disciplines built for it were business cycle analysis and macroeconomics (Schulz-Forberg 2019; Clavin 2013). The economic crisis took visible shape in graphs, lists of countries, rows of data, and tables of prices, values and commodities. The first significant study of the crisis was Bertil Ohlin's report to the League of Nations, *The Course and Phases of the World Economic Depression* (1931). Ohlin and his colleagues (among them the Cold War neoliberal lodestar, Friedrich von Hayek and the Italian fascist, Corrado Gini) tackled the difficult task of analysing and illustrating an unprecedented world economic crisis.

Throughout the 1930s the League used its expert network across the member states and its internal Economic Intelligence Service to publish the *World Economic Survey*. The survey was among the most important publications on the status of the world economy, describing it, analysing it, trying to save it – and firmly establishing the concept along the way. The League showed great concern for the world economy, as it had become clear that peace was not simply a spillover effect of trade. Growth and secure trade routes across the globe were still conceived as a backbone of world peace, as was the conscious organization of political economies and colonial relations (Clavin 2013; Pedersen 2015: 233–60). To flesh out such conditions and pin down the rules of the game, a first economic conference was organized in Geneva in 1927, then still officially called the International Economic Conference in English (and *Conférence Économique Internationale* in French, yet *Weltwirtschaftskonferenz* in German), even though commentaries and publications sometimes called it the World Economic Conference (e.g. Runciman 1927). By the time the next conference took place six years later, 'world economy' was used throughout. At the 1933 World Economic Conference, national interest dominated and a return to the gold standard could not be agreed upon.

The Bank for International Settlements (BIS), an outcome of the Young Plan, played an important role in the decades to come as a bridge-building and reconstructing institution after the Second World War. The annual reports of the BIS are evidence for the legacy of the 1933 conference, which was continuously referenced as a watershed. Yet, 'world economy' as such was used only sparsely in the BIS reports. While the term 'world' increased steeply in frequency through the 1930s (appearing only twice in the first 1931 report), attached to 'trade', 'export', 'supply' and 'demand', 'world economy' appeared for the first time in the 1936 report: 'The past seven years have constituted one of the most disturbed periods through which the world economy has ever passed in times of peace' (BIS 1936: 10).

The League of Nations applied the concept of the world economy to seek global solutions. 'Securing the world economy', as Patricia Clavin illustrated, was among the core tasks of the first world organization (Clavin 2013). The League itself was an active promoter of the concept as were research and policy-making institutions and publishing outlets, such as the *Economist*, that were devoted to an internationalist perspective on world affairs. Here, the 'world economy' featured not as an ideal market or as stable relations between legal actors and countries, but as a space characterized by tensions and hierarchies, particularly between 'agricultural' and 'industrial' countries (e.g. *The Economist*, 28 May 1927: 18). In the context of conceptualizing Eastern European economic and social history, this relationship between agriculture and industry came to illustrate the relationship between developed and developing, or backward and advanced economies (Manoilescu 1929; Boilard and Friis 2022). Within the world economy, this difference was part of Europe's imperial heritage, a form of economic inequality established during the nineteenth century. As the *World Economic Survey* registered: 'The agricultural countries of the world, particularly those more remote from Europe, though equally bound up in the world economy, do not always share the economic changes that are apparent in the industrial countries. At best there is a long time-lag before such changes are fully registered' (Condliffe 1933: 26).

Wilhelm Röpke was among the emerging experts in macroeconomics recruited by the League to work on the relation between agriculture-based and industrialized economies (Röpke 1936, 1942). His study for the League was published during the war and inspired his better-known book on *Internationale Ordnung* (1944, English translation as *International Order and Economic Integration*, 1959). In it, the concept of the world economy took centre stage. Originating from the central power source of European empires, particularly the British Empire, it had existed for centuries (in the sense of onomasiology) despite the absence of a world state. A substitute system had been established, according to Röpke, who conceived of it as a secular version of the *res publica Christiana*, an unwritten *ordre public international*. This unwritten regime with which all so-called 'civilized' states complied had five discernible features: 1) interdependence and communication; 2) multilateralism; 3) a global payments community; 4) the free trade area of the British Empire as its nucleus; and 5) a system of basic freedom regarding the movement of goods, capital and people (Röpke 1959 [1944]: 155–58). Röpke mourned the unquestioned existence of such world economic practice based on imperial relations and agreements. The contractors had lost their moral compass, he thought, and economic interdependence was now problematic instead of promising. He contended that the world economy had to be reorganized and defended more outspokenly.

Further reflections on the condition and concept of the world economy were sparked by the rise in protectionist measures. In particular, Britain's turn to imperial preference, manifested by the 1932 Ottawa Agreement, was cause for much gloom among European economists and internationalists (Bourquin 1936). In the face of multiple political, military and economic crises and the Great Depression as well as protectionist policies by former free traders, the concept of the world economy was increasingly and intensely discussed, to unprecedented levels by 1939. Between 1911 and 1939, 'world economy' is mentioned in the *Economist* eighty-five times (issues available in its web archive). In the 1910s it is mentioned first, but only once in a 1916 book review; in the 1920s six times, mostly in book reviews; and in the 1930s seventy-eight times with a focus on the depression, the turn to policies of imperial preference, the 1932 Lausanne conference where Germany's reparation payments and contribution to 'reconstructing the world economy' were discussed, the rise to power of Adolf Hitler and the National Socialists – and the economic consequences – and of course the 1933 conference.

The *Economist* followed the conference closely; its articles reveal that, also in the eyes of political and economic actors, the world economy was a matter of construction, not a given. The newspaper reflected on the role and immense economic power of the British Empire at the time:

> In the belief that British policy may yet save the world economy from falling to pieces we should say to Europe that, since we regard the maintenance of stability in the gold countries [France, Holland, Belgium, Switzerland and Italy supported the gold standard at the conference, HSF] as of the greatest importance, we will do all we can to prevent speculation and to avoid embarrassing them by movements of the pound. (*The Economist*, 1 July 1933: 4)

In an analysis of Condliffe's second *World Economic Survey* (1933), the *Economist* again pondered the state of the world economy and summarized its significance quite well by calling for the renewal of a common effort at managing currencies, commodity markets and, most importantly, sustainable organization and cooperation among countries. The world economy had to be co-constructed by allowing trade to unfold or else it would be perilous for its participants:

> What remains to be emphasized is the moral of the whole survey: that different ad hoc remedies and solutions in various departments of the world economy may coincide to produce general amelioration, but that no lasting improvement can be expected in any nation until the shackles upon international trade are loosened, and until the insane anarchy of *sauve qui peut* gives place to sane co-operation, ensuring economic safety for all. (*The Economist*, 14 October 1933: 705)

The leading French economic journal, the *Révue d'économie politique*, confirms the general lines of semantic development drawn above. The journal has been published continuously since 1887. *Economie mondiale* is first mentioned in 1923 when a reviewer of Ernst Schultze's book on *Die Zerrüttung der Weltwirtschaft* (the disruption of the world economy) translated the concept from German into French. In 1926, *Weltwirtschaft* is used in its German original within an otherwise French text and the French translation provided in brackets: 'This *Weltwirtschaft* (*économie mondiale*), which some German economists have turned into a compartment of political economy already before the war and to which they have devoted a special journal' (Sauvaire-Jourdan 1926: 1235). Initially, the concept mostly appeared in book reviews. The first research articles to embrace it dealt with the economic situation in South America and with the economic consequences of migration (Burton 1928; Morini-Comby 1932) and in 1936, Wilhelm Röpke, then still in exile in Istanbul, published a paper in the *Révue* he had given at a conference of the Association of Austrian Economists in Vienna. This was the third time the term appeared in a longer article, in Röpke's typical sweeping overview of the economic crisis that coincided with a crisis in terminology and conscious agency that made him one of the leading international economists: 'When looking for the origins of the contemporary chaos of the world economy, one cannot hide the fact that it was the thoughtlessness, the recklessness with which the countries of the first order from an economic perspective have abandoned the stability of exchange rates' (Röpke 1936b: 1295).

In English, the journal *Economica* was fundamentally important for key economic concepts from its foundation in 1921. The concept of the world economy was first mentioned in long academic pieces by one of the journal's co-editors, Stanley Hartnoll Bailey, who argued that the 'mechanism' of the world economy had been misused for the sake of 'exclusive national advantages' (Bailey 1932: 115) and that it needed a new and proper set of rules to avoid political discrimination inflicted by the colonial powers, notably the most-favoured nation clauses and the open-door policy (Bailey 1933). As it was an internationally leading journal, the voices of French, German, Italian and American authors concerned with the world economy were also raised within *Economica* from the 1930s.

One fruit of the efforts of the Carnegie Endowment to carry out vast research, as decided upon in 1911 in Berne, was its publication series, *Studies in World Economy*. Its first publication, introduced by James T. Shotwell, dealt with the – by then more complex – semantics of the concept and asked how enduring prosperity might be achieved, what the critique of capitalism would yield, how the new theories of business cycle analysis and macroeconomics would enter the picture, whether competition bred conflict instead of peace and how the economy related to politics (Shotwell and Fosdick 1931). All these questions were also widely discussed and written about within the League's International Studies Conferences (League of Nations 1932; 1933).

## Conclusion

While the term 'world economy' was coined as law-based relations of nation states and ensuing mutual dependencies, and retained this meaning, the concept was increasingly characterized by a rich and complex semantic field that reflected the political effects of world economic organization. The old liberal assumption that trade was peaceful eroded and the tensions emerging from hierarchical relations within the world economy – both inside and between nation states – led to critical and new perspectives. Instead of taking it for granted or merely describing it as the space for market agency constructed via international legal agreements, the need to measure it properly and to organize it actively in ways that would allow for prosperity, security and peace on a global scale was decisively expressed during the crises of the 1930s. Despite contestations of the assumption that free markets were the nucleus of the world economy and thus the key to peace, liberal positions prevailed and contestation of the concept by Marxist or other perspectives did not topple the free market as the supposedly normal condition – it was not superseded by anything else Schilder (1912) had called 'fantasies'. Between the 1920s and 1940s what dominated was discussion about how the free market heart of the world economy might best be kept beating without causing social strife and violence.

The Bretton Woods order of 1944 built on the established views about organizing a stable world economy, tackling the questions that were teased out in the 1930s. The World Bank, the International Monetary Fund and the General Agreement of Trade and Tariffs (GATT) carefully looked into the issues identified as crucial for a sustainable world economy at the time. Growth was identified as a key component of the world economy and became a hegemonic concept within its semantic field (Schmelzer 2016) and began to be measured in Gross Domestic Product (GDP), a statistical exercise invented in 1934 by Simon Kuznets and broadly applied within the Bretton Woods organizations after the Second World War (Lepenies 2016).

Bretton Woods unravelled in the 1970s. From the 1960s to the 1980s, the second period when usage of the concept 'world economy' increased, the discussion about its very organization picked up again. When 'global economy' superseded 'world economy' in the 1980s, the change in terms seems to have gone hand in hand with a change in meaning. A semantic discontinuity can also be detected in French and German, where the concepts of *économie mondiale* and *Weltwirtschaft* remained in continuous use. Gradually, *économie mondiale* no longer signified organization among a trading set of nations, but one single economy (e.g. Herman 1984). Globalization implied a departure from seeking to make national economies compatible to foster good trading conditions toward an integrated economic space. The World Trade Organization subscribed to a more singular understanding of the world economy, aiming to reach an 'integrated, more viable and durable multilateral trading system' (WTO 1994), ironically turning against its institutional predecessor, the nation-based GATT. Today, the world economy remains a key semantic concept that extends beyond the nation state. The notion of an integrated world economy is challenged both from within its Western core and by differently organized economies like China. Increasing awareness of climate change and social inequalities led some to challenge the growth paradigm with counter-concepts such as sustainability or degrowth and with attempts to measure the economy in other ways 'beyond GDP' (Stiglitz et al. 2010; Lima de Miranda and Snower 2020; Chapter 13).

**Hagen Schulz-Forberg** teaches at Aarhus University. He is interested in the theory and practice of global conceptual history. Recently, his research focused on a global history of neoliberalism since the 1930s. ORCID 0000-0001-5176-2468.

## References

### Primary Sources

Anonymous. 1923. 'Compte rendue critique: Die Zerrüttung der Weltwirtschaft', *Revue d'économie politique* 37(5): 739–41.

Bailey, S.H. 1932. 'The Political Aspect of Discrimination in International Economic Relations', *Economica* 35: 89–115.

———. 1933. 'Reciprocity and the Most-Favoured-Nation Clause', *Economica* 42: 428–56.

Bank for International Settlements. 1936. *Sixth Annual Report*. Basle: Bank for International Settlements.

Baumstark, E. 1835. *Kameralistische Encyclopädie: Handbuch der Kameralwissenschaften und ihrer Literatur für Rechts- und Verwaltungs-Beamten, Landstände, Gemeinde-Räthe und Kameral-Candidaten*. Heidelberg and Leipzig: Groos.

Bernstein, E. 1911. 'Das Grundsätzliche in der Frage der Handelspolitik', *Sozialistische Monatshefte* 15–17(7): 424–31.

Bourquin, M. (ed.). 1936. *Collective Security: A Record of the Seventh and Eights International Studies Conferences*. Geneva: League of Nations.

Bücher, K. 1893. *Die Entstehung der Volkswirtschaft: Sechs Vorträge*. Tübingen: Laupp.

Burton, H. 1928. 'La vie économique en Amérique du Sud', *Revue d'économie politique* 42(6): 1528–73.

Calwer, R. 1903–1912. *Jahrbuch der Weltwirtschaft: Jahresberichte über den Wirtschafts- und Arbeitsmarkt für Volkswirte und Geschäftsmänner, Arbeitgeber- und Arbeiterorganisationen.* Jena: G. Fischer.

Condliffe, J.B. 1933. *World Economic Survey.* Geneva: League of Nations.

'The Economist Economic Conference Supplement', *The Economist,* 28 May 1927.

Fichte, J.G. 1800. *Der geschlossene Handelsstaat: Ein philosophischer Entwurf als Anhang zur Rechtslehre und Probe einer künftig zu liefernden Politik.* Tübingen: Cotta.

Gide, C. 1911. 'La conference de Berne sur les cause et les effets économiques des guerres', *Révue d'économie politique* 25(5): 553–62.

Harms, B. 1912. *Volkswirtschaft und Weltwirtschaft: Versuch der Begründung einer Weltwirtschaftslehre.* Jena: G. Fischer.

———. 1913. 'Weltwirtschaft und Weltwirtschaftslehre', *Weltwirtschaftliches Archiv* 1(1): 1–36.

Herman, B. 1984. 'Revue des livres: Multinationales européennes et investissements croisés'. *Revue d'économie politique* 94(1): 174–75.

League of Nations. 1932. *A Record of a First International Study Conference on the State and Economic Life with Special Reference to International Economic and Political Relations.* Paris: International Institute of Intellectual Co-operation.

———. 1934. *A Record of a Second Study Conference on the State and Economic Life.* Paris: International Institute of Intelletual Co-operation.

Manoilescu, M. 1929. *Théorie de protectionnisme et de l'échange international.* Paris: M. Girard.

Morini-Comby, J. 1932. 'Essai sur les conséquences économiques des migrations', *Revue d'économie politique* 46(1): 74–108.

Ohlin, B. 1931. *The Course and Phases of the World Economic Depression.* Geneva: The League of Nations.

Oppenheim, H.B. 1872. *Der Katheder-Sozialismus.* Berlin: R. Oppenheim.

Rau, K.H. 1825. *Über die Kameralwissenschaft: Entwicklung ihres Wesen und ihrer Theile.* Heidelberg: C. F. Winter.

———. 1847 [1826]. *Grundsätze der Volkswirthschaftslehre.* Heidelberg: C. F. Winter.

Ricardo, D. 1817. *On the Principles of Political Economy and Taxation.* London: John Murray.

Röpke, W. 1931. *Weltwirtschaft und Außenhandel.* Berlin: Spaeth&Linde.

———. 1936a. *Crises and Cycles.* London: W. Hodge & Company.

———. 1936b. 'Tendences actuelles de l'économie politique', *Révue d'économie politique* 50(4): 1284–307.

———. 1942. *International Economic Disintegration.* London W. Hodge and Co.

———. 1959 [1944]. *International Order and Economic Integration.* Dordrecht: D. Reidel.

Rouxèl, M. 1896. 'Revue des principals publications economiques en langues française', *Journal des économistes* 55(1): 187–205, 202.

Runciman, W.L. 1927. 'The World Economic Conference at Geneva', *The Economic Journal* 37(147): 465–72.

Sauvaire-Jourdan, F. 1926. 'La vie économique internationale by Barthélemy Raynaud', *Revue d'économie politique* 40(5): 1235–36.

Say, J-B. 1815. *Catéchisme d'économie politique ou instruction familière qui montre de quelle façon les richesses sont produites, distribuées et consommées dans la société.* Paris: Guillaumin.

Schilder, S. 1912. *Entwicklungstendenzen der Weltwirtschaft. Vol 1: Planmässige Einwirkungen auf die Weltwirtschaft.* Berlin: Franz Siemenroth.

Schmoller, G. 1900. *Grundriss der allgemeinen Volkswirtschaftslehre.* Leipzig: Duncker&Humblot.

Shotwell, J.T. and R.B. Fosdick. 1931. *International Conciliation.* Studies in World Economy 1. New York: Carnegie Endowment for International Peace.

Taussig, F.W. 1905. 'Schmoller on Protection and Free Trade', *The Quarterly Journal of Economics* 19(3): 501–11.

'A World Economic Survey', *The Economist*, 14 October 1933: 705–709.

'A World Perplexed', *The Economist*, 1 July 1933: 3–5.

World Trade Organisation. 1994. *Agreement Establishing the World Trade Organization*, available at https://www.wto.org/english/docs_e/legal_e/04-wto.pdf.

*Secondary Sources*

Ashley, W.J. 2018. 'Socialists of the Chair', in *The New Palgrave Dictionary of Economics.* London: Palgrave, pp. 132–53.

Backhaus, J.G. 1993. 'Gustav Schmoller and the Problems of Today', *History of Economic Ideas* 1/2(3/1): 3–25.

Balabkins, N.W. 1993. 'Gustav Schmoller and the Emergence of Welfare Capitalism', *History of Economic Ideas* 1/2(3/1): 27–42.

Boilard, M.-C. and S. Friis. 2021. 'Development Revisited: The Concept of Development as Space/Time Practice in the Postwar Era', in H. Schulz-Forberg (ed.), *Zero Hours: Politics of Time from Global Perspectives.* London: Palgrave (forthcoming).

Clavin, P. 2013. *Securing the World Economy: The Reinvention of the League of Nations, 1920–1946.* Oxford: Oxford University Press.

Hoffmann, T.S. (ed.). 2018. *Fichtes Geschlossener Handelsstaat. Beiträge zur Erschließung eines Anti-Klassikers.* Berlin: Duncker&Humblot.

Lepenies, P. 2016. *The Power of a Single Number: A Political History of GDP.* New York: Columbia University Press.

Lima de Miranda, K. and D. Snower. 2020. 'Recoupling Economic and Social Prosperity', *Global Perspectives* 1(1): 11867. https://doi.org/10.1525/001c.11867.

Magnusson, L. 2004. *The Tradition of Free Trade.* London: Routledge.

Nokkala, E. and N.B. Miller (eds.). 2019. *Cameralism and the Enlightenment: Happiness, Governance and Reform in Transnational Perspective.* New York: Routledge.

Pedersen, S. 2015. *The Guardians: The League of Nations and the Crisis of Empire.* Oxford: Oxford University Press.

Peukert, H. 2001. 'The Schmoller Renaissance', *History of Political Economy* 33(1): 71–116.

Schmelzer, M. 2016. *The Hegemony of Growth: The OECD and the Making of Economic Growth*. Oxford: Oxford University Press.

Schulz-Forberg, H. 2019. 'Modern Economic Thought and the "Good Society"', in W. Breckman and P. Gordon (eds.), *The Cambridge History of Modern European Thought, Vol. 2: The Twentieth Century*. Cambridge: Cambridge University Press: pp. 361–90.

Stiglitz, J. et al. 2010. *Mismeasuring our Lives: Why GDP Doesn't Add Up*. London and New York: The New Press.

Tribe, K. 2017. 'Jean-Baptiste Say's Footnotes to Ricardo', in J.L. Cardoso et al. (eds), *Economic Analyses in Historical Perspective*. London: Routledge, pp. 113–22.

# Chapter 8

# Ecumene Redefined

## Concepts of (Inter)National Religious Unity in British, Dutch and Swedish Parliamentary Debates, 1880–2020

*Joris van Eijnatten and Pasi Ihalainen*

Although historically often centred on nation states, religion has played an important role in the formation of international relations. The Catholic Church, in particular, has traditionally seen itself as universal and supranational by definition. Increasingly from the early nineteenth century onwards, Protestant churches began to open up to international cooperation and the transfer of ideas. In predominantly Protestant countries, many leading advocates of internationalism were motivated by religious beliefs, while religious organizations have had a strong record in international activities ranging from missionary work to humanitarianism (see Chapter 11) and peace movements (Green 2017: 17).

These changes in perception of the role of religion in the world touch on the complex interrelationship between nationalism and internationalism. Yet the evolving discourse on internationalism has rarely been analysed in terms of religion, which has been all but marginalized since secularization theses became dominant in mainstream historical scholarship. As Hugh McLeod has argued, relations between church and state and long-term experiences of secularization have diverged radically between different national contexts. The connection between secularization and modernization is not 'natural'; it needs to be explored empirically, and the timing of wide-ranging transformations postponed, possibly to the 1960s (McLeod 2000; 2003: 1–26).

This contribution to the long-term conceptual history of internationalism is a first attempt to take a comparative approach to the valence of religion on international issues in political and, more particularly, parliamentary discourse. We have chosen to focus our analysis on parliaments because they have constituted forums in which the representatives of a wide spectrum of values influencing the national political communities – ranging from professional clerics and religious activists to merely cultural Christians and non-believers – have expressed their views. Their arguments have been presented in a highly comparative long-term setting, in the most appreciated forum of political debate in each country – and this extensive data has recently become available digitally, which makes its computer-assisted distant reading possible.

We approach parliamentary debates in terms of religious thought, by focusing on the Christian interpretation of the originally Greek notion of the ecumene (*oikoumenè*, meaning 'the inhabited world'). This is the idea that Christians form a unity, a single religious community that transcends theological and institutional barriers – at first at the denominational and national but later also at the international and even interfaith level. The idea of the ecumene carries with it a spatial dimension, not just because of its etymological origins, but because a territorial understanding of Christendom is integral to most expressions of historical Christianity. That territorial understanding has ranged from the local and national to the global and has always been closely bound up with notions of continuity and truth.

This chapter examines how the relationship between religious unity and territory has been conceptualized in the parliamentary discourse of three Northwest European countries from the late nineteenth century to the present. For the sake of comparability, and based on our previous research on politico-religious discourses in these countries, we have chosen three states that have, historically, identified themselves as Protestant: Britain, the Netherlands and Sweden. Despite the apparent commonality of these 'Protestant' nations, they were in some respects quite different. Sweden was fundamentally Lutheran until the late twentieth century, Britain predominantly Anglican and the Netherlands partly Calvinist.[1] Britain and the Netherlands were multireligious empires that facilitated religious toleration at an early stage in their history, mainly for pragmatic reasons. Sweden was a religiously uniform country where religious pluralism arose late. In the Netherlands, church and state were separated de jure (if not de facto) in 1796, in Sweden only in 2000, while Britain still recognizes a state religion related to the monarchy until the present day.

Until 1922 Britain had to cope with a large majority of Roman Catholics in Ireland and Catholic minorities elsewhere, small but relatively influential Protestant groups outside the Church of England and the non-Christian world religions of the Empire. The Netherlands possessed a substantial Catholic minority (around 35% of the population) and ruled colonies with predominantly Muslim majorities. Sweden became a destination of immigrants with diverse religious backgrounds increasingly from the 1960s onwards. All three societies secularized rapidly during the twentieth century, especially after the Second World War, but at the same time needed to address religious issues both at home (due to immigration) and abroad (where secularization often was not an issue).

To understand how and why, in each of these countries, the relationship between religious unity and territory was conceptualized, at first within and subsequently beyond the nation state, we begin our exploration in the later nineteenth century. Throughout the early modern period and in much of the nineteenth century, the national community had been conceptualized predominantly through the established, dominant or state church. In the late nineteenth century, however, traditional associations between the state and mainstream Protestantism gradually began to weaken. Religion was often still tied explicitly to nationhood, while international aspects of religion began to be put on the agenda more emphatically than before.

### Reading 'Ecumenical' from a Distance

In what follows, we focus on parliamentary debates on 'the ecumene' cropping up every now and then in discussions on the values of the nation. First we traced a number of relevant terms over a longer period of time using a custom-made keyword search method that allowed us to visualize historical patterns.[2] These terms figure in what we expected to be the broad 'semantic field' covering religious unity in relation to territory; the keywords include 'between churches', 'between religions', 'interreligious', 'interfaith', 'religious freedom', 'religious liberty', 'toleration', 'anti-Catholicism', 'state religion', 'state church', 'people's church' and, of course, 'ecumenism' itself. Experimenting with these alternatives – derived from our previous experience in empirical research on religious nationalism (Van Eijnatten 2003; Ihalainen 2005) – we learned that 'ecumenism' best indicated the semantic field of internationalism in the context of religiously motivated debate. We therefore chose to limit our analysis to its uses, rather than to all phrases containing the word 'international' as such, which would not have captured the religious aspects of international thought so distinctly. We decided to explore words that occurred in the same context with 'ecumenical', although we are aware that this approach captures only one aspect of the debates.

In what follows we present two series of visualizations: firstly, a comparison between the number of references to the 'national' church in Britain, the Netherlands and Sweden and the word 'ecumenical' in their respective parliaments between the nineteenth century and the present (Figures 8.1–8.3).

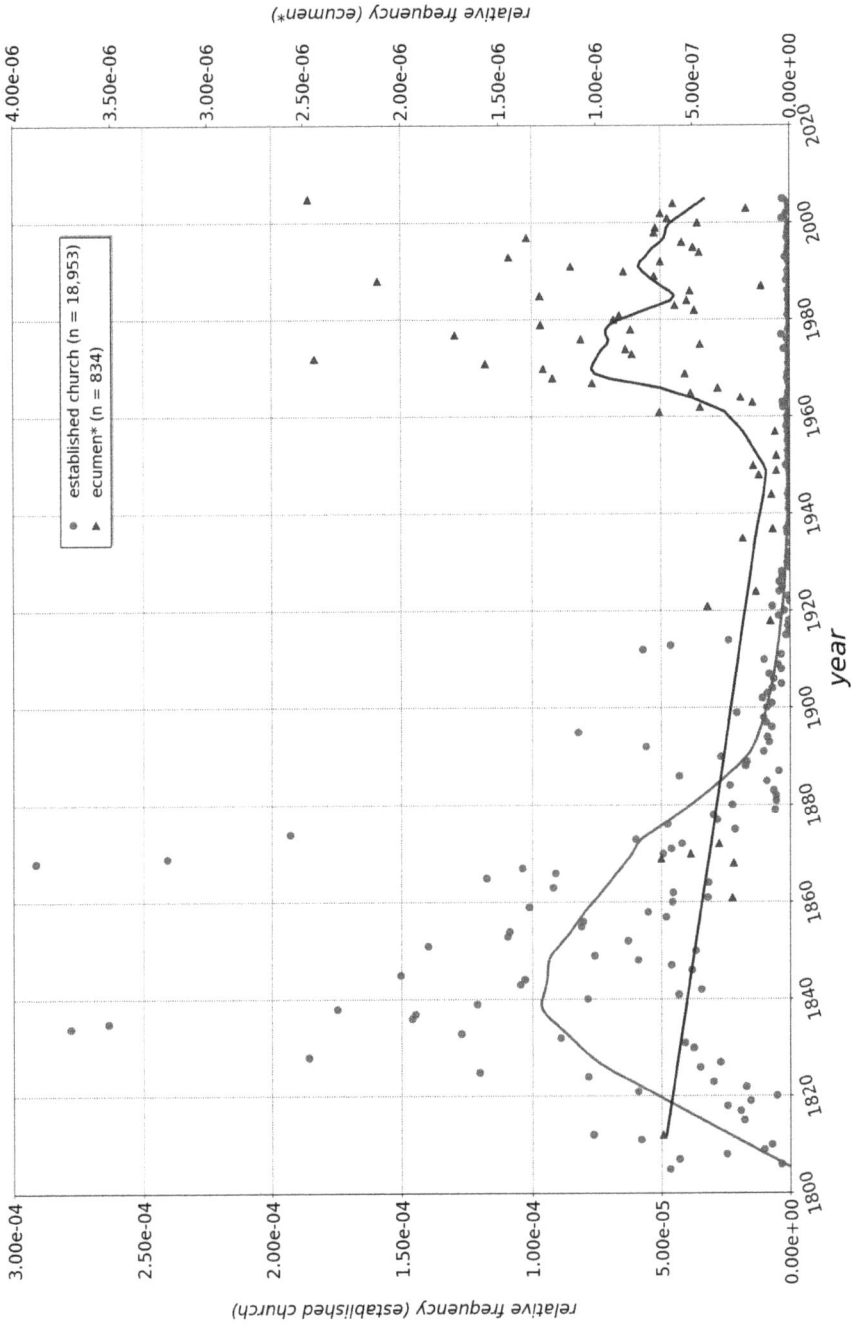

**Figure 8.1** Relative frequencies of 'established church' in relation to the stem 'ecumen*' in the British parliament. © Joris van Eijnatten.

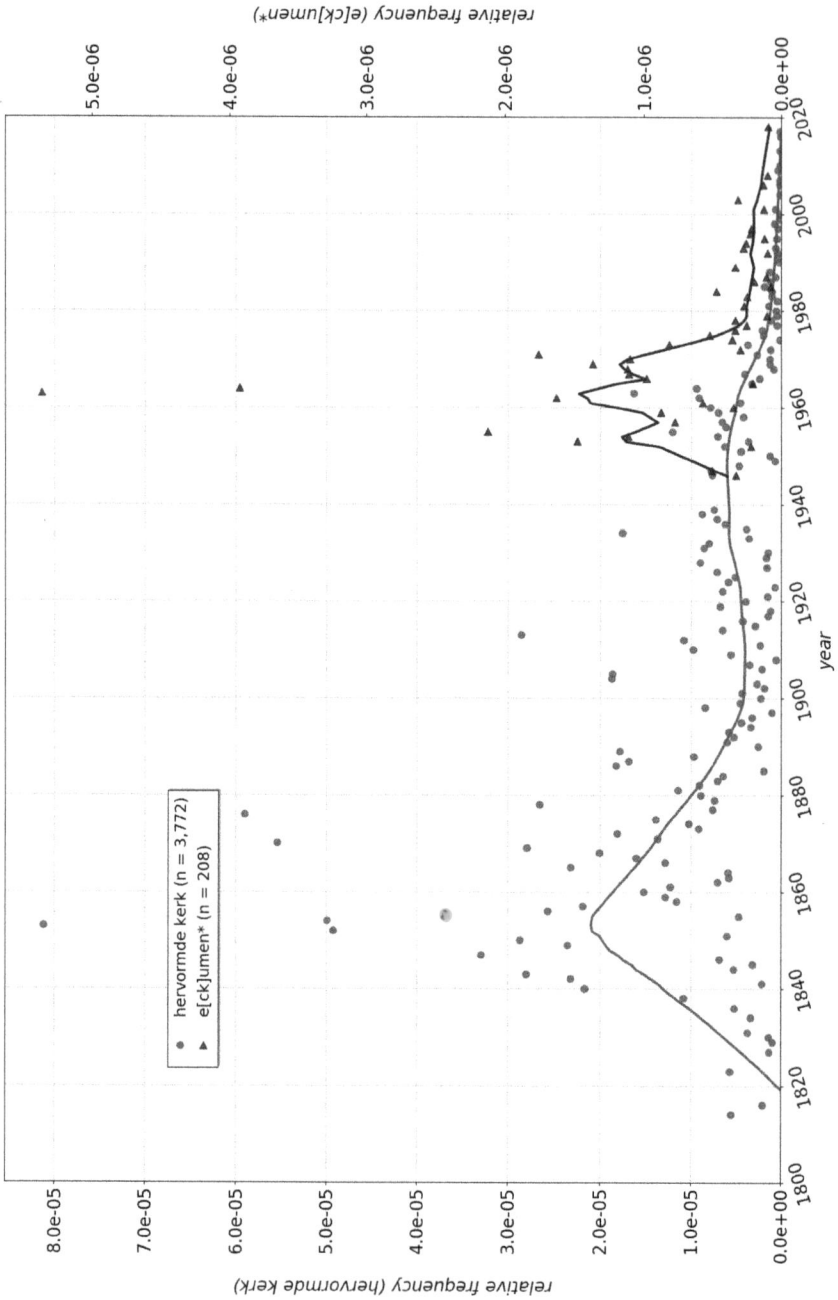

**Figure 8.2** Relative frequencies of *Hervormde Kerk* (Reformed Church) in relation to the stem 'ecumen*/ekumen*' in the Dutch parliament. © Joris van Eijnatten.

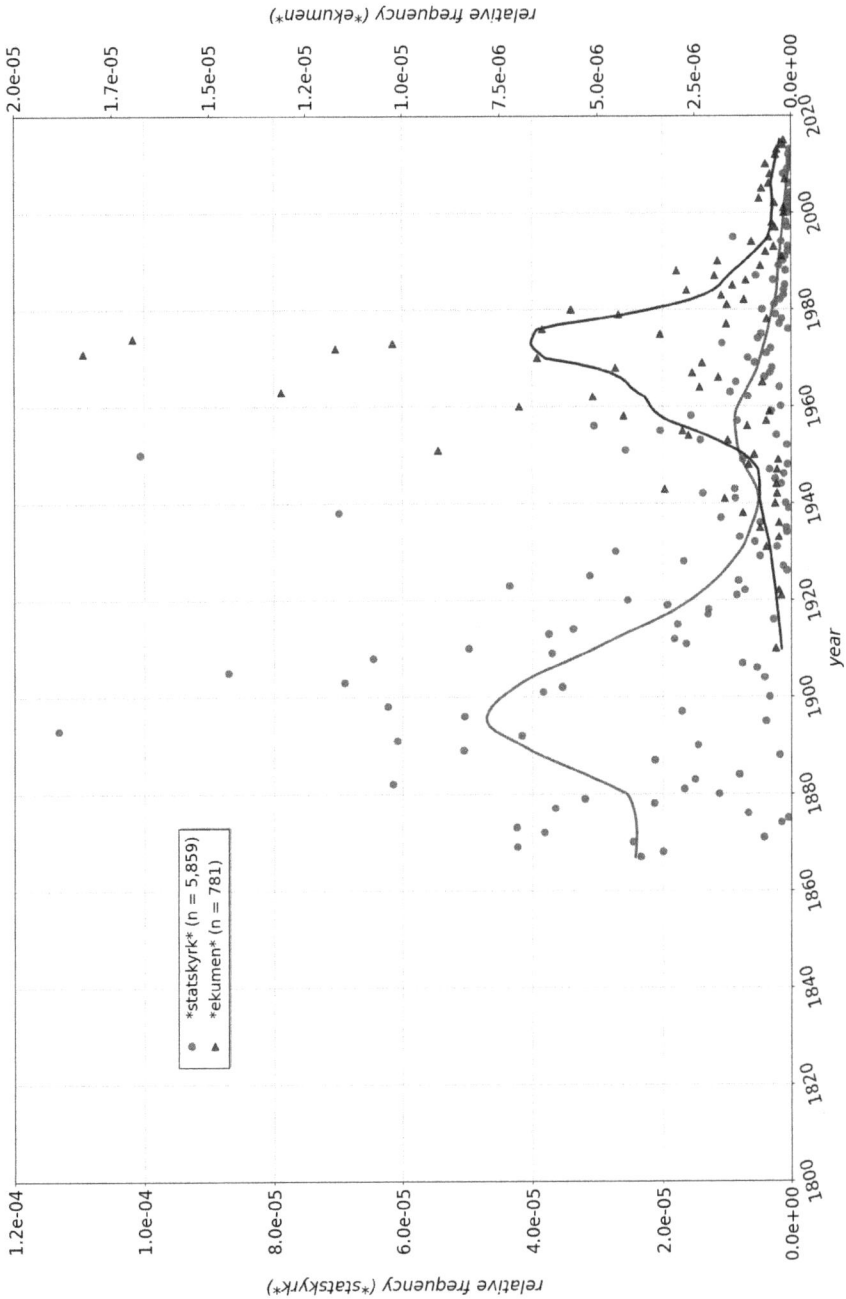

**Figure 8.3** Relative frequencies of '*statskyrk*' ('state church') in relation to the stem 'ekumen*' in the Swedish parliament. © Joris van Eijnatten.

Secondly, we present an analysis of the expansion of the semantic field of the term ecumenical in the British House of Commons (Figures 8.4–8.6). In the figures, the relative frequencies are the number of hits in relation to the total number of words per year. The curve is a 'smoothing' curve based on a local polynomial regression function (LOESS) which allows one to better see patterns. We used the LOESS function in statsmodels v0.12.0. Note that the y-axes differ.

It became possible to conceptualize religion in more international ways in predominantly Protestant contexts once the associations between 'religion' or 'church' and the 'nation' or 'state' that had dominated early modern thought started to weaken. This possibility can be inferred from the extent of the debates on the relationship between church and state in all the three countries studied here. Figure 8.1 illustrates how discourse mentioning the 'established church' peaked in the British parliament in the mid-nineteenth century but declined rather dramatically at the beginning of the twentieth (although by no means disappearing). A similar pattern can be discerned in the Netherlands (Figure 8.2), with parallel timing, though discourse on the Reformed Church remained more common there until the 1980s. At the same time, it will be clear that the Dutch set less store by the idea of a 'national church' than either Britain or Sweden: *staatskerk* was hardly used, and the most common word to denote the historically privileged church, *Hervormde Kerk* (Reformed Church), did not occur as frequently as comparable terms did elsewhere. In Sweden, the four estates conducted substantial debate on the state church (*statskyrkan*), such as in the 1850s, but the real peak in the debate occurred later than in the other two countries, as illustrated in Figure 8.3. Swedish parliamentarians often referred to the state church at the end of the nineteenth century. Debate was still taking place in the 1950s, as in the Netherlands, and in Sweden it waned only with the separation of church and state in 2000.

The word 'ecumenical' as such had already emerged in nineteenth-century parliamentary discourse but its frequency rose in Britain only in the late 1960s. The discourse on ecumenism would remain relevant for some parliamentarians until the early twenty-first century. In the Netherlands the term peaked earlier, in the 1950s, and again in the 1960s, after which it declined. The Swedish parliamentarians joined the discourse on ecumenical matters at the same time as their British and Dutch colleagues, and when they did their usage of the term was quite spectacular – reflecting the rise of the ecumenical movement, to which Swedish activists such as Nathan Söderblom, the Lutheran Archbishop of Sweden, had contributed considerably, both nationally and internationally. As in Britain and the Netherlands there was a peak in word usage in the 1960s in Sweden, but a second, much higher one followed in the 1970s; after that the frequency counts indicate continuity on a lower level. The data thus suggests rather similar patterns for all three countries with some differences in timing. In a nutshell, the dominant discourse on the national church in the nineteenth century was gradually replaced in parliaments with one on ecumenism, especially in the 1960s, after which that discourse too waned. In what follows we explore possible explanations for this through contextualized instances on the microlevel.

Another way of looking at the word 'ecumenical' in the twentieth century is by distant reading to examine words that 'behave' in a similar fashion, i.e. they occur in contexts similar to the one in which 'ecumenical' occurs. Taking the British House of Commons as a case study, we find three patterns (Figures 8.4–8.6). The radial graph shows the similarity score of each word in relation to 'scenario', for all values equal to or higher than 0.45 where the word frequency is higher than 10.

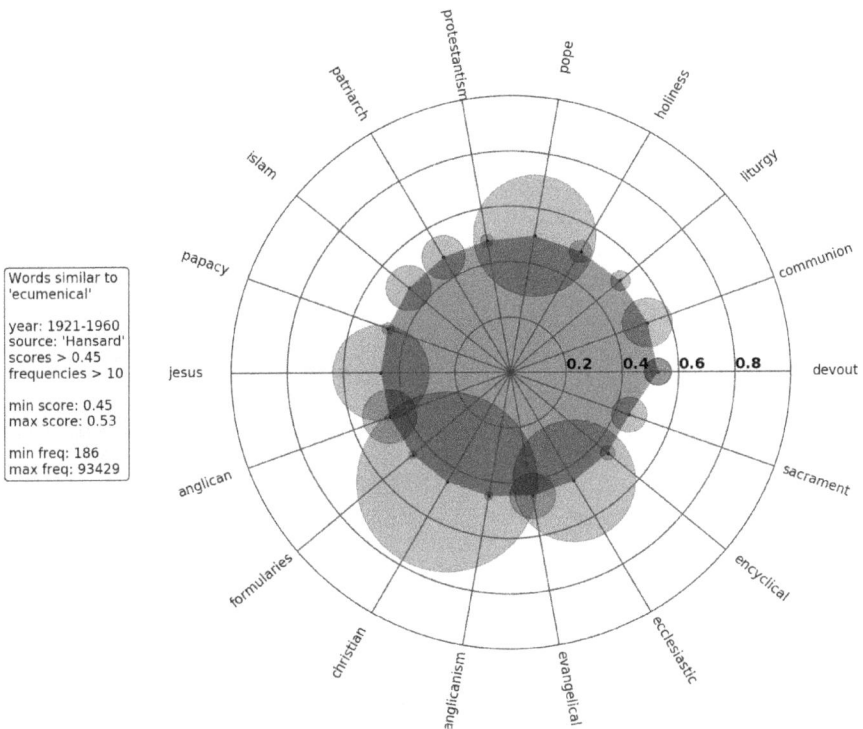

**Figure 8.4** Words behaving like 'ecumenical' in the British House of Commons in 1921–1960, based on word embeddings. © Joris van Eijnatten.

Parliamentary discourse on the ecumenical has gradually become highly diversified and polyvocal in the course of the twentieth century. Between 1921 and 1960 (when the term first starts to occur reasonably often), words that behave similarly to 'ecumenical' begin to be related less exclusively to words which were related to the older conceptualizations of the Protestant nation such as 'Anglican', 'Evangelical' and 'Protestantism'. Increasingly, they also related to 'Christian', 'communion' and 'Jesus'; to 'pope' and 'papacy'; to 'patriarch' and to 'Islam' (Figure 8.4). In the 1960s and 1970s, the list of words expands considerably. The most significant ones refer to ecumenism between the Protestant denominations most relevant to Britain ('Methodism', 'Evangelical'; 'nonconformist' refers to all 'non-established' churches so it includes non-Protestants) although synonyms for ecumenism also began to appear at this point ('Christendom', 'interdenominational'). Antonyms likewise appear, such as 'fundamentalist', 'secular', and 'atheism' and 'atheists', reflecting strong secularist and anti-secularist trends in that period (Figure 8.5). Finally, the period 1981–2005 saw the rise of the word

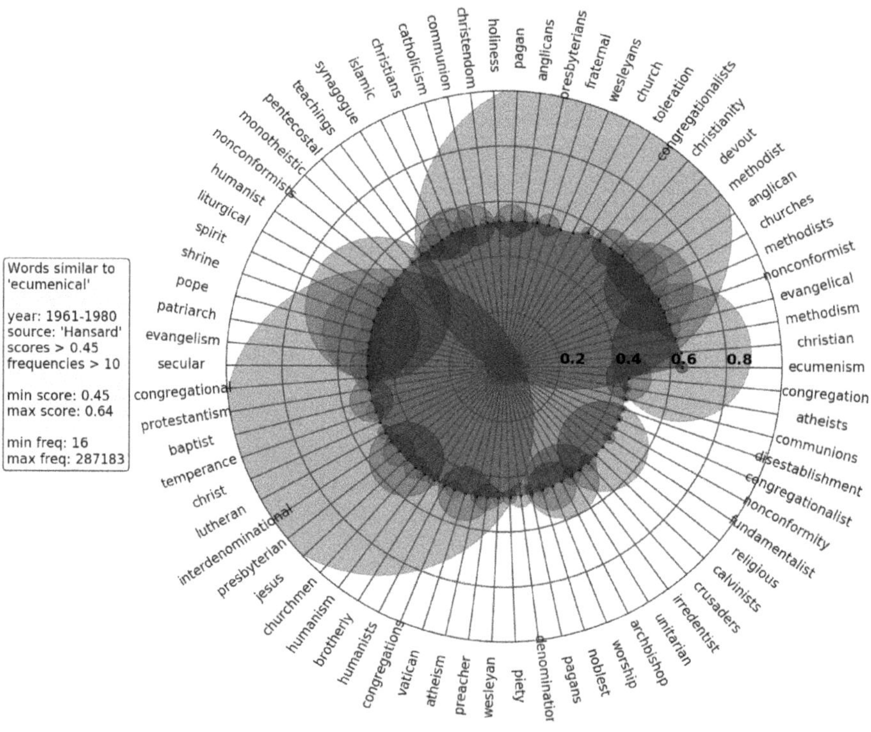

**Figure 8.5** Words behaving like 'ecumenical' in the British House of Commons in 1961–1980, based on word embeddings. © Joris van Eijnatten.

'interfaith' as an alternative for the previously specifically Christian term ecumenism; non-Christian religions now appear in the debates, such as Hinduism, Sikhism and Buddhism. Similarly, the attribute 'Abrahamic' brought Christianity, Judaism and Islam together in a way unthinkable in the nineteenth century (Figure 8.6). Ecumenism had clearly been extended well beyond Protestant denominations within a nation state to concern major world religions.

Our contextualizing close reading starts with typically nineteenth-century conceptualizations of religious nationhood that either supposed an identity between church, state and people and insisted on religious unity or, alternatively, challenged the necessity of complete (Protestant) conformity and called for an ecumenical approach at the national level. We proceed by investigating discourses on an ecumenical spirit, world peace and universal understanding. These emerged in all three national contexts after the First World War with the rise of what could be analytically called religious internationalism, evolving during the 1960s into an outspoken 'ecumenism'.

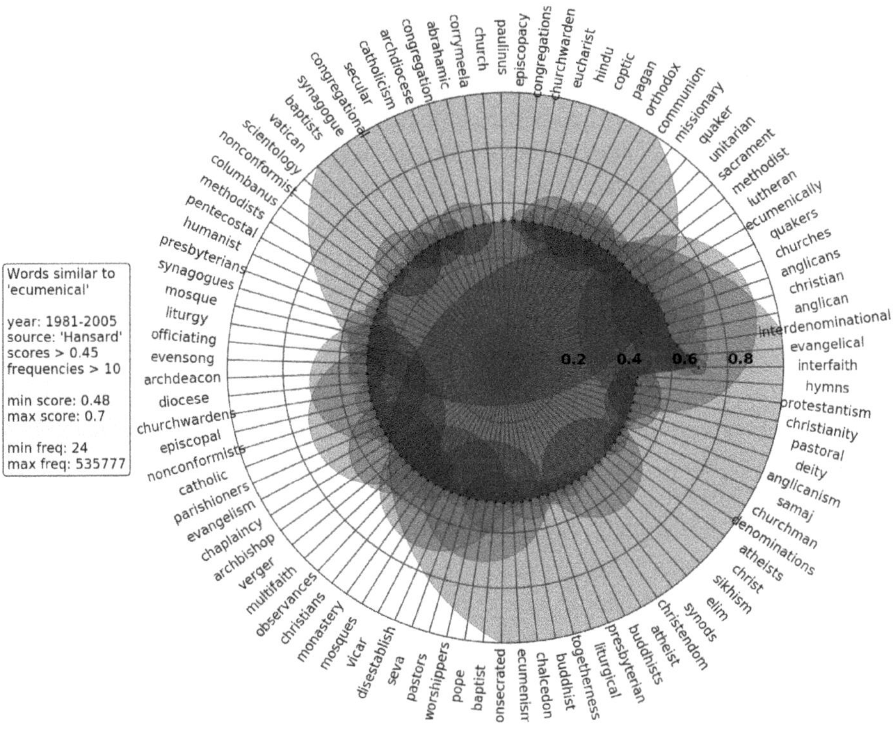

Words similar to 'ecumenical'

year: 1981-2005
source: 'Hansard'
scores > 0.45
frequencies > 10

min score: 0.48
max score: 0.7

min freq: 24
max freq: 535777

**Figure 8.6** Words behaving like 'ecumenical' in the British House of Commons in 1981–2005, based on word embeddings. © Joris van Eijnatten.

The political fragmentation of the world after 1989, together with secular-ization, immigration and multiculturalism, contributed to the waning of Christian discourse on the ecumene, while the need to control religious extremism became a more recent major concern in international relations.

## Religious Nationhood until the First World War: Church, State and People United

Until the nineteenth century, British parliamentarians followed the general European trend inherited from the nation-centred Protestant Reformations by using the terms 'state religion' and 'state church' to denote their con-ceptual understanding of a religious unity that was primarily national. The supposition was that a historically embedded religious unity guaranteed the political continuity of the state, and vice versa (Ihalainen 2005; Van Eijnatten 2003). In Britain, this understanding had traditionally been crit-icized by dissenting Christians who pointed out 'that there are only two pretences on which the state church – the Protestant Church – can exist … The one is religious – the other is political' (John Bright, Liberal and Quaker, HC, 1868: 649). The latter, political (i.e. territorial) conception was usually referred to implicitly: on British soil it was most frequently expressed through official names like 'Church of England' (or of Ireland, of Scotland or in Wales), or characteristically British terms like 'established church'. Although British legislation gave more freedom and equality to dissenting churches, Establishment was supported until the twenty-first century, the most fervent supporters usually being Conservatives: 'it should be borne in mind that the Church of England is our state Church', was something that could still be said in 2014 (Fiona Bruce, Congleton, Con, HL, 2014: 569).

Theological currents such as the Oxford Movement, which approached Catholicism, supported the rise of more ecumenical ways of conceptualizing the national community. Often the USA was used as proof that a reterritori-alized ecumenicity did no harm to the state, as in a rhetorical question posed in 1895: 'What had been the result [there] of the absence of an Established Church upon religious unity?' (F.S. Powell, Wigan, HC, 1895: 91). The answer in this instance was negative: cutting the ties between church and state did not break unity since, in the end, all citizens were Christians. Outside America, however, most nineteenth-century politicians would not have agreed with this position but believed in institutional guarantees for religious unity. A common response from the supporters of Establishment in Britain, as in many Lutheran countries, was 'comprehension', the inclusion of as many opinions as theologically possible within the established church 'by enlarging the terms of ecclesiastical communion',[3] and thus preserving institutional ecumenicity on the national level. 'Nothing could be worse than to curtail the charity and comprehension of our great national Church', said one MP in 1903 (C.A. Cripps, Lancashire, Stretford, HC, 1903: 755).

In a Germanic linguistic context other words were in use to denote the symbiosis of church and state, apart from such obvious terms as *staatskerk* (Dutch) and *statskyrka* (Swedish). In the Dutch parliament, the notion of the *volkskerk* ('people's church') first cropped up in 1887, following a secession from the national *Hervormde Kerk* (Reformed Church). The government then still had every intention of regarding the *Hervormde Kerk* as the 'historical Reformed Church in the Netherlands'. According to dissenting Calvinists, however, its status was based on the unlawful intrusion of the state on church prerogative (Alexander F. de Savornin Lohman, Die Anti-Revolutionaire Partij [ARP], SG2, 6 December 1887: 357–58). Once the shock of the secession had abated, the *Hervormde Church* to all intents and purposes became one (very big) church among others. Yet the idea of a *volkskerk* remained powerful, and sometimes cropped up in parliament in the context of discussions about the state's role in paying the clergy's wages, financing theological faculties, providing access to church buildings and caring for the poor.

Supporters of the *volkskerk* idea had a conservative interpretation of the state of affairs: 'In the last century three principles have influenced the people [*het volksleven*]: liberalism in politics, modernism in the church and [religious] neutrality at school'. They saw the result of this threefold influence as disastrous for Christianity, for the state and for the people (Ankerman, SG2, CHU, 10 December 1913: 671–72). Once in a while books were quoted in parliament, such as one entitled 'The Great Importance of the Reformed Church as the People's Church' (Roessingh, SG2, 8 March 1909: 1466; P.J. Kromsigt, *Het hooge belang der Hervormde kerk als volkskerk*, 1909). Such MPs invariably identified Christianity with their own brand of Protestantism, which they considered to be historically rooted in the nation; religious internationalism, when it emerged after the First World War, came from those less bound to the traditional mainstream confessions. The Calvinist concept of a religious community that was inclusive of core-ligionists elsewhere enabled the rise of international perspectives, especially in comparison with almost uniformly Lutheran Scandinavian countries.

In Sweden, the territorial implications of religious unity were expressed in a similar vein, though uniformity was greater. Only the true Evangelical Lutheran religion that, according to the national narrative, had been defended on battlefields for centuries, was capable of guaranteeing 'the bliss and prosperity of the entire nation' (Herman Reinhold Fleming, Nobility, 20 March 1840: 375, 377). The notion of the people's church (*folkkyrkan*),

borrowed from the Danish and German contexts, was used as a synonym for
the state church: the Swedish Church had 'become a state church or, as our
southern neighbours so characteristically call this, a people's church'. This
implied 'a unification between her and the civic order of this people or the
state' (Frithiof Grafström, FK, 11 April 1877: 23:15). Supporters of free
churches used the expression also in the opposite, deinstitutionalized sense,
the introduction of a people's church implying a separation between church
and state, but the majority rejected such a prospect (Simon Boëthius, AK, 17
February 1898: 7:17). Antipathy towards Catholics was particularly prominent in Sweden's religious monoculture: 'animosity towards popery has
developed almost into a national hate [*nationalhat*]', said one nobleman in
1853 (Gustaf Löwenhjelm, Nobility, 16 June 1853: 211–12). Contemporaries
were aware of the differences in policies regarding toleration, warning that
Sweden was lagging behind 'the happiest and most civilized countries in
Europe, England and Holland' (Lars Vilhelm Henschen, Burgher Estate, 7
January 1854: 354–56; on toleration, see Alwall 2000: 151; incidentally, the
example illustrates the historical relevance of our comparison). But as late as
1920, conservative politicians continued to stress that 'the Swedish Church
has been the Swedish people itself', and lamented attempts to eliminate
'Christianity from our public life, from our societal life' (Karl Johan Ekman,
The Right, FK, 20 March 1918: 23:19; FK, 17 January 1920: 4:9) and abolish
'Christianity as a state religion and to have "religious liberty" instead' (Erik
Räf, AK, 20 March 1918: 31:21). International aspects were rarely referred
to in parliamentary debates on the church. This would change quite dramat-
ically in the interwar era.

## Global Christendom in the Interwar Era: Ecumenism, World Peace and Universal Understanding

Religious unity was increasingly reconceptualized in all three countries after
the tragedies of the First World War, no longer so strongly from a historical
and national perspective, but from a future-oriented and international one.
The visible transcendence of Protestant churches rooted in national pasts
gave way to the worldly immanence of progressive institutions seeking the
redemption of humanity as a whole.

In the Netherlands during the interwar era, this international ecumenism
typically cut across political and religious differences, although outspoken
supporters almost exclusively tended towards the theological and political
left. In 1934, during discussions on the defence budget and when tensions in
international relations were rising due to Hitler's ascendancy, one MP called
upon both the government and the churches to take 'moral disarmament'

much more seriously (Jan Faber, SDAP, SG2, 28 November 1934: 610). He spoke in the context of the League of Nations Conference for the Reduction and Limitation of Armaments (1932–1934) and referred to the difficulties encountered by the 'emerging ecumenical movement', the World Alliance for International Friendship through the Churches and 'The Association Church and Peace'. The latter was *Kerk en Vrede*, the Dutch daughter organization of the International Fellowship of Reconciliation, founded in 1914 by the English Quaker Henry Hodgkin and the German Lutheran Friedrich Siegmund-Schultze. Reflecting an international trend, Jan Faber's plea was meant to put a 'soul' into politics;[4] in theological terms, it was to further God's reign on earth.

Faber represented a substantial constituency of mostly but not exclusively Protestant believers, including many ministers of the church. Church and Peace was the largest Christian pacifist association of the Dutch interbellum. Founded by two theologians, the Remonstrant Gerrit Jan Heering and Johannes Hugenholtz, it counted around 9,000 members in 1933. Heering's inspiration is clear from two of his writings, both of which were quoted during parliamentary sessions: *The Church as Social Conscience* (1921) and the *Fall of Christianity* (1928) (*De kerk als maatschappelijk geweten, Zondeval van het Christendom*, translated into German and English). Hugenholtz, a sympathizer of the Social Democratic Workers' Party (SDAP), founded the International Union of Antimilitarist Ministers and Clergymen in Amsterdam in 1928. This antimilitarism, sometimes larded with ecumenism, was characteristic of those members of parliament who backed a petition for disarmament supported by 80,000 signatories, including Protestants and Catholics, submitted by Church and Peace to parliament in 1930. They included Albert van der Heide, one of the 'red reverends' (*rode dominees*). Pointing to the international dimension of the ethical issue addressed by the petition, he claimed that it represented 'people of different confessions who agreed that they supported national and international disarmament on religious grounds' in Switzerland, England, France, America and 'the Nordic countries' (Van der Heide, SG2, 22 October 1930: 218).

Insofar as they were overtly Christian, these international peace initiatives were voiced only by a minority: such interventions during the interbellum were few. There was rather substantial criticism of this reconceptualization of religious unity based on internationalism. A representative of the largest Protestant party regarded the internationalism of Church and Peace supporters as an unpatriotic sacrifice of national sovereignty, and saw in their antimilitarism a capitulation to foreign aggression. Yet even this MP believed in the immanent work of the spirit: it was the calling of the Dutch people, he claimed, to foster peace between nations, taking recourse to violence if all other options proved fruitless (Paul Briët, ARP, SG2, 17 December 1930: 96–97). Some outspoken supporters of international ecumenism rejected disarmament. A member of the conservative Christian Historical Union (CHU) thought that both the nation and global Christianity were best served, not by shooting down the budget for a couple of cruisers, but by eradicating 'nationalism, mutual friction, economic difficulties, absolute misunderstandings, chauvinism' (J.R. Slotemaker de Bruïne, SG2, 23 October 1930: 234). The response illustrates the fact that religious internationalism cut across confessional and ideological lines.

In the Swedish parliament, in the meantime, debates focused primarily on loosening the ties between church and state as suggested by the political left, but religious unity was similarly reconceptualized, as an immanent force that in principle was not restricted to ecclesiastical institutions sanctified by history. One MP remarked, 'as a free church the Lutheran Church would fulfil a good Christian mission in our country' (Wilhelm Gullberg of the Liberals, a free church preacher, FK, 3 May 1919: 33:49). For a utopian leftist, Christianity in general was a better substitute for 'the pure evangelical religion' in state government (Carl Lindhagen, Leftist Social Democrat, FK, 23 March 1923: 22:73; 27 February 1924: 15:36). The 1930s saw the strengthening of the notion of 'a free and energetic people's church' that constituted an alternative to the church as a visible institution of the state (Axel Lindqvist, AK, 8 May 1938: 35:53) supported by appeals to 'a humanly understood Christianity' and a 'modern spiritual culture' (Rickard Lindström, FK, 13 June 1936: 43:118). Thanks to its conservative origins, this idea of a 'Swedish people's church' was also acceptable to the rightist defenders of 'the Evangelical-Lutheran faith' (Viktor Sandström, FK, 21 April 1937: 26:63). Leading clerics including Archbishop Nathan Söderblom extended this train of thought to the international order, which was not always welcomed by Swedish MPs. Söderblom was engaged in the Young Church Movement (*Ungkyrkorörelsen*), which, inspired by student awakenings in Britain, had initially aimed at remaking the Swedish Church into a tool of God to reach the Swedish people and then, by extension, the world (Aronson 2009). One Social Democrat critic of 'ecumenical politics' regarded Söderblom's efforts as an imitation of Anglican and even Catholic practices, as well as an attempt to combat Social Democracy on the international level (Arthur Engberg, AK, 20 April 1921: 31:90; 15 March 1922: 17:71). Nevertheless, more idealistic visions were also present: a utopian socialist believed in 'a happy agreement between peoples to introduce Christianity into the world order' (Carl Lindhagen, FK, 31 January 1925, motion 182, 4–5). The rise of ecumenism within the Swedish Church is evident from the readiness with which it was associated with Protestantism in general, rather than only Lutheranism as had been conventional (Ernst Klefbeck, a Social Democratic clergyman, FK, 27 February 1932: 15:22).

As a concept, 'ecumenism' spilled over from religion into politics, a metaphorical – often ironic – use of the term that occurred also in the Netherlands and in Britain. Interparty cooperation across ideological divisions was typically styled as 'ecumenical'. Although in some cases it carried the pejorative associations of an unholy alliance, and domination by Social Democrats (Knut Petersson, Liberals, FK, 23 March 1938: 23:108), this conceptual valence was similar to ecumenism proper: unity needed to be achieved to further the cause of a common humanity, and to supersede historically given ideologies and institutions.

Despite the limited acceptance of ecumenist ideas, international ecumenism was heavily indebted to Swedish actors. The Church of Sweden supported the multilateral soft power diplomacy that was typical of Swedish politicians acting through secular institutions in the interwar era. In autumn 1919, the World Alliance convened in Oud Wassenaar in the Netherlands, bringing together representatives from Protestant and Eastern Orthodox Churches. The conference appointed Archbishop Söderblom to organize a formal international ecumenical body. The leader of the Swedish Church launched a meeting in Geneva and an ecumenical conference in Stockholm in 1925, which led to the founding of the Ecumenical Council in Geneva in 1930 and, in 1948, the World Council of Churches (WCC), although agreements had already been reached in 1937 (Thompson 2006: 55–56; Gorman 2010: 58–59). In Britain, similar trends of religiously motivated internationalism were represented by the Oldham group of Christian intellectuals who believed in the potential of Christian faith to support social and cultural renewal in an era of totalitarianism (Wood 2019).

## Changing Concepts of Christendom in a Postwar World

In British parliamentary debates, the first reference to 'ecumenical' international activities appeared rather late, only in 1944 when the late Archbishop Randall Davidson was thanked for his 'ecumenical outlook' by a Labour politician and Methodist lay preacher (Ernest Lamb, HL, 1 November 1944: 771). The term had the connotation of being left-wing and nonconformist, just as in the Netherlands and Sweden, which may explain the reticence expressed in 1961 by the Bishop of Chelmsford when he conceded that the word 'ecumenical' seemed 'to have come to stay for lack of any alternative'. He regarded it as 'a movement towards the recovery of unity, so that we may indeed be a whole Church of Christ, of one world-wide Christian fellowship'. If that was to be achieved, the territorial impact of the spirit would have to extend to all levels of society. But 'so far, the Ecumenical Movement has made its main impact upon the leaders of the Christian Churches: So far, I submit the Ecumenical Movement has made singularly little impact upon ordinary Church members at the local level in the towns and villages of our country' (Falkner Allison, HL, 10 May 1961: 289). This was going to change somewhat during the 1960s.

In the course of the decade several others observed 'the atmosphere of increasing good will between Churches' (Lance Mallalieu, Labour, HC, 5 December 1968: 1944). In the context of the Cold War and the Soviet threat, religious reconciliation within the Western bloc was encouraged. Decolonization, immigration and accelerating secularization led to calls for pragmatic toleration between believers. Even Conservative MPs – the traditional advocates of the established church – noted 'the greater understanding and the infinitely greater tolerance between Churches than ever before', rejoicing in 'the present ecumenical age, with much happier relationships between Churches' (William van Straubenzee, Con, HC, 31 October 1968: 313). By the end of the 1960s, a Roman Catholic MP likewise expressed his fondness for 'this wonderful ecumenical movement which has made such terrific, such unexpected, such staggering progress' (Frank Pakenham, Labour, HL, 30 January 1969: 1303). Church of England bishops talked about 'these days of growing ecumenical understanding' (Gerald Elison, the Bishop of Chester, HL, 8 May 1969: 1303) and Methodists praised interdenominational 'ecumenicity' (Donald Soper, a Methodist minister, HL, 30 January 1969: 1308). A peer supporting the Labour Party hoped 'ecumenism' would change not just educational practices but, ultimately, the world itself (Lord Chancellor Gerald Gardiner, HL, 15 November 1967: 698). MPs welcomed the advances of the ecumenical movement in the form of the WCC (Arthur Gore, Conservative, HL, 10 May 1961: 234; Fletcher, HC, 14 December 1962: 767), 'the ecumenical attitude' of Christians helping refugees (Frank Pakenham, HL, 6 May 1964: 1285) and the gathering force of 'the ecumenical movement all over the world' (Lance Mallalieu, HC, 23 February 1965: 330). Religious unity extended to the whole world in the discourse of the 1960s, as much as the world was assimilated into the nation. Experiences of rising immigration led to the suggestion that church leaders should make an ecumenical appeal against racial and religious hatred (Norman St John-Stevas, Con, HC, 23 March 1965: 411), and that school curricula should cover not only the various Christian denominations but also other faiths, including Judaism (Barnett Janner, a Labour MP with a Jewish background, HC, 4 November 1966: 879).

Surprisingly similar trends can be found in the Netherlands and Sweden. The epochal sense that universal understanding was finally possible had already reached the Netherlands in the mid-1950s. The word 'ecumenical' had cropped up in the Dutch parliament in the context of colonial politics, when an MP admonished the government to choose between the 'solidarity of all religions', emphatically including Islam, and the 'general destructive danger' of communism all over the world (Gijsbert Vonk, SDAP, SG2, 12 November 1946: 176). In the confines of the Cold War metanarrative and decolonization, the idea of inter-Christian and even interreligious dialogue was in the air and soon became a multipurpose tool in the hands of parliamentarians. At the same time, there were those who noted sarcastically that the reason Catholics and Protestants were allowed to give spiritual care, and humanists were not, was not ecumenical dialogue, of which they were incapable, but simply their inescapable social presence (Gerard van Walsum; in 1946 he traded the conservative CHU for the Labour Party, SG1, 16 April 1952: 687–88).

Invoking the Dutch Ecumenical Council, established in 1946 as a domestic expression of the WCC, MPs stressed the need to actively address social issues from the perspective of the churches. This resulted in discussions about disarmament (De Dreu, SG1, 23 March 1954: 385–86), requests for broadcasting time for the churches (Krol, SG2, 10 March 1955: 2564–65), and debates on a great many other topics, ranging from the atomic bomb and the moral drawbacks of economic growth to poverty and reconciliation with communist regimes. Even if discussions were often limited to domestic issues, they emphatically implied a reterritorialized concept of religious unity that included the national in the international. In the debate on broadcasting, references were made to 'ecumenism' as a concept enabling a broader understanding of theological concepts such as 'church' and 'priesthood of all believers' than the institutional churches allowed for. Thus, 'cooperation on an ecumenical level' was not the same as sticking church labels on religious activities, while the 'ecumenical congress' in Evanston (the Second Assembly of the World Council of Churches, 1954) had wise things to say on the nature of mission (Verwey-Jonker, SDAP, SG1, 18 October 1955: 2035–36).

More conservative MPs did not dispute the importance of either television broadcasting or ecumenism, but typically argued that one should not go so far as to put the church on a par with associations supporting 'cultural, artistic, humanitarian and other respectable and friendly objectives'. For now, in our post-materialist era, the church

is the conscience of the people [*volk*]. She now understands her apostolic task, here in this country, and in others beyond it. The churches agree with each other on this task and the 'ecumenical movement' is a powerful and not to be underestimated factor in humanity's passage to a future that, more than ever, will depend on the spirit. (Johannes de Zwaan, CHU, SG2, 18 October 1955: 2038)

In the 1960s, references to a reconceptualized ecumene were also made with respect to another offspring of the WCC, the Foundation for Ecumenical Aid to Churches and Refugees (Stichting Oecumenische Hulp aan Kerken en Vluchtelingen, 1952–2000; e.g. Minister for Agriculture Marijnen, SG2, 19 January 1961: 3617; debate regarding famine in Congo) and to John XXIII, who was remembered as a 'reconciliatory and ecumenical' pope (Jonkman, SG1, 5 June 1963: Buitengewone Zitting, 3). At the beginning of the parliamentary year, churches prayed for parliament in a combined service: 'proof of the progressively developing ecumenical idea' (Jonkman, SG1, 17 September 1963: 5). Only members of a traditional splinter party, the Reformed Political Party (Staatkundig Gereformeerde Partij, SGP), which consciously cultivated the older idea of the ecumene as a unified Dutch national body hallowed by a history that bore the mark of divine leadership, saw in the ecumenical movement a conspiracy to create a united Europe under the leadership of Rome (Van Dis, SGP, SG2, 1 October 1963: 57–59).

After the founding of the Ecumenical Council of Churches (Oecumenische Raad van Kerken) in 1968 as the successor to the Ecumenical Council after the Roman Catholics joined it, the word 'ecumenical' remained laden with progressive meaning: with the pursuit of 'horizontal' salvation and God's reign on earth, and not so much with saving individual souls. MPs with a distinct religious drive, committed to third-world development, liberation theology and human solidarity, invoked the WCC, the Dutch Interdenominational Peace Forum (Interkerkelijk Vredesberaad, IKV) and the Dutch branch of the Roman Catholic peace movement Pax Christi (Dolf Coppes, a Catholic ex-priest, Die Politieke Partij Radikalen, SG2, 26 February 1975: 3055–56).[5] Sweden saw a similar broadening of perspectives, related to the ascendancy of Social Democracy in politics: The churches began to organize an annual 'ecumenical development week' to 'create opinion about the responsibility of Christendom and society in trying to decrease gaps between the rich and poor in the world' (Thorvald Källstad, Liberal, RD, 7 November 1973: 127:74). The ecumenical development week stimulated 'local parishes to deepen their international engagement and intensify efforts to inform and awaken consciousness about the situation of the developing countries and the responsibility of the Swedish people' (Jan-Erik Wickström, Liberal, 8 November 1973: 129:78). Questions such as the atomic weapons and the status of Christians in the Eastern bloc were taken up by the churches, just as in the Netherlands.

In Sweden, aversion to Roman Catholicism survived longer than in either Britain or the Netherlands, as evidenced by a parliamentary controversy on allowing Catholics to establish monasteries as late as the 1950s (On the Religious Liberty Act, 1951). Many members continued to adhere to the unity of the Swedish nation and the Lutheran religion, viewing Catholicism as a foreign other. The Swedish Church went no further than to welcome Finnish Lutherans, who had belonged to the same church until 1809, emphasizing 'the living ecumenicity that has long been characteristic in Evangelical Lutheran Christendom and particularly in the Nordic countries' (Proposal for a Law on Religious Liberty, 23 February 1951: 146). Ecumenicity beyond nationhood became much more acceptable during the 1960s, which reflects a rapid change in values. One MP highlighted the WCC as 'the most extensive and profound international community which we currently have', involving 198 different Christian churches, advancing understanding and community between them, and inspiring the United Nations (Augustinus Keijer, AK, 12 March 1962: 12:57–58). Another praised 'the ecumenical work which now more than ever is needed at the international level', while supporting funding membership of the Lutheran World Union (Eric Nelander, who belonged to the Salvation Army, AK, 29 March 1963: 13:57).

Domestically, Social Democratic MPs who dominated the political scene pressed for 'toleration and an ecumenical inclination' within the Church of Sweden (John Lundberg and Åke Zetterberg, AK, 7 May 1963: 20:22). As one MP and clergyman put it: 'most within the Swedish Christendom welcome ecumenical approaches between churches' (Mårten Werner, Conservatives, RD, 23 February 1972: 27:82). Not surprisingly, the question of separation between church and state returned to the centre of the debate in the last two decades of the twentieth century. Although right-wing MPs continued to view the 'deep relation between church and state' as a key element of Swedish democracy (Gunde Raneskog, Centre, RD, 10 March 1978: 93:56), making use of a concept at the core of Swedish national identity (Göran Åstrand, Conservative, RD, 18 January 1989: 52:58), a majority of parliamentary parties were ready to see 'a divorce between church and state' (Bertil Fiskesjö, Centre, RD, 7 April 1988: 95:98). By 1998, the Social Democrats would conclude that the relationship created between church, crown and state by the Reformation should be changed as 'in our century these bonds have loosened, and modern democracy has given the people and nation the first place in relation to the king and the church'. That was a clear if somewhat belated institutional departure from the ecumene defined as a historical expression of religious nationhood (Parson Pär-Axel Sahlberg, RD, 18 November 1998: 17:50).

As we saw, conceptual and discursive changes since the 1960s typically preceded institutional rearrangements. In Sweden, some had long seen 'an ecumenical consensus' between the churches and the parliament, and had rejected 'a cultural conservative notion' of confessional teaching in schools (Jan-Erik Wikström, Liberals, a free church activist, RD, 21 November 1973: 143:87). Suggestions had been put forward for an ecumenical TV programme that would include non-Lutheran churches and 'even other religions' and 'thereby give a perspective of the world that could increase understanding for other people – and also for immigrants in our country – and for other cultures' (Eva Åsbrink, Social Democrats, doctor of theology, RD, 5 December 1972: 131:106). Rising immigration played an important part in reterritorializing religious unity in Sweden as elsewhere. As early as the 1960s, religious education in schools had been deemed more necessary than ever, in this era of 'internationalization in all fields of life', which called for a deeper knowledge of the 'different directions within Christianity, non-Lutheran orientations within Christendom and not least the rising importance of the ecumenical movement', as well as the 'non-Christian philosophies of religion and life' (Thorvald Källstad, Liberal, RD, 20 March 1963: 11:77). These debates pointed towards a third conceptualization of religious unity in relation to territoriality: the decline of Christianity and the fragmentation of Western dominance.

## A Fragmented World since the 1970s: Immigration, Multiculturalism and the Waning of the Ecumene

In Britain, the process of reconceptualizing the ecumene in terms of global humanity took an interesting turn in connection with debates on membership of the European Economic Community in 1971, when the Bishop of Southwark summarized the reasons for the British Council of Churches to support membership. Two world wars had taught Britons that they were inseparably bound up with Europe, he argued:

> the old European disunity and insistence upon nationalism has shown itself to be disastrous, not merely politically and militarily, but also economically ... one of the losses [of the Reformation] was that we broke away from European Christendom. That was a great disaster, because Christendom is much more than ecumenical relationships between Churches: it is a whole culture. I hope that, as a result of going into Europe, we may be able to share together our common European inheritance. We must think of ourselves first as Europeans and not as Frenchmen or Britishers. (Mervyn Stockwood, HL, 27 July 1971: 260–61)

Protestant Christianity indeed seemed to have shifted from supporting nationalism to advocating international cooperation and even common European identity. In the 1970s Europe, and not least Britain, no longer reflected such ideals. The Christian culture in which the European and global ecumene had been grounded had lost much of its influence.

Nevertheless, like the idea of religious nationhood, the vision of a global Christendom lingered on, though more inclusively towards non-Christian religions. School education was one key area through which the concept of ecumene was operationalized in Britain, as in 1960s Sweden. The Bishop of Guildford argued in 1979 that the curriculum 'needs to be both international in its choice of content and global in its perspective', covering 'the whole ecumene, which we share with people of all other races in all other countries across the world' (David Brown, Bishop of Guildford with a missionary background, HL, 24 January 1979: 1411). A leading Catholic peer concluded in 1977: 'In our ecumenism the religions of the world are getting together and the Christians are finding the same God the Father as the Jews have, and the same God the Father as have the Mohammedans' (Miles Fitzalan-Howard, HL, 18 May 1977: 817–18). At some point, of course, it needs to be asked whether the concept of the ecumene, rooted as it was in Christendom, was still a viable concept in a society where most people hardly could explain what Christianity itself entailed.

The less conservative theologians in parliament were inclined to circumvent this question. Robert Runcie, the Archbishop of Canterbury, insisted in 1988 that 'improved relations between Churches and, in places, between communities of faiths' provided welcome networks of consultation, in addition to the diplomatic ones (Robert Runcie, HL, 23 November 1988: 37–38). Conservative MPs, by contrast, remained critical of a school education that tended to 'blur the distinctions between religions' and disregard the fact that 'the religious traditions in Great Britain are in the main Christian' (Harry Greenway, HC, 19 July 1990: 1175). In their view, such education was 'more obsessed with interfaith dialogue than with any study of our own Christian faith', and neglected the Christian tradition only to prevent Muslims and Jews from being offended (Olga Maitland, HC, 16 July 1992: 1249). This inward turn to a Christianity that no longer had a substantial purchase on society was characteristic of a minority of MPs in all three countries. That the Church of England was 'thoroughly ecumenical in outlook' was hardly to the point (Michael Alison, Con, HC, 21 January 1991: 15). More important was its active role in 'interfaith co-operation' (John Habgood, former Archbishop of York, HL, 22 May 2002: 782) although that observation laid it bare to left-wing criticism concerning the value of a state church in a 'multi-creed society' (Tony Banks, HC, 28 October 1986: 214; Tony Benn, HC, 29 October 1993: 1109).

If the global ecumene had become a relic of the past, there were three ways forward for the future. Firstly, the fragmentation of culture could be accepted as a fact of life. Religious tradition would be kept intact, but could not be used to pursue a territorialized religious unity. The free churches had already proposed this solution in the nineteenth century, with one significant difference: the cultural context was now de-Christianized and secular. Secondly, the fragmentation of culture could be rejected. The pursuit of territorialized religious unity would remain worthwhile, but its religious basis would be extremely tenuous, if not negligible. The third option was simply to keep intact the (fictitious) concepts of the past, and to emphasize either religious nationhood or global Christendom.

Insofar as they were interested in religion at all, most parliamentarians tended to support the second option. After the end of the Cold War and before 9/11, to free Christians from misconceptions about Islam, they advocated 'inter-religious ecumenical dialogue' (Frank Judd, former director of Oxfam, HL, 18 January 1994: 591). It had become British government policy to avoid 'viewing the world as divided between religions' and demonizing Islam (Derek Fatchett, Labour, Minister of State for Foreign Affairs, HC, 18 March 1998: 1264). According to a Muslim peer, 'the interfaith movement throughout the world', especially that between Catholicism and Islam, 'should awaken world leaders to the new spirit of co-operation between the faiths that can be an effective base for peace between nations' (Nazir Ahmed, Labour, HL, 15 October 1999: 686–88). It is worth quoting this de-Christianized version of the global ecumene extensively:

> We can no longer afford to ignore religions as a significant factor in communal and international relations. Many conflicts around the world could be made amenable to resolution if the right religious approach were made. I say 'the right religious approach' because I am mindful of the long history of wars and massacres committed in the name of religion. The protagonists preferred to meet on the field of battle rather than the debating chamber. Humanity appears to be moving away from this painful path of hostility and hatred. Almost all the significant religious leaders of the world are calling for peace among nations and mutual respect between religions. We no longer hear the blood-curdling cry for religious conquest and coercion. The Parliament of the World's Religions gathered in one assembly not long ago the spokesmen of all religions to promote peace and harmony across the religious divide. They celebrated diversity of faiths and underlined the common human values enshrined in all the world's religions. (HL, 15 October 1999: 686–87)

The irony was that the pursuit of territorial unity on the basis of religion was lopsided: while religion appealed to majorities abroad, its hold on the larger communities at home had become insignificant. As one MP put it, in the context of the war on Iraq and Samuel P. Huntington's work on 'the clash of civilizations', 'we have entered into a new hundred years war – a war not between religions, but certainly based on religion' (David Heath, Liberal Democrats, HC, 8 March 2003: 888). Nevertheless, MPs (many of them clergy) invoked a de-Christianized ecumene even in the aftermath of the clash of civilisations exemplified by 9/11, optimistically regarding solidarity as the way to put terrorism to an end (Shirley Williams, Liberal Democrats, HL, 4 October 2001: 124) or welcoming the 'debate between religions as well as between nations' as the way forward (David Smith, the Bishop of Bradford, HL, 4 October 2001: 165). MPs applauded the fact that 'overtures of friendship have been made between churches and mosques' (Kathleen Richardson, a Methodist minister, HL, 4 October 2001: 178) and emphasized that 'dialogue between religions and states, between religions and within religions' was essential to the pursuit of peace and the war on terror (Colin Moynihan, Con, HL, 9 April 2003: 234). Achieving peace between religions was seen as the way to achieve world peace (Peter Forster, the Bishop of Chester, HL, 22 October 2003: 1612).

In Sweden, too, Christian Democrats, striving to avoid confrontations between religions and ethnic groups, created an interreligious council (Helena Höij, RD, 10 May 2006: 120:3). A Conservative MP welcomed the better visibility of 'all the children of Abraham' (Christians, Jews, Muslims) in Sweden and Europe (Hans Wallmark, RD, 26 April 2007: 99:12). Foreign Minister Carl Bildt (Conservatives) even suggested creating a European body that would 'promote dialogue between religions, cultures and nations' (RD, 18 February 2009: 72:6). In 2015, before the immigration crisis of that year, then Foreign Minister Margot Wallström (Social Democrats) expressed respect for the contribution of Islam to 'our common civilisation', claiming that 'we have worked for decades for toleration, diversity and understanding between religions – those in our country and those all over the world' (RD, 20 March 2015: 76:19).

Two terms used in the context of the de-Christianized ecumene were 'multicultural' and 'interreligious' (or interfaith). 'Multiculturalism' cropped up in the Netherlands after 1976, mainly in the context of a policy on minorities concerning such issues as primary education and health care in 'a Netherlands that has become multicoloured and multicultural', 'multiracial and multiform', with different 'cultural ethnic groups', and '260,000 Muslims and 57,000 Hindus' (various MPs, SG2, 13 February 1984: 52:1–71). 'Interreligious' turned up once in 1955 with reference to

French and British colonial law, which gave a fuller legal status to Islam and Christianity than Dutch law did to Catholicism (Lemaire, SG2, 24 November 1955: 2259). The term began to be used only much later in parliamentary discourse, from the very late 1990s onwards, in the context of deradicalization policies abroad and at home. In 2015, Foreign Minister Bert Koenders observed that 'interreligious tolerance is very important. I already mentioned antisemitism, anti-Islam, anti-Christendom; we see that these manifestations of the old wars of religion are returning in the Middle East' (Koenders, 24 March 2015, SG1: 25-8-7). In other words, the erstwhile Christian ecumene had given way to an international policy of containing religious extremism: it had become a secular conversation on mutual forbearance in a fragmented world with some radical communities of faith, devoid of its once deeply Christian overtones.

## Conclusion

In this chapter, we have addressed the role of religion in interdenominational national and international relations and demonstrated how it has been radically redefined during the past 150 years. The key questions were when, how and why mainstream Protestant religion became conceptualized in ways that were inclusive of religious diversity at home and abroad, and how this relates to the overall history of internationalisms. We have explored how politicians in three Northwest European countries traditionally considered 'Protestant' at first reconceptualized the relationship between religion and national identity or political citizenship and then, gradually, the religious aspects of international relations.

We chose to focus especially on 'ecumene' as the most obvious international theological concept of Christianity and on three Protestant countries that have all experienced long-lasting early modern constructions of supposed confessional unity in a nation state but also significantly contributed to the rise of ecumenism in the twentieth century. We analysed four periods of debate – one on the national church in the late nineteenth century, one on emerging ecumenism in the interwar era, one on postwar ecumenism, and one on the fragmented world since the 1970s. These entailed gradual redefinitions of religion with reference to territorial and disciplinary boundaries so that the fiction of a religiously uniform nation state was replaced with attempts to include the fact of diverse religious communities first nationally and then internationally. This process entailed major reconceptualizations of the ecumene and hence the international.

Our analysis, which combined distant reading of big data with contextual close reading, demonstrated that the traditional religious concept of nationhood identifying the church with the nation and state survived for a surprisingly long time in parliamentary discourse; the major changes only began in the 1960s. Christian ecumenical thinking at first made gradual progress within nations, starting with Protestants not belonging to the established, privileged or state church. Forward-looking religiously motivated internationalism, conceptualized as ecumenical cooperation aiming at world peace and universal understanding, only started to emerge after the First World War and long remained a leftist minority phenomenon criticized by conservatives.

Discourses on ecumenism shifted dramatically in all three countries in the fragmenting world of the 1960s at a time when decolonization, immigration, emerging multiculturalism, the disappearance of older religious unity and the secularization of political discourse increasingly challenged traditional religion at home and the context of the Cold War encouraged reconciliation. While the world was at first integrated with the nation, the nation became then increasingly integrated with the world. Since the 1960s, awareness about the coexistence of competing but declining religions in Western societies has supported the rise of more inclusive understandings of ecumenism, extending the initially Christian concepts to cover all faiths. Confrontations with radical Islam have encouraged a search for mutual understanding between religions and the joint international endeavour to confine religious fanaticism.

**Joris van Eijnatten** is Professor of Digital History at Utrecht University and general director of the Netherlands eScience Center. His numerous publications include books and articles on toleration, Dutch religious history, the poet Willem Bilderdijk, sermons, the justification of war, media history and conceptual history. A digital historian, Van Eijnatten specializes in applying digital methodologies to newspapers, periodicals, parliamentary records and other historical data, with a focus on tracing changing concepts over time. ORCID 0000-0002-8865-0002.

**Pasi Ihalainen** is Academy of Finland Professor at the Department of History and Ethnology, University of Jyväskylä, and has previously worked as a visiting professor at the universities of Freiburg, Gothenburg, Leiden and Uppsala. He has published widely on the history of political discourse and the conceptual history of nationalism, democracy and parliamentarism since the eighteenth century, applying comparative and transnational perspectives. ORCID 0000-0002-5468-4829.

## Notes

1. In the Dutch context, 'Calvinism' is somewhat of a misnomer, if only because it was rarely used. Much more common is 'Reformed', which in Dutch comes in several historically quite specific variations (e.g. *hervormd*, *gereformeerd*, *calvinistisch*).
2. The data for the research consists of three sets of plenary debates, made accessible on parliament or other websites, through search interfaces and downloadable datasets for Britain: https://hansard.parliament.uk/; Netherlands: https://zoek.officielebekendmakingen.nl/uitgebreidzoeken/historisch, http://search.politicalmashup.nl; Sweden: http://www.riksdagen.se/sv/riksdagsbiblioteket/litteratur-och-tjanster/sammanstallning-litteratur-och-tjanster/riksdagstryck/, http://www.riksdagen.se/sv/dokument-lagar/. Other search tools used for the sections include the Hansard Corpus – https://www.english-corpora.org/hansard/ – for Britain and the Swedish parliament website. A word on methodology: we have used off-the-shelf technologies in the programming language Python. For Ngrams we removed punctuation, made lists of words (retaining stopwords), and included only Ngrams with a frequency higher than 4, using the NLTK library (http://www.nltk.org/api/nltk.html#nltk.util.ngrams). For word vectors (embeddings) we employed the Gensim library (https://radimrehurek.com/gensim/models/word2vec.html). The following Word2Vec parameters were used: size=160, window=10, iter=12, min_count=3, workers=3.
3. 'Comprehension, n.', OED Online, Oxford University Press, available at https://www-oed-com (accessed 30 May 2019).
4. The World Alliance for International Friendship through the Churches, established in 1914, was regarded by its supporters as a way to give a 'soul' to the League of Nations.
5. *Interkerkelijk Vredesberaad*: the IKV (1974–2004) aimed to influence politics through action groups. The organization made its name by keeping in touch with Christians on the eastern side of the Iron Curtain, and by organizing two impressive demonstrations against nuclear weapons in 1981 and 1983 for which they twice mobilized about a half million protesters.

## References

### Primary Sources
Plenary debates
British parliamentary debates, House of Commons (HC) and House of Lords (HL), available at https://hansard.parliament.uk/; https://www.english-corpora.org/hansard/.
Dutch parliamentary debates, Eerste Kamer (SG1) and Tweede Kamer (SG2), available at https://zoek.officielebekendmakingen.nl/uitgebreidzoeken/historisch; http://search.politicalmashup.nl.
Swedish parliamentary debates, Första Kammaren (FK) and Andra Kammaren (AK), from 1971 Riksdag (RD), available at http://www.riksdagen.se/sv/riksdagsbiblio-

teket/litteratur-och-tjanster/sammanstallning-litteratur-och-tjanster/riksdags-
tryck/; http://www.riksdagen.se/sv/dokument-lagar/.

*Secondary Sources*

Alwall, J. 2000. 'Religious Liberty in Sweden: An Overview', *Journal of Church and State* 42(1): 147–71.

Aronson, T. 2009. *Ungkyrkorörelsen och pingstväckelsen i Sverige – fanns det någon initial kontaktyta mellan de två väckelserörelserna?* Available at https://teologia.fi/2009/11/ungkyrkoroerelsen-och-pingstvaeckelsen-i-sverige-fanns-det-na-gon-initial-kontaktyta-mellan-de-tva-vaeckelseroerelserna/.

Eijnatten, van J. 2003. *Liberty and Concord in the United Provinces: Religious Toleration and the Republic in the Eighteenth Century Netherlands*. Leiden: Brill.

Gorman, D. 2010. 'Ecumenical Internationalism: Willoughby Dickinson, the League of Nations and the World Alliance for Promoting International Friendship through the Churches', *Journal of Contemporary History* 45(1): 51–73.

Green, A. 2017. 'Religious Internationalisms', in G. Sluga and P. Clavin (eds), *Internationalisms: A Twentieth-Century History*. Cambridge: Cambridge University Press, pp. 17–37.

Ihalainen, P. 2005. *Protestant Nations Redefined: Changing Perceptions of National Identity in the Rhetoric of English, Dutch and Swedish Public Churches, 1685–1772*. Leiden: Brill.

McLeod, H. 2000. *Secularisation in Western Europe, 1848–1914*. Basingstoke: Macmillan.

———. 2003. 'Introduction', in W. Ustorf and H. McLeod (eds), *The Decline of Christendom in Western Europe, 1750–2000*. Cambridge: Cambridge University Press, pp. 1–26.

Thompson, D.M. 2006. 'Ecumenism', in Hugh McLeod (ed.), *The Cambridge History of Christianity: Volume 9, World Christianities c.1914 – c. 2000*. Cambridge: Cambridge University Press, pp. 50–70.

Wood, J. Carter. 2019. *This is Your Hour: Christian Intellectuals in Britain and the Crisis of Europe, 1937–49*. Manchester: Manchester University Press.

# Chapter 9

# 'Olympism Is Real Internationalism'

## Conceptualizations of Internationalism(s) in the Olympic Movement from the 1890s to the 1990s

*Antero Holmila*

The rise of the modern Olympic Movement in 1894 was part of the 'first internationalist turn' in the final decades of the nineteenth century that witnessed the birth of a number of international organizations, including the International Red Cross in 1863, the Postal Convention in 1875, the Esperanto Movement in 1887, the Permanent Court of Arbitration in 1899 and the Scouting Movement in 1908, to name but a few of the most important (Hoberman 1995: 1–37; Morgan 1995; Britchford 1996: 139; Preuss and Liese 2011; see Chapter 3). The rise of the Olympic Movement was also related to the globalization of sport more generally from the 1870s onwards, especially in connection with British imperialism when football, cricket and rugby became established in Asia, Europe and South America (Giulianotti and Robertson 2007: 1–2).

While sport was gradually being globalized, meaning that different sports were played all over the world, by the turn of the century it was not yet structured internationally. In other words, few sports had international governing bodies. For example, the International Football Association was founded in 1904, the International Swimming Federation in 1908, athletics (track and field) became regulated through the International Amateur Athletic Foundation in 1912 and tennis organized itself into the International Tennis Federation in 1913.

To a degree, the Olympic Movement was a driving force shaping the birth of these international federations. Indeed, one of the main ideas of the Olympic Movement was to facilitate the internationalization of sport by functioning as a nexus for the renewed ancient Greek sporting festivals, the Olympic Games. As I argue below, the point was not simply to organize sporting events to gather different sports under the umbrella of the same festival but to utilize the event to further international understanding and, ultimately, peace.

Despite some attempts, the forerunner to the Olympic Movement, the British Wenlock Olympian Games – relying on the English tradition of country sports – failed to become international (Beale 2011; Hill 1996: 12–13). However, the Wenlock Games were important, as the founder of the modern Olympic Movement and the creator of the International Olympic Committee (IOC) in 1894, the French baron Pierre de Coubertin (1863–1937), visited the Games in 1890, and became strongly convinced that sport must be internationalized and put to serve the betterment of societies.

The purpose of this chapter is to examine the meanings assigned to the concept of internationalism and closely related words such as 'nationalism', 'cosmopolitanism' and 'global', their evolution and changing meanings over time in the context of the Olympic Movement. The starting point, in the tradition of conceptual history, is to stress the hermeneutical inquiry and therefore the significance of 'the conceptual apparatus, horizons, and self-understanding of historical actors' (Richter 1995: 35). In what follows, I trace how the IOC – as seen in the discourses of the *Olympic Review* – has conceptualized international cooperation and utilized the concept of internationalism to legitimize its place within an international society. As I show, internationalism was never a contested concept within a movement itself. The IOC and its members constructed internationalism as a collective, defending their sporting internationalism against competing and the 'wrong' type of – e.g. socialist – internationalism; in the process they denounced the pejorative political connotations of the term.

The source material consists of the IOC mouthpiece, *Revue Olympique/ Olympic Review* (hereafter *RO*) and the records from Olympic Congresses, as the IOC utilized these forums to define and legitimize its historical purpose. The selected timeframe is roughly the first century of Olympic history, from the first Olympic Congress held in Paris in 1894 to the Paris Congress in 2000. To locate the discourses on internationalism, the *RO* was searched for the following keywords: internationalism* with 115 hits (71 in French/44 in English); nationalism* with 276 hits (149 in French/127 in English); cosmopolit* with 74 hits (46 in French/28 in English); global with 399 hits (108 in French/291 in English). The IOC started to use the concept of global in the 1960s to refer to world affairs or issues that had global reach, but it really rose in prominence during the 1990s. Overall, the figures are only indicative, and in many cases they are duplicates since after 1926 the publication was produced simultaneously in French and English, containing the same texts in translation.

As a publication, *RO* was atypical as it did not only contain articles by journalists and reporters. It was (and still is) a political forum for which many cabinet ministers, sports and business leaders wrote, as, of course, did key figures of the IOC. Occasionally, I also refer to selected materials from other publications, such as Coubertin's writings, insofar as they directly relate to my analysis. As a historical source, *RO* has been underutilized by sport scholars despite the fact that ever since its official inception in 1901 it was aware of its role as the mouthpiece for the Olympic Movement and the main organ through which Olympic ideology would be disseminated (Brown 2005: 82).

In historiography, the Olympic Movement's internationalism has attracted considerable interest. According to John Hoberman, one of the most prominent and critical scholars of its intellectual history, 'Olympic historiography ... has long been inseparable from the Movement's status as redemptive and inspirational internationalism' (Hoberman 1995: 1). What he meant was that through physical education and athletic contests (i.e. the Olympic Games) nations could release their competitive and potentially destructive energies. The sports field was preferable to a battlefield. Coubertin, the father of the Modern Olympic ideology (which he called 'Olympism'), viewed the Olympic Movement's internationalism as 'a kind of moral epistemology' (Morgan 1995: 12) centred on a *religio athletae*. The 'religious athlete' was an enlightened man who was proud of his original national roots but also tolerant and in friendly competition with his fellow sportsmen, acting as inspiration for the masses to follow (Krüger 1993: 93). As Coubertin wrote in 1894, Olympism should appeal to 'all those who truly love sport, to all those who also wish to see the youth of all countries united on the most peaceful of battlefields, the playing field' (de Coubertin 1894a: 1).

While Coubertin and the IOC self-consciously positioned themselves as international, what elements IOC internationalism consisted of has not always been clear. Douglas A. Brown has suggested that 'Coubertin's ideas on internationalism and non-governmental participation in international activity are the most misunderstood and misrepresented dimensions of the IOC and the Olympic Games' (Brown 2005: 24). Following Brown, it could be argued that it is even less clear how IOC internationalism evolved and changed over time.

Both terms – 'Olympism' and 'internationalism' – appeared in the first ever issue published by the IOC in 1894, although 'Olympism' in this case referred to the Greek Games. The front page of the *Bulletin du Comité International des Jeux Olympiques* discussed the Olympic idea as 'the best of Internationalisms' (*le meilleur des Internationalismes*) that every four years brings together the representatives of the nations of the world in peaceful and courteous struggle ('Le Congrés de Paris', *Bulletin* 1, 1894: 1). Evidently, internationalism was a positive concept of peaceful competition between nation states in an environment of mutual respect.

Clearly, then, the concept of internationalism constituted the key part of Olympism from the start. In Olympic discourses these terms (international and Olympic) appeared in -ism form, denoting their politicized status, even if the IOC has consistently downplayed the link between sport and politics (Senn 1999; Guttmann 2002; Boykoff 2016). Coubertin explained the term most thoroughly in 'The philosophical foundations of modern Olympism' in 1935, although he had been using it since the 1890s. For him, the ideology constituted the following elements: 'a religion of sport', 'an aristocracy', 'chivalry', 'truce', 'rhythm', 'the young adult male individual', 'beauty', 'peace', 'participation and competition' (de Coubertin 1966 [1935]: 130–34). Further, as he claimed in his writing, 'Olympism' was 'a religious sentiment' that was 'transformed and widened by Internationalism, Democracy and Science' (de Coubertin 1966 [1935]: 131). The original radio speech was given to German audience prior to the Berlin Olympics (1936). As the movement had endured harsh criticism for granting the Games to Nazi Germany but steadfastly defended the Germans' right to host, Coubertin's conceptualization of Olympism as democracy must be understood as a cultural project: democracy did not mean a form of government or representation, but a process of broadening people's right to have access to and practise sports. Such a message of Olympism was acceptable to both totalitarian and democratic systems.

## Internationalism and Cosmopolitanism

As is argued in Chapters 1–3, the term 'cosmopolitanism' was part of Europe's intellectual, aristocratic and political vocabulary in the eighteenth and nineteenth centuries, although its meaning remained negative or at least ambiguous. Given Coubertin's aristocratic background it is hardly surprising that he, too, adopted the concept in order to discuss certain features of the Olympic Movement. Indeed, the concept of 'cosmopolitanism' was only used and defined by Coubertin within the Olympic Movement, although he never truly espoused it. When he was not the direct source, the concept remained attached to Coubertin's ideas.

The only time cosmopolitanism was given a deeper conceptual meaning was at the turn of the century by Coubertin: 'Properly speaking, cosmopolitanism suits to those people who have no country, while internationalism should be the state of mind of those who love their country above all, who seek to draw to it the friendship of foreigners by professing for the countries of those foreigners an intelligent and enlightened sympathy' (de Coubertin 1898: 429–34).

Although internationalism was favoured over cosmopolitanism, the latter had a limited meaning, that shared characteristics with French eighteenth-century conceptualizations, such as 'one who does not adopt a fatherland' concept (see Chapters 1–2). As Coubertin explained in 1911: 'I owe so much to many cosmopolitan friendships'. He immediately qualified the concept significantly, explaining how these friendships 'never detracted from my love of my own country. But, just as much as I believe in the value of this kind of cosmopolitanism, I feel equally strongly that one must be wary of the brand of cosmopolitanism born of mere travel' (de Coubertin, cited in *RO* August 1977: 498). What is clear from this conceptualization is that cosmopolitanism was questionable, even dangerous if it negated a person's patriotism. As Coubertin was an educator, it is no surprise that his 'true internationalism' was connected with 'study' as the way to combat prejudices born out of ignorance. True internationalism recognized cultural and social differences and respected them.

On the whole, cosmopolitanism remained vague; despite the dangers of anachronism, it could be argued that its meaning was similar to today's terms 'global reach' or 'international character' (like Coubertin's friendships). The cosmopolitan and international could overlap, as in 1903 when Paul Champ noted that sports did not have a 'cosmopolitan character', but continued that major athletic events all over the world adhered to the IOC's international character (Champ, *RO* February 1903: 13).

When 'cosmopolitan' appeared in *RO* after Coubertin (who stepped down as IOC president in 1927 and died in 1937), it was used interchangeably with 'international' and 'global', as a simple qualifier with more neutral tone than Coubertin's. After the Second World War, cosmopolitanism had lost many of its negative connotations. The Olympic Congress in 1951 was held in Vienna, a city that had 'been blessed by nature with a cosmopolitan spirit' and in 1980, the small town of Lake Placid that hosted the Winter Games had acquired 'cosmopolitan flavour' (*RO* January–February 1980: 10). In both cases – while separated by three decades – the meaning of the text would not have been much different if cosmopolitan had been replaced with international. The same could not have been said about Coubertin's use of the concept.

## Internationalism and Nationalism

Although in Olympic historiography the tension between nationalism and internationalism is often defined as 'an Olympic paradox' (Mandell 1976), the fact remains that from its inception, Olympic internationalism was situated within the nation-state framework and nationalism was seen as a positive force. It was part of the progressive vision of Olympism that nationalism was channelled in an 'enlightened way' bearing hallmarks of 'humanity' such as international understanding and friendship (Hoberman 1995: 8). Coubertin discussed the issue in his *Notes sur L'Education Publique* (1901), demonstrating that his version of nationalism was not

> unhealthy, but it would quickly become so if it were not corrected by sincere internationalism. There are two ways of understanding internationalism. One is that of the socialists, revolutionaries and ... utopians; they foresee a gigantic levelling out that will make the civilized universe a state without frontiers ... The second is that of men who observe without bias and take account of reality, rather than their favourite ideas; they have long noted that national characteristics are an indispensable condition for the life of a people and that, far from weakening them, contact with other people strengthens and enlivens them. (de Coubertin 1901: 262–63)

This definition illustrated the antagonism that Coubertin (and by extension the Olympic Movement) felt towards socialist internationalism: in a sense it was seen as a negative extension of cosmopolitan ideology (cf. Chapter 4). The lack of nation states, borders and barriers as well as the inability to recognize national peculiarities distilled the civilized world into 'the most monotonous of tyrannies' (de Coubertin 1901: 262).

A year later, in 1902, Coubertin posed a crucial question in the French political and literature magazine *Revue du Pays de Caux*: 'What is to be thought of socialism?' He defined it as 'a cult', and 'a new religion', although from its basic tenets 'it appears to be eminently respectable, for it proceeds from the best of the human soul, the notion of justice and the impulse of goodness' (de Coubertin 1902: 137). After all, Coubertin's Olympism was also 'a new religion'. In his view, socialism had two key problems: it was dependent on international cooperation and dogmatic misreading of capitalist development (see Chapter 4). As socialism pitted two groups (proletariat versus bourgeoisie) against each other, it could not survive in its current form (unlike Olympism, which at least in theory, if not in practice, wanted to embrace all people from all classes): 'Socialism, in order to live, must be a producer of wealth: and to produce wealth, it must be the result of an understanding between peoples' (de Coubertin 1902: 141). Yet, rather than increasing interaction, Coubertin found socialist internationalism to be in decline: cross-border solidarity among the working class was not strong enough. Blinded by a Marxist view of the economy, socialism could not see that capitalism was not in a steady and permanent crisis, but reforming itself: 'Capitalism is [being] reborn in a new form, very alive, very robust ... If socialism has to wait to overtake it ... it will wait a long time' (de Coubertin 1902: 136–46).

While Coubertin wrote about socialism, 'socialist internationalism' was never discussed on the pages of *RO*. Similarly, the paper remained silent about Marx, communism and the workers Olympiad. As the above citations suggest, unlike Olympic internationalism, which strove to achieve concrete practical international action through contact between peoples, Coubertin disliked 'theorists and utopians'. He applied this vision to the Olympic context when speaking at the 1905 Olympic Congress in Brussels: out of 'all the internationalisms ... ours ... is the most healthy and normal. Athletics, in fact, brings peoples closer together, making them more aware of those essential differences of temperament and mentality which characterize their national existence: it organizes peace on the basis of legitimate and fruitful rivalries' (Olympic Congress Report 1905: 16).

In Coubertin's vision, the Olympic was unlike any other type of internationalism (whether socialist or not, pacifist or women's) that had permeated urban culture in fin-de-siècle Europe. Above all, it was more than the main competing form, the socialist one. Olympic internationalism represented a 'healthy' ideal. Unlike its socialist counterpart, Olympic internationalism was capable of both recognizing and respecting national differences; it used friendly competition to steer national passions and natural competitive impulses towards peaceful coexistence. This view recognized rivalry as an essential feature of international life. As the discussion on cosmopolitanism has established, for Coubertin, love of one's country was a natural sentiment. Like many internationalists after the First World War, he concluded that patriotism and internationalism were not opposites but needed one another (MacAloon 2008: 112; Holmila and Ihalainen 2018; Chapter 6).

Indeed, Coubertin argued that while in the Ancient Olympics the athlete was honouring his gods, 'In modern times, the athlete in his achievement honours his country, his race and his national flag' (*Bulletin du Comité International Olympique* 1956: 52). In other words, true patriotism was not incompatible with internationalism, as Coubertin made very clear: 'internationalism should be the state of mind of those who love their country above all, who seek to draw to it the friendship of foreigners by professing for the countries of those foreigners an intelligent and enlightened sympathy'

(Morgan 1995: 14). Such a position between the socialist and nationalist sentiments was precarious and Coubertin faced strong criticism. The inter-war French right (see Chapter 6) was especially suspicious of Coubertin's internationalism.

The symbolic meaning of the Olympic flag further illustrates the early entwined and positive relationship between internationalism and national-ism. As Coubertin noted in 1913 in preparation for the 1914 Congress:

> five interlaced rings in different colours – blue, yellow, black, green, red – stand out against the white background. These five rings represent the five parts of the world that Olympism has now acquired and are ready to accept its fertile rivalries. Moreover, the six colours thus combined reproduce those of all nations without exception. The blue and yellow of Sweden, the blue and white of Greece, the French, English, American, German, Belgian, Italian and Hungarian tricolours, the yellow and red of Spain, the yellow and red of Spain, the Brazilian and Australian innovations, the old Japan and the young China. This is truly an international emblem. (*RO* August 1913: 5)

As this citation makes clear, the meaning of internationalism was con-stituted through nation states. After the Second World War, however, Coubertin's original vision of 'enlightened nationalism' and 'fruitful rival-ries', which had become mainstream in the interwar liberal discourse, no longer held much conceptual power.

In general, converging with wider discourses from 1945 to the 1970s, nationalism as a concept almost exclusively denoted something negative in postwar Olympic discourse. For example, the editorial 'Olympism and Nationalism' lamented that classification tables were 'undoubtedly written with the intent of serving national if not nationalistic ends' (*RO* March 1952). In another editorial, published in 1964, Swiss journalist Frederic Schlatter commented how 'sport is used everywhere as an instrument for nationalism; only the circumstances and methods vary. Now this use of sport for political and nationalistic ends is, since Coubertin revived the Olympic Games, in conflict with the strong tendency to make of sport a means of contact between nations' (*RO* February 1964: 89).

By the mid-1970s, the movement was facing a crisis: 'The ideal extolled by Coubertin has lost its purity and it can even be stated that the ideal of the modern Games is exactly the contrary to that of Coubertin ... Nowadays, the Olympic Games have been transformed into a sports "war" – a "war" aimed at winning the greatest number of medals' (*RO* May 1978: 296).

By the 1970s Coubertin's Olympic vision was lost under the pressures of a post-industrial and postmodern world. Supposedly 'healthy' nationalism was almost bankrupt due to the Second World War, and commercialism had become a key conceptual struggle for the IOC (Holmila 2020). Nevertheless, internationalism remained the cornerstone of the movement. During the decades of Cold War détente, a modest attempt was made to hang on to the original concept of positive nationalism. This can be seen in the discourse about the loss of Coubertin's ideal and the lamentations over nationalism that often came with semantic qualifications such as 'blind nationalism', 'excessive nationalism', 'chauvinistic nationalism' and 'narrowminded nationalism', to cite just a few examples. Therefore, Olympic discourse still implicitly recognized Coubertin's notion of 'enlightened nationalism' even if contemporaries argued that it had vanished from the sporting field.

The final semantic shift in the concepts of inter/nationalism was related to increasing globalization: sport felt the impact of this, not least with the rise of TV, satellite communications and commercialization. Although nationalism remained a negative counter-concept to internationalism after the Second World War, with the growing global connectedness following the Cold War, internationalism regained prominence within the Olympic discourse: 'Progressive internationalism about which the Baron spoke has ... become even more tangible today', argued the rector of Quebec University in 1990 (*RO* July 1990: 312). The socialist bloc was crumbling at the time of writing, and the Olympic Movement also caught the tailwind of the liberal democratic triumphalism following the end of the Cold War. Writing under the title 'The Olympic Movement and International Understanding', Kiwi journalist and historian Ron Palenski argued that 'the Olympic Movement, and especially as manifested in Games opening and closing ceremonies, serves the cause of internationalism rather than nationalism as the world stage draws all together so one can learn and better understand another' (Olympic Congress Report 1994: 68). For T.A. Bhuvanendra, a Sri Lankan triple jumper and academic, by the 1990s, 'The concept of internationalism as an ethical proposition [had overtaken] all other ideologies and systems that once stood astride the fulcrums of history'. This change meant that nationalism had 'become obsolete in the political framework [while] [m]ost of the erstwhile national problems have assumed global proportions' (T.A. Bhuvanendra, *RO* 24, 1998: 15).

These new global problems included health, environmental concerns and drug abuse. Although difficult to back up with strong empirical evidence, the above statements are indicative of a brief 'end of history' optimism at the end of the Cold War, which gave birth to a movement known as Sport for Development and Peace. Importantly, these initiatives were not only supported by the IOC but also business corporations and multilateral organizations like the United Nations (Keys 2019: 6–7).

## Internationalism, Peace and Friendly Rivalry

The modern Olympic Movement had its roots in the first Olympic Congress held at the Sorbonne University in Paris in June 1894 (Mandell 1976; Guttmann 2002; Goldblatt 2018). It included seventy-eight delegates from nine countries (Brown 2005: 24). Dietrich Quanz has argued that the Olympic Movement originated much less in Coubertin's love of Antiquity than in his timely concern for peace and practical involvement with contemporary peace movements (Quanz 1993: 9–10). For instance, when the founding congress of the IOC gathered in Paris in 1894, five future Nobel Peace laureates were its honorary members (Quanz 1993; Hoberman 1995).

Thus, it is hardly surprising that Olympic internationalism was first mentioned in explicit connection with peace promotion, on the first page of the first IOC publication. During the 1880s Paris was the international centre for pacifists. The first annual Universal Peace Congress under the auspices of the International Parliamentary Union was held in Paris in 1889, an event which Coubertin followed with much interest, from which he developed personal contacts with peace movement activists (Quanz 1993: 5–11). Although the Olympic motto *citius, altius, fortius* (faster, higher, stronger) is well-known today in sporting circles and beyond, Coubertin originally planned for it to be *ludus pro pace*, or 'games/sport for peace' (de Coubertin 1894b: 177; Quanz 1993: 11).

Coubertin's concern for peace also formed a key discourse in the Olympic press. He wrote how every four years the Olympic Games brought together athletes and it was possible 'to believe that these peaceful and courteous struggles constitute the best of internationalisms' (de Coubertin 1894a: 1). The following year he reformulated 'peaceful and courteous' as 'peace and fraternity' with an important link to nationalism: Olympic internationalism promoted peace in practice by bringing athletes together in the Games in mutual respect and ready to form friendly relations. Olympic internationalism had been 'born in the great need for peace and fraternity that rises from the depths of the human heart' (*Bulletin du Comité International des Jeux Olympiques* 1895: 4).

Over the following century, the discourse on 'peace through friendship' has remained largely stable as expressed in the Olympic discourse. In 1938, the IOC president, the Belgian Henri de Baillet-Latour, stated that peace would soon be re-established and that, 'through happy interpretation of sport, concord and harmony will be restored among the youth of the world' (*RO* July 1938: 32). In 1978, Nadia Lekarska, a member of the Bulgarian Olympic Committee, similarly argued that 'the basic Olympic principles ... promote ... mutual esteem and friendship among the sporting youth all over the world in a climate of goodwill, peace and understanding' (*RO* July 1978: 461). When, in 1952, the socialist bloc was admitted to the 'Olympic family', it adopted the Olympic language. Essentially, this was easy to do since at least in principle the movement opposed commercial intrusion into sport and advocated peace as a social force, practiced by amateurs. Paradoxically, given that the early history of the movement was defined by its opposition to Marxist socialism, Olympic rhetoric after the Second World War was closer to socialist discourse than to the capitalist discourse in the West. As a consequence, the representatives from the Eastern bloc did not need to refer to Marxist principles per se – it was enough to embellish the original rhetoric of peace, friendship and solidarity to adhere to socialist doctrines.

While such Olympic discourse has always been more aspirational than actual, obviously incapable of preventing wars and conflicts in practice, the core principle has remained: Olympic internationalism aimed at functional ends not abstractions, and the movement's spokespersons were usually explicit about this. Tackling this issue, Mohamed Mzali, Prime Minister of Tunisia and member of the IOC, argued: 'Olympism is a real internationalism. The moral portrait of the Olympic athlete is a portrait in which universality holds a choice place. Friendship among races, among peoples, and among men must always be the last word of Olympism' (*RO* August–September 1982: 475). As Juan Antonio Samaranch put it, sport should be placed 'at the service of the harmonious development of humankind with a view to encouraging the establishment of a peaceful society concerned with the preservation of human dignity' (*RO* June–July 1999: 3).

These conceptualizations of Olympic internationalism make constant reference to youth. Making the world a better (and more international) place was put discursively in the hands of young people – essential to the *religio athletae* – not of heads of states, politicians or corporations. Young people gathering denoted tangible internationalism which transferred into lived practice in daily life, as people 'with a greater understanding of the Olympic Movement and its enhanced role in international understanding know that the movement and its ideals can and should impinge on the daily lives of everyone' (Palenski, Olympic Congress Report 1994: 68).

The embodiment and lived practice of Olympic peace and friendship was the Olympic village in which the athletes lived together during the Games. The 1924 Games in Paris was the first to have a village, but the practice was only consolidated in the 1932 Games at Los Angeles. William May Garland, the President of the Los Angeles Organizing Committee, greeted the athletes by asking them to demonstrate how they 'can produce a record of peace and happiness' during and after the Games (Baker 2016). Decades later, Greek Epaminondas Petralias noted the same spirit when he argued how Olympism transcended 'national boundaries and our very own "Olympic village" proves this'. In a tone which belittled the many problems the movement was facing (writing in 1977 when the Games were suffering from a cycle of boycotts and the lack of cities to compete for hosting it), he continued to note that although there had been 'incidents of political rivalry and sporting tension', they were 'tiny compared to the internationalism and friendship we have enjoyed and serve to reinforce our pragmatic approach to the problems of internationalism today' (*RO* January 1977: 25; see also Philip M. Bruebaker, *RO* May 1984: 321).

## Internationalism in a Global Era

Finally, the concept of 'global' also became a fixture in the Olympic discourse in the 1990s, although sporadic uses of the term can be found from the 1960s onwards. For example, the Olympic Congress records from Varna (1973) and Baden-Baden (1981) have few references to 'global' while the Paris centennial Congress in 1994 is suffused with the term. *RO* shares the same pattern. While in the 1960s, there were few random references to 'global', in the 1970s there were twenty-seven hits, in the 1980s sixty-two hits, and in the 1990s 192 hits, reflecting the diversification of the ways in which internationalism was constructed.

The first time the term 'global' appeared in the *RO* was in 1960 with reference to the IOC's financial aid to international federations (*RO* November 1960: 63). The following year 'global' was used as a technical term, when Ernst Jokl examined 'a global analysis of data' on 'a global scale' (*RO* November 1961: 37). In the 1970s, global remained a technical term. Semantics like 'global evolution', 'global development' (*développement global*) and 'global dimension of sport' were used purely descriptively as a short-hand for 'worldwide', without any attempts to define their meaning (*RO* October–November 1978: 601; *RO* September–October 1975: 371; *RO* October 1979: 573).

In the 1980s, 'global' started to gain wider meanings and conceptual significance, although primarily it was still used as a technical term. Louis Leprince-Ringuet, a French scholar, was worried that 'at certain moments of great rugby or football matches, one catches a glimpse of this feeling of global hostility in the form of an enemy to be beaten, as if the players were waging war against each other' (*RO* September–October 1981: 547) while Don Anthony discussed sport as a communal activity referring to a 'global family of sports' (*RO* July 1987: 326). By the 1988 Seoul Games, the idea of a 'global sports family' had clearly taken root and as a concept, 'global' was fixed to Coubertin's Olympic discourse. As Seh-Jik Park, the President of the Organizing Committee, mentioned in the opening ceremony of the Seoul Games: 'vigorous competition will lead to harmony which will grow into friendship and in this way, each member of the global family will receive the most precious of all gold medals – the gold reward of love and peace' (*RO* November 1988: 490). At the Paris Congress in 1994, Tapio Korjus, a Finnish sports administrator and Olympic gold medallist in javelin (Seoul, 1988), argued in a line not dissimilar to Park: 'Sport is an influential factor on the international forum. Communication through athletes, sports organizations, and sports competitions contributes to global understanding' (Paris Congress Report 1994: 81).

While 'global' had come to signify similar issues to 'internationalism', it did not mean that the latter term was becoming less used or being replaced by the former. In essence, 'global understanding' represented the same idea as 'international understanding' but was less Eurocentric. While for a long time 'internationalism' had operated as a hierarchical term, linked to a world order led by Europe and the United States, 'global' was more universal in its connotation. In a 1995 article, the Swedish Social Democratic Prime Minister Ingvar Carlsson wrote how 'the concept of global village is a reality. Our entire planet had become our neighbourhood'. In the same article he claimed that 'internationalism has always been a Swedish key concept. This is why we feel a natural sense of affinity with the Olympic Movement, which creates the frontierless [*sic*] meeting places of increasing important today' (*RO* August–September 1995: 27). As the article neatly illustrates, the terms were used interchangeably but with universal tones as indicated by the words 'frontierless' and 'planet'.

## Conclusion

Although the texts discussed above do not represent the sum total of Olympic internationalism, they constitute its most important conceptualizations. Over the course of a century, certain semantic fields were related to the term, which changed over time and due to external pressures (including two world wars, the Cold War and technological change) while other elements remained stable. Cosmopolitanism, for example, was never truly a part of Olympic discourse beyond Coubertin's writings at the turn of the twentieth century. On the whole the baron constructed it in a fairly negative way. Based on these conceptualizations we could argue that the IOC did not semantically construct itself on the premises of cosmopolitanism (or universalism) but on internationalism and on nationalism.

Above all, in any decade, these discourses on Olympic internationalism relied on and adhered to Coubertin's vision that internationalism was healthy as it encouraged practical interaction between different people and nations who respected one another. At no point were Coubertin's views challenged or alternative conceptualizations even offered within the Olympic Movement. Yet, if the source material were enlarged to other forums such as the European and US daily and sports press, a more variegated view would no doubt emerge.

The most stable semantic field which gave meaning to internationalism was the discourse on peace, friendship, mutual understanding and tolerance: themes which paralleled the movement's progressive and eminently educational perspective on Olympism. While Olympic internationalism drew its inspiration from the ideas of peace and friendship, nationalism remained another key concept. Only after the Second World War did nationalism begin to appear as a counter-concept to internationalism, but even then the *Olympic Review* sought to highlight 'bad' nationalism. Tacit in this construction was that 'good' nationalism (in other words, Coubertin's vision of it) remained somewhere in the background. Indeed, for Coubertin, nationalism was positive as long as it was directed towards progressive goals, such as respect for other peoples' nationalisms and love of their homelands. The internationalism of the Olympic Movement was situated in precisely this type of nationalistic framework. Originally, the concepts were not mutually exclusive but compatible and mutually dependent. In the 1990s the term 'global' emerged as an alternative to (but not a substitute for) 'internationalism'. Importantly, the semantics of the global immediately adopted Coubertin's language of 'friendship, toleration and peace' and the two concepts, internationalism and global, came to be used interchangeably.

While the statements on Olympic internationalism were more aspirational than actual – Olympic solidarity, friendship and toleration have hardly been a sufficient antidote to war and conflict – they were nevertheless genuine attempts to participate in the process of building a tolerant international community. For the IOC, the concept of internationalism was never a technical formulation, mere catchphrase or empty concept to which they paid lip service. It was an idea and practice embodied in both symbolic rituals (the Olympic hymn, flag, oath, and opening and closing ceremonies) and material practices, such as the Olympic Games itself, the Olympic villages, the Olympic Congresses and International Olympic Academy. As a fitting closure to this century of Olympic internationalism, Seiuli P. Wallwork argued how Olympism promoted 'fair play, international understanding, tolerance, friendship, and respect for the language and culture of others. It enhances morality. Like religion, it is a way of life with a spiritual quality, creating a sense of inner unity and promoting camaraderie and friendship' (*RO* February–March 1998: 73).

**Antero Holmila** is Associate Professor of Modern History at the Department of History and Ethnology, University of Jyväskylä, Finland. He has published widely on the histories of the era following the Second World War, including the transition from war to peace, the emergence of the Holocaust in British and Nordic collective memories, the birth of the United Nations, geopolitical thinking and the International Olympic Committee during the Cold War era. ORCID 0000-0003-2456-7223.

# References

*Primary Sources*

*Revue Olympique / Olympic Review* (under different titles on the following dates):
  *Bulletin du Comité International des Jeux Olympiques* (1894–95)
  *Supplément du Messager d'Athéns* (1896)
  *Revue Olympique* (1901–14)
  *Bulletin du Comité International Olympique* (1915)
  *Bulletin Officiel du Comité International Olympique* (1926–38)
  *Revue Olympique / Olympic Review / Olympische Rundschau* (1939–44)
  *Bulletin du Comité International Olympique* (1946–67)
  *Newsletter* (1967–69)
  *Olympic Review* (1970–)
*The American Monthly Review of Reviews*
*Revue du Pays de Caux*
*La Revue de Paris*


Olympic World Library, Lausanne, Switzerland
  Olympic Congress Reports, 1894–2009
  The Papers of Pierre de Coubertin
  The Papers of Avery Brundage
  The Papers of Lord Killanin
  The Papers of Juan Antonio Samaranch

Pamphlets, memoirs:
de Coubertin, P. 1894a. 'Chronique', *Bulletin du Comité International des Jeux Olympiques* 2.
———. 1894b. 'Le Rétablissement des Jeux Olympiques', *La Revue de Paris*, 15 June: 177.
———. 1898. 'Does Cosmopolitan Life Lead to International Friendliness?', *The American Monthly Review of Reviews* 17: 429–34.
———. 1901. *Notes sur L'Education Publique*. Paris: Hachette.
———. 1902. 'Que faut-il penser du socialisme?', *Revue du Pays de Caux* 4 (September).

————. 1966 [1935]. *Olympic Idea: Discourses and Essays*. Stuttgart: Olympischer Sport-Verlag.

## Secondary Sources

Baker, P. 2016 'A History of Athletes' Villages at an Olympic Games from 1924 to 2016', *Inside the Games*. https://www.insidethegames.biz/articles/1038893/a-history-of-athletes-villages-at-an-olympic-games-from-1924-to-2016.

Barney, R.K. and K.V. Meier (eds). 1994. *Critical Reflections on Olympic Ideology*. London, ON: University of Western Ontario.

Beale, C. 2011. *Born out of Wenlock – William Penny Brookes and the British Origins of the Modern Olympics*. Derby: DB Publishing.

Boykoff, J. 2016. *The Power Games: A Political History of the Olympics*. London and New York: Verso Books.

Britchford, M. 1996. 'Avery Brundage and the Internationalization of the Olympic Games', in *Olympic Perspectives: Third International Symposium for Olympic Research*. London, ON: Western University, pp. 139–44.

Brown, D.A. 2005. 'The Olympic Games Experience: Origins and Early Challenges', in K. Young and K.B. Wamsley (eds), *Global Olympics: Historical and Sociological Studies of the Modern Games*. New York: Elsevier, pp. 19–42.

Giulianotti, R. and R. Robertson (eds). 2007. *Globalization and Sport*. Oxford: Blackwell.

Goldblatt, D. 2018. *The Games: A Global History of the Olympics*. New York: W. W. Norton & company.

Guttmann, A. 2002. *The Olympics: A History of the Modern Games*. Champaign: University of Illinois Press.

Hill, C.R. 1996. *Olympic Politics: Athens to Atlanta 1896–1996*. Manchester: Manchester University Press.

Hoberman, J. 1995. 'Toward a Theory of Olympic Internationalism', *Journal of Sport History* 22(1): 1–37.

Hobsbawm, E. 1990. *Nations and Nationalism since 1780*. Cambridge: Cambridge University Press.

Holmila, A. 2020. 'Olympialiikkeen kriisi(t) ja transformaatio 1970-luvulla', *Suomen urheiluhistoriallisen seuran vuosikirja 2019*. Helsinki: Suomen urheiluhistoriallinen seura, pp. 13–37.

Holmila, A and P. Ihalainen 2018. 'Nationalism and Internationalism Reconciled? British Concepts for a New World Order During and After the First and Second World War', *Contributions to the History of Concepts* 13(2): 25–53.

Keys, B. (ed.). 2019. *The Ideals of Global Sport From Peace to Human Rights*. Philadelphia: University of Pennsylvania Press.

Krüger, A. 1993. 'The Origins of Pierre de Coubertin's Religio Athletae', *Olympika* vol.II: 91–102.

MacAloon, J.J. 2008. *This Great Symbol: Pierre de Coubertin and the Origins of the Modern Olympic Games*. London: Routledge.

Mandell, R.D. 1976. *The First Modern Olympics*. Berkeley: University of California Press.

Morgan, W.J. 1995. 'Coubertin's Theory of Olympic Internationalism: A Critical Reinterpretation', in R.K. Barney and K.V. Meier (eds), *Critical Reflections on Olympic Ideology*. London, ON: University of Western Ontario, pp. 10–25.

Quanz, D.R. 1993. 'Civic Pacifism and Sports-Based Internationalism: Framework for the Founding of the International Olympic Committee', *Olympika: The International Journal of Olympic Studies* 2: 1–23.

Pound, D. 2004. *Inside the Olympics: A Behind the Scenes Look at the Politics, the Scandals and the Glory of the Games*. Hoboken, NJ: Wiley.

Preuss, H. and K. Liesel (eds). 2011. *Internationalism in the Olympic Movement: Idea and Reality between Nations, Cultures, and People*. Wiesbaden: Springer.

Redihan, E.E. 2017. *The Olympics and the Cold War, 1948–1968: Sport As Battleground in the U.S.–Soviet Rivalry*. Jefferson, NC: McFarland & Company.

Richter, M. 1995. *The History of Political and Social Concepts: A Critical Introduction*. Oxford: Oxford University Press.

Senn, A.E. 1999. *Power, Politics and the Olympic Games*. Champaign, IL: Human Kinetics.

Steinmetz, W., M. Freeden and J. Fernández-Sebastián (eds). 2017. *Conceptual History in the European Space*. New York: Berghahn.

Young, K. and K.B. Wamsley (eds). 2005. *Global Olympics: Historical and Sociological Studies of the Modern Games*. New York: Elsevier.

# Chapter 10

# European Unity and the Nation State

*Mats Andrén and Joris van Eijnatten*

❖

In contemporary Europe, the concept of the nation has derived its meaning in part from its entanglement with the project of European integration. Because they are embedded in cooperation and multilateralism within the frame of European decision making and law, ideas of sovereignty and independence no longer have the implications they had before. On the one hand, the European Union has a parliament, a foreign office and a commission that to some extent acts like a cabinet. The citizens of the member states have European citizenship, which brings with it certain rights, while the Union has instituted a range of signifiers that includes a European passport, a flag and an anthem. On the other hand, the postwar development of a European governing structure has by no means led to a dismissal of the nation state, which continues to be the main entity within the EU, or to a removal of nationality and nationhood. Even if it were possible to discern a European identity, it remains an open question how strong such an identity actually is; it is indisputable that a robust national identity still exists among the citizens of the member states.

From the outset, the idea driving the general thrust towards European integration was to reconcile the interests of the nation states with their cooperation in common legal, political and economic frameworks. In the official rhetoric of the EU, this has often been referred to as the ingenious innovation of the French statesman Jean Monnet. From the perspective of the early postwar years, this 'innovation' should rather be considered as a rational way of managing the shortcomings of the states. These were generally exhausted economically, while the victors had to deal with Germany in a way that would not feed revanchist sentiments. Taken with the threat of further communist expansion and the fear of a third world war fought with nuclear weapons, it was no surprise that initiatives for closer cooperation were taken within Western Europe. From 1948 the USA clearly pushed for Western European integration as a way to stabilize and advance the European economy. It was also part of British and US policy to knit the West more closely together in a security and defence arrangement.

Alan Milward's seminal study on the integration process clearly demonstrated how the initiators of postwar integration and the European Economic Community (EEC) – like Konrad Adenauer, Hendrik Brugmans, Robert Schumann and Paul-Henri Spaak – never dropped the concept of the nation state but saw an opportunity for rescuing and even strengthening it by partly giving up national sovereignty and the step-by-step integration of law, the economy and politics (Milward 2000: 318–44). In contrast to the politicians, intellectuals did not require external pressure to affirm the quest for European unity. Immediately after the war, writers, philosophers and scholars looked for ways to continue the transnational intellectual exchanges of the interwar period, and they engaged in an intense and creative discourse (Spiering and Wintle 2011; Hewitson and D'Auria 2012; Andrén and Costa 2020).

It was clear to all that the postwar unification of Western Europe had to take a different course than that of the Nazi-led Europe the victors had just overcome. Formerly occupied nations enjoyed their re-established independence. Thus, giving up the idea of nationhood was not on the agenda; European unity necessarily had to be reconciled with the nation state. This mindset, then, determined the nature of the integration project (Andrén 2020).

In this chapter, we take a twofold approach to the study of concepts that extend beyond nation states by examining the concept of the nation in the context of European integration and identity. First, we examine how a number of intellectuals wrestled with the problem of how to adopt and/ or develop the idea of the nation to fit with the new European project. In their articles, essays and books these intellectuals write about core ideas that define Europe as a concept beyond the nation state. We consider their ideas in two periods. First, the early postwar years were key in shaping a political language of European unification and the nation state. In fact, pleas for a world government were often heard among these intellectuals; European unification was only their second choice or a step in the direction of supranational governance. Thus, the pleas for European unity and integration represented a kind of internationalism more limited than that of the interwar period, but it included a wider political spectrum of liberals, conservatives and social democrats (Chapter 6). Second, whereas the early postwar period is characterized by the closing of the borders between Eastern and Western Europe, the period from the late 1980s to the new millennium saw them open up again. In the decade between 1985 and 1995, the political language of European unification was refreshed in the context of a drive for further integration and a renewal of the European idea that transcended the rift between East and West.

The intellectuals discussed here were well-known in their own time and their works have been translated into major and minor European languages. As public intellectuals they made their ideas known to the larger public. Consequently, the second approach we take in this chapter is to examine how these ideas about integration and identity were conceptualized by politicians in parliamentary debates in Britain, the Netherlands and Sweden. Parliamentary debates generally offer compact argumentation and therefore tend to put differences into a sharper perspective. The choice of parliaments as historical sources is in part based on practicalities: the parliamentary debates for each country have been fully digitized. The countries were selected because they represent three stages in the development of the EU: the Netherlands was a founding member, Britain a new member from the 1970s to 2020, and Sweden joined in the 1990s. As we shall see, the way in which parliamentarians approached concepts that extended beyond nation states was determined in part by the history of their own state's relation to the EU. We focus on the conceptualization of 'European integration' and 'European identity', and how these concepts relate to that of nation.

Previous researchers have paid much attention to the efforts to enhance a European awareness and identity by including cultural politics in the European integration project from the 1980s onwards (Shore 2000; Hansen 2000; Fornäs 2012). As we show here, this discourse was already present immediately after the Second World War. We demonstrate that conceptions of European unity that went beyond the nation state while supporting the relevance of nations and their states were nevertheless prevalent among both intellectuals and politicians.

## European Unity in the Early Postwar Period

In the intellectual discourse on European unity that surfaced immediately after the Second World War several notions that had already arisen in the interwar period gained prominence. At the conference *L'esprit européen* held in Geneva in 1946, the French intellectual Julien Benda stressed the need for a common European spirit that both transcended and retained divisions; he envisioned one spirit that included individual nations. Several speakers reiterated his argument while stressing the tensions between nations and calling for their reconciliation so as to rebuild Europe after the war and promote a 'European spirit' and a 'European civilization' (Benda 1947).

The idea of a United States of Europe was promoted by several postwar groups, while that of a European nation was emphasized by some intellectuals, for instance the Spanish philosopher Jose Ortega y Gassett who posited the existence of a European nation with a common culture (Gray 1989: 339ff; Villacanas Berlanga 2005: 177–98). In a 1946 essay, the Spanish historian and novelist Salvador de Madariaga, who was also an Oxford professor of literature, called for a European nation that would differ from most existing nations of Europe; he suggested that it should be modelled on the Swiss state, a federal entity of different languages and cultural dissimilarities. Such an accomplishment would require the creation of a 'European commonwealth' and the implementation of 'European standards'. He pointed out that common sense, intelligent progress and 'the European spirit' were prerequisites to this project (Madariaga 1946: 152–59).

Underlying this plea for unity was the belief in a cultural unity that transcended differences. This in turn resulted in a number of values that were deemed to reflect this unitary culture. Thus, we also find the idea of a 'European awareness' or a 'consciousness of Europe', to be promoted through media and education, together with a number of tensions: independent states versus a European political body, cultural unity versus national diversity, European consciousness versus national histories and state-bound educational systems (Congress of Europe 1999). This blending of unity with diversity has remained on the European agenda ever since.

Such amalgamations often cropped up in arguments for peaceful cooperation or unification. In his talk on the unity of Europe, Eliot defended the richness of the national cultures and stressed the gains of keeping intact their variety (Eliot 1948). In a portrait of Europe from 1952, Madariaga described 'the play between unity and diversity which is typical of Europe' (Madariaga 1952: 22). For the intellectuals, the call to protect the national diversity of Europe went together with reflections on the dual character of the concept of the nation. Spender (1946: 279ff) talked about nationalism as outdated while he affirmed that true glory came from national culture. De Rougemont rejected nationalism as a romantic disease that led to fascism and totalitarianism. Instead of adhering to absolute sovereignty and keeping armies to defend borders and wage war, the nation should be open towards its neighbours, suppress frontiers and develop cultural uniqueness for the good of both the national and the European community. Within a federation, Europe would find a fruitful way of overcoming the principle of the nation state (Rougemont 1947: 104–15; 1956: 157, 177–78).

The concept of an effective European integration was not yet on the agenda, even if occasionally mentioned. It took some time for it to become a catchword. The term itself was already in use in the late nineteenth century, as when the British philosopher Wordsworth Donisthorpe, inspired by Herbert Spencer, talked about political integration in Europe. He saw a long and dominating trend towards larger states and within them 'a constant tendency towards increasing integration'. For him, however, 'European integration' occurred within the states and not between them (Donisthorpe 1889). Later, in the interwar period, the concept of economic integration was presented as a recipe for overcoming recession (see also Chapter 7). Many states had become severely indebted and suffered from the economic consequences of the First World War. In addition, the economies had to adapt to the new national borders that followed the principle of national self-determination advanced by the victors at the Paris Peace Conference. The collapse of the Habsburg, Ottoman and Romanov Empires left Central and Southeast Europe with a range of new border checks, currencies and tariffs that had a deleterious influence on trade and communications. In part the quest for economic integration followed from the transformation of a continent dominated by a few empires to one consisting of many nation states. Moreover, in the early 1930s, economists described the precarious state of Europe, with industries concentrated in a few countries while the rest provided raw materials. Economists argued that the situation of new state borders, continuing interdependence and the need for cross-border trade required management through economic integration (Machlup 1977; Weber 1946: 4ff, 235–36).

Subsequently, 'European integration' was set out as a doctrine for a new grand project and became a key concept in the political language, largely superseding the earlier semantics that preferred 'European federation', 'United States of Europe' and 'European Union'. At the very beginning of the period, the German economist Alfred Weber put integration on the agenda for the process of restructuring Europe and establishing a civilized order in Germany (Weber 1946: 234–35). British economist Barbara Ward related it to practical issues of transport, trade and common market facilities (Ward 1948: 186–95).

## 'European Integration' in the Parliaments

How did this debate on European unity in the early postwar years emerge in the British, Dutch and Swedish parliaments? As Table 10.1 shows, of the various political terms coined in the early postwar years, 'European integration' caught on most. Interestingly, in all parliaments the term attained its greatest popularity only in the 1990s. No less interestingly, the other terms show different patterns across the three parliaments.

**Table 10.1** The frequency per decade of the political terms 'European federation', 'European integration', 'people's Europe' and 'United States of Europe' in the British, Dutch and Swedish parliaments, from the 1940s onwards. © Joris van Eijnatten.

| Britain | European | | Europe | |
|---|---|---|---|---|
| | federation | integration | people's | united states of |
| 1940–1949 | 28 | 3 | 0 | 74 |
| 1950–1959 | 51 | 48 | 0 | 24 |
| 1960–1969 | 22 | 59 | 0 | 93 |
| 1970–1979 | 28 | 104 | 0 | 89 |
| 1980–1989 | 17 | 85 | 48 | 117 |
| 1990–1999 | 46 | 447 | 86 | 349 |
| 2000–2005 | 28 | 262 | 10 | 95 |
| | **220** | **1,008** | **144** | **841** |
| **Netherlands** | (west) Europe(e)s(ch)e | | Europa | |
| | federatie | integratie | van de mensen* | vere(e)nigde staten van |
| 1940–1949 | 64 | 4 | 0 | 16 |
| 1950–1959 | 71 | 578 | 0 | 31 |
| 1960–1969 | 6 | 330 | 0 | 21 |
| 1970–1979 | 17 | 289 | 8 | 8 |
| 1980–1989 | 5 | 398 | 1 | 8 |
| 1990–1999 | 17 | 969 | 4 | 28 |
| 2000–2009 | 9 | 347 | 3 | 31 |
| 2010–2018 | 11 | 182 | 0 | 93 |
| | **189** | **2,915** | **16** | **143** |
| **Sweden** | (väst) (all) Europeisk(a) | | Europa(s) | |
| | federation(en) | integration(en) | folkens | förenta stater |
| 1940–1949 | 0 | 0 | 0 | 23 |
| 1950–1959 | 0 | 1 | 0 | 14 |
| 1960–1969 | 0 | 5 | 0 | 18 |
| 1970–1979 | 0 | 5 | 0 | 2 |
| 1980–1989 | 2 | 141 | 1 | 8 |
| 1990–1999 | 3 | 177 | 6 | 68 |
| 2000–2009 | 3 | 56 | 4 | 70 |
| 2010–2017 | 7 | 22 | 1 | 31 |
| | **15** | **407** | **12** | **234** |

* The literal Dutch translation of 'people's Europe' is *Europa van de volkeren*, but this occurs only twice (in 1986 and 1991).

## British Parliament: Continental Threat

The Conservative Somerset De Chair was one of the British MPs who, like Winston Churchill, supported the idea of a United States of Europe that had been propagated before the war by the Austrian Count Coudenhove-Kalergi. In a debate in 1944 he referred to the British ambassador Lord Lothian, who had put forward the idea of a 'European Federation' in a speech at St Louis, as well as General Smuts who had recently revamped the idea of 'United States or Commonwealth of Europe'. Given the complete devastation of the continent, it would be up to Britain, Russia and the United States of America to decide whether to implement this European federative framework. Comparing 'the nations of Europe' to 'a clowder of cats', he did not seem to put great store by individual nationhood: 'The cats, as it were, can all be put into the bag. There will be a good deal of yowling and scratching for a while, but I am hopeful that, under the powerful super-vision of the three great Powers I have mentioned, the situation inside the bag will sort itself out in time'. Britain, of course, would be kept out of the bag (Somerset de Chair, Con, HC, 25 May 1944: 979). Labour MPs likewise argued for 'some form of European Federation, Union or Commonwealth', on the assumption that the various nationalities on the continent would merge into a 'new form of European nationality' (Stephen King-Hall, Con, HC, 28 September 1944: 571–72).

Although after the war ideas of a 'United States of Europe, a European Federation and European unity' were still on the agenda (Ernest Bevin, Secretary of State for Foreign Affairs, Labour, HC, 19 June 1947: 2336), support for it declined among both Labour and Conservative MPs (Ernest Davies, Under-Secretary of State for Foreign Affairs, Labour, HC, 13 November 1950: 1401–402). By the early 1950s, it was clear that a 'European Federation' was seen to conflict with Britain's position within the British Empire or Commonwealth. However, the notion of 'a United Europe, developing on what we might call Commonwealth lines in which this country would join as a full member' was seen as a better way of achiev-ing the balance between the universal and the particular (Julian Amery, Con, HC, 14 May 1952: 1525). In some cases, 'European federation' and 'United States of Europe' were seen as projections of the American con-stitutional model onto a continent where such a model would simply not work. 'I think that the great pride of each European nation in its separate existence is indeed an obstacle to federal union in Europe, but it can be a source of strength to union of another kind' – a common market. 'It is true that nationalism has revived, but nationalism is not always a destructive force' (John Biggs-Davison, Con, HC, 23 July 1956: 75).

In the early 1970s, the idea of 'European federation' was still associated with the choice 'between a national identity and a European one', although supporters of Britain's membership of the EEC argued that the choice was a false one, since the federation simply did not exist (Norman St. John-Stevas, Con, HC, 20 January 1971: 1164; Richard Wood, Con, HC, 30 October 1969: 487). Diehard supporters of British EEC membership did tend to worry less about the preservation of national sovereignty. 'The questions we ought to be facing are: do we wish to build a European federation? Do we wish our generation to be the Founding Fathers of the United States of Europe?' (John Pardoe, Liberal, HC, 5 November 1974: 922).

*Dutch Parliament: A Shared Project*
In the postwar Netherlands, as elsewhere, it was taken for granted in the context of discussions about European integration that historical developments were such that nations and peoples were bound to become part of larger connections. Whether one adhered to the idea of a European federation or not, the point, according to one MP, was that 'the wealth of spiritual and cultural diversity' of the European tradition was incorporated into a larger unity. Federalism stood for 'greater unity', albeit one without 'complete collectivism'. In other words, 'the principles of subsidiarity, sphere sovereignty and functional decentralization' should be applied to the international community (Geert Ruygers, Labour Party [PvdA], SG2, 4 December 1946: 653). This way of combining the particular with the universal, i.e. the nation with Europe, was interpreted by some as a temporary measure. The question for these MPs was not whether a European federation should be brought about, but how. Because of the 'spiritual-cultural connection' between the European nations this should be done on the basis of international law, with the sovereign states as the political actors. Historically, federations commonly developed in this way, with constitutional structures arising naturally in the course of time. Nobody wanted to impose a Bismarckian *Blut und Eisen* policy that forced Europe into a federal constitution (Sieuwert Bruins Slot, ARP, SG2, 5 July 1949: 1622).

This view of gradual development from international to constitutional law, which the British tended to regard as a threat, served for Dutch MPs as a reason for leaving the British out of the unification process for the time being. Britain had 'historical and traditional' reasons not to be interested. Its position with regard to continental Europe had always been based on divide-and-rule politics on the one hand, and its role as mediator between the USA and Europe on the other. Its interest lay in the balance of power, not in unification, and its loyalties were slanted towards the United States. Once Europe was federalized, however, the British were bound to enter the

European fold (Johannes Reijers, CHU, SG1, 24 April 1950: 661). On the whole, Dutch MPs around the 1950s held positive views of a centralized European federation based on what the Catholics among them called the principle of subsidiarity. 'Europe with its great diversity of traditions and cultures' should not be forced into a unitary state. On the contrary, the various European peoples enriched the community with 'their own nature, culture and character' (Marga Klompé, The Catholic People's Party, SG2, 30 October 1951: 166). In the end, the British refusal to proceed rather dampened Dutch enthusiasm. As one MP expressed it, quoting Anthony Eden, 'without England a political European federation is merely a French–German tête-a-tête' (Willem Wendelaar, The People's Party for Freedom and Democracy [VVD], SG1, 11 March 1952: 379). In the 1970s, conservative MPs belonging to the smaller Christian parties would take a critical stance, referring to the lack of realism of the postwar plans for a European federation based on a 'common European civilization' (Bart Verbrugh, The Reformed Political Union [GPV], SG2, 13 September 1972: 4268). Meanwhile, in the mainstream interpretation, the 'European federation' remained an end goal to be reached; but opinions differed as to what it ought to look like.

*Swedish Parliament: Belated Response*

In Sweden the term 'European federation' first cropped up in 1950, when the leader of the Liberal People's Party, Bertil Ohlin, expressed support for the government's reticence in subscribing to a 'Western European Federation or similar agreement' (Bertil Ohlin, Liberals, RD, 21 March 1950). Sweden had a long-standing policy of neutrality, and 'European federation' only began to be used regularly quite late in parliamentary discourse, after warnings that the European federation was developing rapidly, and that Sweden should take care not to be left behind. Others expressed doubts whether any federation that guaranteed all freedom could ever be realized in prac-tice (Hädar Cars, Liberals, RD, 15 May 1986; Lars Norberg, The Greens, RD, 22 March 1990). After Sweden was hit by an economic crisis and the Soviet Union collapsed in the early 1990s, the Social Democrats gave up their previous resistance to joining the EU and made common cause with the Liberals and conservatives in having Sweden apply for membership. In 1992 Prime Minister Carl Bildt gave assurances that the constitution of the 'new European federation of nations' would be decided democratically in each nation state (Carl Bildt, Conservatives, RD, 10 June 1992). The Swedish conservatives had come a long way from their general interwar stance of hesitance to accept parliamentary democracy and international cooperation. Critics on the left and the right saw the European Monetary Union as the herald of a unitary European federation, and the EU as a means of realizing it, without anybody being aware of how rapidly advances were being made (Peter Eriksson, The Greens, RD, 23 January 1997; Kurt Ove Johansson, Social Democrats, RD, 29 April 1998; Lars Ohly, Leftist Party, RD, 10 June 2003; Johnny Skalin, Sweden Democrats, RD, 10 June 2013). Such critics could be found in all three countries.

## The Quest for European Identity

Our second case concerns the notion of European identity. This took off as a concept that extended beyond the nation state in the 1980s, in the wake of the general interest in identities, which impacted on political thinking no less than it did on artistic performance. Intellectuals soon made themselves heard, in either positive or negative terms. In some parliamentary debates the term was already being used in the late 1960s, in connection with European integration. The European Community approved a document on European identity in 1973, in which a communal identity was conceived as an outcome of economic integration. However, the European Community definition of identity remained vague and the document was of minor significance in the 1970s (Shore 2000; Stråth 2016: 377–78).

A large amount of research demonstrates that the European Commission began to promote a common European identity in the 1980s and 1990s by launching notions such as a 'European culture' and a 'European heritage' that could foster a shared 'European conscience' and 'European identity'. Soon enough the Commission focused on strengthening the EU's legitimacy, in a period in which it faced criticism for its seemingly exclusive focus on economic and legal issues. The Commission therefore looked for ways to speed up economic integration, based on the idea that the only way for it to win support was if citizens began to feel European. The national politicians needed to demonstrate loyalty to a community that extended beyond the nation state, and citizens needed to be imbued with a feeling, a sense, a consciousness of being European. The explicit aim was to build a 'European identity'. 'Unity in diversity' became a key slogan, indicating that Europe flourished thanks to its diversity but that one common history and culture underlay its cultural variety (Lähdesmäki and Wagener 2015).

*Responses by Intellectuals*
From the 1990s onwards, intellectuals contributed substantially to the idea of European identity. In the first place, they promoted it by applying it in writings intended for a broader public. The French medievalist Jacques Le Goff (1996), for example, presented an essay demonstrating the long heritage of the European identity. The future pope, Cardinal Joseph Ratzinger

(2005), criticized contemporary culture in a speech that made use of the notion. The British historian Timothy Garton Ash (2007) wrote about 'European identity' in a popular magazine.

In the second place, intellectuals offered definitions of the notion. We can distinguish three kinds of definitions of European identity. Le Goff's was in accordance with the take on history characteristic of the French *Annales* school, which stressed the significance of the *longue durée*. According to Le Goff, European identity had evolved over many centuries, influenced by Greek philosophy, the Roman idea of empire, and Christianity. European identity was the result of historical processes, in particular the development of internal divisions within Christianity and between states, the quest for unity through the exclusion of groups such as heretics, witches and Jews, and the expansion of European power through conquests and colonial ventures. Thus, Le Goff defined the shared identity of Europe as a combination of the pursuit of unity and the struggle for diversity (Le Goff 1996: 53). Ratzinger likewise identified a long historical tradition from which a Europe distinct from other cultures had grown. He acknowledged the value of Enlightenment ideas and a rationalistic culture but also stressed their limits and excesses, arguing that the former was rooted in Christianity and the latter led to the atomic bomb. For him, the essence of European identity was Christianity (Ratzinger 2005: 62–84). Delanty and Garton Ash represented the third view of European identity. They both celebrated a modernist conception that emphasized its late advent in history. Delanty defined it in terms of a post-national consciousness that, in contrast to national identities, was self-critical and cosmopolitan. Garton Ash suggested a new narrative that emphasized the goals of 'freedom, peace, law, prosperity, diversity and solidarity' and avoided the mythologies of national histories. In this case, European identity was closely linked to the construction of the supranational legal and political bodies of the EU after the Second World War (Delanty 2009; Garton Ash 2007).

Other intellectuals contested the relevance of the concept. In the early 1990s, Anthony D. Smith, a leading historian of nationalism, discussed the attempt of the European Commission to strengthen the sense of a shared European culture by emphasizing a common heritage based on Antiquity and Christianity. He warned that the notion of a European identity implied a 'logic of cultural exclusion' and imposed 'the defects of each of Europe's national identities, precisely because it has been built in their images' (Smith 1992: 76). The philosopher Étienne Balibar similarly argued that the idea of a European identity was exclusionary and limited democracy; it created obstacles to the expansion of citizenship rights and established a kind of apartheid, an exclusion of people who were part of the workforce and economy but lacked a European passport (Balibar 2009).

**Table 10.2** The frequency per decade of the culture-related terms European 'spirit', 'heritage', 'culture', 'identity', 'consciousness', 'nation', 'standards' and 'values' in the British, Dutch and Swedish parliaments, from the 1940s onwards. © Joris van Eijnatten.

| Britain | spirit | heritage | culture | identity | consciousness | nation | standards | values |
|---|---|---|---|---|---|---|---|---|
| | | | | | European | | | |
| 1940–1949 | 0 | 0 | 11 | 0 | 0 | 0 | 10 | 0 |
| 1950–1959 | 1 | 3 | 9 | 0 | 1 | 0 | 14 | 0 |
| 1960–1969 | 3 | 2 | 8 | 7 | 0 | 2 | 23 | 1 |
| 1970–1979 | 13 | 19 | 30 | 29 | 7 | 3 | 70 | 4 |
| 1980–1989 | 9 | 16 | 20 | 7 | 3 | 0 | 179 | 2 |
| 1990–1999 | 3 | 19 | 65 | 69 | 1 | 10 | 226 | 10 |
| 2000–2005 | 1 | 5 | 11 | 25 | 0 | 2 | 124 | 19 |
| | **30** | **64** | **154** | **137** | **12** | **17** | **646** | **36** |

| Netherlands | geest | erfgoed | cultuur | identiteit | bewustzijn | natie | norm(en) | waarden |
|---|---|---|---|---|---|---|---|---|
| | | | | | (west)Europe(e)s(ch)e | | | |
| 1940–1949 | 8 | 0 | 22 | 0 | 1 | 0 | 0 | 1 |
| 1950–1959 | 28 | 0 | 34 | 0 | 1 | 4 | 1 | 1 |
| 1960–1969 | 15 | 2 | 13 | 0 | 2 | 3 | 2 | 0 |
| 1970–1979 | 5 | 0 | 20 | 34 | 4 | 2 | 8 | 1 |
| 1980–1989 | 9 | 3 | 41 | 59 | 2 | 1 | 36 | 0 |
| 1990–1999 | 0 | 2 | 33 | 71 | 1 | 2 | 47 | 4 |
| 2000–2009 | 2 | 0 | 27 | 67 | 4 | 3 | 105 | 56 |
| 2010–2018 | 4 | 9 | 14 | 23 | 0 | 1 | 179 | 112 |
| | **71** | **16** | **204** | **254** | **15** | **16** | **378** | **175** |

| Sweden | (väst)Europ(eisk)(a)(as) | | | | | | | |
|---|---|---|---|---|---|---|---|---|
| | anda | arv(et)(s) | kultur | identitet(en) | medvetande | nation | normer | värden(a) |
| 1940–1949 | 0 | 0 | 0 | 0 | 0 | 1 | 0 | 0 |
| 1950–1959 | 0 | 0 | 0 | 0 | 0 | 0 | 0 | 0 |
| 1960–1969 | 0 | 0 | 0 | 0 | 0 | 0 | 0 | 0 |
| 1970–1979 | 1 | 0 | 2 | 10 | 0 | 1 | 0 | 0 |
| 1980–1989 | 0 | 2 | 1 | 15 | 1 | 0 | 0 | 1 |
| 1990–1999 | 0 | 3 | 3 | 66 | 3 | 7 | 3 | 1 |
| 2000–2009 | 1 | 1 | 0 | 15 | 0 | 0 | 1 | 3 |
| 2010–2017 | 0 | 1 | 0 | 4 | 0 | 0 | 3 | 4 |
| | 2 | 7 | 6 | 110 | 4 | 9 | 7 | 9 |

## 'European Identity' in the Parliaments

As Table 10.2 shows, of the various culture-related terms coined in the postwar period, 'European identity' was the most popular across the three parliaments. 'European culture' also has relatively high scores (the highest in Britain) but hardly figures in Sweden. Incidentally, the highest absolute score is for 'European standards', but because this term has a strong bearing on technical issues, rather than only on cultural ones, we have opted to neglect it and focus on 'identity'.

### *Britain: Choosing Between European and Atlantic*
In the British parliament, 'European identity' was first debated in 1969 in the context of a stronger European pole within the Atlantic Alliance and NATO, the other pole being the USA. This usage of the term continued in the 1970s, but by then a related theme had cropped up: European identity as an end in itself, thus superseding national identities (cf. Ihalainen and Sahala 2020). Some MPs remained down to earth: economic policies should be seen as a means of bringing about greater economic unity, and not 'as M. Pompidou seem [*sic*] sometimes to think, as a means of establishing a sort of metaphysical European identity' (Austen Albu, Labour, HC, 15 February 1972: 333). Others were optimistic, noting a year after Britain's accession that the EEC was 'well along the road to agreeing and defining the basis of our European identity', which strengthened the basis for transatlantic relationships (John Davies, Con, HC, 27 November 1973: 231).[1]

Only in the 1990s did the notions of 'culture' and 'values' enter into the debate (see Van Eijnatten 2019). This was in part the result of Article 128 of the 1993 Maastricht Treaty, which called for 'the flowering of the cultures of the Member States' and 'bringing the common cultural heritage to the fore'.[2] As one MP put it, 'I am not sure whether I know what a common cultural heritage is, but I suspect that it is grounded in the ideas and values of the Renaissance, in the Enlightenment Project and in liberal political thought'. She believed that approaching commonality from this perspective was much better than defining the European heritage 'in terms of ethnic origin, racial background or some spuriously defined European identity' (Ann Clwyd, Labour, HC, 19 January 1993: 272). Others (mostly post-Thatcherite Conservatives) rejected the whole idea of a common heritage and argued that it was 'national and regional diversity' that mattered. 'It would be utter nonsense to expect the French to blur their cooking with fast foods, supermarket frozen foods, McDonalds and so on'. Such 'interlocking circles' as 'country, political party, village, firm, religion or whatever' are natural units to which people adhere in and of themselves; but 'it is not a natural human instinct to want to belong to a continent or to feel some sort of European identity' (Toby Jessel, Con, 19 January 1993: 287–88). Pro-Europe Labourites countered with statements such as: 'With European integration, we are not losing identity; we are gaining a new identity. In addition to our Scottish, English, Welsh and British identities, we will develop a European identity' (Calum Macdonald, Labour, HC, 1 March 1995: 1124).

The two themes – 'European identity' as complementary to either the 'American' or the national one – gave rise to a third one: a European identity as opposed to an Atlantic identity. Some argued that the opposition was false, and that the British national identity was allied to geopolitical entities on both sides of the Atlantic (Malcolm Rifkind, Secretary of State for Foreign and Commonwealth Affairs, Con, HC, 16 November 1995: 137). Others emphasized that 'the people of Britain do not want a European identity, but identify more readily with the English-speaking world and the Commonwealth' (Petrie Bowen Wells, Con, HC, 11 December 2000: 427). So, the original tension between Europe and nationhood remained subject to different interpretations. Europhiles retained the tension, suggesting that 'it is now time to get behind the common European identity of a united Europe, a union of nation states working together to solve common problems with common solutions' (Mark Hendrick, Labour, HC, 21 May 2003: 1078).

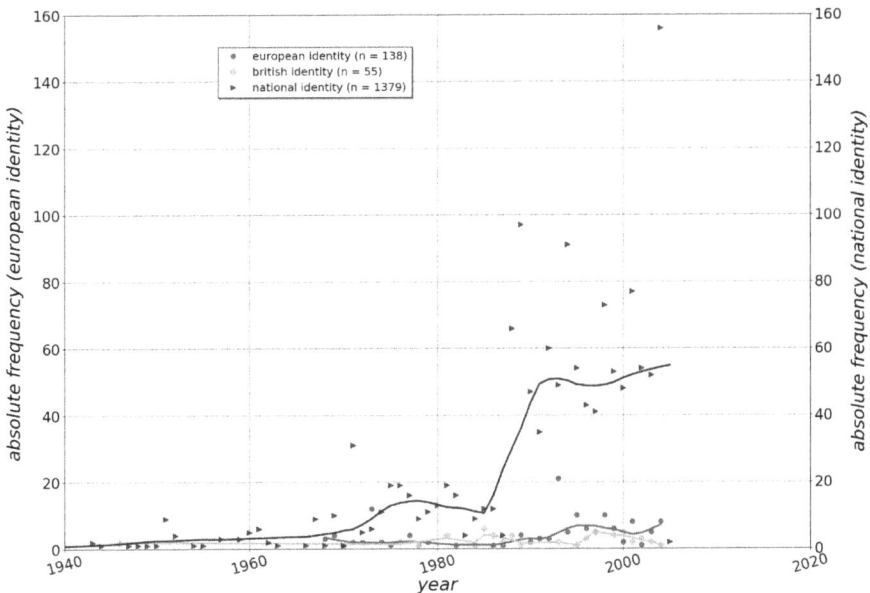

**Figure 10.1** Usage of the terms 'European', 'British' and 'national' identity in both houses of the British parliament after 1940. © Joris van Eijnatten.

Critics rejected the attempt 'to foist' a European identity on the nation, as if Europe were a nation state: 'We have a European Parliament, a European Court, a European currency, a European anthem and a European flag' and now 'driving licences have to have the Euro symbol' (Gerald Howarth, Con, HC, 24 April 2001: 270). As Figure 10.1 shows, 'national identity' remained high on the agenda; the term was increasingly used after about the mid-1980s.

*Netherlands: Debates on a Tenuous Construct*
The first instance of 'European identity' in the Dutch parliament was very much a cultural issue: it concerned the choice of a second European language next to the national one. The MP in question rejected English, since it was a global language that would do little to establish a specifically European identity (Hendrik Jan Louwes, VVD, SG1, 16 May 1972: 892). As in Britain, discussion about the USA's proposal for a new Atlantic Charter arose in the early 1970s, and here too the more conservative (traditionalist Protestant) MPs were not happy with Henry Kissinger's suggestion that the Netherlands should integrate into 'a regional European identity' (Bart Verbrugh, GPV, SG2, 28 November 1973: 1265). They also wondered what the difference between the European and American identities was supposed to be, given that 'Americans descend from the British, French, Germans and Dutch' (Bart Verbrugh, GPV, SG2, 28 January 1974: Vaste Commissie voor Buitenlandse Zaken, B2). Communists too rejected the 'inflated sense of superiority called "European identity"' (Marcus Bakker, CPN, SG2, 28 January 1974: Vaste Commissie voor Buitenlandse Zaken, B5). The majority, however, were more eager to expand the 'cultural component of the European identity', which offered opportunities for 'nation and community building': 'We have a Eurovision and we have an intensive interest in sport, music and literature, but we hardly have any EEC cups, trophies, medals or prizes' (Hendrik Jan Louwes, VVD, SG1, 19 March 1974: 423).

That is as far as the debate then reached. When it surfaced again in the 1980s it mostly concerned the security a European–American alliance would guarantee. In this instance the Christian Democrats represented the original balance between continental and national identities. 'A single European identity does not in my view exist. It is mostly the sum of national identities' (Marten Beinema, Christian Democrats [CDA], SG2, 9 February 1987: Vaste Commissie voor Buitenlandse Zaken, 47–17). Another MP, noting that culture and education were rising up the agenda, framed the issue more positively, if only to counter the 'Americanization' of popular culture: 'Culture is the expression of a regional or national identity. Communal expressions of culture can advertise a European identity with respect to expressions of culture from other continents' (Joost van Iersel, CDA, SG2, 29 June 1988: 95–5279).

In and around the 1990s much of the discussion focused on the need for a European identity, without much thought being devoted to the continued existence and the character of the nation. Some people supported 'the dream of Compostela', while others, such as Peter Sloterdijk, harked back to a unified empire.[3] Christian Democrats such as Jos van Gennip speculated on a 'specific European identity, the result of 2,000 years of collective and partly Christian history'. The answer to the question of what a European identity was ranged from 'a Christian Occident to a multicultural immigration territory'. Debate on this issue would be crucial for the kind of Europe we were going to live in, argued this MP (Jos van Gennip, CDA, SG1, 28 March 2000: 22–1000). As a minister observed, while in the 1950s debates on Europe attracted a full house, half a century later, only a couple of spokespersons turned up during debates (Jan Peter Balkenende, Prime Minister, SG1, 4 November 2003). Subsequent discussions returned to the original mantra: 'We should not relinquish national identities for a European identity', but we must take care to strengthen the latter (Atzo Nicolaï, State

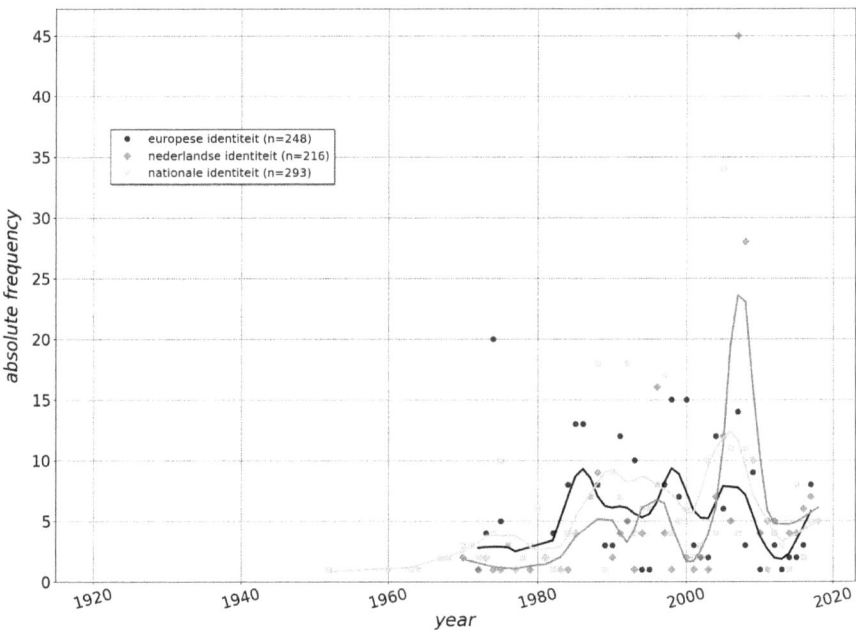

**Figure 10.2** Usage of the terms 'European', 'Dutch' and 'national' identity in both chambers of the Dutch parliament after 1940. © Joris van Eijnatten.

Secretary, VVD, SG2, 9 November 2004: 4–116).[4] Figure 10.2 demonstrates the rise of the national argument in parliament, parallel to developments in Britain. In 2009 there was a debate on whether the European flag ought to be placed next to the Dutch flag on the roof of the Second Chamber. In the line of argument that won the day, many people believed that 'national identity is very important and that the European identity can exist next to it, and even that the European identity can contribute to the conservation of the Dutch identity' (Henk Jan Ormel, CDA, SG2, 1 December 2009: motie van de leden Ormel en Pechtold, 32 125, nr. 3).

*Sweden: In Defence of Global Foreign Policy*
In Sweden, too, the term 'European identity' first materialized around 1970, when a right-wing MP strongly supported the European project, stressing Sweden's historical, cultural, ideological and economic ties to Europe, and citing Dag Hammarskjöld's commitment to 'Western democratic identity' (Gösta Bohman, Conservatives, RD, 3 November 1971).[5] Social Democrat Prime Minister Olof Palme confirmed Sweden's European identity but argued that continued neutrality was the best way to do it justice (Olof Palme, RD, 2 December 1971). This set the contours of the debate until the fall of the Soviet Union, when Sweden's accession to the EU began to be discussed. 'Our own foreign policy', said Prime Minister Carl Bildt in 1991, 'must therefore be a foreign policy with a clear European identity' (Carl Bildt, RD, 14 June 1991). He repeated that statement in a speech in Bonn in November 1991, and supporters reiterated in parliament that 'the European issue is a question of our nation's identity. It is about belonging, a community, which is so essential that it should also shape and influence our foreign policy positions' (Nic Grönvall, Conservatives, RD, 12 December 1991). That statement resulted in a debate on Sweden's neutrality, on the value of the country's contacts with the 'Third World' and on the disadvantages of narrowing its foreign policy to Europe alone. A distinction surfaced between the transatlantic right versus a pro-Third World 'global' left. 'When we talk about a European identity in our foreign policy, it must be that we see European cooperation as a way of promoting our foreign policy goals, which are largely global in nature' (Pär Granstedt, Centre Party, RD, 14 October 1992). The violence in the former Yugoslavia made a big impact on Swedish MPs, who felt that Europe as a whole shared in the responsibility for the conflict. 'I am a warm supporter of a union between the people of Europe, but right now it feels difficult to speak of a European identity' (Pierre Schori, Social Democrats, RD, 22 April 1994).

In the end, the rather gratuitous invocation of a balance between the national and the European carried the day, presumably because it was politically the safest thing to say: 'We are made up of many countries, each with its own special cultural heritage but also with a common background – a European identity' (Charlotte Cederschiöld, Conservatives, RD, 19 October 1994). Sweden joined the Union in 1995 and several years later the Minister of Foreign Affairs could say unabashedly: 'Sweden has a European identity and a European responsibility' (Anna Lindh, Social Democrats, RD, 10 February 1999). Indeed, of the three countries, judging by their use of the term 'Swedish' and 'national' identity, Sweden seems to have been least given to nationalist rhetoric (see Figure 10.3, with its clear spike at the debates on joining the EU). After the turn of the millennium, however, some serious criticism arose from the right as well as the left. No longer couched in terms of Swedish neutrality, it echoed the hesitations about (if not rejection of) the European project in other EU countries. 'In Europe, there are many people. There is no common public space for a European debate, no clear European identity … Therefore in my opinion the notion of a federalist superstate is an extremely risky idea [imposed] from above. The alternative is a Europe of democracies' (Sven Bergström, Centre Party, RD, 6 December 2001). Another MP pointed out that the EU lacked the institutions for democratic development: 'There is no European press, no

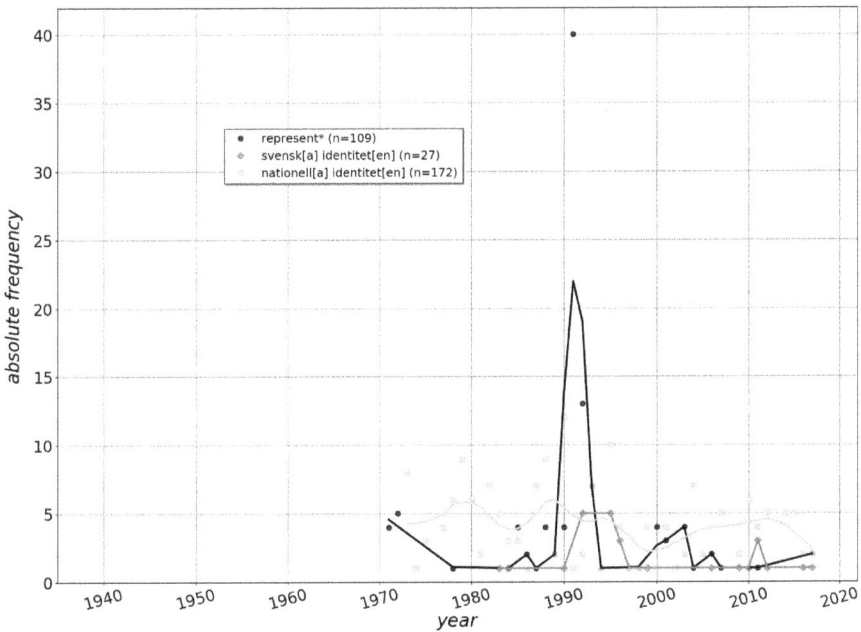

**Figure 10.3** Usage of the terms 'European', 'Swedish' and 'national' identity in the Swedish parliament after 1940. © Joris van Eijnatten.

European debate, no European identity'. The EU failed to create European citizens. 'Europeans are united in their countries, not in a superstate' (Gustav Fridolin, The Greens, RD, 20 November 2003). The government's answer to such criticism was the same as elsewhere: to be European means to be diverse. 'What is so distinctive about European identity? It is that, over the centuries, after all, we have allowed each other to be different' (Göran Persson, Social Democrats, RD, 18 December 2004).[6]

## Conclusion

In this chapter we have demonstrated how intellectuals in discourses on European unity and politicians in parliaments conceived of the balance between the 'national' and the 'European', between the nation state and the European project. Our examination of intellectual discourse shows how this duality was conceptualized by the leading thinkers of the period. Our analysis of the parliamentary debates gives insight into the way in which politicians used these concepts. Various terms were coined in the postwar period to address the commonalities and tensions between the 'national' and the 'European'. Of these, 'European integration' and 'European identity' were the most important, because they were the most frequently used and the most central to the postwar EU institutions. The way in which 'European integration' and 'European identity' were conceptualized in the three parliaments can be understood in terms of a balance. MPs usually took the 'national' to imply the 'European', and vice versa: rarely did they opt for either the one or the other alone.

European intellectuals regarded themselves as representatives of internationalism, thus continuing the ambitions regarding intellectual cooperation between nations and across borders characteristic of the interwar years. Many intellectuals focused on Europe as a second best when it became clear that global government would not come about, and that the UN would remain only a weak semblance of it. Our material reflects how, in the era of anti-communism and the division of Europe between East and West, many intellectuals and politicians considered the European idea and transatlantic cooperation as the viable options for internationalism.

Identity discourse enjoyed an upswing at the beginning of the 1980s, in the context of the rise of the 'New Right'. In Britain national identity (British, English, Scottish or Welsh) came markedly to the fore. This fits well with Menno Spiering's research on cultural Euroscepticism in Britain (Spiering 2015). Recent studies underline the fact that British Euroscepticism has a long history and is deeply anchored in British culture (O'Toole 2018; Spiering 2015; Saunders 2019). However, our study shows that the 1980s were not only crucial for concern about national identity in Britain, but that the British parliament in this period showed a lack of interest in European identity (see also Ihalainen and Sahala 2020). By contrast, in the Netherlands and Sweden concern for national and European identities went hand in hand, and it even seems that interest in European identity arose slightly before the idea of national identity was addressed explicitly.

**Mats Andrén** is Professor of History of Ideas at the University of Gothenburg, associated with the Centre for European Research (CERGU). His recent publications include 'Europe of Nations, Europe of Nationalism' in *History of European Ideas* (2020); *Cultural Borders of Europe* (eds Andrén et al., Berghahn, 2017). Recently, he edited special issues for *European Review* (2020), *History of European Ideas* (with Ettore Costa, 2020) and *Global Intellectual History* (with Ben Dorfman, 2020). ORCID 0000-0002-2053-9674.

**Joris van Eijnatten** is Professor of Digital History at Utrecht University and general director of the Netherlands eScience Center. His numerous publications include books and articles on toleration, Dutch religious history, the poet Willem Bilderdijk, sermons, the justification of war, media history and conceptual history. A digital historian, Van Eijnatten specializes in applying digital methodologies to newspapers, periodicals, parliamentary records and other historical data, with a focus on tracing changing concepts over time. ORCID 0000-0002-8865-0002.

## Notes

1. Mr Davies was the Chancellor of the Duchy of Lancaster. The reference was to the Declaration on the European Identity (1973).
2. http://data.europa.eu/eli/treaty/tec_1997/art_151/oj (accessed 15 June 2021).
3. The book they referred to was Sloterdijk 1994. The reference to Compostela presumably concerns the Council of Europe's elevation of the Camino de Santiago to the first European Cultural Itinerary in 1987.
4. One year later: 'I don't really believe in a European identity, but I do believe in European values' (6 December 2005).
5. A month later (2 December 1971) Bohman referred directly to Dag Hammarskjöld's article on 'choosing Europe': '*Att välja Europa*', published in *Svensk Tidskrift* 38.
6. The debate concerned Turkey's accession to the EU.

# References

## Primary Sources

The data for this article was automatically extracted as XML files directly from online databases in the course of 2019, using the following APIs:

Britain:
British parliamentary debates, House of Commons (HC) and House of Lords (HL), available at http://www.hansard-archive.parliament.uk/ (1803–2004).

Netherlands:
http://jsru.kb.nl/sru (1814–1994; search parameters are described in https://www. kb.nl/sites/default/files/docs/snelstart-sgd.pdf; data is also available through https://doi.org/10.17026/dans-xk5-dw3s).
Dutch parliamentary debates, Eerste Kamer (SG1) and Tweede Kamer (SG2).
https://zoek.officielebekendmakingen.nl/sru/Search (1995–2017; search parameters are described in https://www.koopoverheid.nl/documenten/instructies/2017/ 09/08/handleiding-voor-het-uitvragen-van-de-collectie-officiele-publicaties).

Sweden:
Swedish parliamentary debates, Första Kammaren (FK) and Andra Kammaren (AK), from 1971 Riksdag (RD).
https://weburn.kb.se/riks/tv%c3%a5kammarriksdagen/xml/ (1867–1970).
https://data.riksdagen.se/data/dokument/ (1971–2017).

## Secondary Sources

Andrén, M. 2017. 'The Controversial Concept of European Identity', in M. Andrén et al. (eds), *Cultural Borders of Europe*. New York: Berghahn Books, pp. 159–69.
———. 2020. 'Europe of Nations, Europe without Nationalism', *History of European Ideas* 46(1): 13–24. https://doi.org/10.1080/01916599.2019.1703853.
Andrén, M. and E. Costa. 2020. 'Introduction: Transnationalism in the 1950s Europe, Ideas, Debates and Politics', *History of European Ideas* 46(1): 1–12. https://doi. org/10.1080/01916599.2019.1703856.
Balibar, É. 2009. *We, the People of Europe? Reflections of Transnational Citizenship*. Princeton: Princeton University Press.
Benda, J. (ed.). 1947. *L'esprit européen*. Neuchâtel: Éditions de la Baconnière.
Congress of Europe. 1999 (1948). Council of Europe, available at http://www.coe. int/t/dgal/dit/ilcd/archives/selection/thehague/default_en.asp.
Coudenhove-Kalergi, R. 1953. *Die europäische Nation*. Stuttgart: Deutsche Verlags-Anstalt.
Delanty, G. 2009. 'Models of European Identity: Reconciling Universalism and Particularism', *Perspectives of European Politics and Society* 3: 345–59.
Donisthorpe, W. 1889. *Individualism: A System of Politics*. London: MacMillan.
Eijnatten, J. van 2019. 'On Principles and Values: Mining for Conservative Rhetoric in the London Times, 1785–2010', in *Digital Scholarship, Digital Classrooms: New*

*International Perspectives in Research and Teaching*. Farmington Hills, MI: Gale, pp. 1–26, available at https://www.ris.uu.nl/ws/files/69946365/DSDC_1_On_Principles_and_Values.pdf.

Eliot, T.S. 1948. *Notes Towards the Definition of Culture*. London: Faber and Faber.

Fornäs, J. 2012. *Signifying Europe*. Bristol: Intellekt.

Garton Ash, T. 2007. 'Europe's True Stories', *Prospect* 131 (February), available at https://www.prospectmagazine.co.uk/magazine/europestruestories.

Goff, J. Le. 1996. *Das alte Europa und die Welt der Moderne*. Munich: Beck.

Gray, R. 1989. *The Imperative of Modernity: An Intellectual Biography of José Ortega y Gasset*. Berkeley: University of California Press.

Grinell, K. 2017. 'Ilm al-Hududiyya: Un-Inheriting Eurocentricity', in M. Andrén et al. (eds), *Cultural Borders of Europe: Narratives, Concepts and Practices in the Present and the Past*. New York: Berghahn Books, pp. 54–70.

Hansen, P. 2000. *European Only? Essays on Identity Politics and the European Union*. Umeå: Umeå University.

Hewitson, M. and M. D'Auria. 2012. *Europe in Crisis: Intellectuals and the European Ideas, 1917–1957*. New York: Berghahn Books.

Ihalainen, P. and A. Sahala. 2020. 'Evolving Conceptualisations of Internationalism in the UK Parliament: Collocation Analyses from the League to Brexit', in P. Paju et al. (eds), *Digital Histories: Emergent Approaches within the New Digital History*. Helsinki: Helsinki University Press, pp. 199–219.

Lähdesmäki, T. and A. Wagener. 2015. 'Discourses on Governing Diversity in Europe: Critical Analysis of the White Paper on Intercultural Dialogue', *International Journal of Intercultural Relations* 44 (January): 13–28. DOI: https://doi.org/10.1016/j.ijintrel.2014.11.002.

Machlup, F. 1977. *A History of Thought on Economic Integration*. New York: Columbia University Press.

Madariaga, S. 1946. *Victors, Beware*. London: Jonathan Cape.

———. 1952. *Portrait of Europe*. London: Hollis & Carter.

Milward, A.S. 2000. *The Rescue of the Nation State*. London: Routledge.

O'Toole, F. 2018. *Heroic Failure: Brexit and the Politics of Pain*. London: Head of Zeus.

Ratzinger, J. 2005. 'Europa in der Krise der Kulturen', in M. Pera and J. Ratzinger (eds), *Ohne Wurzeln: Der Relativismus und die Krise der europäischen Kultur*. Augsburg: Sankt Ulrich Verlag.

Rougemont, D. 1947. *The Last Trump*. New York: Doubleday.

———. 1956. *Man's Western Quest: The Principles of Civilization*. New York: Harper & Brother.

Saunders, R. 2019. *Yes to Europe! The 1975 Referendum and Seventies Britain*. Cambridge: Cambridge University Press.

Shore, C. 2000. *Building Europe: The Cultural Politics of European Integration*. London: Routledge.

Sloterdijk, P. 1994. *Falls Europa erwacht: Gedanken zum Programm einer Weltmacht am Ende des Zeitalters ihrer politischen Absence*. Frankfurt am Main: Suhrkamp.

Smith, A.D. 1992. 'National Identity and the Idea of European Unity', *International Affairs* 68(1): 55–76.

Spender, S. 1946. 'Stephen Spender 11 septembre 1946', in *L'esprit européen: Rencontres internationales de Genève*. Neuchâtel: Les Éditions de la Baconnière, pp. 267–77.

Spiering, M. 2015. *A Cultural History of Euroscepticism in Great Britain*. London: Palgrave.

Spiering, M. and M. Wintle (eds). 2011. *European Identity and the Second World War*. Basingstoke: Palgrave Macmillan.

Stråth, B. 2016. *Europe's Utopias of Peace: 1815, 1919, 1951*. London: Bloomsbury.

Villacanas Berlanga, J.L. 2005. 'Europe hora zero: meditación Europea de Ortega', ÁGORA: *Papeles de Filosofia* 24(2): 177–98.

Ward, B. 1948. *The West at Bay*. Allen and Unwin: London.

Weber, A. 1946. *Abschied von der bisherigen Geschichte: Überwindung des Nihilismus*. Bern: Verlag A. Francke AG.

# Chapter 11

# Universalism in Emergency Aid before and after 1970

## Ambivalences and Contradictions

*Norbert Götz and Irène Herrmann*

❖

On 8 October 1965, the Twentieth International Conference of the Red Cross Movement, the world's oldest and most significant humanitarian organization, adopted seven fundamental principles.[1] These were meant to guide its members and inform the world at large about the ways of conceiving and organizing emergency aid. The most important principle, namely humanity, reflected the humane dedication at the core of humanitarianism and hinted at both the wideness of this generous feeling and the comprehensiveness of its consequences. While humanity may be seen as 'the one concept that humanitarianism cannot exist without' (Radice 2018: 158; see also Klose and Thulin 2016), it may also be understood as one of the emotive concretizations of a more abstract concept: universality (Feldman and Ticktin 2010: 1, 3, 7).

This concept (*universalité* in French, *Universalität* in German and *универсальность* 'universalnost' in Russian) was also officially endorsed by the Red Cross as the seventh principle, pertaining to its own structure as a global federation of equal national societies. At the same time, the Red Cross doctrine as such, including all seven principles, was regarded as universal, as a cross-cultural moral substratum with a 'lasting character [that] is perhaps a sign of its superiority over everything that happens here on earth' (Pictet 1979: 11). The Red Cross appeared therefore not only as a 'world-wide institution' but also as a supreme body that possessed 'a universal doctrine, a humanitarian basis common to all peoples' (ICRC 1965a: 569; 1965b: 574).

There was no further definition of the principle of universality at the time. Neither was there any explanation for the choice of the term, and all participants who used it during the discussions in the conference seemed to harbour no doubt about its meaning (ICRC 1965a). At no point was it compared or contrasted to linguistic variants such as universalism. The speakers, in accordance with French lexical use (and conceptual history), presumably considered universality as a reality and universalism as a doctrine (Robert 1969: 720) – without spelling out that the former can be seen as an outcome of the latter, or vice versa.[2] Equally noteworthy is the absence of any reference to counter-concepts, of which particularity and particularism may be the most obvious.

Such a lack of antonyms is relevant for both systematic and historical reasons. Hence, universality (and universalism) is a term that is best defined by elenchus, namely by stating what a phenomenon lacks to be considered universal. Humanitarianism is particular in the sense that it is a corrective in an emergency situation and therefore ideally would not be required. Moreover, the claim to universalism is easily challenged when confronted with practice (Balibar 2014 [2007]). If humanitarianism is supposed to have a universal aim of helping all people in need, it ought to be rooted in the realities it aspires to change. By definition, these realities are conditions of more or less overwhelming crisis, so humanitarian aid causes need to be selected and prioritized, that is, triaged. This applies both to medical treatment hierarchies and to the decision to – or how far to – adopt any particular aid cause (Götz, Brewis and Werther 2020; Ten Have 2014). Thus, in humanitarian efforts universal ideals become inseparably intertwined with differentiating practices (Fassin 2010).

More generally speaking, emergency aid is a set of practices, encompassing routines forged by experience and contingencies dependent on the actors and the situation. While humanitarianism aims at helping human beings in general, each individual is distinct, and each situation is in some way unique. Here again, there seems to be a contradiction in terms. Humanitarian doctrines of many organizations encompass universal aims in such a paradoxical manner, but only the International Red Cross Movement (to be renamed International Red Cross and Red Crescent Movement from the 1980s) can plausibly claim to represent a universal structure. Therefore, they tend to address universality as something referring to dissemination and local embeddedness throughout the world rather than to an overarching doctrine or generalized scope of action. In these latter fields the concept of humanity has a more concrete appeal than is implied by universality or universalism, for any organization. While the notion of humanity is almost tautological as a mission statement of humanitarianism, it exonerates the latter from the suspicion of the narrow-minded zeal inherent in any 'ism'. This is a liability even for the term universalism, which, due to the 'universalising rationale' of the ism suffix as such (Kurunmäki and Marjanen 2018: 244), may be regarded as the ultimate 'ism'.

Nonetheless, declaring the universality of Red Cross aid as a reality still poses fundamental problems, which may be concealed either deliberately or because of blinding certitudes. This in turn begs questions such as why the ambiguity was concealed, how particularism was handled, how other actors reacted and what this management reveals, both from a conceptual and from a humanitarian point of view. Due to the prominent role of the Red Cross, we take its case as an indicator of the impact of 'universalism' in emergency aid in general. Considering the broad scope of the proposed overview, we restrict the analysis to a period during which these issues were especially visible. Around 1970, when humanitarianism was undergoing profound changes, there was a sudden proliferation of organizations and undertakings with divergent approaches in the wake of the particularism-sensitive decolonization process – only a few years after the Red Cross Movement officially proclaimed its universality and while the Cold War continued as a context of competing universalisms.

## The Temptations of Universalism Until the End of the 1960s

The inclusion of universality among the seven fundamental principles in 1965 was the first occasion on which the Red Cross gave it such explicit official prominence. However, as an ambition it had always been key to the Red Cross since its foundation in 1863. The idea of universality was confirmed in 1918 and 1921, and after the Second World War when they were presented as such, it became one of the fundamental principles (Palmieri 2015).

In fact, since time immemorial, bystanders and (religious) corporations have provided emergency aid on an ad hoc basis. This was notably the case for assistance to wounded soldiers, while the ineffectiveness of such aid often contributed to true humanitarian disasters (Destexhe 1993). This insight struck Henry Dunant on the battlefield of Solferino in 1859 and incited him to propose that so-called civilized states sign an international pact in which they would agree to form neutral associations dedicated to helping wounded and sick soldiers, without regard to which camp they belonged. He believed that such help, organized at the national and international level, would be more effective than the system prevailing until then. He resented the fact that the fate of the victims depended on peculiar circumstances, such as the degree of hatred between belligerents, the existence of prior agreements, the number of doctors or the goodwill of civilians. From this point of view, the universalization of emergency help was the best way to avoid the contingencies of particularism.

The founders of the International Committee of the Red Cross (ICRC), inspired by Dunant's ideas and idealization of universality, were eager to help any victim of any international war in the world (Hutchinson 1996; Moorehead 1998). Although their undertaking was novel, its theoretical and practical premises were not entirely original and corresponded to the contemporary way of solving crucial international issues. During the last third of the nineteenth century, the number of international conferences increased steadily – a good number of them being held in neutral Switzerland. They were supposed to manage and regulate various societal issues, from prostitution and abandoned youth to postal communication and technical standardization. This provided the context in which the first international organizations were founded, facilitating a multilateralism that seemed to offer solutions to most problems around the world (Lyons 1963; Reinalda 2009).

During the first half of the twentieth century, the belief in the necessity of international collaboration was even considerably reinforced, not least because of the globalization of conflicts. The two world wars, with their military and civilian casualties, genocide and refugees, forced governments' attention to the humanitarian field. Here again, it was apparent that human needs and suffering had to be addressed by general rules and practices. This kind of reflection was at the core of the creation of the League of (national) Red Cross Societies in 1919, which was to complement the League of Nations in the humanitarian field. It was meant to be the main and possibly even the only humanitarian structure after the First World War, aimed at playing a leading role in peace time humanitarianism, among other similar organizations such as the ICRC (a board made up exclusively of Swiss citizens), and newcomers to the field, such as the Save the Children Fund (SCF) or the American Relief Administration (ARA). The members of the ICRC perceived this attempt as sheer usurpation, based on the appropriation of the symbolic capital their institution had built up over the decades. They fiercely defied their unwanted counterparts and succeeded in remaining the principal humanitarian body until the creation of various UN humanitarian agencies after the Second World War (Herrmann 2012–2013: 13).

This conflict prompted deep reflection that put universality and universalism at centre stage. Having defeated National Socialist Germany, the leading powers worked on the hypothesis that peace would be better maintained on the condition that states were speaking to and negotiating with each other. Opposing war was not only of general concern; it was also to be solved by using general means. This is exemplified by the Universal

Declaration of Human Rights, which embodies the idea that no action 'to make peace secure had more power and a wider scope than the formulation and effective implementation of an international bill of rights'.[3]

This period was also a time when the ICRC was subjected to harsh criticism that was indirectly and a posteriori linked to this state of mind. Whereas most belligerents had praised the institution's action during the hostilities, the victors – who no longer needed its help – changed their position. Western countries now criticized ICRC inaction on the massacre of European Jewish populations, the emerging symbol of ultimate human suffering. The communist states criticized its lack of initiative to help partisans and Soviet prisoners of war (POWs), who were considered as fighting for human values against inhumane ones.

These reproaches were tendentious, as the ICRC had no legal basis to alleviate the fate of Soviet POWs as the USSR had refused to sign the 1929 Geneva Convention that would have protected them. Moreover, despite their military means, the victors had shown little inclination to rescue Jewish victims during the war and even continued to display antisemitism after it. Many borders remained closed so that displaced Jews often had little choice than to go to Palestine. Blaming the ICRC allowed the critics to turn a blind eye to inhumanity more broadly (Herrmann 2018: 117).

Nonetheless, the ICRC took the accusations seriously. One of the most decisive countermeasures was to officially embrace the credo and reaffirm the term that was then so promising and popular: universality. In the mid-1950s, the jurist and future member of the governing body of the ICRC, Jean Pictet, suggested that the universalism of the Red Cross Movement should be officially proclaimed and acknowledged by everybody, not least by the national Red Cross societies that were organized along the same scheme, respected the same principles and whose actions had to be homologated by the Red Cross Conferences (Pictet 1955 [Eng. transl. 1956]: 82): 'The very idea of universality implies identity in certain respects. The name and emblem of the Red Cross can have only one and the same meaning everywhere... For we must again emphasize here that everyone can acknowledge that ideal, whatever his views on life and man's destiny' (ibid. 86ff).

Pictet's recommendation had two related effects. First, it countered the reproach that the ICRC had deliberately abandoned some categories of victims by implying that others were responsible for this failure. Second, it suggested a dominant position for the Red Cross, which claimed to be universal, contrary to other humanitarian organizations that did not (and usually could not plausibly) apply this rhetorical argument: once it had branded itself as universal, the Red Cross made its competitors appear as non-universal, and hence inferior, organizations.

## Reasons for Crafting Universality

Owing to the ICRC's humanitarian field of action and the significance of its moral capital for the continuation of its activity, political and mundane reasons for adopting universality as a doctrine were not openly discussed. They would have impaired the image of benevolent humanitarianism. Therefore, discussions about the universality of the Red Cross were subtended by other strategies of altruistic reason. Most significantly, both from a historical and ethical perspective, was the argument that human suffering is universal (Blondel et al. 1996: 2). Whereas this assertion may seem unproblematic, it presupposes that the experience of suffering is the same, whenever and wherever one lives. Yet, anthropologists have shown that the perception of pain depends on numerous factors; it varies with context, from society to society, from epoch to epoch, and from person to person (Hinton 2015: 505–506).

Second, the claim to universality emanated from the observation that war may occur at any time and in any place (ICRC 1958: 57). Again, this depends on how war is defined. The Red Cross Movement espoused a traditional understanding centred on international conflicts of opposing state armies and therefore envisioned dialogue only within the framework of the nation state. Less formalized variants of armed conflict were not taken into account, including massacres of civilians, genocide (defined as a crime after the Second World War), violent fights involving non–official combatants (as seen during the Second World War) and most internal hostilities. Moreover, the leaders of the ICRC obviously did not consider that their neutral homeland might ever become a belligerent country. Thus, they revealed a biased understanding of universality: it was limited and did not necessarily include themselves.

The third point shows that such exceptionalism, particularly of themselves, was not entirely intentional. Both the founders of the Red Cross and their twentieth-century heirs reckoned that it was their task to alleviate universal suffering. This self-assigned mission was profoundly rooted in religious belief, as most religions value dedication to one's fellow human in need. Henry Dunant and his co-founders belonged to a specific branch of Calvinist Protestantism, the Awakening (*le Réveil*, see Warner 2013). This movement pleads for an intimate private relationship with God and professes that each individual has a moral duty and sacred responsibility to do good. Even in the mid-twentieth century, most leaders of the Red Cross perpetuated this belief and acted by virtue of their Christian Messianic ideal. In this framework, humanitarianism was triggered by an ambiguous mix of (nonexclusive) superiority complex and a wish for universality.

Finally, there was the widely shared conviction among nineteenth-century political elites that a universal means to regulate war, human suffering and the whole planet already existed, namely international law. This confidence was also rooted in the ICRC's history and *raison d'être*. The institution was created at a time when many Western intellectuals aspired to regulate and manage the contacts between states through a body of law, respected by all its signatories. Even this idea might be called Messianic as it aimed at unifying so-called civilized countries and inciting others to join them to forge a 'civilized world'. On these premises, the Red Cross contributed to the elaboration of international humanitarian law (Quataert 2014). Between 1864 and 1949, it decisively participated in drafting the four Geneva Conventions, meant to protect an increasing number of victims and categories of victims. At first, this body of law protected only wounded or sick soldiers, but by 1929 it also addressed prisoners of war and finally, as of 1949, it included civilians.

## Challenges after the Second World War

In the years between 1949 and 1965, when universality was proclaimed as a guiding principle of the Red Cross, the world changed considerably. Not only did the Cold War unfold, but it was echoed and reinforced by the dynamics of decolonization. These developments thwarted the smooth resolution of tensions with the Eastern bloc, for which the ICRC had hoped; they even worsened its position in international relations, with marked consequences for the claim to universality.

The liberation wars that started after the Second World War profoundly challenged the idea of humanitarian universality, which was tied to the recognized sovereignty that was still concentrated in Europe. International humanitarian law, even as it had recently been improved and extended, was ill adapted to anticolonial uprisings. This body of law was still principally designed to regulate classic state-to-state armed conflicts, and the humanitarians' only official interlocutors remained the governments. Therefore, emergency aid during the decolonization wars depended on the goodwill of the European empires – on an issue in which they were inclined to display none. In its official communications, the ICRC (e.g. 1961: 17) tended to downplay the problem by presenting it as merely temporary impediments.

Moreover, the very rationale of decolonization proved that the goal was difficult to reach as such, because of the tenacious persistence of irreducible particularisms. Initially, the colonial powers considered these armed conflicts as mere internal problems that confronted legally constituted armies with insurgent groups. They intended to manage these situations without interference of humanitarian organizations that might prolong the uprising and give it publicity, which, in turn, might spread revolutionary 'ideas' among neighbouring peoples. For some time, the ICRC seemed to share the imperial point of view and remained passive, considering these issues as temporary difficulties. As the number and the duration of armed conflicts for independence increased, the Red Cross considered taking serious action. However, it soon discovered that it lacked effective tools to help the victims of this type of war (Branche 1999).

In addition, the organizational principle that had allowed the Red Cross to intervene in internal conflicts until then, namely the ramification into national societies, proved ineffective. This shortcoming was not totally novel: during the Second World War, the Deutsches Rotes Kreuz had diligently served the National Socialists and thereby demonstrated that the existence of national societies was not always sufficient to cope with particularities (Merkenich and Morgenbrod 2008). Moreover, the international humanitarian law promoted by the ICRC based on the principle that *Pacta sunt servanda* among 'civilized states' – and hence assuming that the signatory states would honour their commitments – proved ineffective in totalitarian states. What was new, however, was that such an instrumentalization of the Red Cross machinery did not only occur under authoritarian regimes but in democracies as well. Hence, despite claiming universality, the Red Cross failed to reach all persons in all countries, especially outside Europe.

The end of anticolonial wars did not put an end to the refutation of universalism. In some countries the ICRC faced peculiarities it had not imagined until then. It came across civilizations, for instance in Kenya and in Somalia, in which 'war' was a common and accepted ritual. There, 'low average' suffering was not only admitted but even desired. The populations concerned had no intention of stopping their culturally embedded feuds just to please a Western organization, however disturbed the latter was (Palmieri 2003).

The leaders of the ICRC were aware of the difficulties, to which the Eastern bloc added a second dividing line, be it through the Soviet societies of the Red Cross and Red Crescent, through the national societies of the countries included in the Warsaw Pact, or through the (sometimes) independently acting Yugoslav society. Even with the 'thaw' following the death of Stalin in 1953, communist criticism of the International Red Cross continued. Somewhat counterintuitively, USSR animosity mostly stemmed from a similarity in values and objectives. Like the Red Cross, the Soviet regime claimed that its ultimate goal was peace. However, the Eastern bloc did not regard international humanitarian law as sufficient to oppose war and, more generally, regarded the Red Cross approach to armed conflict and human suffering as bourgeois and merely palliative. In their opinion, the ICRC was too removed from the wider realities of war and provided insufficient remedies to a systemic problem.

Despite this fundamental disagreement, the Eastern bloc did not question the universality of the Red Cross Movement and even admitted that 'the humane purpose of the Red Cross Society commands respect throughout the world' (*Izvestya*, 18 June 1963: 4). Irrespective of how sincere this concession might have been, it provided the socialist states with an efficient rhetorical tool. At the International Red Cross Conference in Vienna, in 1965, they deplored the fact that most capitalist countries did not respect the fundamental principle of universality, as they had not invited the Red Cross Society of Communist China (ICRC and LRC 1965: 49, 77, passim). By presenting themselves as guardians of Red Cross universality, they gained a moral advantage and used it to promote what they suggested was the true universal goal of humanitarianism, namely peace. Under this pressure, in 1969 and in 1975, the ICRC participated in a number of East–West conferences, but without changing either methods or its universalist objectives (Herrmann 2019).

The reactions of both the Eastern bloc and the Red Cross are telling. The USSR and its allies challenged not the notion of universality as such, but the kind of universality the Red Cross represented. They were convinced that socialist ways of internationalism and ultimately communist universality had precedence over any alternative (see also Chapter 4). This not only illustrates that there may not be any true universality in humanitarianism, but even shows that the claim to universality may serve as a rhetorical move that imposes a specific universality. Thus, the suggestion that something is universal, or that a (humanitarian) reality has a general quality, can never be more than a claim to universality. It is a doctrine, rather than an observation, as the ICRC itself acknowledged. Whereas the decolonization wars challenged the universality of the Red Cross as they revealed its particularism, the Cold War had a similar effect, but on the basis of an allegedly superior universalism. In this context, it is intriguing how fiercely the ICRC stuck to its claims.

## The Dialectics of Universalism and Particularism Since the 1970s

In the mid-1960s, when the Red Cross Movement enshrined universality as one of its fundamental principles, drawing on a centennial tradition, Western societies began to embark on a trajectory that left the universalism of the twentieth century behind. The 1970s saw a move towards post-material, increasingly individualistic values, post-Fordist or neoliberal economics and the emergence of a postmodern and narcissistic culture. The growing endorsement of reality as a fragmented site of contention might even be due to lessons learned from the twentieth century's wrecked totalitarian projects, implying that 'today no cause can be universalized' (Finkielkraut 2000: 97). In humanitarian studies these trends are encapsulated in the figure of the ironic spectator and the humanitarian so-called NGO that struggles to 'maintain consumer [i.e. donor] loyalty under conditions of compassion fatigue' and frequently submits to the vested interests of a facilitating government (Chouliaraki 2013: 52, 49).

While the discretionary reality of aid entailed by these prototypes was far from new, a striking change occurred in the reference and scaling of humanitarianism. Concrete relief efforts had traditionally been framed as expressions of a universal commitment to humanity at large, despite the always more or less selective background of donors and recipients. In the course of the twentieth century, aid causes had been deliberated extensively in various societal contexts, the experience and gratitude of aid beneficiaries had been valued and the circle of compassion had expanded greatly beyond Europe and the North Atlantic (Götz, Brewis and Werther 2020). By the end of the 1960s, a situated and utilitarian way of expressing solidarity began to take hold that was more unequivocal in its self-referential aspiration and salvation than theretofore. The growing frankness about the motives of aid, including assumed win-win outcomes of apparently altruistic behaviour, accompanied the loss of a transcending universal narrative suited to highlighting the entitlement claims raised by those suffering from disaster. Thus, there was a marked departure from the ideals of a mass society and its generalizing models and solutions. The latter had included global teleologies such as modernization theory, development optimism and the assumption that capitalism and communism would eventually converge. Major humanitarian efforts during and after the First World War, such as Herbert Hoover's Commission for Relief in Belgium or the ARA (both of which collaborated with the American Red Cross), had maintained spatially and temporarily limited objectives. However, like the SCF's focus on 'enemy children' at the time, ARA relief to a hostile, famine-ridden Soviet Russia demonstrated a universal zeal. SCF also learned that isolated initiatives for children were not always feasible and therefore coordinated its work with food programmes for adults funded by other organizations. After the Second World War, the United Nations Relief and Rehabilitation Administration supported Jewish refugees on the assumption of universal suffering, ignoring the particularity of antisemitism. The Cooperative for American Remittances to Europe (CARE) became a permanent multi-purpose organization that soon changed its full name to Cooperative for American Remittances to Everywhere. The conceptual shift from Europe to 'everywhere' reflected the shouldering of global responsibility by a pseudo-continental, but essentially national humanitarian enterprise (Wieters 2017: 63).[4] Similarly, Oxfam, initially a local committee tasked with alleviating the Greek famine during the Second World War, rapidly evolved into a transnational agency with worldwide activities (Black 1992). However, while CARE, Oxfam and other organizations became globally engaged and adopted doctrines of universal scope, they rarely used the terms universality or universalism and did not, like the Red Cross, draw on a structure of national branches across the world.

Organizations such as the Red Cross, Oxfam and CARE continue to pursue their at least implicitly universal claims, further accentuated by the increased internationalization of the 1970s and the expansion of the humanitarian field in the wake of vanishing Cold War blockades in the 1990s (Sluga 2013; Paulmann 2013). However, this trend of governments outsourcing official functions and degrading aid agencies to the status of 'force multipliers' restricted the latter's latitude and vision. Compared to earlier times, fundraising drives increasingly emphasized the role of relief providers and disregarded the causes of the need for aid. Brand maintenance and celebrity profiling became crucial elements of fundraising, whereas the gratitude of aid recipients – which was important to humanitarian donors of earlier times – has lost significance in parallel with an increasing distance from the beneficiaries.

This development has reinforced the overall tendency for circles of beneficiaries to widen over time, as in the Western popular engagement for the secessionist Eastern Region (Biafra) against the Federal Military Government of Nigeria at the end of the 1960s (Götz forthcoming) or for victims of famine in Ethiopia in the mid-1980s. However, what emerged could be called a 'thin universalism', dependent on contingencies of mobilization, in which the beneficiaries of aid mattered less to the donors and had a more limited agency than in earlier efforts targeted at culturally closer groups of people (Götz, Brewis and Werther 2020). The little-discussed example of famine in Yemen 2018–2019, qualified by UN officials as rapidly becoming the worst in living memory (UN and Partners 2019), shows how muted an international response to a humanitarian disaster can be when notions of religious and ethnic strife go along with an understanding that the support of one party by the US president and the military intervention of powerful neighbours will inhibit impartial humanitarian action. The sex scandals practically all humanitarian agencies faced after the 2018 revelation of abuses of Oxfam representatives in the wake of the Haiti earthquake signify another type of particularistic aberration (Charity Commission 2019).

## Universality as Unlimited Particularity

The early 1970s proved to be a watershed, with far-reaching consequences for the Red Cross, the humanitarian sector's semi-official flagship organization whose fundamental principles remain a benchmark of humanitarian action. The Biafran War (1967–1970) was a postcolonial conflict; the federal government of Nigeria's policy was to maintain it as a domestic internal conflict that would not be negotiated at the international level, whereas the ultimately unsuccessful Biafran leadership skilfully rallied public opinion across the world to its own separatist cause. Conditions in Biafra became quasi-universal because they were on display as the first televised famine, but also through mobilizing slogans such as '"A" as in Auschwitz, "B" as in Biafra' (Heerten 2015). The relation of these sites of mass destruction appeared universal in the sense of them both being manifestations of genocide and the 'infinitely particular' (Kouchner 1991: 45). The problem, that famine conditions in Biafra were largely self-inflicted and deliberately exploited to discredit the military enemy, was not widely understood at the time.

The Red Cross as a whole stuck to its traditional neutrality, avoiding alienation of the recognized government on which it depended to access the larger conflict area. Most of its activity therefore benefitted areas controlled by Nigerian forces, though this permitted some relief to be given to the insurgent province. At the same time, the flood of horrifying images from Biafra and their personal experiences on the ground made several Red Cross representatives uncomfortable with the cautious manoeuvring of their organization. Staff from the French Red Cross formed the Comité de lutte contre le génocide au Biafra, and although their empathy for this abortive nation was initially voiced and appreciated within a polyphonic Red Cross discourse, this group was the nucleus of what became a defecting organization from the Red Cross: Médecins Sans Frontières (Doctors Without Borders, MSF; Desgrandchamps 2011).

The French doctors inaugurated a new style of humanitarianism in contrast to the lowkey and supposedly confidential approach of the Red Cross. By means of a strategic use of media, the organization of protest marches and especially an effective rhetoric renouncing silence, they made Biafra a symbol resembling 'a second Solferino' (Finkielkraut 2000: 84). When MSF was formally founded in 1971 they answered the call for 'a new Dunant' (Davey 2015: 35–36) and their choice of name was programmatic. 'Without borders' signalled a 'distinctly universal ambition' (Redfield 2013: 1) that departed from the status quo of a world seen as a composite of nation states. Within a few years the organization also came to challenge the traditional understanding of humanitarian neutrality and to champion advocacy (*témoignage*) on behalf of sufferers, including denunciation of human rights abuses by governments. This emphasis on engagement and transgression of the governmentality of the Red Cross agency expanded the scope of humanitarian action. The irony was that the foundational moment of MSF was flawed as the universal cause contemporaries saw in Biafra – despite reasons for discontent with the federal government of Nigeria – in hindsight appears as an idiosyncratic crisis that had been manufactured by cynical secessionist exploiters of aid (Barnett 2011: 134–35).

## Continuities and Ruptures: MSF Universalism and Beyond

The Red Cross Movement had been torn apart over the shortcomings of neutrality and the existing system of sovereign states as gauges and placeholders for universality. Despite this schism, not only did the principle of universalism survive unscathed, but even neutrality and statism continued to be held in high esteem. Hence, it was difficult to distinguish the concise charter that MSF adopted in 1971 from the doctrines of the Red Cross. It included defensive statements framing MSF as an apolitical organization with the sole object of providing humanitarian assistance and an article that reconciled neutrality and universalism:

> Operating on a strictly neutral and independent basis, refraining from interference in internal affairs of state, governments and parties in the areas where they are called to serve, the members of Médecins Sans Frontières demand, in the name of the association's universal mission [*vocation universelle*], full and unhindered freedom in the exercise of its medical functions. (Binet and Saulnier 2019: 24)

The fact that the MSF charter was framed in such conventional terms reflects the foundational alliance of Biafra activists with more established groups alongside a newcomer's (and perceived 'medical hippie's') quest for respectability (Redfield 2013: 57). At the same time, it shows that action preceded conceptual change, both in a temporal sense and as a perceived priority over formal codification.

While the baseline of the 1971 charter was the submission to established patterns of international affairs, the essence of *sans-frontiérisme* and the recognition of the paradox that parties formed significant elements of the universal opened a back door to circumnavigate national sovereignty. As the structure of this order was in flux until the mid-1970s (and again in the 1990s), such an understanding was sensitive to shifting realities on the ground. It subtly challenged the working hypothesis of the Red Cross, namely that the universal was sufficiently approximated as an aggregate of official totalities. The MSF became more discriminating, more considered and more boldly involved in shaping the particular realities that had a bearing on the universal at a given point in time. By the mid-1970s, the organization began to build on aspects of the Biafra legacy of witnessing and speaking out, denouncing governments if need be, which eventually became its trademark, alongside the transgression of borders and media spectacle. This included the strident withdrawal from aid projects such as in Ethiopia in 1986 or later in Congo and North Korea (Weissman 2011; Binet and Saulnier 2019: 27; Vallaeys 2004: 189), but also from a global event like the World Humanitarian Summit in 2016. Since the late 1970s, MSF has conducted clandestine missions without approval of the government in charge, drawing conflicts that were difficult to address otherwise into the humanitarian realm (Tanguy 1999: 239). While all this can be interpreted as a universal approach that served principles higher than that of consensus, it was also akin to the ICRC's 'Western' and 'Northern' bias and its troubled relationship with the communist bloc and the global South during the Cold War.

When they redrafted their charter in 1989 to its current form (adopted in 1991), MSF abandoned the principles of confidentiality and non-intervention, although they were still cautious to stipulate a document that would function as a 'business card' vis-à-vis authorities and not complicate their access to humanitarian calamities. Key conceptual moves were MSF's claims to act in 'the name of universal medical ethics' ('au nom de l'éthique médicale universelle') and of anyone's 'right to humanitarian assistance' (Binet and Saulnier 2019: 145). Although different from the Red Cross in style and approach, MSF has nevertheless been seen as 'defending the great timeless principles that inspired Dunant, the naive universalism of the organization's moral code' (Finkielkraut 2000: 86–87).

MSF permeated borders even within its professional field. In the early 1970s, when the newly founded organization did not yet command the means to run its own programmes, it 'functioned like a placement agency' that sent volunteers abroad through other organizations, including the Red Cross and SCF (Redfield 2013: 57; see also Binet and Saulnier 2019: 24). Such permeability exemplifies an overall compatibility and division of labour within the humanitarian sector that transcends the quarrels over different approaches, the coexistence of particular interpretations of universalism and the assumption of specific humanitarian missions. It can partly be explained by the difference between pragmatic field work and headquarters dogmatism: despite the latter's claims to universality, practitioners may have a greater inclination towards universalism than those who govern them.

Coordination has been an issue throughout the twentieth century and the humanitarian sector has attributed increased significance to it after failures in response to the 2004 Indian Ocean tsunami. In this sense, the overworked concept of a worldwide 'NGO community' had and continues to have some bearing as an overarching ideal. What is more, over the past decades MSF and the Red Cross have become close collaborators again and their agendas have reconverged (Brauman 2012: 1533–34).

Nonetheless, MSF itself soon split, in 1979, over the pursuance of a more charismatic or bureaucratic line of action. Former frontman Bernard Kouchner left MSF and founded the more emphatically political *Médecins du Monde* (Doctors of the World, MDM). His perspective, recognizing the universality of conflict and disequilibrium rather than that of harmony and countering it with a minimal universalism of sorts based on response to suffering, remained very much in line with that of MSF (Kouchner 1986: 13–16). In addition to the organizational breakup, throughout the 1980s the relationships among national MSF sections were highly conflictual, including legal battles concerning the ownership of the movement (Redfield 2013: 60–63). The fact that an organization that claimed to transcend borders organized itself in national branches with particular profiles and responsibilities was a contradiction in terms (Pallister-Wilkins 2019: 148). Moreover, the term 'French doctors' has become a brand name for MSF and MDM at large.

More generally, the 1970s saw a marked proliferation of humanitarian organizations, each with its own specific background and profile (O'Sullivan 2014). By the 1980s, the rise of identity politics and the recognition of a fragmented reality came to the fore in an official redescription of the Red Cross system as the International Red Cross and Red Crescent Movement – a move designed to accommodate major particularities under their universal umbrella. In 2005, a third official symbol was added (but not included in the name): the Red Crystal. This ultimately neutral, perhaps genuinely universal, symbol comes at the price of a reduction in meaning for large audiences and is henceforth seldom used (Bugnion 2007).

Apparently, MSF was an eminently secular organization, and some observers stress this legacy (Redfield 2013). Others suggest that MSF rather merged a secular leftist tradition of humanitarianism with a Catholic one, thereby developing 'a new universalism that transcends the right–left divide' (but is also distinctly French; see Taithe 2004: 147). Still others see it as an eschatologically oriented 'parareligion' that has successfully propagated its credo and myth by wrestling with the ICRC as Luther or Calvin once did with the Catholic Church, while it continues to stand aloof of other humanitarian organizations in the manner of a sect (Benthall 2008).

Be this as it may, humanitarian engagement in the last decades of the twentieth century was far from a predominantly secular – and in this sense supposedly universal – matter. Rather, missionaries and churches remained crucial intermediaries, for example in mobilizing public opinion in the global north for Biafra (with its Christian population; see Omaka 2016; Chapter 8). Moreover, many new aid agencies still had religious backgrounds. The most prominent example that emerged from solidarity with Biafra was the Irish organization Africa Concern, which after a few years changed its name into Concern Worldwide (O'Sullivan 2012; thereby resembling the universalization of CARE two decades earlier).

By 1977, the Geneva Conventions were extended with two additional protocols, improving the protection of victims of international armed conflicts and introducing detailed rules for civil war. Thus, endorsed by most nation states in the world, in the 1970s the ICRC began to chart domestic territory. According to the ICRC, these amendments 'were adopted ... to make international humanitarian law more complete and more universal' (and to adapt it better to the demands of modern conflicts) and created an opportunity for newly independent countries to contribute to developing international humanitarian law (ICRC 2009). Nonetheless, the form of protocols was chosen because the ICRC anticipated that governments around the world might accept a lowkey format more easily than additional conventions. While this strategy may have been successful, the presumption of a lack of universal appeal was confirmed by the subsequent development. Although the protocols have been ratified by the vast majority of states, they have not achieved the same universal outreach as the four Geneva Conventions. The US and a compact belt of South Asian countries stretching from Turkey to Papua New Guinea remain outside the orbit of the protocols – suggesting the existence of separate 'Asian' values (ICRC 2018).

## Conclusion: Stubborn Conceptual and Historical Contradictions

From the founding of the Red Cross, universal principles have dominated the self-understanding of humanitarian organizations. The opposite – partiality – is widely considered to be incommensurable with modern humanitarian aid, and practical work with specific groups tends to be justified by arguing that their disadvantaged position defies the general standards of humanity. Hence, universality as a maxim, universalism as a practice and universal as an attribute all remain key concepts. The growth and ramifications of the humanitarian sector, illustrated by the rise of MSF in the past half-century, corroborate this observation in a paradoxical manner.

However, they also highlight the contradictions inherent in the universal claims of humanitarianism.

Despite its spread across the globe, the Red Cross has faced major challenges to its proclaimed universality, which have not led it either to reconsider the principle or to change its self-understanding. The organization's conceptual rigidity when encountering new conjunctures and other civilizations reflects its religious and moral European heritage and postcolonial leanings. Moreover, it was characterized by intrinsic anticommunism: Eastern bloc arguments remained alien to the Red Cross, which promoted discretionary humanitarianism rather than socialism. Furthermore, its difficulties with legislation proved that its universality was a goal rather than a baseline. More broadly, the Red Cross perceived particularism as a backward orientation that its altruistic universality bypassed in order to improve emergency aid.

Ultimately, what made the ICRC slightly reconsider its view on universalism was not any of the elements typical of the Cold War, such as communism, anticolonialism or the evidence of legal shortcomings. It was the rivalry with new humanitarian organizations, which either advocated special interests or, like MSF, made alternative claims to universality, thus challenging the ICRC's conceptual prerogative. This tension between variations on the concept of universalism came to the fore around 1970 in a context of social transformation and cultural change (see also Chapters 8, 9 and 12). The defection of former colleagues in the 1970s and their founding of MSF, with its propagation of a border-transcending universalism and departure from the old consensus-seeking approach, was a major blow to the universal ambition of the Red Cross.

In competition with the Red Cross, MSF even assumed the role of mouthpiece for the humanitarian sector as a whole – and was awarded the Nobel Peace Prize for its 'pioneering humanitarian work'. James Orbinski, in his 1999 Nobel lecture on behalf of MSF, declared that 'humanitarian action is by definition universal, or it is not' (Binet and Saulnier 2019: 199). This proposition tied humanitarian efforts and universalism intimately together. As we have shown, this was the phrasing of an ideal, rather than an account of actual practice. MSF's claim to universality disregards several persistent contradictions that haunt the humanitarian sector as a whole.

There is a tension between humanitarianism and universality as, of necessity, any organization aiming at helping victims has a specific social basis and historically anchored reasons to be engaged (see also Lidén 2020). Contrary to what most humanitarians believe, these reasons are only partially universal; transcending these particular contexts is always difficult. This points to the ontological factor that humanitarian aid is generally provided by those who are not in need of it, because they are outsiders to the problem they come to mitigate or solve. They help by virtue of specific interests or principles. The latter are, by definition, non-particular and tend to be considered universal. Finally, the tensions between humanitarianism and universalism reveal contradictions pertaining to humanitarianism as such. On the one hand humanitarianism, which is supposed to help people and to be triggered by human dedication and a wish to do good, is the result of discrimination (triage). On the other, given the legitimacy conveyed by the claim to universality, any speech-act involving the 'universal' entails a clear dimension of domination and power. From this conceptual perspective, the permanence of humanitarians' claims to universality stems not only from their desire to be humane towards humanity, but also from the fact that they too belong to the human race – and may be all too human.

Thus, universalism is a hegemonic concept. It is mainly rooted in European efforts to transcend the nation state and reveals the internal contradictions of humanitarian organizations and of the world that needs them. Based on European and North Atlantic situatedness and bias, the concept of universality is used as an instrument of power – and might also be challenged. In fact, any universalism not only clashes with various particularisms, but also with competing universalisms based on deviating presumptions about what could constitute benchmark values. Ultimately, the inevitable entrapment of any human body and practice in particular circumstances makes the European dream of universalism and universality an illusion.

While late modernity in Europe and elsewhere is characterized by growing individualism and the decline of grand narratives, this is happening in an increasingly interconnected world. As we showed in this chapter for the Red Cross Movement and other organizations such as MSF, the humanitarian sector is exposed to both tendencies and has undergone a major transformation in the half-century since the Biafran War. Despite increasing fragmentation and a consideration of the different backgrounds of aid agents, however, the conceptual map of humanitarianism has remained remarkably stable.[5] European notions of universality guided the work of the Red Cross Movement from the beginning and – one hundred years after its inauguration – were codified as fundamental global principles. Ironically, this was done when the phantasmagoria of universalism became increasingly apparent, when the Red Cross Movement was about to split and a surge of new organizations shaped a myriad of new aid demands. Nevertheless, the concept of universalism as such survived in the humanitarian sector. However partial the realization of emergency aid may have been, its main rationale was considered and presented as universal, or at least universalistic.

**Norbert Götz** holds the Chair in Contemporary History at Södertörn University, Stockholm, Sweden. He has worked on global civil society, UN diplomacy and Nordic collaboration. His latest book is *Humanitarianism in the Modern World: The Moral Economy of Famine Relief* (Cambridge University Press, 2020, with G. Brewis and S. Werther). He is currently working on the Nordic humanitarianism during the Biafra Crisis. ORCID: 0000-0002-8788-101X.

**Irène Herrmann** is Professor of Swiss Transnational History at the University of Geneva, Switzerland. She graduated in both Russian and history at the University of Geneva. She was visiting professor at the University Laval, Canada, lecturer at the Graduate Institute of International Studies, Geneva, SNF Fellow at the Russian State University for Humanities, Moscow, and SNF Professor at the University of Fribourg, Switzerland. She has published more than 100 scientific articles, ten edited books and five monographs. Her work focuses mainly on solidarity, humanitarianism, conceptual history, conflict management and the political uses of the past in Switzerland and in post-Soviet Russia. ORCID 0000-0002-6046-2392.

## Notes

1. These principles are: humanity, impartiality, neutrality, independence, voluntary service, unity and universality.
2. '[T]he Red Cross must extend to all men, in all countries … In doing this, the principle will take on its full meaning, that of universalism' (Pictet 1979: 87, 89).
3. Archive of the United Nations, SOA 317/1/01(1), C: Draft for a speech to be presented by Charles Malik at the plenary session of the General Assembly, written by Edward Lawson, November 1948, f°2. This affirmation, formulated within the framework of the UN, reflects a general state of mind and, as such, can be generalized.
4. A more balanced universalization, at least nominally, was undertaken in 1993, when the organization was renamed Cooperative for Assistance and Relief Everywhere.
5. For the general tension between the limited normative validity of human agency and the unlimited aspiration of meaning in universalisms, see also Albrecht (2019: 41).

## References

*Primary Sources*
ICRC (ed.). 1958. *Final Record Concerning the Draft Rules for the Limitation of the Dangers Incurred by the Civilian Population in Time of War*. Geneva: ICRC.
———. 1961. *Rapport d'activité pour l'année 1960*. Geneva: ICRC.

————. 1965a. The XXth International Conference of the Red Cross. *International Review of the Red-Cross* 56 (November): 567–69.

————. 1965b. Resolutions adopted by the XXth International Conference of the Red Cross. *International Review of the Red-Cross* 56(November): 570–98.

————. 2009. Protocols I and II additional to the Geneva Conventions. Geneva: ICRC, available at https://www.icrc.org/en/doc/resources/documents/misc/additional-protocols-1977.htm (accessed 16 August 2019).

————. 2018. States Party to the Geneva Conventions and Their Additional Protocols. *Annual Report*. Geneva: ICRC.

ICRC and LRC. 1965. *XXe Conférence internationale de la Croix-Rouge, Vienne, 2–9 octobre 1965: Compte rendu*. Geneva: ICRC and LRC.

### Secondary Sources

Albrecht, C. 2019. 'Universalismen – Partikularismen: Zur Kultursoziologie von Geltungsansprüchen', in P. Geiss, Dominik Geppert and J. Reuschenbach (eds), *Eine Werteordnung für die Welt? Universalismus in Geschichte und Gegenwart*. Baden-Baden: Nomos, pp. 27–43.

Balibar, E. 2014 [2007]. 'Sur l'universalisme – Un débat avec Alain Badiou'. Allocution inaugurale d'une rencontre organisée par la School of Social Sciences, University of California, Irvine, le 2 février 2007. *Mediapart*, available at https://blogs.mediapart.fr/segesta3756/blog/091214/etienne-balibar-sur-l-universalisme-un-debat-avec-alain-badiou.

Barnett, M. 2011. *Empire of Humanity: A History of Humanitarianism*. Ithaca: Cornell University Press.

Benthall, J. 2008. *Returning to Religion: Why a Secular Age is Haunted by Faith*. London: I. B. Tauris.

Binet, L. and M. Saulnier. 2019. *Médecins Sans Frontières, Evolution of an International Movement: Associative History 1971–2011*. s.l.: MSF.

Black, M. 1992. *A Cause for Our Times: Oxfam: The First 50 Years*. Oxford: Oxfam.

Blondel, J.-L. et al. 1996. *The Fundamental Principles of the Red Cross and Red Crescent*. ICRC publication N° 0513. Geneva: ICRC.

Branche, R. 1999. 'Entre droit humanitaire et intérêts politiques: Les missions algériennes du CICR', *Revue Historique* 301(1): 101–25.

Brauman, R. 2012. 'Médecins Sans Frontières and the ICRC: Matters of Principle', *International Review of the Red Cross* 94(888): 1523–35.

Bugnion, F. 2007. *Red Cross, Red Crescent, Red Crystal*. Geneva: ICRC.

Charity Commission. 2019. *Inquiry Report Summary Findings and Conclusions – Oxfam*. London: Charity Commission.

Chouliaraki, L. 2013. *The Ironic Spectator: Solidarity in the Age of Post-Humanitarianism*. Cambridge: Polity.

Davey, E. 2015. *Idealism Beyond Borders: The French Revolutionary Left and the Rise of Humanitarianism, 1954–1988*. Cambridge: Cambridge University Press.

Desgrandchamps, M.-L. 2011. 'Revenir sur le mythe fondateur de Médecins sans frontières: Les relations entre les médecins français et le CIRC pendant la guerre du Biafra (1967–1970)', *Relations internationales* 146: 95–108.

Destexhe, A. 1993. *L'Humanitaire impossible, ou Deux siècles d'ambiguïté*. Paris: Armand Colin.

Fassin, D. 2010. 'Moral Commitments and Ethical Dilemmas of Humanitarianism', in I. Feldman and M. Ticktin (eds), *In the Name of Humanity: The Government of Threat and Care*. Durham: Duke University Press, pp. 238–55.

Feldman, I. and M. Ticktin. 2010. 'Introduction: Government and Humanity', in I. Feldman and M. Ticktin (eds), *In the Name of Humanity: The Government of Threat and Care*. Durham: Duke University Press, pp. 1–26.

Finkielkraut, A. 2000. *In the Name of Humanity: Reflections on the Twentieth Century*. New York: Columbia University Press.

Götz, N. Forthcoming. 'Towards Expressive Humanitarianism: The Formative Experience of Biafra', in F. Balestracci, Ch. v. Hodenberg and I. Richter (eds), *An Era of Value Change: The Seventies in Europe*. Oxford: Oxford University Press.

Götz, N., G. Brewis and S. Werther. 2020. *Humanitarianism in the Modern World: The Moral Economy of Famine Relief*. Cambridge: Cambridge University Press.

Heerten, L. 2015. '"A" as in Auschwitz, "B" as in Biafra: The Nigerian Civil War, Visual Narratives of Genocide, and the Fragmented Universalization of the Holocaust', in H. Fehrenbach and D. Rodogno (eds), *Humanitarian Photography: A History*. Cambridge: Cambridge University Press, pp. 249–74.

Herrmann, I. 2012–2013. 'Décrypter la concurrence humanitaire: Le conflit entre Croix-Rouge(s) après 1918', *Relations internationales* 151: 91–102.

———. 2018. *L'humanitaire en questions: Réflexions autour de l'histoire du Comité international de la Croix-Rouge*. Paris: Éditions du Cerf.

———. 2019. 'Humanitaire et paix: Une équation impossible?', in F. Bugnion et al. (eds), *Humanitaire et quête de la paix*. Geneva: Éditions Georg, pp. 28–45.

Hinton, A. 2015. 'Violence', in D. Fassin (ed.), *A Companion to Moral Anthropology*. Malden: Wiley Blackwell, pp. 500–18.

Hutchinson, J.F. 1996. *Champions of Charity: War and the Rise of the Red Cross*. Boulder: Westview.

Klose, F. and M. Thulin (eds). 2016. *Humanity: A History of European Concepts in Practice from the Sixteenth Century to the Present*. Göttingen: Vandenhoek & Ruprecht.

Kouchner, B. 1986. *Charité Business*. Paris: Le Pré aux Clercs.

———. 1991. *Le malheur des autres*. Paris: Éditions Odile Jacob.

Kurunmäki, J. and J. Marjanen. 2018. 'A Rhetorical View of isms: An Introduction', *Journal of Political Ideologies* 23(3): 241–55.

Lidén, K. 2020. 'Universality', in A. De Lauri (ed.), *Humanitarianism: Keywords*. Leiden: Brill, pp. 220–22.

Lyons, F.S.L. 1963. *Internationalism in Europe, 1815–1914*. Leyden: Sijthoff.

Merkenich, S. and B. Morgenbrod. 2008. *Das Deutsche Rote Kreuz unter der NS-Diktatur 1933–1945*. Paderborn: Schöningh.

Moorehead, C. 1998. *Dunant's Dream: War, Switzerland and the History of the Red Cross*. London: Harper Collins.

O'Sullivan, K. 2012. *Ireland, Africa and the End of Empire: Small State Identity in the Cold War, 1955–75*. Manchester: Manchester University Press.

———. 2014. 'A "Global Nervous System": The Rise and Rise of European Humanitarian NGOs, 1945–1985', in M. Frey, S. Kunkel and C.R. Unger (eds), *International Organizations and Development, 1945–1990*. Houndmills: Palgrave Macmillan, pp. 196–219.

Omaka, A.O. 2016. *The Biafran Humanitarian Crisis, 1967–1970: International Human Rights and Joint Church Aid*. Madison: Fairleigh Dickinson University Press.

Pallister-Wilkins, P. 2019. 'Médecins Sans Frontières and the Practice of Universalist Humanitarianism', in R. Jones (ed.), *Open Borders: In Defense of Free Movement*. Athens: University of Georgia Press, pp. 141–55.

Palmieri, D. 2015. *Les principes fondamentaux de la Croix-Rouge: Une histoire politique*, available at https://www.icrc.org/fr/document/les-principes-fondamentaux-de-la-croix-rouge-une-histoire-politique.

———. 2003. 'Le temps pour comprendre la violence de guerre: L'exemple de l'Afrique', *RICR* 85(852): 775–90.

Paulmann, J. 2013. 'Conjunctures in the History of International Humanitarian Aid during the Twentieth Century', *Humanity* 4(2): 215–38.

Pictet, J. 1955. *Les principes fondamentaux de la Croix-Rouge*. Geneva: ICRC.

———. 1979. *The Fundamental Principles of the Red Cross Proclaimed by the Twentieth International Conference of the Red Cross, Vienna, 1965: Commentary*. Geneva: Henry Dunant Institute.

Quataert, J.H. 2014. 'International Law and the Laws of War', in U. Daniel et al. (eds), *1914–1918-online: International Encyclopedia of the First World War*. Berlin: Freie Universität.

Radice, H. 2018. 'Humanity', in T. Allen, A. Macdonald and H. Radice (eds), *Humanitarianism: A Dictionary of Concepts*. London: Routledge, pp. 158–67.

Redfield, P. 2013. *Life in Crisis: The Ethical Journey of Doctors Without Borders*. Berkeley: University of California Press.

Reinalda, B. 2009. *Routledge History of International Organizations: From 1815 to the Present Day*. London: Routledge.

Robert, P. (ed.). 1969. *Dictionnaire alphabétique et analogique de la langue française*. Vol. 6. Paris: Société le Nouveau Littré.

Sluga, G. 2013. *Internationalism in the Age of Nationalism*. Philadelphia: University of Pennsylvania Press.

Taithe, B. 2004. 'Reinventing (French) Universalism: Religion, Humanitarianism and the "French Doctors"', *Modern & Contemporary France* 12(2): 147–58.

Tanguy, J. 1999. 'The Médecins Sans Frontières Experience', in K.M. Cahill (ed.), *A Framework for Survival: Health, Human Rights and Humanitarian Assistance in Conflicts and Disasters*. New York: Routledge, pp. 226–44.

Ten Have, H. 2014. 'Macro-triage in Disaster Planning', in D.P. O'Mathúna, B. Gordijn and M. Clarke (eds), *Disaster Bioethics: Normative Issues when Nothing Is Normal*. Dordrecht: Springer, pp. 13–32.

UN and Partners 2019. 'UN and Partners to Hold Conference Seeking Urgently Needed Funds to Save Millions in Yemen from "Horrific Plight"', *UN News* (24 February 2019), available at https://news.un.org/en/story/2019/02/1033401 (accessed 21 July 2019).

Vallaeys, A. 2004. *Médecins sans frontières: La biographie*. Paris: Fayard.

Warner, D. 2013. 'Henry Dunant's Imagined Community: Humanitarianism and the Tragic', *Alternatives: Global, Local, Political* 38(1): 3–28.

Weissman, F. 2011. 'Silence Heals…: From the Cold War to the War on Terror, MSF Speaks Out: A Brief History', in C. Magone, M. Neuman and F. Weissman (eds), *Humanitarian Negotiations Revealed: The MSF Experience*. London: Hurst, pp. 177–97.

Wieters, H. 2017. *The NGO CARE and Food Aid from America, 1945–80: 'Showered with Kindness'?* Manchester: Manchester University Press.

Chapter 12

# Defining 'the Third Way'

Oppositional Internationalisms of Finnish,
Swedish and West German Student and New Left
Movements in the 1960s

*Juho Saksholm*

The sixties are often seen as a 'transnational moment of change', and the global reach of 1968 is an integral part of the symbolic nature of the year that for a brief moment seemed to change everything (Horn 2004). Beyond simple, often anecdotal notions of new popular culture and global TV networks, more tangible indicators of mobility seem to justify such a view; the number of exchange students in European universities doubled between 1960 and 1973, travel in general increased, and global trade reached new levels (Klimke and Nolan 2018; Schildt 2006). These tangible factors have often meant that the increase in political internationalism, especially amongst the social movements of the period, has been taken for granted; but were the 1960s really a period of 'the global before the internet?' (Suri 2003: 262). How did increased mobility in the sixties affect the politics of its social movements? To understand the meaning and significance of international-ism as a political concept, we need to see how contemporary activists used it in different contexts, which is my conceptual historical approach here.

Studies on the social movements of the sixties have taken into consider-ation both cultural and political processes and agents. Yet, interpretations of the internationalist and global character of these movements have often focused on the framework of the Cold War, despite the fact that sixties activists often directly opposed the contemporary international system (Klimke and Scharloth 2008; Thomas 2003: 236). Recently, scholars of global history have challenged the Eurocentric perspective of traditional Cold War history, and transnational studies have broadened the focus from diplomatic history to show how dissident movements participated in defining the international system.

The sixties movements redefined existing definitions of Cold War politics by: 1) politically transcending the boundaries of the Cold War and its binary logic; and 2) questioning the role of the state as the de facto agent of foreign policy and forming their own transnational connections and networks.

In this chapter, I highlight the diverse ways in which global and local political influences and traditions were intertwined when the social activists of the sixties defined their own, oppositional version of internationalism both as a political concept and as a practice for transnational political cooperation (Kalter 2017).

Global and transnational processes, agents and discourses were certainly an important part of the movements in West Germany, France, the US and other canonized examples of 1968 (Klimke and Nolan 2018). Focusing on other national and local contexts relativizes these established historical narratives and provides a much needed contrast to them. The neutral Nordic countries of Finland and Sweden lacked many of the factors that became key points of social movement criticism in the canonized cases, such as ruling Christian Democratic parties or NATO membership. The Nordics were internationally known for their welfare policies, mixed economies, neutrality and, in the case of Sweden, liberal public morals (Kurunmäki and Strang 2010; Arnberg 2012). This progressive reputation made exchanges with 'Third World' countries a compelling option (Hellenes and Marklund 2018). The contrast with West Germany, where the student movement vehemently opposed the official Western alliance of the government, is thus clear.

Comparing the Finnish, Swedish and West German histories of the sixties is also an exercise in analysing transnational entanglements. The historical and spatial proximity of these North European nation states is clearly visible in the context of university students and academics. The German cultural sphere has been the traditional scholarly centre for the Nordic intelligentsia. Throughout the early twentieth century, many of their political discourses were adapted from German discussions, regardless of political position (Kortti 2014; Ihalainen 2017: 23–37). Simply showing how political influences moved from the radical centre of Berlin to the periphery of the Nordic countries would not capture the dynamic nature of transnational entanglements between the social movements of the sixties. The agents in these smaller Nordic countries acted not only as adapters but also as discursive innovators; focusing on them adds a different transnational perspective to the well-researched West German debates (Marjanen 2017; Bauer 2010).

As this volume exemplifies, internationalism is a fluid, changing and disputed political concept. In the context of the 1960s, international politics

was certainly not the only sphere where internationalism and related concepts were used and redefined. Internationalism could be associated with a
wide variety of phenomena from the economy to television and pop culture.
In these uses, the concept often functioned as a modifier that defined the
phenomena in question as modern and significant. The buzzwordy nature
of the concept makes studying its political uses challenging; yet, from a
conceptual history perspective, ambiguity also signals significance. One
could talk of a 'super-concept' (Freeden 2017: 121). While it generally functioned as a positive epithet, perhaps for the first time in European history,
internationalism was an important concept of self-definition. Small political
movements often attached themselves to a wider international scene as a way
of highlighting their importance (Jørgensen 2011: 52).

I pay particular attention to transnational discursive connections that
shaped the conceptualizations of internationalism within the sphere of North
European student and New Left movements. Including shared experiences,
texts and symbols in the study of physical cross-border entanglements exemplifies how different national dynamics and contexts shape transnational
history. Agents who used internationalism as a political concept did not
necessarily share any single political tradition, and groups working under
shared transnational concepts like the New Left often had rather different
theoretical premises and political views (Vinen 2018: 201; Horn 2007).

In this chapter, I analyse the debates in Finnish, Swedish and West
German student and New Left papers which were independent of party
politics. While published in different political contexts, all of these papers
had the fundamental role of providing a forum for the inner debates of the
social movements in the sixties. Transnational exchange featured in travel
reportages, translations of radical texts and news stories borrowed from
secondary sources. Thus, these papers give a good overview of the diverse
conceptualizations of internationalism and the reactions to the transnational
events experienced by social movements of the decade.

## Liberal and Radical Discourses of Internationalism

Different national and local political traditions had a significant influence
on the political language of the movements of the 1960s. Two different
discourses had a particular effect on the meaning of internationalism and
on how it was used as an oppositional concept in national and transnational
political debates in Northern Europe. Contemporary concepts were used to
self-define and position different strands of radical politics in relation to each
other. In practical discourses, these definitions were often fluid and at times
even convergent; yet they were fundamentally based on two different ideas

on how to accomplish political change. For this analysis, I categorize these discourses as follows:

1) *Liberal* discourses included definitions of internationalism that were based on universalism and global, general solutions. Discourses that highlighted the universality of individual rights were particularly important for Nordic discourses in the early 1960s. These discourses shared a strong faith in Western values and the UN as the protector of global peace and progress. By highlighting the shortcomings of nation-alist policies and attitudes in the domestic context, liberal definitions of internationalism were in clear opposition of existing definitions of international politics.

2) *Radical* internationalism was a leftist discourse, but through its empha-sis on 'Third World' issues it critically reflected on established forms of socialist internationalism. No single conceptualization of 'Third World internationalism' among different movements ever existed, as both national and internal differences and disputes between New Left groups in the 1960s had a marked effect on their internationalist perspective.

While both spheres incorporated a wide variety of different agents, the essential difference between these two discourses of internationalism can be defined through their attitudes towards 'Western values' such as individual rights, freedom of speech, the market and parliamentary politics (Gilcher-Holtey 2018). Liberal activists saw these Western values as universally appli-cable and thus promoted their wider and more radical application. Radical New Left activists were much more critical towards the universality of Western values. Interpretations have often emphasized the latter's extreme 'Third World' associations with guerrilla warfare and revolutionary politics, but while they were highly visible in mainstream media, these ideas were hardly the only or even the primary political programme of any European New Left group. National issues, like the West German *Notstandsgesetze* (emergency powers acts) or university reform debates, often took significant amounts of political space in the day-to-day activities of social movements in the sixties (Brown 2013: 100–105; Sedlmaier 2014).

## A 'World Society' as a Challenge to National Sovereignty

The 1960s saw a new type of politics emerging in many parts of Europe and indeed the world, as new political movements and agents challenged the established ways of making political decisions. Postwar societies seemed to need a completely new form of politics, better suited to the technological, cultural and political transformations that had followed the Second World War. Such arguments were key components in the Nordic 'cultural radicalism' of the early 1960s. A small but high-profile group of intellectuals, cultural figures and students emphasized antitraditionalism, antinationalism, individual rights, and rational modernism in both politics and culture (Östberg 2002: 44–45; Kolbe 1996: 27–31, 55–56, 93–97). Since the nationalist policies of the 1930s offered a straightforward explanation for the devastations of the war, a more internationalist outlook proffered a modern alternative.

An 'international standpoint' was one of the key definitions supported by Nordic liberal activists (LibD 2/58, B.M., 70–71); the era of the bomb meant that foreign policy was a matter that suddenly concerned everyone (LibD 1/56, T.V., 25–26). Technological advances that increased communication and contacts between different groups could provide a new era of more participatory foreign policy. The Swedish liberal students in particular wanted to accelerate these developments with political means; a 'drive to active internationalism' would lead to increased international dependence and to the creation of a 'world society' (LibD 3/60, Mats Kihlberg, 14–16; LibD 2/60, Hans Hederberg, 1–2; LibD 6/61, Björn Beckman, 23–26). In Finland too, changes in the surrounding society were seen as legitimizing more active international communication as the new 'state of affairs' (*Aikalainen* 4/64: 3–6). A sense of progressive teleology was central to liberal definitions of internationalism; belief in a particular Zeitgeist inspired predictions that the 1960s would be 'the real breakthrough period of international cooperation', characterized by international 'solidarity' and 'tolerance' (LibD 4/58).

In Finnish student circles, liberal notions were crystallized in the conceptualization of 'new patriotism', a new, more international focus that differed from Swedish universalist definitions in that it was still primarily legitimized by the benefits it would guarantee for the nation state (Saksholm 2020). The Swedish liberal tradition was more outspokenly international. Welfare economist Gunnar Myrdal saw the new nationalisms stirring up in the midst of decolonization as a political awakening that would increase international contacts and solidarity and thus ensure 'awakening to internationalism' as a practical political model that would support global economic and political integration (LibD 3/58, David Wirkmark, 96–100). While Myrdal was highly revered in socially liberal circles, he was often a rather moderate voice in the debate. Swedish liberal students were more partisan and clearly emphasized the value of internationalism as self-evident and absolute.

Swedish debates frequently used the -ism form from the early 1960s, thus redefining the concept as an epithet of a particular political ideology (LibD 3/60, Mats Kihlberg, 14–16; LibD 1/61, 39; LibD 6/61, Björn

Beckman, 23–26; Kurunmäki and Marjanen 2018). Some liberal students explicitly rejected combinations of national and international perspectives: 'The internationalism of the Sixties makes national borders increasingly obsolete ... it is our duty to reconsider the idea of (national) sovereignty' (LibD 7–8/61, Hans Hederberg, 1–4). Definitions of internationalism in opposition to national sovereignty would surface in Finland only after the student movement took a leftist turn later in the 1960s (Tuomioja 1967).

Some Nordic student activists saw the UN as the basis for a future 'world society' that would expand its existing peace-keeping forces to the level of a global police force. These notions were founded on a firm belief in the neutrality of the organization (LibD 6/56, Hans Blix, 157–60; LibD 2/60, Hans Hederberg, 1–2). Member states were responsible for any shortcomings in the present practices of the UN (LibD 6/58, K.H., 191). The focus on the UN was part of a more general discourse, as the UN was the prime forum of neutral foreign policy in all Nordic countries (Hellenes and Marklund 2018; Koikkalainen 2010). As a testament to this, Student UN Associations were important organizations especially in the Finnish student scene. They worked in close connection with the Finnish Committee of 100, a radical pacifist organization known for its demands for unilateral disarmament and antimilitaristic, antinational politics (Kolbe 1996: 84–85).

In Sweden, organizations supporting South African liberation movements were a more prominent early form of international activism; they also had more direct links to parties and the government. They turned internationalism into political practice through the grassroots organization of exchange programmes and development aid projects, a clear example of direct student participation in the international sphere (Sellström 1999). Some Nordic activists demanded that the internationalist goals of these programmes be generalized and expanded (JYL 31/62, PK, 3; LibD 2/60, Hans Hederberg, 1–2; LibD 6/61, Björn Beckman, 23–26; YL 4/67, Maunu Harmo, 12). In West Germany, student organizations likewise demanded a more universal application of human and political rights (Slobodian 2012: 11, 18–21). Radical press was also used to further these goals. In West Germany and Sweden, New Left activists focused on making universal human rights more tangible by publishing personal stories of oppression (Slobodian 2012: 26; Saksholm 2020). One factor in this were travel reportage books that had been an important phenomenon in Sweden since the early 1960s. Volumes like Jan Myrdal's *Report from a Chinese Village* (1963) were not only instrumental in spreading information on global issues but also inspired activists (Hedén 2008; Johansson 2010).

For an outright politicization of global issues, economic analysis was an important catalyst. From the late 1950s onwards, leftist and liberal Swedish papers emphasized structures of the global economy and its effects on the future of developing nations (*Clarté* 1/56, Erland con Hofsten, 7–10; LibD 1/60, Torsten Gårdlund and Åke Ortmark, 22–25; LibD 4/60, Hans Blix, 40–41). As 'the Swedish model' gained some international attention as a compromise between socialism and capitalism, Swedish agents were ready to promote their national model as a global solution. The international applicability of the Swedish model was also part of domestic political debate; for the Swedish liberals, international equality was a response to the claimed national isolationism of Swedish social democracy (LibD 7–8/61, Hans Hederberg, 1–4; Hellenes and Marklund 2018). Hence, concepts like 'international social policy' were common, and signified a change in sphere of internationalism from foreign policy to international social and economic cooperation (LibD 6/58, Utrikesminister Östen Undén, 192; LibD 4/58, S.A. Birger Möller, 120–121; LibD 3/60, Mats Kihlberg, 14–16). Gunnar Myrdal's role as a transnational global political economist at least partly inspired these discussions; in his work, he focused on the economic aspects of wider social and cultural factors (LibD 3/58, David Wirkmark, 96–100; *Clarté* 3/58, Bo G. Gustafsson, 2–4). Through Myrdal's writings, theoretical models of the global economy that pointed out the contradiction between Western abundance and 'Third World' poverty quickly became a practical concern leading to calls for ordinary Swedish citizens to take action.

More political reading of the global economy and its structures coincided with the adaptation of socialist concepts during the latter part of the 1960s. The escalation of war in Vietnam was an important catalyst that turned internationalist discourses into an explicit criticism of US imperialism and made new political arguments possible (Salomon 1996; Mausbach 2010). The West German student Left, for example, had supported many of the US policies during the Kennedy era, but the war in Vietnam quickly eroded the support the US had enjoyed since the Second World War. In the new situation, humanitarian justifications for action became irrelevant, as they lacked a structural analysis of global power relations (Slobodian 2012: 78–81, 204–205).

## The 'Third World', Global Structures and the New Left

In existing literature, the criticism on both capitalism and Marxism expressed by Herbert Marcuse and other Frankfurt school scholars are often repeated as de facto theoretical inspiration for the sixties movements (Rothenhöfer 2011; Garavini 2007). While direct links between the Frankfurt School and sixties activists remain elusive, the core concepts of the Marxist theory like class, hegemony and imperialism could certainly easily be applied to every context without justifying their capability as analytical tools. Together with a structural approach to the global economy, these Marxist concepts profoundly affected the way in which student and New Left activists saw the global role of Western Europe and the USA. The ideological shift from the division between East and West to one between the rich North and poor South was important in readjusting the focus of radical social movements (Jørgensen 2011; Thomas 2003: 65; Klimke 2008: 101).

While New Left papers like the West German *Konkret* featured anti-colonial reporting early in the 1960s (Slobodian 2012: 1), more theoretical and universal debates became frequent after the war in Vietnam escalated. In a 1967 interview, Jean-Paul Sartre reminded *Konkret* readers that class struggle would be fought 'on the international level' (*Konkret* 2/67: 22–26). Rudi Dutschke, one of the intellectual leaders of the West German student movement, also repeatedly emphasized the interconnectedness of the 'Third World' and Western societies as the precondition for a revolutionary moment (*Konkret* 6/67: 24–26; Klimke and Nolan 2018). While the global focus of European radical thinkers has often been seen as a form of political appropriation, Quinn Slobodian has argued that it was part of the 'radical imagination' of sixties movements and thus a more complicated process of adaptation and redefinition (Slobodian 2018: 74).

In the transnational network of the New Left press, European agents were not the only ones emphasizing the theoretical entanglement of global oppression. The Swedish New Left press had several links to Black Power leaders, who paralleled 'Third World' movements with the Black struggle based on their joint fight against US imperialism. Swedish New Leftists followed the global focus set by their liberal counterparts but added Marxist concepts to their analysis. These approaches were profoundly inspired by contacts with non-European activists. Translations from Chinese and Latin American sources frequently featured in the Swedish radical papers, and Western publishers complemented these efforts: *Les Damnés de la Terre* by Francis Fanon was translated into Swedish immediately after its publication, before the English and German versions were in print. In addition to textual transfers, Swedish New Left press invested considerable resources in sending their own reporters to witness conditions outside of Europe (Östberg 2002: 38–39; Sellström 1999; Saksholm 2020).

West German student activists not only had access to transnational texts, but also formed tangible transnational encounters with 'Third World' agents. Quinn Slobodian has argued that these personal contacts were the main factor that inspired protests on global issues (Slobodian 2012: 3, 51). Exchange students took an active part in organizing protests; beginning as early as 1964, in the rally against the Congolese president Moïse Tshombe, they culminated in the Shah protests of 1967 (Brown 2013: 7–8, 21–23, 38, 72). The ultimate goal of these protests was cooperation with 'Third World' activists that would eventually help to shift the balance of global politics (Slobodian 2012: 2). The protests were important not only because they were organized in cooperation with non-European activists; they exemplified how the violence already discussed in theory could become a reality in a Western context such as Berlin (Thomas 2003: 107–16).

With the emergence of new universal concepts, the personal contacts with 'Third World' activists that had been so instrumental slowly became less important, as local particularities within the 'Third World' began to be seen as mere building blocks for a universal political theory. Changes in political practices also had their effect. Increasing protests against the war in Vietnam not only mobilized student activists, but also profoundly shifted the student perspective on the 'Third World' towards more abstract explanations (Slobodian 2012: 79, 154, 192). These changes are reflected in the concepts used. Ulrike Meinhof, the editor of *Konkret*, emphasized the interconnectedness by talking about Vietnam as 'a new type of world war' (*Konkret* 11/67, Ulrike Meinhof). Parallels between Saigon and Berlin or Newark and Vietnam were frequent, and exemplified how images of resistance and violence could make the locality of the events almost irrelevant. Universal theories robbed the 'Third World' of its agency and turned active individuals into passive placeholders (*Konkret* 8/67; Mausbach 2010; Slobodian 2012: 12). These tendencies found their logical endpoint in the explicit anti-Nazi rhetoric of the radicalized West German student movement in the late 1960s; this rhetoric mostly bypassed any of the theoretical nuances that the Frankfurt School used to describe similar cases (Abromeit 2010; Schmidtke 2006). Comparisons with National Socialism removed the global multiplicity from the discourse and reverted the discussion back to domestic, German issues (Slobodian 2012: 135). It is worth noting that even the West German Sozialistischer Deutscher Studentenbund (Socialist German Student Union), often seen as one of the most important European student organizations, never fully endorsed violent guerrilla tactics. Some members saw the focus on 'Third World' issues as a hindrance to their domestic political goals (Slobodian 2012: 98). Transnational connections and comparisons not only created new alliances but also challenged existing ones.

The Vietnam War Crimes Tribunal, perhaps better known after its chief organizer as the Russell Tribunal, is an interesting example of the different layers present in transnational activism of the 1960s. Part of the radical antiwar movement, and incorporating some of the most noticeable figures on the Left, it still used liberal ideas of international justice to legitimize its actions. As a committed communist and Tribunal member, Jean-Paul

Sartre argued that while the Tribunal was judicially irrelevant, it was still an important part of the political struggle; it was 'giving a judicial dimension to international politics' (*Konkret* 2/67: 22–26). In practice, Sartre saw the international press as the main audience of the Tribunal (*Konkret* 1/68, Dagobert Lindlau, 29–33). Sartre's uneasiness with the liberal premises of the Tribunal shows how strongly left-wing radicals criticized its legitimization with international neutrality. *Konkret* pushed Sartre to the point of acknowledging his opposition the 'petit bourgeois' moralism of the Tribunal.

Although the role of thinkers like Dutschke in the West German context is perhaps a little overblown (Klimke and Nolan 2018), in the Nordic countries radical celebrities were a natural point from which to approach European activism in general. Acquiring, adapting and translating political texts took a lot of time and effort (Brown 2013: 6). Dutshcke was one of the few leaders of the West German student movement that had concrete contacts with 'Third World' activists (Slobodian 2012: 52–53), so encounters with Western intermediators like Dutschke provided Nordic activists with access to a network of transnational activism. These contacts turned abstract internationalism into concrete political practice. This was the case during Dutschke's visit to Uppsala University in March 1968: his speech was translated into Swedish and published in *Kommentar*, a Swedish New Left paper. Emphasizing the hidden fascism of Western societies and the political nature of the university, Dutschke argued strongly against specific university-level solutions or actions. While Dutschke was not explicitly pointing to the fascism of Swedish society as such, his remarks on the ties between capitalism and fascism were so general that it was easy to draw conclusions about their applicability to the Swedish context (*Kommentar* 4/68: 3–9). Dutschke clearly pushed for the internationalization of the student movement on the West German model.

While personal connections were important, they were often slow to establish. Thus, media reports of protests of 1968 were often more accessible and easier to use when compared to personal transnational contacts, inspiring Nordic radicals to interpret their own local context as part of a global movement. Marxist concepts were once again useful to them. For instance, they interpreted the May 1968 protests in France through the framework of class; the radical groups inside the Swedish New Left in particular emphasized the global nature of the events by presenting all labour and student protests as a 'worldwide phenomenon' together resisting 'capitalism, imperialism and bureaucracy' (*Clarté* 4/68, Lena and Claus Brunderius, 17–19). The war in Vietnam, the violence during the 1968 Mexico Olympics and the civil rights movement in the US were all presented as parts of the same revolutionary entity.

Swedish domestic protests were also compared and contrasted with global events. *Kårhusockupationen*, the takeover of the student building of Stockholm University in May 1968, was interpreted as the domestic sign of a global rise in political consciousness, resistance against US influence and increase in class antagonism (*Clarté* 4/68, Göran Eriksson and Gunilla Wettersjö, 37–41). Indeed, papers like *Clarté* wrote about the revolutionary struggle in the singular, thus conceptually tying together movements from all over the world (*Clarté* 5–6/68, Lena Brundenius, 44–47). Countering 'neocolonialism' was a conceptual alternative to internationalism, because of its explicit focus on global economic exploitation. Once it turned towards a Maoist line, *Clarté* became a prime forum for these conceptualizations. Using Chinese sources to present protests from West Germany, the UK, Belgium, Italy, Denmark, Luxemburg, Switzerland, Yugoslavia, the Netherlands, Spain, Turkey, the USA, South Africa, Japan, Congo, Brazil, Chile, Mexico, Argentina, Bolivia and Uruguay as part of the same global phenomena (*Clarté* 4/68, 43–47), *Clarté* exemplified how the transnational elements of the 1968 protests were used, circulated and reused politically. In fact, *Clarté* was in direct contact with the Chinese embassy in Sweden, which provided much of the political material the paper used (Johansson 2010).

## Conclusion

The 1960s discussions on internationalism in the student and New Left press were diverse and intersected with numerous national and transnational political trends. 'Third World internationalism', which aspired to launch a new global revolutionary movement, was certainly important; Nordic, liberal definitions of internationalism add another perspective to the heterogeneous nature of the concept. These discourses not only complemented established definitions of international cooperation, they radically challenged the status quo in their rejection of national sovereignty. Through transnational transfers and texts, agents on the peripheries outside continental European nexuses of radical thought implemented their own visions of radical internationalism as a political discourse and practice. An examination of European nation states can still show how the global sixties were present in European contexts, and how global events and ideas were used to situate local political movements into the global arena of radical imagination. In many ways, later social movements have faced similar challenges; as globalization has become ever more politically important, the question of how to organize antiauthoritarian, global protests have become even more pressing.

**Juho Saksholm** has a PhD in History from the University of Jyväskylä, Finland. His dissertation deals with the transnational conceptual history of Finnish and Swedish student movements and the New Left. His research interests include conceptual, transnational and global history, particularly in the postwar North European context. ORCID 0000-0001-8192-929X.

## References

### Primary Sources

Finnish student papers
*Jyväskylän Ylioppilaslehti* (JYL)
*Oulun Ylioppilaslehti* (OYL)
*Turun Ylioppilaslehti* (TYL)
*Ylioppilaslehti* (YL) from Helsinki
*YyKoo/Aviisi* from Tampere

New Left papers
Sweden
*Clarté*
*Häften för kritiska studier* (HfKS)
*Kommentar*
*Konkret*
*Tidsignal* (TiS)
*Zenit*

Finland
*Aikalainen*
*Ajankohta*
*Tilanne*

Federal Republic of Germany:
*Konkret*
*Liberal Debatt* (LibD)

Pamphlets
Tuomioja, Erkki. 1967. *Tahditon rauhanmarssi*. Helsinki: Weilin+Göös.

### Secondary Sources

Abromeit, J. 2010. 'The Limits of Praxis: The Social-Psychological Foundations of Theodor Adorno's and Herbert Marcuse's Interpretations of the 1960s Protest Movements', in B. Davis et al. (eds), *Changing the World, Changing Oneself: Political Protest and Collective Identities in West Germany and the U.S. in the 1960s and 1970s*. New York: Berghahn Books, pp. 13–38.

Arnberg, K. 2012. 'Under the Counter, Under the Radar? The Business and Regulation of the Pornographic Press in Sweden 1950–1971', *Enterprise & Society* 13(2): 350–77.

Bauer, K. 2010. 'From Protest to Resistance: Ulrike Meinhof and the Transatlantic Movement of Ideas', in B. Davis et al. (eds), *Changing the World, Changing Oneself: Political Protest and Collective Identities in West Germany and the U.S. in the 1960s and 1970s*. New York: Berghahn Books, pp. 171–88.

Brown, T.S. 2013. *West Germany and the Global Sixties: The Antiauthoritarian Revolt, 1962–1978*. Cambridge: Cambridge University Press.

Etzemüller, T. 2006. 'A Struggle for Radical Change? Swedish Students in the 1960s', in A. Schildt and D. Siegfried (eds), *Between Marx and Coca-Cola: Youth Cultures in Changing European Societies, 1960–1980*. New York: Berghahn Books, pp. 239–57.

Freeden, M. 2017. 'Conceptual History, Ideology and Language', in W. Steinmetz, M. Freeden and J. Fernandez Sebastian (eds), *Conceptual History in the European Space*. New York: Berghahn Books, pp. 118–38.

Garavini, G. 2007. 'The Colonies Strike Back: The Impact of the Third World on Western Europe, 1968–1975', *Contemporary European History* 16(3): 299–319.

Gilcher-Holtey, I. 2018. 'Political Participation and Democratization in the 1960s', in J. Kurunmäki, J. Nevers and H. te Velde (eds), *Democracy in Modern Europe: A Conceptual History*. New York: Berghahn Books, pp. 257–80.

Hedén, A. 2008. *Röd stjärna över Sverige: Folkrepubliken Kina som resurs i den svenska vänsterradikaliseringen under 1960- och 1970-talen*. Lund: Sekel Bokförlag.

Hellenes, A.M. and C. Marklund. 2018. 'Sweden Goes Global: Francophonie, Palme, and the North-South Dialogue during the Cold War', *Histoire@Politique* (35).

Horn, G. 2004. 'The Working-Class Dimension of 1968', in G. Horn and P. Kenney (eds), *Transnational Moments of Change: Europe 1945, 1968, 1989*. Lanham: Rowman & Littlefield Publishers, pp. 95–118.

———. 2007. *The Spirit of '68: Rebellion in Western Europe and North America, 1956–1976*. Oxford: Oxford University Press.

Ihalainen, P. 2017. *The Springs of Democracy: National and Transnational Debates on Constitutional Reform in the British, German, Swedish and Finnish Parliaments, 1917–1919*. Helsinki: Finnish Literature Society.

Johansson, P. 2010. 'Mao and the Swedish United Front Against USA', in Z. Yangwen, H. Liu and M. Szonyi (eds), *The Cold War in Asia: The Battle for Hearts and Minds*. Leiden: Brill, pp. 217–40.

Jørgensen, T.E. 2011. 'National Ways to Socialism? The Left and the Nation in Denmark and Sweden, 1960–1980', in M. Klimke, J. Pekelder and J. Scharloth (eds), *Between Prague Spring and French May: Opposition and Revolt in Europe, 1960–1980*. New York: Berghahn, pp. 49–63.

Josefsson, S. 1996. *Året var 1968: Universitetskris och studentrevolt i Stockholm och Lund*. Göteborg: Historiska institutionen i Göteborg.

Kalter, C. 2017. 'From Global to Local and Back: The "Third World" Concept and the New Radical Left in France'. *Journal of Global History* 12(1): 115–36.

Klimke, M. 2008. 'West Germany', in M. Klimke and J. Scharloth (eds), *1968 in Europe: A History of Protest and Activism, 1956–1977.* New York: Palgrave Macmillan, pp. 97–110.

———. 2011. *The Other Alliance: Student Protest in West Germany and the United States in the Global Sixties.* Princeton: Princeton University Press.

Klimke, M. and M. Nolan. 2018. 'Introduction: The Globalization of the Sixties', in *The Routledge Handbook of the Global Sixties.* Abingdon: Routledge, pp. 1–9.

Klimke, M. and J. Scharloth. 2008. '1968 in Europe: An Introduction', in M. Klimke and J. Scharloth (eds), *1968 in Europe: A History of Protest and Activism, 1956–1977.* New York: Palgrave Macmillan, pp. 1–9.

Koikkalainen, P. 2010. 'From Agrarian Republicanism to the Politics of Neutrality: Urho Kekkonen and "Nordic Democracy" in Finnish Cold War Politics', in J. Kurunmäki and J. Strang (eds), *Rhetorics of Nordic Democracy.* Helsinki: Finnish Literature Society, pp. 238–61.

Kolbe, L. 1996. *Eliitti, traditio, murros: Helsingin yliopiston ylioppilaskunta 1960–1990.* Helsinki: Otava.

Kortti, J. 2014. 'Intellectuals and the State: The Finnish University Intelligentsia and the German Idealist Tradition', *Modern Intellectual History* 11(2): 359–84.

Kurunmäki, J. and J. Marjanen. 2018. 'Isms, Ideologies and Setting the Agenda for Public Debate', *Journal of Political Ideologies* 23(3): 256–82.

Kurunmäki, J. and J. Strang. 2010. 'Introduction: "Nordic Democracy" in a World of Tensions', in J. Kurunmäki and J. Strang (eds), *Rhetorics of Nordic Democracy.* Helsinki: Finnish Literature Society, pp. 9–36.

Marjanen, J. 2017. 'Transnational Conceptual History, Methodological Nationalism and Europe', in W. Steinmetz, M. Freeden and J. Fernandez Sebastian (eds), *Conceptual History in the European Space.* New York: Berghahn Books, pp. 139–74.

Marwick, A. 1999. *The Sixties: Cultural Revolution in Britain, France, Italy, and the United States, c.1958–c.1974.* Oxford: Oxford University Press.

———. 2006. 'Youth Culture and the Cultural Revolution of the Long Sixties', in A. Schildt and D. Siegfried (eds), *Between Marx and Coca-Cola: Youth Cultures in Changing European Societies, 1960–1980.* New York: Berghahn Books, pp. 39–56.

Mausbach, W. 2010. 'America's Vietnam in Germany – Germany in America's Vietnam: On the Relocation of Spaces and the Appropriation of History', in B. Davis et al. (eds), *Changing the World, Changing Oneself: Political Protest and Collective Identities in West Germany and the U.S. in the 1960s and 1970s.* New York: Berghahn Books, pp. 41–64.

Mishkova, D. and B. Trencsényi. 2017. 'Conceptualizing Spaces within Europe: The Case of Meso-Regions', in W. Steinmetz, M. Freeden and J. Fernandez Sebastian (eds), *Conceptual History in the European Space.* New York: Berghahn Books, pp. 212–35.

Östberg, K. 2002. *1968 när allting var i rörelse: sextiotalsradikaliseringen och de sociala rörelserna.* Stockholm: Prisma.

Peifer, E.L.B. 2006. 'Public Demonstrations of the 1960s: Participatory Democracy or Leftist Fascism?', in P. Gassert and A.E. Steinweis (eds), *Coping with the Nazi*

*Past: West German Debates on Nazism and Generational Conflict, 1955–1975*. New York: Berghahn Books, pp. 194–209.

Rothenhöfer, A. 2011. 'Shifting Boundaries: Transnational Identification and Disassociation in Protest Language', in M. Klimke, J. Pekelder and J. Scharloth (eds), *Between Prague Spring and French May: Opposition and Revolt in Europe, 1960–1980*. New York: Berghahn Books, pp. 116–31.

Saksholm, J. 2020. *Reform, Revolution, Riot? Transnational Nordic Sixties in the Radical Press, c. 1958–1968*. PhD thesis, University of Jyväskylä: Jyväskylä University Press.

Salomon, K. 1996. *Rebeller i takt med tiden: FNL-rörelsen och 60-talets politiska ritualer*. Stockholm: Rabén Prisma.

Schildt, A. 2006. 'Across the Border: West German Youth Travel to Western Europe', in A. Schildt and D. Siegfried (eds), *Between Marx and Coca-Cola: Youth Cultures in Changing European Societies, 1960–1980*. New York: Berghahn Books, pp. 149–60.

Schmidtke, M. 2006. 'The German New Left and National Socialism', in P. Gassert and A.E. Steinweis (eds), *Coping with the Nazi Past: West German Debates on Nazism and Generational Conflict, 1955–1975*. New York: Berghahn Books, pp. 176–93.

Sedlmaier, A. 2014. *Consumption and Violence: Radical Protest in Cold-War West Germany*. Ann Arbor: The University of Michigan Press.

Sellström, T. 1999. *Sweden and National Liberation in Southern Africa: Formation of a Popular Opinion (1950–1970)* (Vol. 1). Uppsala: Nordic Africa Institute.

Slobodian, Q. 2012. *Foreign Front: Third World Politics in Sixties West Germany*. Durham, NC: Duke University Press.

Slobodian, Q. 2018. 'The Meanings of Western Maoism in the Global 1960s', in *The Routledge Handbook of the Global Sixties*. Abingdon: Routledge, pp. 67–78.

Suri, J. 2003. *Power and Protest: Global Revolution and the Rise of Detente*. Cambridge: Harvard University Press.

———. 2009. 'The Rise and Fall of an International Counterculture, 1960–1975', *American Historical Review* 114(1): 61–68.

———. 2010. 'Ostpolitik as Domestic Containment: The Cultural Contradictions of the Cold War and the West German State Response', in B. Davis et al. (eds), *Changing the World, Changing Oneself: Political Protest and Collective Identities in West Germany and the U.S. in the 1960s and 1970s*. New York: Berghahn Books, pp. 133–52.

Thomas, N. 2003. *Protest Movements in 1960s West Germany: A Social History of Dissent and Democracy*. Oxford: Berg.

Vinen, R. 2018. *The Long '68: Radical Protest and Its Enemies*. London: Allen Lane.

## Chapter 13

# 'The Vision of an Undivided, Habitable World'

### International Climate Policies in German, British and European Parliamentary Debates on Conceptions of Justice, 1992–2019

*Miina Kaarkoski*

For centuries, in the processes of formulating international laws and treaties, discourses of fairness and conceptions of justice have caused disputes when states have debated their rights and duties and the international order (Armstrong 1999: 547–49). The United Nations Framework Convention on Climate Change (1992), the Kyoto Protocol (1997) and the Paris Agreement (2015) are examples of international agreements whose efficacy depended on the willingness of nation states to ratify and to enforce them. These treaties included a conception of justice that the nations were able to agree on, and which reflected their ideas about international cooperation and the world order.

Scholars have argued that in international climate politics, discourses about the historical responsibility of the wealthier states flourished in the 1990s, whereas in the twenty-first century, environmental safety as a universal human right was increasingly important in debates about justice. Tensions between the global North and South, or developing and advanced industrial countries, have been discussed in the scholarship of climate justice. In this tradition, justice provides an analytical frame to study international cooperation from the perspectives of distribution, recognition and representation in international relations (Anand 2004; Di Chiro 2016; Joshi 2014, Kortetmäki 2016).

However, 'justice', 'fair/ness' and 'solidarity' deserve attention as meaningful empirical political concepts that were used when debating principles of internationalization and the meanings of 'worldwide' or 'global' in international climate politics. I analyse competing ways of using these concepts in the German, British and European parliament when the parliamentarians debated the necessity, content or ratification of international climate policies and treaties. The scholarly field of climate justice originated from the US citizens' movement of the late 1980s and has since then emphasized justice especially from the viewpoint of the poorer and less-developed parts of the world (Di Chiro 2016: 100–105; Joshi 2014: 677–91; Scholsberg 2017: 309–18). Conceptual analysis of political language in the German, British and European Union contexts from 1992 to 2019 brings a European perspective to the conception of justice.

Both Germany and Britain, as well as the EU, have been profiled as supporters of international climate policies. The following provides more a nuanced analysis of the tensions and complexity of the evolution of international climate policies. It shows that in the 1990s, political ideas were highly idealistic and concepts of 'global', 'worldwide', and 'humanity' were used to emphasize a new world starting after the Cold War. Gradually, the tone became more pessimistic although historical references to the international settings established after the Second World War were frequently used to motivate international policies. Rhetoric about guilt evolved when conceptions of the historical responsibility of the advanced industrial countries were partly left aside and 'fair/ness' and 'social justice' of international climate policies were defined in a situation where all the countries had to make binding commitments.

Below, I discuss three cycles of the debates on the conceptions of justice. In the 1990s and early 2000s, the world was rhetorically divided, and political rhetoric highlighted the responsibilities of the wealthier countries in international politics. After a phase when the analysed concepts were used less frequently, their frequency began to increase again at the end of the 2000s, when conceptions of justice evolved towards requiring a larger number of countries to commit to international climate action. Finally, in the period following the 2015 Paris Agreement, transnational social aspects of justice and human rights competed with the nationalist ideas.

## Internationalization of Climate Politics, 1992–2004

Before international attention turned to global warming in the late 1980s, the diminishing ozone layer was an issue that was quite successfully addressed by international agreements. The international system of environmental treaties expanded significantly in the United Nations Conference on Environment and Development in Rio de Janeiro on 3–14 June 1992. The Framework Convention on Climate Change signed at this conference set the course for new international climate policies, although the targets were non-binding. Five years later, the Kyoto Protocol (1997) included legally binding obligations for developed countries for 2008–2012.

The internationalization of environmental policies forced countries to review the benefits of international cooperation, since environmental policy was a more direct matter of national interest than many other foreign policy issues (Hanf 2000: 9). Both the UN Climate Convention and the Kyoto Protocol reflected a sense of justice based on the historical responsibility of advanced industrial countries. In Germany and Britain, parliamentarians used concepts of the global, humanity, worldwide and responsibility to categorize countries based on their politics, society and economy. In addition, the concept of solidarity expressed the attitude required from the wealthier countries.

German and British traditions of framing climate change as a political problem diverged in the late 1980s and early 1990s. In (West) German debates climate change was portrayed as a serious threat demanding an international and a domestic response. In British politics, economic aspects had more weight and the attitude of the British political leadership was more reluctant towards specific international targets (Cass 2007: 34–47). Political conceptualizations also differed. In the German parliament, member attitudes towards climate change were relatively deterministic. Climate change was widely conceptualized as a worldwide question. For example, in May 1992, just before the Earth Summit, Chancellor Helmut Kohl argued for the internationalization of environmental issues by stating that the task was to solve 'the pressing questions about the future of humanity' and that 'small-minded provincial thinking' was not enough. The Chancellor spoke about the 'work of justice' and 'global responsibility', which meant promoting peace between nations in a world where the Cold War had ended (DB, 20 May 1992: 7575–79). At this point, Germany had already set a national target of reducing $CO_2$ emissions by 25–30% from the 1987 level by 2005.

Green and Leftist politicians, including Gregor Gysi (PDS/Left list) and Klaus-Dieter Feige (Alliance 90/The Greens), used crisis talk, including expressions such as 'huge environmental crisis' and 'threatening climate catastrophe' when demanding international policies that would change economic structures more fundamentally than the majority favoured (DB, 20 May 1992: 7583–85). Such expressions were used to raise the status of issue, but also reflected party ideological positions on the relationship between the economy and environment. Simultaneously, the British MPs focused more on scientific results when they debated the internationalization of environmental policies. Lord McIntosh of Haringey saw that it was justifiable to take 'an apocalyptical view' on the environmental agenda of the Rio Summit, which he validated by referring to the book *Beyond the Limits* (1992) by Meadows, Meadows and Randers (HL, 20 May 1992: 610–12).

Geopolitical changes after the end of the Cold War raised the priority of environmental issues in international relations (Detraz and Betsill 2009: 304). The North–South discourse constituted a traditional part of environmentalism: wealthier parts of the world were blamed for having caused the vast majority of worldwide environmental problems (Rice 2009) and this discourse continued in conceptions of international climate politics. In this rhetoric, the term 'South' referred to countries and people who shared historical experiences of being subject to colonial and imperial powers, which framed their social and economic conditions (Anand 2004). North–South framing has been criticized for several reasons such as state centrism, Third Worldism and neoliberal economic globalization (Joshi 2014: 677). In addition, categorizing countries as either 'developing' or 'Western' reflected ideas concerning their power relations, conditioned by cultural factors in the post-Cold War international system.

Notions of economic imbalance between the countries of the world set the frames for a sense of justice in international climate politics. For example, in May 1992 the Lord Bishop of Southwark, Roy Williamson, spoke about 'major issues of injustice in the distribution of wealth and resources', which had to be sorted out before 'developing countries' could be expected to cooperate in environmental matters. Baroness Eirene White even called the USA, Europe and Japan 'the ecological imperialists' who had caused the 'sharp division between the countries'. According to Lord Roy Jenkins, 'the developing world' saw 'with some justice' that 'industrialised nations' had caused most of the Earth's pollution. He conceptualized environmental issues as 'lofty global concerns' which the wealthier countries could afford whereas poorer countries were concerned with poverty, famine and disease (HL, 20 May 1992: 620, 626, 638). In the German context, Social Democrat Harald B. Schäfer (SPD) used expressions of 'threatening climate catastrophe' and 'global economic, ecological and social crisis' caused by 'the Western industrial nations', which had violated 'the principle of justice' since billions of people suffered from poverty. Schäfer emphasized the concept of 'solidarity' as a 'maxim' of politics, which meant that the international climate treaty had to include binding targets for the industrial nations and their commitment to change their production methods (DB, 20 May 1992: 7579–83).

These speeches in the British and German parliaments demonstrate central elements of the sense of justice of the period, which highlighted the historical responsibilities of the wealthier countries and climate policies primarily as their duty. However, the relationship between economic and climate policies caused tensions in the ways that parliamentarians viewed international cooperation. Schäfer's opinion on economic reform represented a more radical understanding than the majority of the Social Democrats favoured and came closer to those of the Green and Leftist speakers. More mainstream ideas were articulated, for example, by Christian Democrat Ulrich Klinkert (CDU/CSU) who spoke about 'global threats to our natural livelihood', but proposed introducing technological innovation as a solution (DB, 20 May 1992: 7579–83). In the environmental discourses of the earlier decades, including the 1970s oil crisis, contemporaries had explicitly recognized that Western countries had to make some reforms in production and consumption in order to prevent environmental degradation (Graf 2014).

In the early 1990s, after the end of the Cold War, reorganization of the world's economic relations was clearly expected by many members of both parliaments. References to the Marshall Plan, for example, reflected expectations that a new era would begin after the Earth Summit. In May 1992, Baroness Inga-Stina Robson spoke about the necessity to agree on 'a global Marshall Plan'. This reference to the European Recovery Programme initiated by the USA to help Western Europe recover from the Second World War evoked expectations that the internationalization of environmental policies required new mechanisms of balancing the world economic situation (HL, 20 May 1992: 616, 623–25). In the German context, Klaus Kübler (SPD) spoke about 'an eco-deal', which presumably referred to the American New Deal programme established in the 1930s to stimulate economic and societal recovery after the Great Depression. According to Kübler, the industrial and developing nations needed to agree on a system to improve the ecological situation (DB, 22 April 1993: 13006–69). Later on, the idea of a 'green deal' expanded and aspects of it have been institutionalized in the European Green Deal programme.

The attitude of the US government towards international climate politics was a key factor in the debates about internationalization. The political tradition of framing climate change as scientifically uncertain was strong and prevalent in the USA (Cass 2007: 23–47), which has a long tradition of not committing to international treaties. The US government resisted any binding targets for the Climate Convention. Many German and British MPs hoped for stronger commitments and they used rhetoric of international leadership as a political tool. The rhetoric about Germany being an international leader or forerunner reflected the aspiration to raise the country's foreign policy profile in the field of environmental policy (Kaarkoski 2019:

47–63). The British political rhetoric of international leadership was connected with their special relationship with the USA, emphasized especially by Tony Blair's Labour government (HC, 29 March 1995; HC, 30 March 1995; HC, 9 June 1999). International law was commonly favoured by British parliamentarians, but USA involvement was considered important (DB, 5 November 1999; HC, 1 May 2001; HL, 4 April 2001; DB, 24 January 2002). Russia's ratification of the Kyoto Protocol was welcomed as a positive sign for international climate policies and 'multilateralism', although the USA refused to ratify it (DB, 2 December 2004).

The rhetoric about justice was evolving. In December 2004, Germany's Green Minister of the Environment, Jürgen Trittin, argued that some tighter limitations for poorer countries were needed since the world's climate could not cope if these countries grew economically without reducing emissions. More precisely, guilt rhetoric now focused more not only on the USA but also on China, whose increasing energy consumption made the efforts 'in the Western World' useless, argued Klaus W. Lippold (CDU/CSU). In this context, Lippold shared 'the vision of an undivided, habitable world', quoted in the title of this chapter, when arguing that every effort had to be made to ensure that the Kyoto Protocol would be implemented. In this context, this expression also illustrated noteworthy scepticism (DB, 2 December 2004: 13415–20).

Altogether, from 1992 to 2004, the advanced industrial countries understood quite clearly that they were responsible for climate policy. Conceptual aspects of internationalization were mainly debated before and after the Earth Summit of 1992. At that point, debates were idealistic and they were mainly concerned over the important issues such as world order and justice. Towards the end of the time period, negative attitude of the USA towards environmental justice became dominant in analysed debates.

## Evolving Conceptions of Responsibilities, 2008–2011

A new cycle in the political debates began when the international community started to negotiate an agreement for the post-Kyoto period. Eventually, countries were on the whole meeting the targets agreed in the Kyoto Protocol, but emissions were still increasing worldwide. The concept of climate justice was evolving to include 'fair/ness' and 'social justice'; the new argument was that it was not only advanced industrial countries who were responsible for attempting to tackle climate change.

The Economist Nicholas Stern's report, 'The Economics of Climate Change', published in October 2006, was noticed all over the world. It highlighted the imminent economic costs of climate change if sufficient actions were not taken. German and British MPs referred to this report to justify the need for further international agreements (DB, 17 January 2008; HC, 5 November 2009). Rebecca Wills concludes that in Britain in the late 2000s, the Labour Government framed climate change in economic terms. This approach contributed to the successful passage of the Climate Change Act that was internationally ambitious (Wills 2017: 215). Arguments for a radical change in prevailing economic thinking to save the world's climate were more muted than in the early 1990s. For example, the German Federal Minister of Environment of the Grand Coalition of 2005–2009, Sigmar Gabriel (SPD), and his successor in Christian Democratic–Liberal coalition, Norbert Röttgen (CDU), argued that climate protection had to be connected to economic growth. Gabriel used the expression 'dangerous climate collapse' to describe the danger if climate conservation and economic growth could not be linked (DB, 17 January 2008: 14261–65; DB, 3 December 2009: 590–92).

In the 2000s, climate justice discourse moved towards a rights-based approach, in which a sustainable environment was considered a universal human right (Joshi 2014: 679–80). As part of this development, the concept of 'social justice' emerged in the British and German parliaments. This rhetoric was especially, but not exclusively, adapted by the Leftist, Green and Social Democrat parliamentarians. When using this concept, MPs pointed at economic gaps between the countries. In January 2008, Leftist Eva Bulling-Schröter (Die Linke) presented climate policy as a matter of 'social justice'; in her argument this meant that more money should be transferred to developing countries to prevent 'the climate GAU' (DB, 17 January 2008: 14269–70). GAU (*größte anzunehmende Unfall*), or worst-case scenario, was a central concept of the German conflict over the use of nuclear energy (Kaarkoski 2016: 73). In the context of international climate policies, it was now an expression of crisis talk.

Scholars have used the term 'distributive justice' to describe the idea that in international environmental policy, developing countries deserve financial support (Armstrong 1999: 547–50). In the political debates, this train of thought was connected with the conception of 'fair/ness' in international politics. For example, in the European parliament in January 2008, Satu Hassi (Greens/EFA) defined 'fairness' as 'the real Gordian knot with regard to international negotiations on climate', since saving the 'planet' required 'the big developing countries, like China and India' to limit their emissions. This situation was 'fair' only if the wealthier countries found a way 'to compensate developing countries for the fact that our emissions per head of population are many times greater than those in the developing countries' (EP, 30 January 2008). A competitive definition of 'fair' was presented by

German right-wing liberal Michael Kauch (Free Democratic Party, FDP) in December 2009 when he spoke about 'the principle of shared but differentiated responsibility'. This meant international cooperation in which all countries had to do their share, but the process was gradual for the 'middle-income' countries such as China, Brazil, India and South Africa. Kauch favoured a solution based on 'fair share of burden on the basis of equality in competitiveness'. In this context, Kauch saw 'international responsibility' and 'international solidarity' as the guiding concepts in the efforts to bring emissions per person towards a similar sustainable level within a longer period (DB, 3 December 2009: 594–95).

In some instances, speakers wondered if the UN process in international climate politics was workable. In the European Parliament in January 2008, Stavros Dimas (European People's Party, EPP) mentioned Brazil, South Africa, the USA, China and India as countries that had to be encouraged in 'all the available international forums' although 'the UN would evidently remain the main negotiating forum' (EP, 30 January 2008). In Britain in November 2009, the Secretary of State for Energy and Climate Change, Edward Miliband, highlighted that 'a history of mistrust in the negotiations between developed and developing countries' explained partly why the UN negotiations were moving so slowly. Therefore, the concept of 'fair' was crucial in the international agreement, so countries such as India could find ways to enjoy the benefits of economic growth without following the environmentally damaging path taken by advanced industrial countries. Therefore, 'global public finance' was a central tool for fairness and, hence, for the success of the UN process of formulating international climate policies (HC, 5 November 2009: 1011–14).

Expectations of the Copenhagen Climate Change Conference of 2009 were high, although less idealistic than during the previous decade. Historical references to the postwar settings were again used in political argumentation. In November 2009, Greg Clark (Conservative) highlighted the importance of the upcoming conference for the whole twenty-first century by comparing it to the Bretton Woods Summit which heralded 'a new internationally agreed order governing the way in which our economies interact with each other' and which 'has, since the second world war [*sic*], guided the way in which we interact globally'. According to Clark, the Copenhagen agreement had to have a similar level of ambition since it guided the way towards 'the global shift that we all desire towards a low-carbon economy over the next 40 years' (HC, 5 November 2009: 1016–17). This was one of the strongest speeches highlighting the crucial importance of the Copenhagen Summit, but members of other parties also took similar tones. Elliot Morley (Labour) considered the conference as one of the most important international negotiations ever. References to the Paris Peace Treaties after the Second World War and Bretton Woods Conference were made by Simon Hughes (Liberal Democrats) who considered Copenhagen as the last opportunity to 'reverse the pattern of behaviour' (HC, 5 November 2009: 1022–28). However, while the creation of the Bretton Woods system was led by the USA, it has been far more reluctant to play a role in formulating international climate policies. Thus, these speeches referring to the Bretton Woods should perhaps be considered more as an expression of disbelief and attempts to motivate the US government, than a whole-hearted anticipation of US leadership.

Compared with the expectations prior to the conference, the outcome of the Copenhagen Conference was modest. More headway was achieved two years later at the Durban Conference in 2011 when the participants agreed on a road map to a new global legally binding agreement to replace or supplement the Kyoto Protocol. This agreement was to incorporate emissions targets for all countries, other than the poorest and least developed. When the Durban Conference was still going on, in the German parliament Frank Schwabe (SPD) expressed frustration with the UN process, calling the situation 'a crisis of legitimation' and 'a crisis of credibility of the whole process'. He saw a gap between the scientific results of climate change and worldwide action (DB, 1 December 2011: 17363–64). This rhetoric expressed the constant challenges of international climate politics. Figures produced by bodies such as the Intergovernmental Panel on Climate Change made it clear that emissions had to be reduced radically, but the world's nations were unable to find any agreement within the frameworks of the UN, the leading forum for international cooperation. As Andreas Jung (CDU/CSU) replied to Schwabe, there were no real alternatives to the UN process, despite its difficulties (DB, 1 December 2011: 17364–65).

On 12 December 2011, the House of Commons also discussed the results of the Durban Conference in terms of the credibility of the UN and international law. The Secretary of State for Energy and Climate Change, Chris Huhne, said that Durban had 're-established the principle that climate change should be tackled through international law, not through national voluntarism'. The path was open for 'a new, more comprehensive and more ambitious global agreement' than the Kyoto Protocol (HC, 12 December 2011: 568–69). The decisive point in this rhetoric on the success of the Durban Conference was the fact that 'for the first time everyone in the world, including major emitters – the United States, India and China', were committed to the process of a legally binding agreement, as Tony Baldry (Con) put it (HC, 12 December 2011: 573). MPs such as Caroline Lucas (Green) said that despite the success of reaching international agreement, its content was not enough to limit global warming (HC, 12 December 2011: 575).

During this period, expressions of duties and responsibilities began to refer to all countries. The pendulum of 'responsibility' clearly swung from advanced industrial nations alone to include emerging economies. Yet, the former were still seen as having a duty to show 'solidarity' and 'fairness' to the latter as they came into the fold of international obligations.

## Raising Nationalist Voices, 2015–2019

At the Paris Climate Conference in December 2015, representatives of 196 states negotiated the Paris Agreement with the goal of keeping the increase in global average temperature to below two degrees. Nationalist parties had become stronger in many countries, including Germany and Britain, which raised the weight of arguments concerning national interests when considering the conceptions of justice in international climate policies.

The use of concepts such as 'social justice' focused political attention on the requirement to balance the economic situation between the wealthier and poorer countries. Human rights were another important factor, especially in the European Parliament. In October 2015, several MEPs considered the meaning of justice in relation to human rights and social living conditions. According to Jude Kirton-Darling (Socialists and Democrats, S&D), 'social justice' was at the heart of the Paris Agreement, which had to guarantee 'a just transition' to a cleaner future. This meant that while tackling 'dangerous climate change', it was crucial to create decent jobs (EP, 14 October 2015). Heidi Hautala (Greens/EFA) demanded that the EU endorse 'a human-rights-based approach' to climate change. This notion of human rights extended to 'climate mitigating activities, including climate financing' since, according to Hautala, these activities had to be formulated in ways that did not cause 'environmental and social harm to people' (EP, 14 October 2015). This rhetoric, emphasizing aspects of climate policy that were not clearly economic, was presented by other MEPs affiliated to the Green or Social Democratic parties. For example, Julie Ward (S&D) emphasized that human rights and climate policy had to go hand in hand (EP, 22 October 2018).

The use of the concept of 'solidarity' by German and British MPs underlined the attitude that this what was required from the wealthier countries in international climate policies. In December 2015, a speech by the German Federal Minister of Environment Barbara Hendricks (SPD) on 'solidarity' and 'fairness' revealed how conceptions of the world order had evolved. According to her, 'worldwide solidarity' was required because not all the countries were suffering the consequences of climate change in the same way. Therefore, 'fairness' in international climate policies meant that wealthier countries had to give financial support to those countries who needed it. However, Hendricks argued, division of the world into poor and rich countries, as was done in the 1990s, was no longer correct since some prosperous countries in the South had higher incomes per person than some EU member states. She argued that the understanding of solidarity and fairness reflected in the Paris Agreement had to be different from the one in the Kyoto Protocol (DB, 4 December 2015: 14128–31). In practice, this meant binding targets for every country.

The German Leftist party, Die Linke, demanded international cooperation on climate policies that reflected the party's ideology and had somewhat different features from the mainstream political ideas of the period. In September 2016, Eva Bulling-Schröter argued that 'international law' in which 'international solidarity' was expressed by transferring money from the rich North to the disadvantaged South was noteworthy as a historical world agreement (DB, 22 September 2016: 18838). This conceptualization followed the traditional lines of the North–South discourse of environmentalism. Another member of the party, Katja Kipping, commented on the relationship between economic growth and climate policy to argue that the largest 'global injustice at this world' was the situation in which poor countries suffered most from the consequences of global warming. She doubted whether this situation could be improved through prevailing economic structures. Kipping referred to Naomi Klein's criticism of globalization when arguing that the choice was between preventing climate change and maintaining capitalism (DB, 4 December 2015: 14317–40).

'Climate justice' was a more widely used political concept in the British context, where many NGOs adopted it as a framework for their campaigning agenda (Agyeman and Evans 2004: 155). This argumentation on climate justice was presented especially by MPs of the Scottish National Party (SNP). The party even had a spokesperson for climate justice; during the second half of the 2010s this was Chris Law. John McNally (SNP) used the expression 'the present climate emergency' and asserted that Scotland had established 'the world's first climate justice fund' which, according to McNally, sought to mitigate the damage caused by climate change on the world's poorest communities (HC, 16 January 2019: 443–50). Justice was, once again, advanced through financial means.

Expressions of the urgency of climate change had become more common. 'Climate emergency', quoted above, was one example of this crisis talk and McNally connected it with the possible long-term security and military implications of climate change (HC, 16 January 2019: 450). This connection between climate change and global security had been pointed out earlier by the Parliamentary Under Secretary of State, Department of Energy and

Climate Change and Wales Office, Lord Bourne of Aberystwyth (Con), in his argument for the Paris Agreement (HL, 15 December 2015: 1970–72). In November 2015, just before the Paris Climate Conference, Edward Miliband (Labour) used the expression 'catastrophic' to describe the situation in 2100 if the world faced three-degree warming (HC, 19 November 2015: 866). In the German parliament, the concept of 'climate crisis' was used as well (DB, 4 December 2015).

However, in Germany, the emphasis on climate change as a threat to humanity was not as clearly or widely articulated as in the 1990s. After the federal election of 2017, the right-wing populist party Alternative für Deutschland (AfD) had seats in the federal parliament, and international climate policies evidently went against the party's ideological basis. Karsten Hilse (AfD) was especially vocal in his criticism of the credibility of climate change caused by human behaviour. In November 2017, Hilse argued that the German share of greenhouse gas emissions was marginal worldwide and there was no trustworthy justification for trying to 'achieve some utopic climate targets' in Germany. Members of other parties challenged this climate sceptical opinion with arguments in favour of international cooperation, and the ideological differences were debated. Lukas Köhler (FDP) even labelled the attitude expressed by Hilse as 'climate nationalism' which he considered as wasted time. Instead, he favoured 'a global viewpoint', which in terms of climate policy required considering emissions levels in 'the worldwide' context instead of focusing on the limited scope of one nation. A Christian Democrat, Andreas Jung, used religion to oppose the AfD's standpoint when he defined climate policies as being about taking care of 'creation' and Christian values. Lorenz Gösta Beutin (Die Linke) included elements of Leftist ideology in his speech, when he used the concept of 'climate justice' to express another conception of the world. His argumentation about the 'global South' and the rich North included the idea of a 'change of system' referring to economic structures and thought (DB, 21 November 2017: 134–37).

The tone of the German parliamentary debate evolved after the IPPC 1.5-degree report was published in October 2018. Those speakers who in principle favoured international climate policies also used argumentation highlighting German interests more clearly than during earlier decades. For example, Oliver Krischer (Alliance 90/The Greens) called global climate warming 'an existential question' for Germany, which had many coastal areas. From this perspective, climate policies were a matter of German interest too, and not just about protecting others in the world. The fact that the German parliamentary discourse on international climate policies was evolving to give greater weight to German national interests becomes even clearer in a speech by Marie-Luise Dött (CDU/CSU). She called the Greens 'a climate conservation party' that did not care about the German economy, unlike her own 'people's party'. She used the concept of 'climate justice', but in an untypical sense. In Dött's view, 'social justice' meant that climate policy had to be formulated in a way that did not put an economic burden on people (DB, 10 October 2018: 5839–41). This reflected an important change in the German discourse on international environmentalism, where every party (excluding the AfD) had used environmentally friendly rhetoric since the 1980s at the latest. Dött was not against international climate policies or attempts to meet their targets, but the fact that strengthening nationalist attitudes changed the rhetoric on international cooperation and national concerns could not be ignored.

The AfD made it clear that national economic concerns were their priority. Hilse argued that German climate policy efforts endangered the car industry, energy industry, economy, consumption and 'nature and cultural landscape', which probably referred to wind and solar energy (DB, 10 October 2018: 5841–42). The German Federal Minister of Environment, Svenja Schulze (SPD), spoke about 'just transition' as an international guideline, which meant emphasizing aspects of social policy such as jobs when executing climate policies (DB, 10 October 2018: 5843–44). In these conceptions, justice was reduced from concerning the world order that had dominated the discussions on international climate policies in the 1990s to being about national, everyday issues.

At the same time, British MPs were focused on Brexit – an issue which crept into the debates concerning international climate policy. On 16 January 2019, speeches concerning the Katowice Climate Package (December 2019) that provided guidance for the implementation of the Paris Agreement were connected to the Brexit vote. On 15 January 2019, the House of Commons voted against the prime minister's Brexit deal. The following day, Anna McMorrin (Labour) highlighted the importance of Britain being a full EU member by arguing that 'Brexit also threatens to have hugely negative consequences for our climate action here in the UK'. She called the situation a 'climate crisis', which a single nation could not solve, and argued that this strengthened the case for Britain remaining in the EU (HC, 16 January 2019: 439–44). Other British MPs also framed climate change as a 'crisis'. Caroline Lucas (Green) used the concept of 'climate crisis', which required 'the global North' in particular to change its ways of consuming and recycling, and even to focus on 'dematerialisation' (HC, 16 January 2019: 448–49).

## Conclusion

Various conceptual expressions of justice to justify international cooperation evolved from the 1990s to the end of the 2010s. In the early phase, 'responsibility' was a central expression. Discussions about the 'global', 'worldwide', and 'humanity' were interweaved with the idea that wealthier countries were obligated to support the internationalization of climate politics. 'Humanity' was a prominent concept in the early phase of international climate policies but vanished later on. After 2000, 'fair/ness', social aspects of justice and human rights were used to turn attention to living standards and to the people living in those poorer countries that also had a duty to implement international climate policies. In the 2010s, nationalist voices reduced the debates to everyday policy issues, and global aspects had to compete with domestic ones. The concept of 'solidarity' appeared every now and then and was especially used to motivate international cooperation.

Altogether, debates concerning the conceptions of internationalization brought out fundamental challenges that have set the course for international climate agreements. Scientific evidence has undeniably proved that climate change can lead to a crisis that will gradually shake the foundations of the liberal world order and its institutions. Comparisons of the UN climate conferences with the situation after the Second World War highlighted how crucial the situation was. Yet, this sense of urgency has not turned into ambitious international climate policies. Perhaps the crisis has not yet been felt concretely enough in Britain, Germany and the EU, or their politicians have failed to connect evidence of physical reality with the crisis talk. Crises related to the global climate have been largely speculative and not perceived as imminent enough to motivate a shift in the international order towards 'a vision of an undivided, habitable world'.

Simultaneously, despite all the setbacks, the United Nations as the core international institution has managed to maintain its ability to face this crucial global problem. International agreements within the UN frame have proved to be the most effective available way to push towards international solutions. In this process, politicians have defined the concept of justice and related conceptual expressions in ways that have sufficiently resonated with the ideas of the world's nations about the acceptable world order. In the field of climate change, the concept of worldwide 'solidarity' between countries has remained important to express an attitude that helps to maintain suitable living conditions, peace and prosperity. During the Covid-19 pandemic, European leaders and politicians who aimed at motivating cooperation also used the concept of 'solidarity', but in the context of the European Union. It remains to be seen how this will influence global solidarity on an issue that has continued to feel less pressing despite the science and increasingly recurring events like the fires in the Amazon, California and Australia.

**Miina Kaarkoski** is a postdoctoral researcher at the National Defence University, Finland. Her main research areas are environmental and climate policies and security policies and she has published several articles on these topics. She is an expert on conducting conceptual analysis of political language and debates. Her publications include 'Political Meanings of Climate Change in Security and Defence Policy Reports and Parliamentary Debates in Finland, 1995–2017' (*Kosmopolis* 50[3], 2020) and 'Conflicting Conceptualisations of "Democracy" in the German Bundestag during the Anti-nuclear Demonstrations, 1995–2001' (*Parliaments, Estates and Representation* 38[1], 2018). ORCID: 0000-0003-4489-2998.

# References

## Primary Sources

Deutscher Bundestag (DB), available at https://pdok.bundestag.de/.

European Parliament (EP), available at https://www.europarl.europa.eu/sides/getDoc.do?type=CRE&reference=20080130&secondRef=ITEM-020&language=GA; https://www.europarl.europa.eu/doceo/document/CRE-8-2015-10-14-ITM-014_FI.html; https://www.europarl.europa.eu/doceo/document/CRE-8-2018-10-22-ITM-013_FI.html

House of Lords (HL) and House of Commons (HC), available at https://hansard.parliament.uk/.

## Secondary Sources

Agyeman, J. and B. Evans. 2004. '"Just Sustainability": The Emerging Discourse of Environmental Justice in Britain?', *The Geographical Journal* 170(2): 155–64.

Anand, R. 2004. *International Environmental Justice: A North-South Dimension*. Burlington, VT: Ashgate.

Armstrong, D. 1999. 'Law, Justice and the Idea of a World Society', *International Affairs* 75(3): 547–61.

Cass, L.R. 2007. 'Measuring the Domestic Salience of International Environmental Norms: Climate Change Norms in American, German, and British Climate Policy Debates', in M. E. Pettenger (ed.), *The Social Construction of Climate Change: Power Knowledge, Norms, Discourses*. Aldershot: Ashgate, pp. 23–50.

Detraz, N. and M.M. Betsill 2009. 'Climate Change and Environmental Security: For Whom the Discourse Shifts', *International Studies Perspectives* 10: 303–20.

Di Chiro, G. 2016. 'Environmental Justice', in J. Adamson, W.A. Gleason and D.N. Pellow (eds), *Keywords for Environmental Studies*. New York: NYU Press, pp. 100–105.

Graf, R. 2014. *Oil and Sovereignty: Petro-Knowledge and Energy Policy in the United States and Western Europe in the 1970s*. New York: Berghahn Books.

Hanf, K. 2000. 'The Domestic Basis of International Environmental Agreements', in A. Underdal and K. Hanf (eds), *International Environmental Agreements and Domestic Politics: The Case of Acid Rain*. Aldershot: Ashgate, pp. 1–19.

Joshi, Shangrila. 2014. 'Environmental Justice Discourses in Indian Climate Politics', *GeoJournal* 79(6): 677–91.

Kaarkoski, M. 2016. *'Energiemix' Versus 'Energiewende': Competing Conceptualisations of Nuclear Energy Policy in the German Parliamentary Debates of 1991–2001*. Jyväskylä: Jyväskylä University Press.

———. 2019. 'German and British Parliaments and Conceptions of the Global Climate Threat during the United Nation Earth Summit of 1992', *Parliaments, Estates and Representation* 39(1): 47–63.

Kortetmäki, T. 2016. 'Reframing Climate Justice: A Three-dimensional View on Just Climate Negotiations', *Ethics, Policy and Environment* 19(3): 320–34.

Rice, J. 2009. 'North-South Relations and the Ecological Debt: Asserting a Counter-Hegemonic Discourse', *Critical Sociology* 35(2): 225–52.

Schlosberg, D. 2017. 'Theorising Environmental Justice: The Expanding Sphere of a Discourse', in C. Schlottmann et al. (eds), *Environment and Society*. New York: NYU Press, pp. 309–18.

Wills, R. 2017. 'Taming the Climate? Corpus Analysis of Politicians' Speech on Climate Change', *Environmental Politics* 26(2): 212–31.

Chapter 14

# Dynamics of the International and National in Finnish and Hungarian Higher Education, 1990–2020

*Viktória Ferenc, Petteri Laihonen and Taina Saarinen*

❖

## Universities as National and International

This chapter presents a discourse analysis of the terms 'national' and 'international' in Finnish and Hungarian higher education legislation from the 1990s to the present day. We conduct the analysis by applying linguistic and textual methods in the study of conceptual and political history as argued by Ihalainen and Saarinen (2019). We compare the conceptual contextualizations of the words 'international' and 'national' in the political motivations presented in the preambles to the Hungarian Acts, and in the government proposals for the Finnish Acts. We analyse the relevant discursive and societal practices (see Fairclough 2003) linking occurrences of the national and international in our data to the discursively cycled practices and the societal contextualization of the legislation and their motivations. We approach the national and international as parts of long- and short-term discourse cycles, which reconstruct and recycle sedimented language ideological debates (Hult and Pietikäinen 2014; see Saarinen and Ihalainen 2018 on language policies) and produce new cycles (Saarinen 2020) that are still visible in today's discourses of the national and international roles of higher education.

With our chapter, we contribute to the methodological development of conceptual history. As higher education scholars, applied linguists and sociolinguists, we share the need of comparative historians to unpack linear, apparently self-evident national(ist) histories and stories (see Ihalainen 2017), and to look for historical layers (Välimaa 2019) and contingencies (Stråth 2016), not least in research on histories of higher education policy.

*Analysing the National and International in Higher Education Legislation*
To understand how the 'international' and 'national' are conceptualized and what meanings are attributed to these terms, we touch upon the classic semantic triangle of Ogden and Richards (1989) that links 'words, thoughts, and things' or symbols, references and referents in relation with each other. The word 'internationalization' may refer to different ideas and be realized in various kinds of activities. Our empirical focus is the legislative reforms of 1997 and 2010 in Finland and of 1993, 2005 and 2011 in Hungary. We thus focus on the practical side of concepts beyond nation states as opposed to ideological discourses (on the entanglement of European integration and the nation state, see Chapter 10).

There are three Acts on higher education in Hungary: the first was adopted in 1993, the second in 2005 and the current one in 2011. Before the first Act, higher education was included in the Act on Education. The overall trend has been an increase in references to the national as opposed to the international. The Finnish data consists of two universities Acts: the 1997 Universities Act (645/1997) and the 2009 Universities Act (558/2009). Since the Hungarian legislation includes lengthy preambles explaining the background and motivation of the Acts, to get a comparative view on Finland, the Finnish government proposals on both Acts were added to the data and analysed (HE 263/1996 and HE 7/2009). The government proposals are standard preparatory documents that briefly describe the main content of the proposal, general and more detailed motivations, and the draft Act (Rantala 2016). Here, too, the primacy of the nation over the international community can be observed, although not on the same scale as in Hungary.

Our data is presented in Table 14.1.

*Methodology*
We combined deductive and inductive approaches. Following Mayring (2000), we started by deductively analysing our data by looking for key-words pertinent to our research questions, which were themselves a result of an inductive-deductive process. The specific keywords (or categories, following Mayring 2000) that we deemed relevant for our data were international and nation(al); i.e. in Finnish *kansa\**, *kansain\** and in Hungarian *nemzetközi\** and *nemzeti\**. The asterisk (\*) denotes a root word; for instance the Finnish *kansa\** can refer to *kansa* (nation, people), *kansalainen* (citizen),

*kansalaisuus* (citizenship), closed compounds such as *Kansalliskirjasto* (National Library) or collocations such as *kansallinen kulttuuriperimä* (national cultural heritage).

This allowed us to narrow down the relevant themes in connection to our topic. While doing this, it became necessary to conduct an inductive analysis of our data (Mayring 2000): after the first round of analysis, we found that domestic*/local* as well as foreign*, global* and citizen* were related concepts (in Finnish *kotimai*/*paikall*, *globaali*, *ulkomaalai*, *kansalai*; in Hungarian *hazai*, *idegen*, *külföldi*, *állampolgár*) which needed to be taken into account, as well as *suomalai* (Finnish) and *magyar* (Hungarian), and their collocations. The last round of context analysis circled back to the discourses of international* and national*, their occurrences and their relationships. It needs to be noted that the Finnish *kansa* includes notions of both 'people' and 'nation', and in some contexts 'common people' and 'citizenship'. In Hungarian the term *nemzet* more often refers to ethnicity (e.g. *nemzetiség*) or to the ethnic Hungarian nation, but it can also be a general reference to the state as 'national' for Hungary – for example, *Nemzeti bank*: National Bank (of Hungary). *Kansainvälinen* (Finnish) or *nemzetközi* (Hungarian), or 'international', mainly refers to activities between countries, without ethnonational implications.

Based on this preliminary analysis, it seems that conceptions of internationalization in higher education discourse vary; it was viewed as a commodity, cooperation or a threat (see, for instance, Saarinen 2012; Saarinen 2020; Nokkala 2007; Välimaa 2019; Scott 2011). This insight led us to our research questions. What appears to be the motivation for internationalization in the higher education documents from the 1990s to the 2020s in Hungary and Finland? How is internationalization conceptualized? Which discourses of internationalization are recycled and reproduced in the higher education

**Table 14.1** Frequencies for national (*nemzet* or *kansa*) and international (*nemzetközi* or *kansainväli*) in the data.

| Country | Document | Year | Word counts | nation* | internation* |
|---------|----------|------|-------------|---------|--------------|
| Hungary | Act | 1993 | 25,492 | 6 | 15 |
| Hungary | Act | 2005 | 60,827 | 21 | 24 |
| Hungary | Act | 2011 | 61,640 | 55 | 31 |
| Finland | Government proposal | 1996 | 11,794 | 6 | 2 |
| Finland | Act | 1997 | 6,196 | 3 | 1 |
| Finland | Government proposal | 2009 | 42,875 | 68 | 60 |
| Finland | Act | 2009 | 15 942 | 18 | 7 |

legislation and which are not? Internationalization also seems highly local-ized, with national goals intertwined in the internationalization goals (see Vares 2020; Saarinen 2020; Scott 2011; Välimaa 2019). This raised further questions: how do national and international aspects meet in the documents? What are the localized conceptualizations of internationalization in Finland and Hungary?

## On the Conceptualization of National and International in Higher Education

In line with this volume as a whole, we approach the national and inter-national as interdependent and constituting each other historically. As we speak of national higher education and its different instantiations, it is also necessary to discuss dynamics between the national (often operationalized from the nation state) and cross-national activities of higher education as an institution. Wimmer and Glick Schiller (2002) point out that, paradoxically, focusing on the nation state has made us blind to its dynamics. They draw our attention to two kinds of methodological nationalism (Wimmer and Glick Schiller 2002): ignoring the national framing of modernity; and taking national discourses and agendas for granted.

We take the dynamic nature of this relationship into account (Häkli 2013: 347), suggesting that while the national and international are often concep-tualized as territorially bounded (the national as occurring inside the nation state's borders and the international outside them), this is not helpful for analysing the societal dynamics of higher education. The relationship is more complex than mere juxtaposition; both the national and the interna-tional operate within various fields of higher education policy.

Häkli (2013) theorizes the 'state space' by proposing the concept of the 'transnational field' as a more nuanced way of understanding the inter-relationship of the national and international, and continues to criticize the understanding of the territorial space as 'a natural container of social relations and the concomitant dichotomy between national "inside" and international "outside"' (2013: 343). Emerging new nationalist politics in Europe and elsewhere appear to recycle and reproduce understand-ings of 'international' that centre on the nation state (e.g. Weimer and Barlete 2020). In Finnish higher education, the discourses of 'inside and outside' are mainly internal to the nation state, recently visible particu-larly in relation to framing English as a threat to Finnish and Finnishness or the Swedish-speaking minority as not Finnish (Saarinen 2020). In the Hungarian case, since 1920 Hungarian-medium higher education in the neighbouring countries has blurred the picture of the Hungarian higher education space, at least in comparison with the Finnish one. The relevance of Hungarian higher education beyond the country's borders is established in the Hungarian Acts, analysed below: 'The scope of this Act covers all persons and organizations involved in the activities and governance of higher education, as well as the higher education activities performed by Hungarian higher education institutions *outside the territory of Hungary*' (2011 Act on National Higher Education, emphasis added).

The notion of universities as 'national' institutions stems in part from the fact that, with their students and teachers, they have often been strong national actors in many countries. *Universitas*, originally referring to the guilds or societies of students (Välimaa 2019), started to refer to university-like organizations in the Middle Ages, predating nation states. In fact, Scott (2011: 59) points out that rather than being international (a term only coined in the late eighteenth century, see Chapters 1–3), the early universities can be characterized as pre-national, having roles as universal societies of mobile students and scholars, but also as agents of state formation.

The national nature of universities became even more prominent in the early modern period (Scott 2011), and by the early nineteenth century, universities played an ideologically, culturally, politically and economically strong role in nation-building all over Europe, not least in the Nordic countries (see e.g. Adriansen and Adriansen 2018). The university institution expanded in Europe in the early nineteenth century and was more closely tied to the educational and information needs of emerging nation states (Jalava 2012) as well as to the vernacularization of societies, particularly in Finland.

Before the First World War, when Hungary was a part of the Austro-Hungarian Dual Monarchy, such tendencies were combined with cutting-edge scientific development in various fields (Tarrósy 2002: 13). In the Hungarian historical narrative, the loss of vast territories and about three million ethnic Hungarians to foreign rule in 1920 constitutes a truly nationalistic turn in the history of Hungarian higher education (see e.g. Tarrósy 2002: 13). At that point, the universities of Kolozsvár (now Cluj Napoca) and Pozsony (now Bratislava) were evacuated to Hungary (Tarrósy 2002: 13). As Papp Z. (2011: 481) noticed, the higher education systems of Hungary's new or reinstated neighbours around 1990 (Slovakia, Ukraine, Serbia, etc.) had the uneasy threefold task of fostering the new ethnolinguistic national identity and loyalty of their citizens, reforming the Soviet legacy of higher education, and adapting to European Union (EU) expectations. For Hungarians, the higher education policies and funding of institutions of the large Hungarian-speaking minorities in these countries have been a recurrent topic in the post-Soviet era.

Both political push and pull factors can be seen in higher education internationalization, as exemplified by numerus clausus, wars and language policies in Russia (Finland was an autonomous Grand Duchy of the Russian Empire until 1917) that pushed students to become mobile in Europe before the Second World War (Dhondt 2008: 50). Germany lost its position as a receiving country after the First World War and, in the 1930s, became a source of forced mobility and/or migration because of antisemitism, economic crisis and wars. In the historical narrative of Hungarian higher education, the numerous Nobel Prize laureates are often mentioned (e.g. Tarrósy 2002: 20–21, lists 11) as proof of a golden era in interwar Hungarian education. Yet all of them migrated, most to North America, and received the Nobel Prize for their work there.

Increasing globalization and transnational cooperation after the Second World War, and particularly following the Cold War, took new forms that were seen as blurring the boundaries of nation states. This was perceived as a global market opportunity (neoliberals) or a threat to either nation state interests (statists or neoconservatives) or local communities (radicals) (Held and McGrew 2007). While the legitimation project of nation states more or less ended in Western Europe with the Second World War, and in the Cold War period Hungary was surrounded by three major European multinational states (the USSR, Czechoslovakia and Yugoslavia), the conceptualization of nation states as the 'constant unit of observation through all historical transformations' (Wimmer and Glick Schiller 2002: 305) continued.

Yet universities have always been international, at least in their knowledge base, teaching staff and activities (Scott 2011). Additionally, scientific disciplines and research have a universal basis (see Clark 1983 on the fundamentals of disciplines; Becher and Trowler 2001 on the nature of disciplines); a single path explanation has never sufficed in the analysis of universities in society (Scott 2011). Thus, before entering the analysis, we provide a brief historical contextualization of higher education in the two countries.

## Finland and Hungary from the 1990s to the 2000s

Hungary and Finland lie on the periphery of the Anglo-American hegemony so prevalent in higher education research. The populations of both countries mostly speak non-Indo-European languages with a relatively small readership outside their (historical) borders. Both turned westwards following the fall of the Soviet Union, but from different historical and societal backgrounds and with different outcomes. Present-day Finland can be framed as a Nordic welfare state, which joined the Council of Europe in 1989, the EU in 1995, and became a signatory to the Bologna Process in 1999. Unlike other

Nordic countries, Finland is a member of the Eurozone. However, joining NATO has not gained popularity in Finland, which cherishes a narrative of military neutrality and self-sufficiency.

In the last twenty-five years, Hungary has rushed through the development trajectory of higher education accompanied by tensions between national and international interests, often to impose immature ideas in haste (Polónyi 2015). Hungary swiftly joined all available Western and European alliances, including NATO in 1997 and the EU in 2004, only to turn into a maverick member of these alliances in the 2010s. Like Finland, Hungary has been a full member of the Bologna Process and European Higher Education Area since 1999.

After the end of the Cold War and the collapse of the Soviet Union in 1991, both Finland and Hungary experienced political, economic and social changes that shaped their higher education. The westward turn was strongly reflected in the 'internationalization' agenda of higher education. That being said, the Hungarian case is more complex due to the (higher) educational needs and market of about three million Hungarian speakers living in neighbouring states (see Papp Z. 2011). According to Papp Z. (2011: 482), all major Hungarian minority regions in Romania, Slovakia, Serbia and Ukraine had established separate Hungarian-medium private and/or state universities by the new millennium, often with Hungarian funding and cooperation with institutions in Hungary.

As early as the 1980s, systematic policy measures had changed the landscape of higher education internationalization, as organizations and individuals were expected to 'internationalize' in ways that have been operationalized as student mobility (see also Chapter 12), networking, research cooperation and publishing activities. These activities have both national and international implications and have always played a role in higher education (Scott 2011), but the increase in transnational cooperation programmes initiated by supranational organizations since the 1980s has made mobility-based internationalization a systematic part of higher education. A neoliberal turn (see e.g. Rhoades and Slaughter 2006) in higher education policy has brought an emphasis on global markets of intellectual capital; competitive international funding schemes; a comparative and global ethos of excellence; and a formal depoliticizing and outsourcing of higher education to consultants and experts, as well as to intergovernmental and transnational policy networks.

*Finland: Internationalization Needed to Protect National Commercial Interests*

Finnish society and consequently its educational system have faced relatively major changes since the late 1980s (Saarinen 2020). Educational steering and regulation have been formally decentralized at all educational levels, including higher education, and softer forms of regulation such as funding based on internationalization measures have replaced centralized normative steering (Simola et al. 2017). After the economic boom of the 1980s, several factors led to a severe recession in the early 1990s. The liberal fiscal politics of the late 1980s and early 1990s, the consequent overheating of the economy, the dissolution of the Soviet Union and the consequent decline in Soviet trade combined with problems in international trade were a massive blow for Finnish society (Kiander 2001; Välimaa 2019) that was so dependent on exports (on internationalization and the national economy in the interwar era, see Chapter 6).

The above developments have been described as the first 'globalization shock' as Finland's relatively closed economy and exports sector that had been strongly dependent on Soviet bloc trade met the harsher realities of Western markets (Välimaa 2019: 213). The prevalence of economic factors in societal and political developments has also been visible in higher education policies (Välimaa 2019; Saarinen 2020). The first Finnish internationalization strategy of higher education was drafted during the economic boom, in 1987 (Nokkala 2007). It linked the internationalization of higher education to economic and cultural prosperity, mirroring the traditional national function of the university institution to provide *Bildung* (Jalava 2012; Saarinen 2020). In practice, internationalization was operationalized as staff and student mobility; particularly in the EU, this became the tool for combining the European goals of freedom of mobility of goods, capital, services and labour, by creating a workforce that was ready, willing and able to be mobile.

The 2001 internationalization strategy introduced the concept of competitiveness in internationalization, as a powerful national (economic) basis was seen as indispensable for international competition. The strategy underlined the importance of national legislation protecting the universities, apparently in response to the ongoing Bologna Process. The 2001 strategy thus contrasted the national and international, implying that Finnish higher education needed protection and that legislation would secure this (Saarinen 2020).

The 2009 internationalization strategy continued the economic discourse by naming higher education as a nationally significant export product. Since Finnish universities generally did not charge tuition fees at the time, it seems that this export argument was linked to Finnish higher education as a brand rather than as a commodity.

The increasing attention to national needs was apparent in the latest internationalization guidelines of 2017. The strategy balanced the need for 'international' languages (increasingly spoken also in Finland) with the importance of Finnish national languages for international students and staff. To summarize, it seems that – despite their aim of internationalization – these strategic documents of 1987, 2001, 2009 and 2017 tend to reinforce a protectionist discourse of national economic interests. The recent rise in neo-nationalism in higher education policy has added a layer to the tensions between the national and international roles of higher education (Saarinen 2020).

*Hungary: From Soviet Bloc to a Sovereign Nation in Free Europe*
The centralized ideological and planned labour market approach under state socialism has been characterized as 'a Soviet type of education system marked by strong centralization, a predominance of technical subjects in secondary and higher education, and compulsory secondary education coupled with a shortage of higher education and early, largely irreversible, specialization' (Papp Z. 2011: 481). According to Polónyi (2015: 8) the task of higher education was to ideologically nurture an intelligentsia (e.g. Marxism was a compulsory subject for all disciplines) and to educate experts for the needs of a socialist economy based on heavy industry.

Until the end of the 1990s, the primary goal of higher education in Hungary was to reach the level of Western European countries, to foster academic autonomy and expand student cohorts (see Kozma 1990). In the 1990s, both international, private universities (e.g. the English-medium Central European University, 1991) and state funded church institutions (Pázmány Péter Catholic University and Károli Gáspár University of the Reformed Church, 1993) were established in Hungary (see Tarrósy 2002).

In the early 2000s, the right-wing politics of Viktor Orbán's first government (1998–2002) emphasized training a competitive workforce as a new goal in higher education. Later, the left-wing governments (2002–2010) also emphasized international competitiveness and meeting labour market needs. The second and third Orbán governments (2010–2014, 2014–2018) once again formulated a strongly ideological approach (shaped in the Act on National Higher Education 2011): national economic progress and the intellectual development of the nation, as well as serving the needs of the national and, to a lesser degree, international labour market. As a sign of this new orientation, the University of Public Service, Ludovika, was established in 2012. Due to a conflict with the fourth Orbán government (2018–), the Central European University is now (2020) being relocated to Vienna.

Catching up with 'developed democratic societies' (Preamble to the 1993 Hungarian Act on Higher Education) since the end of the Cold War had been a fundamental endeavour in the political aspirations of Hungarian governments. This reform appeared in higher education policy in the 1990s in terms of increasing the number of students and strengthening the autonomy of universities (e.g. the universities retained the right to award internationally compatible doctoral degrees). In the first decade of the 2000s it was increasingly reformulated as serving an economic catch-up. Most remarkably, the 2005 Act described joining the EU in 2004 as joining the neoliberal economic competition in higher education. It seems that there is no long-term, coherent concept of internationalization in Hungarian higher education policy. The concepts of different governments compete with, rather than build on, each other (for a recent discussion, see Parson and Steele 2019).

## Results of the Discourse Analysis of National versus International

### *Finland: International and National Intertwined*

The 1996 government proposal on higher education made two explicit references to *kansainvälin\** (internation): in the context of international benchmarking of degrees, and in the context of international cooperation of evaluation. Typically, these were measures to develop the transparency of higher education degrees and studies; since the EU's first education policy measures, they have ultimately been devised to make free movement of labour easier (Corbett 2005). While the original goal of this proposal only covered vocational education, by the time the government programme was drafted, the Maastricht Treaty had been signed in 1992 and Finland had joined the EU in 1995.

The goals of benchmarking and cooperation were designed very specifically to develop Finnish higher education – i.e. its degree structure and evaluation systems – to more explicitly respond to EU needs. For approximately fifteen years, the lowest higher education degree in most fields had been a master's. With the establishment of a polytechnic sector from earlier post-secondary vocational institutions, and the international benchmarks, bachelor's degrees were reinstated. The Finnish Higher Education Evaluation Council had been established in 1995 (Välimaa 2019). In other words, the arguments for international benchmarking and cooperation were expressed somewhat after the fact. Thus, it seems that arguments referring to internationalization were a combination of internalized European competitiveness goals and national reforms, both of which had been normalized in Finnish higher education by the mid-1990s, when the new university legislation was drafted. In the 1996 government proposal and the original 1997 Act, 'internation' denotes a dynamic of national and European higher education politics and policies. It also refers to international comparisons both as a vehicle for national benchmarking and as means to argue for or demonstrate the convergence (see Chapter 3) of Finnish higher education with (ideal or imaginary, see Chapter 10) European higher education policies. The 1997 Universities Act was amended several times before the next major reform in 2009. In the amendments, two additions had an effect on conceptualizations of nation* and internation*. These were related to the tasks and administration of the National Library and the new task of universities to provide commissioned education. The National Library was expected to advance the 'domestic and international' cooperation of libraries. The amendment made in 2007 referred to providing education to foreign organizations and students that is paid for by a foreign state, international organization, domestic or foreign public organization, foundation or private society. This controversial addition to the free education for traditional target groups paved the way for the legislative reform in 2009 (Välimaa 2019) and was seen as a fundamental change in the logic of university funding and operations.

Coming to the conceptualizations of people or nation* (*kansa**), the concept appears in the 1996 government proposal mainly in compounds like *Kansalliskirjasto* (National Library) or *kansalaisopistot* (Civic Adult Education). All in all, there were six mentions of *kansa* in this proposal, three of which (references to *Kansalliskirjasto* and to citizenship [*kansalaisuus*] in a section on language requirements for non-native Finnish citizens [*kansalaiset*]) ended up in the 1997 Universities Act. As the references to citizen(ship) often appear in collocations like Finnish, foreign or EU citizens, it seems that in this context the *kansa** is a part of the demarcation between national and international, or us and the others.

With the latest amendments to the 1997 Act, the number of references to *kansa** had increased to twelve. This was mainly due to more frequent mentions of the National Library and to universities' added task of commissioned education in the 2000s. As these additions affected discussion of the international, next we look at nation* and internation* together. Both these concepts or related ones largely appear in collocates such as 'domestic or international' (*kotimaista ja kansainvälistä*) or in defining which organizations and other actors can commission education from universities – a Finnish or foreign state (*Suomen valtio, ulkomaan valtio*) or a Finnish or foreign public authority (*suomalainen tai ulkomainen julkisyhteisö*). While references to internation* are less frequent, they still appear to respond to a need to demarcate national activities from international ones; a differentiation that was not apparent earlier.

By the 2009 Universities Act, references to internation* and nation* had increased significantly. This Act presented a major change in higher education in Finland. Amendments between 1996 and 2009 had mainly related to universities' funding and their societal tasks and had been benchmarked from international examples (Välimaa 2019: 252).

In our analysis of the international and national, this shift in the nature of university legislation is reflected in increased references to international cooperation, competition and comparison (*yhteistyö, vertailu, kilpailu*) and particularly to international high-level (*korkeatasoinen*) rankings and comparisons. All in all, all these indicate a need to benchmark the Finnish system against presumably high(er) level international universities. International, used in this way, positions the Finnish higher education system in a hierarchy of other (Western) systems, as lower internationally, but aspiring to reach the high ranks. An interesting detail in this perspective is the change from the wording in the 1996 proposal and 1997 Act to the 2009 proposal and Act – 'reaching' (*saavutetaan*) becomes 'assuring' (*varmistetaan*) the high level of universities, the implication being that while in 1996/7 Finland still had not reached the top, in 2009 the aim was to maintain the highest level which had been achieved.

All in all, the ethos of comparison, cooperation and competition is strong in the most recent government proposal. Internatio* appears as the benchmark against which the Finnish system is compared. International competitiveness, in turn, appears as a goal to be reached and is ultimately the reason for the renewal of higher education administration and funding. The preparation for the 2009 reform was led by Ministers of Education who were members of the market liberal National Coalition Party.

Coming to conceptualizations of the nation and its derivatives, reference to national organizations and actors continues to be a way of demarcating the international and the national. While the 1996 government proposal had mentioned nation seven times in the three contexts of the National Library (*Kansalliskirjasto*), citizenship (*kansalaisuus*) and adult education institutions (*kansalaisopisto*), the 2009 proposal refers to nation* sixty-eight times, mostly still in compound names such as the National Library (sixteen times), or other compounds such as national goals, innovation systems or research universities. 'National properties' and 'national regulations' emerge in a context in which international comparison of higher education systems is beginning to include competitive elements, again based on international examples. While the references to the international largely relate to competition, markets and rankings, the references to national concern matters within Finland's borders, including national knowledge base, *Bildung* and cultural heritage. Internationalization is countered by a concept of the national as being in need of protection or strengthening.

What stands out again in 2009 are the compound name of the National Library and the references to citizens (of Finland and other countries).

Individual mentions are given to national cultural heritage (*kansallinen kult-tuuriperintö*), national collection (*kansalliskokoelma*) and national services (*kansalliset palvelut*). The latter reference is in the context of the services provided by the National Library, as opposed to local municipal, university and other libraries. The former two imply something separable from 'others' that needs to be preserved; in other words, *kansallinen* (national) here refers to something that is deemed valuable and in need of protection.

*Hungary: From International to National*
The analysis indicates that *nemzetközi* (international) was present in the 1993 Act and it can be found more often in later Acts, partly due to the growing length and detail of the Hungarian Acts on Higher Education. The term *nemzet* (nation) has been on the rise, and outnumbers *nemzetközi* in the 2011 Act for the first time. The term *nemzeti* (national) is of a different character; it has replaced earlier expressions such as *magyar* (Hungarian), *hazai* (domestic) or *Magyarország* (Hungary), which have sometimes been translated as national in the English translations of the Acts. This is especially notable in the 1993 Act, which barely includes six occurrences of *nemzet(i)*, whereas the English translation has over fifty hits for nation*.

In general, the word frequencies display a tendency for *nemzeti* (national) to become a less rare and more general expression, gradually outnumbering *nemzetközi* (international); this tendency has grown with every extension of the Act. That is, by sheer numbers of occurrences, the 1993 Act is more 'international' and the 2011 Act more 'national'.

The general justification of the Hungarian Parliament's first Act on Higher Education (1993), in addition to maintaining quality and adapting the system to Western European standards, was to increase the proportion of people receiving higher education in each age cohort, which is below the Western and Northern European average (Polónyi 2015; Kozma 1990). Based on the preamble, the Act can be characterized as liberal, in the sense that it refers to academic freedom and autonomy of universities, research and study, teachers and students. Furthermore, it expresses Hungary's need to join the 'developed democratic societies', which seem to have a higher number of students in higher education. That is, in 1993 there was a need to transform higher education from an elite privilege to an opportunity for the masses (cf. Kozma 1990). Nation is mentioned once in the preamble to the 1993 Act; the principles and values are similar to those of the Magna Charta Universitatum, signed by 388 European university rectors in Bologna in 1988.

There are only six references to *nemzet** (nation*) in the 1993 Act on Higher Education. Two of these are expressions that are paired with an international term, such as 'national and universal culture'. The term international appears more frequently – fifteen times – in the 1993 Act, with most occurrences in a section entitled International Academic Relations. The first Act on Higher Education in Hungary has an international focus, mostly concentrating on international situations and relations. What is more, there are references to structures, such as the system of international higher education. Such references anchor Hungarian higher education in international structures, networks, norms, practices and standards.

The theme of admitting foreign students to Hungarian universities, the process of recognizing diplomas acquired abroad, and the increasing requirement to prove foreign language skills (e.g. for appointment as a university lecturer or obtaining a PhD) also appear several times in connection to internationalization.

In conclusion, the meanings, connotations and contexts of the occurrences of the terms *nemzeti* (national) and *nemzetközi* (international) display an international orientation in the 1993 Hungarian Act on Higher Education. On the basis of these meanings and connotations, values, relationships, agreements, structures, system and practices and norms are fundamentally international in this first Act.

The 2005 Higher Education Act was elaborated under a left-wing government. The introduction to this Act states that higher education must be able to create and transfer up-to-date knowledge in order to maintain the desired level of social cohesion, sustainable development, international competitiveness and technological innovation. In the justification of the amendment to the law (2007), the goal of higher education is to provide professional training that is in line with labour market needs, competitive at European level and high quality, in institutions that are successfully involved in national and international research development, innovative, efficiently economically and academically managed, and open in their relations (Polónyi 2015).

The preamble to the 2005 Act extends the 1993 preamble with many references to international phenomena. Hungary's accession to the Bologna Process (1999) and to the EU (2004) seem to be the starting points of the Act. References to the term European in the 2005 Act increased to seventeen (in the 1993 Act it was mentioned only twice) in connection with the EU, the European Economic Area, European Higher Education Area, European Research Area and Common European Framework of Reference for Languages. The relevant passages discuss integration into EU structures and compliance with EU law. In sum, 'international' can often mean 'EU' in the 2005 Act, linking the Hungarian discussion to the post-1960s Europeanization debates (see Chapter 10).

Economic competition and efficiency are mentioned several times, making it a distinct marker for this Act. From the economic point of view, the 2005 Hungarian Act on Higher Education could be characterized as neoliberal; freedoms and autonomies are now accompanied by an emphasis on participating in international economic competition and fiscal efficiency.

The term *nemzet* (nation) appears approximately as frequently as *nemzetközi* (international) in the 2005 Act. Nation appears in the naming of certain country-wide phenomena and institutions such as the Hungarian state budget (national budget, *nemzeti költségvetés*). As in the 1993 Act, the rights of national minorities are mentioned in the 2005 Act, in fact the most mentions of *nemzet* in this Act are in the collocation 'national minorities' (*nemzeti kisebbség*) inside Hungary's borders. A new term is Hungarian nationality (i.e. ethnicity) beyond Hungary's borders (*határon túl élő magyar nemzetiségű*).

According to the 2005 Act, higher education should prepare the students to acknowledge and commit themselves to national, European and universal values. It includes an abundance of meanings and connotations for the word 'international'. A new expression since the 1993 Act is 'international competitiveness'. The preamble to the 2005 Act specifically links internationalization to 'academic capitalism', which according to Piller and Cho (2013: 31) is often introduced in the disguise of 'global academic excellence' and similar terms erasing the commodification of higher education. Another new term, again with neoliberal (see Rhoades and Slaughter 2006) connotations, is 'international labour market'. International student mobility is now mentioned in the law. The international structures are now more specific, perhaps as a token of deepening international integration.

According to Piller and Cho (2013), a main force in enhancing neoliberal structural reforms in higher education in Asia has been the International Monetary Fund (IMF) crisis relief. In 2008, Hungary received an IMF loan of €12.5 billion. This loan was soon turned into a political weapon in the hands of the Fidesz (Hungarian Civic Alliance) and its leader, Viktor Orbán, who won the elections by a landslide in 2010, 2014 and 2018. Orbán soon argued for an anti-liberal turn in politics. In the second year of their practically one-party reign – with two thirds of the seats in parliament needed to change the constitution at will – Fidesz delivered its Act on National Higher Education.

The preamble of the current 2011 Act is true to its new name: On National Higher Education. In the preamble, discourses about the nation have replaced references to educational and academic freedoms, international and European values, and economic competitiveness and efficiency. In the current (neo)nationalistic preamble, an ethnonational historical narrative is constructed. Higher education should be a tool for the Hungarian nation's children and grandchildren to bring about a national renewal which could restore Hungary to its past glory of numerous Nobel laureates (see Tarrósy 2002: 20–21) and internationally renowned inventors.

Since the preamble has been formulated around the notion of the Hungarian nation, its naming practices have also changed to favour references to *nemzeti* (national) Acts and institutions. In the previous Acts, the system of higher education institutions was international, now it is termed as national. In the 2011 Act, a national scholarship is established (*nemzeti felsőoktatási ösztöndíj*). A national strategy is also mentioned. As in the previous Acts, national minorities are mentioned fairly often. Provisions with International Relevance contain the same sections as in 2005. In this part, international agreements are mentioned several times. International recognition is still deemed important in some cases in the newest Act. New meanings are contained in the expression 'international commitment' referring to foreign policy commitment, which might be a sign of tightening political control and the primacy of (neo)national(istic) political interests over the universal academic freedom and autonomy that was so strongly expressed in the 1993 Act.

As a result of these changes in the legislation, Hungarian higher education is being thoroughly transformed: from a classical Humboldt-type system with high autonomy, established to educate the broad masses and train intellectuals, to a highly centralized, narrowly autonomous vocational training system to serve national labour market purposes (cf. Polónyi 2015). In the 2010s, the labour market was no longer perceived as international; what is more, Orbán's first government introduced a system of tuition-free higher education for students who agreed to work in Hungary after graduation for a predetermined number of years (Polónyi 2015: 6).

## Conclusion

Our chapter has demonstrated how systematic analysis of two closely related concepts, the national and international, illustrates the contextual differences in different national systems, thus pointing at the inherently national nature of international comparisons in Europe at the turn of the twenty-first century. The methodological flip side of this approach to comparative and conceptual history would be that, done unsystematically and without proper contextualization, focusing on a narrow selection of political concepts could lead to linear and even superficial interpretations. Thus, close discourse analysis of concepts always has to be complemented by research into the political and historical context. We do not claim to present an overarching analysis of the conceptual fields of these concepts and the neighbouring ones; rather, we discuss what happens and what is done particularly with the concepts of the national and international (in Finnish, *kansa\** and *kansainvälin\**; in Hungarian, *nemzet\** and *nemzetközi\**).

Analysis of national and international in the Finnish and Hungarian contexts from the 1990s to the 2010s empirically depicts a development from liberal to neoliberal, or postnational to new national in both countries. However, this occurred at different speeds and on different scales. The global neoliberal turn in higher education (Rhoades and Slaughter 2006) is visible in both cases. The Finnish developments appeared to occur more slowly, however, not just in global comparison but also in comparison to Hungary, which made a speedy move from liberal higher education (1993), briefly to neoliberal/postnational (2005) and then to clearly and strongly new nationalist policy (2011). Finland, in turn, was still in a largely liberal phase in 1996–1997 while in the 2000s the country quickly transitioned to a postnational and neoliberal phase. The new national phase emerged only later and is not visible in our data (Saarinen 2020).

In the Finnish data, the national and international appear intertwined, particularly in the 2009 data (and the amendments to the 1999 Act), where they demarcate each other's space. This demarcation of the inter/national appeared to have the purpose of hierarchizing higher education systems, but also assuring the Finnish higher education community that the national (alongside the international) was still there and not about to disappear. This implies that the new nationalist tendencies that surfaced in Finnish higher education only after 2010 (Saarinen 2020) were already emerging around 2009.

The Finnish conceptualization of internationalization in our data is mainly pragmatic and economic. In the Hungarian data, the values and principles of higher education were universal in the first Act of 1993. The goals were to (re)integrate Hungarian higher education into Western European academic traditions and practices. In the 2005 Act, this was combined with an incentive to (neoliberal) international economic competitiveness. It no longer sufficed to join Western academia with its freedoms; Hungary was supposed to compete internationally in making a profit and commercializing its higher education. Finally, in 2011 all this changed; internationalization or universal academic freedom and neoliberal global virtues were no longer values or goals for Hungarian national higher education. Internationalization was now subordinated to national interests and in practical terms to the foreign political preferences of the government negotiating (bilateral) agreements. Internationalization is sometimes conflated with national interests, at other times, particularly in the Hungarian case, with European identities (see also Chapter 10).

Hungary is at the forefront of a global nationalistic trend, in which higher education management is centralized in political hands. The fourth Orbán government has just finished taking over research institutions from the Hungarian Academy of Sciences. It has also established its own 'alternative' research centres in so-called national studies (see Kamusella 2019). On the global scene, Hungary is moving from multilateral relationships to bilateral agreements both with other countries and with global corporations. Even though the EU remains a major multilateral alliance for Hungary, both economically and in higher education, Hungary is entering into bilateral cooperation with China, Russia, Turkey and other partners in the 'illiberal' world. There are no signs of change in the overwhelming popularity of the Orbán regime; the left-wing and liberal opposition was decimated by the economic crisis in 2008 and has not yet resurged.

Whether Finland will follow Hungary's path, or whether the neoliberal trend will prove stronger than the emerging nationalist one, remains to be seen. Finland has already witnessed a new nationalist turn with higher education strategies turning inwards, and higher education policies being conducted with the national interest in mind. The dynamic in the relationship of international and national higher education is likely to tilt towards the national, and the spaces of internationalization may become more narrowly nation-centric.

**Viktória Ferenc** is a researcher at the Research Institute for Hungarian Communities Abroad (Budapest), who focuses on Hungarian language use and education beyond the border of Hungary. Her work has been published in several edited collections and international journals such as *Nationalities Papers*. Recently, she contributed to the project Linguistic Minorities in Europe Online as an author of the resource published by de Gruyter. ORCID 0000-0002-5849-204X.

**Petteri Laihonen** is an Academy of Finland Research Fellow (2016–2021) at the Centre for Applied Language Studies of the University of Jyväskylä, Finland. His research deals with educational language policy in multilingual contexts. It develops sociolinguistic theory, extends into Eastern Europe and has societal impact on the life of the investigated communities. His publications include articles in the *Journal of Sociolinguistics*, *Visual Communication* and *International Journal of Bilingual Education and Bilingualism*. ORCID 0000-0002-3914-0954.

**Taina Saarinen** is Research Professor of Higher Education at the University of Jyväskylä, Finland. She has published widely on internationalization and language policies in higher education, as well as on contemporary and historical language policies, recently in journals such as *Higher Education*, *Rethinking History* and *Language Policy*. Her monograph *Higher Education, Language and New Nationalism in Finland: Recycled Histories* was published by Palgrave in 2020. ORCID 0000-0002-5117-2756.

# References

*Primary Sources*
Finland:
Universities Act 1997, 645/1997. Yliopistolaki 1997, available at https://www.finlex.fi/fi/laki/alkup/1997/19970645.
Universities Act 2009, 558/2009. Yliopistolaki 2009, available at https://www.finlex.fi/fi/laki/alkup/2009/20090558.
Government Proposal on Universities Act 1996, HE 263/1996. Hallituksen esitys yliopistolaiksi, available at https://www.eduskunta.fi/FI/vaski/sivut/trip.aspx?triptype=Valtiopaivasiat&docid=he+263/1996.
Government Proposal on Universities Act 2009, HE 7/2009. Hallituksen esitys yliopistolaiksi, available at https://www.finlex.fi/fi/esitykset/he/2009/20090007.

Hungary:
1993. évi LXXX. törvény a felsőoktatásról / Act LXXX of 1993 on Higher Education, available at https://mkogy.jogtar.hu/jogszabaly?docid=99300080.TV
2005. évi CXXXIX. törvény a felsőoktatásról / Act CXXXIX of 2005 on Higher Education, available at https://mkogy.jogtar.hu/jogszabaly?docid=a0500139.TV
2011. évi CCIV. törvény a nemzeti felsőoktatásról / Act CCIV of 2011 on National Higher Education, available at https://net.jogtar.hu/jogszabaly?docid=A1100204.TV

*Secondary Sources*
Adriansen, H.K. and I. Adriansen. 2018. 'A Political Geography of University Foundation: The Case of the Danish Monarchy', in P. Meusburger, M. Heffernan and L. Suarsana, *Geographies of the University*. New York: Springer, pp. 193–217.
Becher, T. and P. Trowler. 2001. *Academic Tribes and Territories: Intellectual Enquiry and the Cultures of Disciplines*. Buckingham: Open University Press.
Clark, B. 1983. *The Higher Education System*. Berkeley: University of California Press.
Corbett, A. 2005. *Universities and the Europe of Knowledge: Ideas, Institutions and Policy Entrepreneurship in European Union Higher Education Policy, 1955–2005*. Basingstoke: Palgrave Macmillan.
Dhondt, P. 2008. 'Difficult Balance Between Rhetoric and Practice: Student Mobility in Finland and Other European Countries from 1800 to 1930', in M. Byram

and F. Dervin (eds), *Students, Staff and Academic Mobility in Higher Education*. Cambridge: Cambridge Scholars Publishing, pp. 48–64.

Fairclough, N. 2003. *Analysing Discourse: Textual Analysis for Social Research*. London: Routledge.

Gal, S. 2011. 'Polyglot Nationalism: Alternative Perspectives on Language in 19th Century Hungary', *Langage & société* 136: 31–53.

Held, D. and A. McGrew. 2007. *Globalization/Anti-globalization: Beyond the Great Divide*. Cambridge: Polity.

Hult, F. and S. Pietikäinen. 2014. 'Shaping Discourses of Multilingualism through a Language Ideological Debate', *Journal of Language and Politics* 13(1): 1–20.

Ihalainen, P. 2017. *The Springs of Democracy: National and Transnational Debates on Constitutional Reform in the British, German, Swedish and Finnish Parliaments*. Helsinki: Finnish Literature Society.

Ihalainen, P. and T. Saarinen. 2019. 'Integrating a Nexus: The History of Political Discourse and Language Policy Research', *Rethinking History* 23(4): 500–19, https://doi.org/10.1080/13642529.2019.1638587.

Häkli, J. 2013. 'State Space – Outlining a Field Theoretical Approach', *Geopolitics* 18(2): 343–55.

Jalava, M. 2012. *The University in the Making of the Welfare State: The 1970s Degree Reform in Finland*. Frankfurt am Main: Peter Lang.

Kamusella, T. 2019. 'The Fallacy of National Studies', in J. Fellerer, R. Pyrah and M. Turda (eds), *Identities In-Between in East-Central Europe*. London: Routledge.

Kiander, J. 2001. *1990-luvun talouskriisi. Suomen akatemian tutkimusohjelma: Laman opetukset. Suomen 1990-luvun kriisin syyt ja seuraukset*. Helsinki: Valtion taloudel-linen tutkimuskeskus.

Kozma, T. 1990. 'Higher Education in Hungary: Facing the Political Transition', *European Journal of Education* 25(4): 379–90.

Nokkala, T. 2007. *Constructing the Ideal University – the Internationalisation of Higher Education in the Competitive Knowledge Society*. Tampere: Tampere University Press.

Ogden, C.K. and I.A. Richards 1989. *The Meaning of Meaning*. (Published originally 1923). New York: Harcourt Brace Jovanovich.

Mayring, P. 2000. 'Qualitative Content Analysis', *Forum: Qualitative Social Research* 1(2): Art. 20.

Papp Z., A. 2011. 'The Education Issue', in N. Bárdi, C. Fedinec and L. Szarka (eds), *Minority Hungarian Communities in the Twentieth Century*. New York: Columbia University Press, pp. 480–92.

Parson, L. and A. Steele. 2019. 'Institutional Autonomy and Academic Freedom in Hungary: A Historiography of Hungarian Higher Education', *College and University Journal* 94(4): 10–24.

Piller, I. and J. Cho. 2013. 'Neoliberalism as Language Policy', *Language in Society* 42(1): 23–44. doi:10.1017/S0047404512000887.

Polónyi, I. 2015. 'A hazai felsőoktatás-politika átalakulásai' ['Transformations of National Higher Education Policy'], *Iskolakultúra* 25(5–6): 3–14, https://doi.org/10.17543/ISKKULT.2015.5-6.3.

Rantala, K. 2016. 'Argumentaatio hallituksen esityksissä: keskeiset ehdotukset ja vaikutusten arviointi', *Oikeus* 45 (2): 159–83.

Rhoades, G. and S. Slaughter. 2006. 'Mode 3, Academic Capitalism and the New Economy: Making Higher Education Work for Whom?', in P. Tynjälä, J. Välimaa and G. Boulton-Levis (eds), *Higher Education and Working Life – Collaborations, Confrontations and Challenges*. Oxford: Elsevier, pp. 9–33.

Saarinen, T. 2012. 'Internationalization and the Invisible Language? Historical Phases and Current Policies in Finnish Higher Education', in S. Ahola and D. Hoffman (eds), *Higher Education Research in Finland: Emerging Structures and Contemporary Issues*. Jyväskylä: Jyväskylän yliopisto, pp. 235–48.

———. 2020. *Recycled Histories: Higher Education, Language and New Nationalism in Finland*. London: Palgrave.

Saarinen, T. and P. Ihalainen. 2018. 'Multi-sited and Historically Layered Language Policy Construction: Parliamentary Debate on the Finnish Constitutional Bilingualism in 1919', *Language Policy* 17(4): 545–565.

Scott, P. 2011. 'The University as a Global Institution', in R. King, S. Marginson and R. Naidoo (eds), *Handbook on Globalization and Higher Education*. Cheltenham: Edward Elgar, pp. 59–75.

Simola, H. et al. 2017. *Dynamics in Education Politics: Understanding and Explaining the Finnish Case*. London: Routledge.

Stråth, B. 2016. *Europe's Utopias of Peace: 1815, 1919, 1951*. London: Bloomsbury Academic.

Tarrósy, I. (ed.). 2002. *Higher Education in Hungary: Heading for the Third Millennium*. Budapest: Ministry of Education.

Vares, V. 2020. *Turun yliopiston historia. Kansallinen tehtävä 1920–1974*. Turku: Turun yliopisto.

Välimaa, J. 2019. *A History of Finnish Higher Education from the Middle Ages to the 21st Century*. Dordrecht: Springer.

Weimer, L. and A. Barlete. 2020. 'The Rise of Nationalism: The Influence of Populist Discourses on International Student Mobility and Migration in the UK and US', in L. Weimer and T. Nokkala (eds), *Universities as Political Institutions: Higher Education Institutions in the Middle of Academic, Economic and Social Pressures*. Leiden: Brill, pp. 33–57.

Wimmer, A. and N. Glick Schiller. 2002. 'Methodological Nationalism and Beyond: Nation-state Building, Migration and the Social Sciences', *Global Networks* 2(4): 301–34.

# Conclusion

## Long-Term Patterns in the Vocabulary of Internationalisms

*Antero Holmila and Pasi Ihalainen*

### 'Universal' and 'Cosmopolitan' before 'International': Philanthropy or World Domination?

As Charlotta Wolff (Chapter 1) and several other authors point out, ideas about borderless and universal communities within Europe predate the modern notions of nation state and conceptualizations of such communities as 'international'. In the cultural practices of eighteenth-century intellectuals, cosmopolitanism remained a practical concept, lacking ideological content. The attribute 'cosmopolitan' stood for a mundane or philanthropic attitude, while imageries of what might today be called transnational communities and organizations were not based on the concept of cosmopolitanism. Towards the end of the eighteenth century, cosmopolitan ideals became challenged by the rise of patriotic and national discourses, which tended to politicize the understanding of both cosmopolitanism and cosmopolitan practices.

This can be most distinctly seen in the revolutionary 1790s, when the interests of individual great powers such as the British or French were contrasted with the interests of all humankind. As Friedemann Pestel and Pasi Ihalainen show (Chapter 2), world discourse remained highly contested during the French Revolution. In French revolutionary assemblies, cosmopolitanism was seen as a negative concept and terms such as 'cosmopolitan', 'fraternity' (*fraternité* in French), 'humankind', 'universe' and 'the world' were used to include the proper revolutionaries and to exclude groups such as women, émigrés, aristocrats, priests, Jews, people of colour or enslaved people. The revolutionaries welcomed foreigners only as far as they recognized the principles of the Revolution and cooperated with it. British reactions to the Revolution justifying war also gave universalism nationalist connotations: French universality and fraternity were taken as euphemisms for world domination, whereas the British were defined as the champions of the law of nations within Europe and the 'civilized' world. Such ways of speaking were supportive of the emergence of international law in the European context but also of imperialist endeavours.

In the eighteenth and early nineteenth centuries, discourses on international communities remained relatively rare, and confined to the learned elite or to discussions on relations between nations concerning law, trade and diplomacy. Such discourses continued to be based on older vocabularies of the universal and cosmopolitan. An institutional framework for what was to be called 'international' relations began to take shape at the Congress of Vienna in the aftermath of the Napoleonic Wars.

## The First Wave of 'International' and 'Internationalism' Before the First World War: Nation States Enforced

Quantitative data compiled by Jani Marjanen and Ruben Ros (Chapter 3) demonstrates that the term 'international' started to occur more frequently in the 1860s. Strengthening of the national perspective during the nineteenth century made it easier to understand matters as international, reinforcing the role of nation states in international politics. 'International' gained new meanings, becoming more abstract and political as international matters were often contested, provoking hopes and fears about the future. The period from the 1860s to the First World War constituted the first wave of 'international', with several organizations adopting the attribute to their name. This wave was complemented by an 'internationalist turn' visible at the turn of the century in the greater use of the term 'internationalism' – simultaneously with its emerging counter-concept 'nationalism'. Internationalism could refer neutrally to practices of crossing borders or the state of affairs in the sense of 'internationality' but was also used as a synonym of socialism, which made the concept highly contested, particularly after the Bolshevik Revolution (Chapters 3, 4 and 6).

'International' stood not only for crossing borders in various contexts, it also enforced nation states. In general, as previous studies and most authors in this volume point out, the concepts of international and national were often symbiotic; the one contributed to defining the other. The first wave of international feminism and the Olympic movement both illustrate the practices of deliberately constructing an international community by bringing national entities and their symbols together and amalgamating them with the new international symbols of unity – such as the Olympic flag

(Antero Holmila in Chapter 9). As Tiina Kinnunen (Chapter 5) shows, the concept of internationalism was essential for empowering women and creating cross-border unity in demands for women's rights in various national contexts. In short, the issue of women's rights went beyond nation states. While male-dominated discourses on internationalism tended to focus on material questions, women's internationalism typically emphasized human and social rights.

The interdependency of national and international discourses is also illustrated by Pauli Kettunen's (Chapter 4) suggestion that, in socialist theoretical discourse, 'internationalism' as an 'ism', referring to ideological agency aiming at changing the world, actually preceded 'nationalism' as an ideologically loaded term. The notion of nations as the main category of the world order was also reinforced within socialist theory and the labour movement – based on national organization. Even though world peace was a major goal, revisionist socialists increasingly viewed patriotism as compatible with internationalism. From the late nineteenth century onwards, internationalism became generally associated with socialist challenges to capitalist nation states – this tension between nation states and the international dominated interwar debates in practically all European parliaments and non-socialist public discourse.

## The Second Wave of Internationalism in the Interwar Years: Idealism, Pragmatism and Extreme Nationalism

Internationalism had established itself as a disputed political concept by the First World War, and the founding of the League of Nations in 1919 supported the rise of its new, second wave. As Pasi Ihalainen and Jörn Leonhard show (Chapter 6), the 1920s saw the connotations of internationalism multiply, either going back to the more descriptive language of international cooperation of the nineteenth century, or developing towards more ideological ideas on the world economy and legally bound international order.

While many previous researchers have approached international relations of the interwar era from the perspective of liberal internationalism, Ihalainen and Leonhard (Chapter 6) show that in parliamentary party-political contexts the category proves ambiguous and the liberal/conservative divide fluid. Internationalism had acquired meanings that went beyond any simple dichotomy of liberal and communist. Liberal parties often welcomed economic and practical internationalism supportive of individual nation states while remaining sceptical about ideological internationalism, while the conservatives associated the latter with all brands of socialism. Stable international order was seen as a means to protect small nation states or to help to maintain a large empire. Hence, it was considered compatible with patriotism, which made some conservatives in the Nordic countries and Britain support it, while French and German conservatives remained highly anti-internationalist. In Western parliaments, socialists were divided into revisionists who idealized the reconciliation of internationalism and patriotism, and pro-Soviet communist internationalists. By the early 1930s, internationalism had become highly contested. As Pauli Kettunen (Chapter 4) shows, even the Communist International combined internationalism with patriotism while rejecting cosmopolitanism and nationalism.

An often-neglected dimension of more idealistic interwar discourses on internationalism relates to the transition from conceptions of religion centred on the nation state to more international ones, particularly in Protestant contexts (the traditionally transnational Catholic Church being a different case). Joris van Eijnatten and Pasi Ihalainen (Chapter 8) show how, in liberal and leftist-leaning religious circles, the experiences of the First World War and search for world peace supported an ongoing move away from confessional definitions of the nation state. In Britain, the Netherlands and Sweden the relationship between religious and political belonging was reconceptualized in more tolerant terms at the national level – these ways of thinking were then extended to international contexts. However, conservative political discourse continued to be doubtful about ecumenicity, and the traditional religious concept of nationhood identifying the church with the nation and state survived at least until the 1960s.

Hagen Schulz-Forberg (Chapter 7) argues that the semantic field with regard to the 'world economy' became increasingly rich and varied in its meanings since the turn of the twentieth century, despite retaining its basic function as law-based order regulating the interaction between states. The transformation of internationalism as a result of the Second World War was eased by international financial structures such as the Bank for International Settlements. This transformation was not only structural, enabled by the Bretton Woods system, but also conceptual: the 'world economy' increasingly stood for an integrated economic system as opposed to the web of trading activity conducted by nation states.

## The Second and Third Waves of Internationalism from the 1960s: International as European or Global?

From the nineteenth century, European political elites had conducted international activities by bringing together their respective nation states, often under an ideational banner of European unity, peace and cross-border cooperation. Discourses on the international community have been characteristically Eurocentric. The labour, feminist and Olympic movements, to name just three, started as communities of European 'civilized' nations and the United States and were only gradually, after the Second World War and decolonization, extended beyond Europe and North America. More global aspects of internationalism were long overshadowed by the interests of colonial powers. This has led us to recognize the inherent Eurocentric tint of discourses on internationalism and to critically view its consequences: the marginalization of international cooperation efforts by non-Europeans. These were addressed more seriously only after decolonization in the 1960s and 1970s. Even later, 'international' in European political discourse has often primarily meant European cooperation.

Mats Andrén and Joris van Eijnatten (Chapter 10) explore ways of conceptualizing Europe after the Second World War in intellectual, cultural and more general political discourse, the latter in national parliaments. Many European intellectuals regarded themselves as the representatives of internationalism. The ultimate goal for many – a UN-based world-government – became a practical impossibility during the Cold War, so they saw a European project combined with transatlantic cooperation as the second best option. While some enthusiasm for European integration has appeared at times, typical parliamentary debates, particularly from the 1980s onwards and especially in the British parliament, have focused on tensions between European integration and 'European identity' on the one hand, and the nation state and national identity on the other.

Extending European models of international cooperation beyond Europe in the context of the Cold War was not without its challenges. As Norbert Götz and Irène Herrmann (Chapter 11) illustrate regarding the International Committee of the Red Cross, the supposedly universal principles remained Eurocentric, conditioned by Judeo-Christian traditions and dominant anti-Bolshevist ways of thinking. Discourses on universality and everyday practices of assistance, conditioned by local particularities, diverged, which meant that for the Red Cross 'universality was a goal rather than a baseline'.

If emergency aid was hardly going to challenge the notions of national sovereignty, the student movements of the sixties, especially the New Left radicals, were keen to break ties with 'universal Western values'. As Juho Saksholm (Chapter 12) argues, diverse discourses on internationalism often took globally contested issues such as the Vietnam War or South African apartheid as their rhetorical centres and sought to radically challenge notions of national sovereignty to replace it with 'world community'. These New Left Movements used global events and ideas to situate local movements in the context of global radical imagination. For them, internationalism functioned as a signal that gave significance and prestige to the discourse.

Similarly conditioned by decolonialization and the Cold War détente, as Antero Holmila (Chapter 9) illustrates, the International Olympic Committee also sought to expand its rhetoric beyond Western and Eurocentric premises. For the Committee, internationalism was not merely a discourse but a lived practice of pursuing peace and global solidarity – a goal which the Soviet bloc was quick to accept. Reflecting the wider social, political, economic and cultural transformations in the 1960s, the concept of 'global' started to slowly emerge within the movement and by the 1990s, it appeared as an alternative to 'internationalism' in Olympic discourse – yet, the two concepts were typically used interchangeably.

Discourses on internationalism also met with recurring accusations of elitism – often with good reason, though that by no means removes the need to understand them. Cosmopolitan attitudes were highly elitist in the eighteenth century and continued to be so in the nineteenth and early twentieth centuries. Even in movements challenging the established order such as the first wave of international feminism, activists able to cross borders, meet fellow activists from other national backgrounds and create a transnational community were mostly members of the elite. Within the Olympic movement, advocates of cosmopolitanism faced the accusation that they were ignorant of non-European cultures, that they supported elitist practices by idealizing amateur sportsmen, and that their organization was led by members of elites.

The popularization of internationalisms to larger publics beyond the labour movement began with the creation of national associations linked to the League of Nations, which supported the emerging second wave of internationalisms – only to be washed away under the currents of extreme nationalism in the 1930s and gradually revived by the United Nations after 1945. The United Nations offered a new framework for international cooperation but initially failed to fulfil many expectations due to the Cold War. Its utility as a facilitator of internationalism became more visible during what we call the third wave of internationalisms from the 1960s. International thinking expanded with decolonization, rising immigration, emerging multiculturalism, transformations of the media, increasingly international outlooks among student generations and the relatively broad parliamentary representation of the left.

A case study of these developments is offered by Joris van Eijnatten and Pasi Ihalainen (Chapter 8) who demonstrate a shift in discourses on ecumenism since the 1960s – a period when religious unity in European nation states fragmented. Awareness on the coexistence of competing but declining religions supported the rise of more inclusive understandings of ecumenism, extending initially Christian concepts to cover all faiths. Changing notions of ecumenism and internationalism encouraged practical demonstrations of global solidarity such as awareness-raising about injustices around the world and collecting funds for development projects. Later, confrontations with radical Islam inspired a search for mutual understanding between religions in order to counter religious fanaticism.

## Internationalism after the Cold War: Global Challenges and Neonationalist Trands

Further global challenges, particularly global warming and resource scarcity, have increasingly affected discourses on international cooperation since the 1990s. Environmentalist discourses are rooted in the 1970s oil crisis and reports from the Club of Rome on diminishing natural resources on the one hand and rapid population growth on the other, as illustrated in the popular *Limits to Growth* (1972) pamphlet. Miina Kaarkoski (Chapter 13) analyses how expressions of justice in international cooperation surrounding climate policies have evolved in Britain, Germany and the European Parliament since the 1990s. She shows how discussions about global justice linked with the international relations typically led by the 'wealthier North' to sponsor the environmental policies of the 'poorer South'. After 2000, 'fair/ness' and the social aspect of justice and human rights were used to turn the attention towards living standards. Alongside this discourse, demand grew for poorer nations to participate in shaping and implementing international climate policies. Nationalist voices often reduced the debates on global matters to everyday domestic policy issues. The sense of urgency in some political circles has not turned into ambitious international climate policies. International agreements within the UN framework have proved to be the most effective means for reaching international solutions. During the process, politicians have defined the concept of justice in ways that have sufficiently resonated with ideas about the acceptable world order.

Education policies, too, are typically rooted in nation-state perspectives. Viktória Ferenc, Petteri Laihonen and Taina Saarinen focus on universities as simultaneously national and international institutions, showing how conceptualizations of national and international have evolved in the Finnish and Hungarian higher education discourses since the 1990s. Following the Cold War, Finnish and Hungarian higher education have experienced similar discursive phases, moving from liberal and pro-integration to neoliberal, or postnational to neonational, though at differing paces. While internationalization has been a central rhetorical standpoint, towards the end of the 2010s, internationalism has increasingly become subordinated to national, at least economic, interests. This reminds us of the long-term and ongoing confluence between national and international tendencies.

Together, the fourteen case studies in this volume demonstrate the historical multilayeredness and polyvocality of internationalisms. They illustrate the considerable potential for conceptualizing phenomena that transcend nation states in a variety of political struggles and national contexts, at different levels of political, economic and cultural discourse. In the long term, quantitative rises and qualitative diversifications in discourses on internationalisms have reflected optimism about peaceful political development between nations. In contrast, as quantitative data and more detailed case studies have demonstrated, the decline in internationalist rhetoric is a precursor to or indication of crises between nations and the related uncertainty. Thus, this conceptual history of internationalisms aids our understanding of profound processes in world history that links the past with the national and global concerns of today and of the future.

**Antero Holmila** is Associate Professor of Modern History at the Department of History and Ethnology, University of Jyväskylä, Finland. He has published widely on the histories of the era following the Second World War, including the transition from war to peace, the emergence of the Holocaust in British and Nordic collective memories, the birth of the United Nations, geopolitical thinking and the International Olympic Committee during the Cold War era. ORCID 0000-0003-2456-7223.

**Pasi Ihalainen** is Academy of Finland Professor at the Department of History and Ethnology, University of Jyväskylä, and has previously worked as a visiting professor at the universities of Freiburg, Gothenburg, Leiden and Uppsala. He has published widely on the history of political discourse and the conceptual history of nationalism, democracy and parliamentarism since the eighteenth century, applying comparative and transnational perspectives. ORCID 0000-0002-5468-4829.

# Afterword

*Glenda Sluga*

These days the uncertainty surrounding the fate of the existing international order is accompanied by a strange absence of debate about the international component of that order. This absence is even more curious when we consider that, at crucial turning points in the twentieth century, the discourse of politics between states was constructed out of concepts beyond nation states. There are some current exceptions to the relative shallowness of these concepts, most notably the vital political laboratory that is the EU. While social scientists might be better placed to make such an assessment, for historians weighing up words, the absence of international discourse is most obvious in the responses to the global Covid-19 pandemic. Initially, the spread of infection defeated even EU governance, midwifing instead concepts such as 'vaccine nationalism', and plunging one of the oldest intergovernmental institutions, the World Health Organization, into disgrace in populist discourses. In the early twenty-first century, the organs of international governance face unprecedented existentialist challenges; this applies equally to the 1870s Universal Postal Union, with its technocratic ambitions, or the 1970s World Trade Organization, a bastion of neoliberal sensitivities. The volume *Nationalism and Internationalism Intertwined* intervenes in this moment of international amnesia as a reminder of the value of history and the historical scope of international thinking.

The chapters in *Nationalism and Internationalism Intertwined* confirm a multi-layered history of the contested concept of the international, and a chronology of concepts beyond nation states – how they have been debated, and by whom – embedded in European history, and the histories of European nation states. Into the genealogy of concepts beyond the nation state, this volume folds eighteenth-century terms such as 'cosmopolitan' that preceded the popularity of the words 'international' and even 'nation state' itself, but intimated similar ideas about lives lived beyond borders. It reconfirms that before the coinage of the nineteenth-century word internationalism, before the establishment of intergovernmental institutions, there were border-crossing imaginaries. These imaginaries were asserted in multiple languages – including Dutch, Finnish and English. They took root in legal discourse, becoming more popular by the 1840s, when we find them constitutively entangled in the mutually reinforcing politics of nationalism and imperialism. By the late nineteenth century, as the chapters here show, the concept 'international' was indicative of connections and interdependencies between nations, and 'internationalism' was interpreted as an ideological commitment to increasing that connectivity; both terms traversed the spectrum of political ideologies and provoked positive and negative responses.

For non-European readers, the starting point of this volume, conceptual history (*Begriffsgeschichte*) might be unfamiliar. As Holmila explains in Chapter 9, citing Melvin Richter, this is meant 'to stress the hermeneutical inquiry and therefore the significance of "the conceptual apparatus, horizons, and self-understanding of historical actors"'. The method employed in several of these chapters brings to this conceptual history the resources of the 'Ngram' and 'discourse data'. This data is used as a window allowing us to peer into the trove of European publications and public debate since the eighteenth century, and to measure the social fate of words. The authors use linguistic and grammatical variations of concepts – such as cosmopolitan, universal, international, national, patriotism and even ecumenical – to map out their contextually diverse and interdependent interpretations and meanings. Across the chapters, the benefits of the simultaneously broad and close readings of this data include their exposure of false assumptions about the internationalisms that have been debated. Who knew that the word 'internationalism' does not appear in *The Communist Manifesto* (1848), 'the book that came to serve as the foundation of "proletarian internationalism"'? (see Chapter 4). We can also look at this conceptual analysis another way, as a contribution to our historical understanding of the wealth of imaginaries that have shaped the responses of Europeans to their social existence, and the possibilities of politics within and between states. In the modern era, the more borders became important means of managing societies, the more individuals and political movements imagined practical and theoretical alternatives.

While the framing of studies of concepts beyond nation states in this collection is explicitly European, we are offered a slightly different view onto Europe, with northern European states added, especially Finland and Sweden. This expanded European story tells us that the push and pull of the national and international was woven into the fabric of modern European thinking and experience from the Enlightenment (at least). At the same time, through the nineteenth century, historians assembled the institutions of their profession out of the fabric of the nation state alone. In doing so, they cut away at conceptions of the politics between states, at least other than the *Realpolitik* of national foreign policies. This national bias in historiography reinforced the invisibility of political actors who engaged in the politics between states, even if their motivation was the lack of political representation in nation states – as was the case commonly for women and colonized subjects. Intentionally or not, the chapters here reiterate implicitly what feminist historians have long known – namely that when women have faced the failures of the nation state to address their political ambitions beyond their roles as mothers, they have turned to the international sphere. In some cases, women have been led to socialist internationalism, and, in others, to liberal internationalist institutions. In the context of historiographical trends that fetishized nation states, acknowledging the longue durée of concepts beyond nation states has returned our analytical attention to why and how such concepts were mobilized by those seeking power, as well as those in power.

It is clear from *Nationalism and Internationalism Intertwined* that from the later nineteenth century, the rhetoric of internationalism was deployed by conservatives, liberals, progressives, the enfranchised and disenfranchised alike – although we do not always know their gender or social position. Through the twentieth century, beyond-national concepts were embraced and spread by imperialists and anti-imperialists, economists and student radicals. The concept of internationalism could be tied to the pursuit of universal good, and to the antitheses of that 'good'. While the concept of a world economy can be traced to the cause of a global arena of radical imagination, as we discover, it was also pertinent to the liberal, and later neoliberal, advocacy of free trade and commerce, over and above human rights or social justice. The evidence here suggests that national and inter-national pasts have been mutually interdependent in these distinctive ways, just as, historically, imperialism, nationalism and internationalism have been interlocked. Even in the economic arena, the invention of national account-ing not only coincided with but also relied upon the conceptualization of a world economy. In practical terms, the world economy was a critical framing for comparative and connected studies of national economies, often paying little attention to the imperial forms of economic sovereignty, including gender or race biases, that belonged in that same mapping. Through the historical parsing of terminology and 'semantic clusters', *Nationalism and Internationalism Intertwined* also exposes the specific national (or at least lan-guage-specific) histories of internationalism and contexts in which concepts beyond the nation state were debated. The long history of German-language engagement with a 'world economy' (*Weltwirtschaft*), for instance, can be contrasted with the French understanding of 'global-ization', which has rarely veered from its depiction as *mondialisation*, or 'world-ization'. The languages of internationalism are not just conceptualized but articulated in dialects; they are culturally and linguistically emplaced.

Inevitably, at a crisis point in an international order constructed on the foundations of nineteenth- and twentieth-century nationalist and internationalist thinking, this volume returns to the question, why does the history of concepts beyond nation states matter? At the very least, these chapters establish that over the last two centuries and more, concepts beyond the nation state have been politically malleable, and nationally ineluctable; they have been profoundly entangled in European lives, and in the complex national/international legacies that are Europe's modern political inheritance. In this way, the volume contributes significantly to the growing historiographical interest, since at least the 1990s, in correcting the national bias in historical studies, and advocating for transnational framings, whether international or global.[1] More specifically, it is published at an important moment in the development of international history, with its focus on international institutions and internationalism as a concept.

*Nationalism and Internationalism Intertwined* enhances our understanding of the variety of concepts beyond nation states, not only how they have been debated, but also in terms of the need to continue debating them, their chronologies and their themes, as bases for contemporary conversations. We know from this volume that, in the transnational space that is Europe, concepts beyond nation states, like nation states, have been debated since the eighteenth century, and internationalism has been an important political tradition. That said, the chapters also entice us with the possibility of capturing political language not uttered in books, pamphlets or even newspapers, especially where the sites of speech and thought are not or could not be digitized. Even when drilling down into digitized data (such as newspapers) can tell us that in 1919 the League of Nations was a magnet for diverse ambitions and expectations, it cannot always specify the breadth of the idea and space of Europe that it is describing, unless we notice the specificity of voices. Australian historian Fiona Paisley has done this elsewhere by unearthing the lost history of an Indigenous Australian, Anthony Martin Fernando who went to Geneva to petition the League in 1921. Fernando's voice can be tracked in the Swiss papers, asking the League to transform reserve lands in Australia into mandates governed by Switzerland or the Netherlands in order to secure the 'just future of the Aboriginal race' in Australia – hearing that voice requires us to notice and identify his individual speech act (Paisley 2008: 196, see also Paisley and Holland 2005). The stories of Fernando's pilgrimage to the League are rehearsed in the private correspondence of other individuals such as African-American Ralph Bunche, who went to hear the Haitian delegates lecture the world on its violent treatment of colonial subjects. However, we only know of his visit if we immerse ourselves in Bunche's personal papers, which are not digitized. When we add other kinds of archival evidence, such as personal papers or even oral history, it becomes harder to argue that debates about internationalism only reflect the dominance of European powers, or even the Eurocentrism of international institutions in the first half of the twentieth century. Instead, the evidence of individual, often marginalized, voices reinforces the significance of concepts beyond nation states as a vital subject of historical study.

The narratives of a new international history are now exposing the extent to which – before and after the creation of the League of Nations – the concept of internationalism established important precedents for international institutions as sites of political agency and agitation, for and against the promise of Europe, among non-Europeans as much as Europeans. South Asian scholars such as Sunil Amrith have been able to excavate a rich history of this thinking, comparable to the new work on the Habsburg Empire and post-1919 experiments with the idea of sovereignty. When we acknowledge this non-European historical research, the interwar history of concepts beyond nation states can include Mohandas Gandhi's vision for the solution to the problems of the modern world in 'a world federation of free nations': 'Such a world federation would ensure the freedom of its constituent nations, the prevention of aggression and exploitation by one nation over another, the protection of national minorities, the advancement of all backward areas and peoples, and the pooling of the world's resources for the common good of all' (Bhagavan 2013: 8).

The historian Manu Bhagavan has argued that Gandhi's conception of internationalism was more radical than the idea of a communion of self-interested nation states, 'rather a siblinghood of equal states answerable both to their people and to the larger world community' (Bhagavan 2013: 17). He sees continuity too in developments after independence, as national internationalism became a motif of India's first Prime Minister, Nehru, who rendered Indian national unification the mirror of the One World idea that made international institutions a mainstream idea in the Anglosphere, including the United States. In this period Nehru reconciled India's ambitions with 'real internationalism', whereby 'the successful consolidation and unification of postcolonial India would, or at least might, herald the viability of his scheme at the international level' (Bhagavan 2009: 429). In this same vein, we should not be surprised to find that in 1945, the world that gathered in San Francisco to formally debate a charter for a new postwar United Nations Organization included African-American and colonial rights activists keen to be involved, despite their marginalization, and despite the European dominance of international institutions, let alone of internationalist narratives. The evidence of their international thinking is often to be found in samizdat newspapers, the surveillance reports of government ministries or even, occasionally, in published photographs of events, all of which require research methods that can supplement and contextualize the tracking of digitized words and expand our idea of what counts as a European context.

We already know quite a lot about the social and political history of European women and the colonial subjects of European empires organizing on behalf of internationalism and debating international thinking, even in order to petition for national rights. However, historians of internationalism more generally have found it harder to incorporate these marginalized voices or distinguish between their use of concepts such as cosmopolitan, international and internationalism, whether in European or non-European languages, particularly if their voices or languages are less represented in publications that have been digitized. As I have tried to suggest, the examples we do have are the tip of a global international history iceberg that could at the very least complement a more conventional European story, and even subvert its chronologies. They point historians to the possibilities of collaborative research between scholars who count themselves as international or global in their outlook, and imperial, colonial and national historians of minorities, diasporas and non-European communities. Building on the work of volumes such as these, the inclusion of these voices points the way towards new environmental and economic themes in global international history, and prompts us to nuance our chronologies of European debates. These chronologies might challenge European timelines that limit any non-European engagement in internationalism to the national period of decolonization in the second half of the twentieth century. Instead, they underline a longer, broader, even thicker history of thinking and acting beyond the nation state.

In the face of multi-faceted threats on a global scale today – whether we think of health, the environment or economics – the long and varied history of debating internationalisms matters, in conjunction with our growing awareness of the double heart of nationalism, and the gender, ethnic and racial legacies of European transnational politics. *Nationalism and Internationalism Intertwined* does the important work of encouraging us to start out on a broadened path of discovery, uncovering a variegated spectrum of internationalisms and connected political movements intertwined with liberal, illiberal and antiliberal thinking and ambitions. This same history of concepts beyond nation states might be the momentum we need for a broader understanding of national and European histories as bases for debating internationalism.

**Glenda Sluga** is Professor of International History and Capitalism at the European University Institute and ARC Laureate Fellow at the University of Sydney. Recent publications include *Internationalism in the Age of Nationalism* (with Patricia Clavin) and *Internationalisms: A Twentieth Century History*, and *The Invention of an International Order*. In 2020 she was awarded an ERC Advanced Grant to work on Twentieth Century International Economic Thinking. ORCID 0000-0002-2481-3394.

## Note

1. See the introduction to this volume for a useful survey of this literature.

## References

Bhagavan, M. 2009. 'Princely States and the Making of Modern India', *The Indian Economic and Social History Review* 46(3): 427–56.

———. 2013. *India and the Quest for One World*. London: Palgrave.

Paisley, F. 2008. 'Mock Justice: World Conservation and Australian Aborigines in Interwar Switzerland', *Transforming Cultures e-journal* 3(1): 196–226, available at http://epress.lib.uts.edu.au/journals/TfC.

Paisley, F. and A. Holland. 2005. 'Fernando, Anthony Martin (1864–1949)', in *Australian Dictionary of Biography*, Supplementary Volume. Melbourne: Melbourne University Publishing, available at http://adb.anu.edu.au/biography/fernando-anthony-martin-12918.

# Index